the Nature of Love and Relationships

Generally Acceptable Relationship Principles
for the New Era

Tom Omidi, Ph.D.

Copyright © 2011 by Tom Omidi

All rights reserved. No part of this book may be reproduced, translated, or transmitted in any form or by any means—graphic, electronic or mechanical, including photocopying, recording, taping or information storage or retrieval systems—without the prior written permission of the publisher or the author.

Library and Archives Canada Cataloguing in Publication

Omidi, Tom, 1945-
The nature of love and relationships: generally acceptable relationship principles for the new era / Tom Omidi.

ISBN 978-0-9783666-1-2

1. Man-woman relationships. 2. Couples. 3. Love.
4. Interpersonal relations. I. Title.

HQ801.O45 2011 306.7 C2011-905501-5

Published by Eros Books,
Vancouver, British Columbia
Canada
contact@erosbooks.net

Printed in the United States

Dedicated to my mysterious soul mate,
Who is so perfect, pretty, and passionate.

I keep looking for her!

List of Books by This Author

(As of June 2014)

Non fiction

The Nature of Love and Relationships **2012**
Doubts and Decisions for Living:
   Volume I: The Foundation of Human Thoughts **2014**
   Volume II: The Sanctity of Human Spirit **2014**
   Volume III: The Structure of Human Life **2014**

Fiction

Persian Moons (First Edition) **2007**
Midnight Gate-opener **2012**
My Lousy Life Stories **2014**
Persian Moons (Second Edition) **2014**

Table of Contents

Page

List of Diagrams and Tables
Foreword 1

PART I: Personal Issues in Relationships

Introduction: **Relationship Obstacles** 15
   Three Cautionary Points 15
   Adjusting to the Changing World 17
   The Book Structure 27

Chapter 1: **Personal Needs versus Relationship Needs** 31
   Personal Needs (Motives) behind Love 39
   Satisfying Our Needs in Relationships 41
   Relationship Needs 48
   Compatibility Limitations 51
   The Forces of Evil 55
   Need Setback Hysteria 58

Chapter 2: **Inner and Outer Forces Affecting Personality** 61
   I. Inner Forces of Personality 63
     A. Instinctual Forces 65
       i. Need for Dependence vs. Independence . . . 65
       ii. Need for Control 76
       iii. Need for Sex 77
       iv. Need for Love 78
     B. Genetic Forces 79
     C. Conditional Forces (Habits) 80
     D. Reactional Forces (Impulses) 82
   II. Outer Forces 84

Chapter 3: **Personality Aspects** 89
   Personality Model 93
   Interactions of Personality Aspects 102
   Learning about Our Personality Aspects 108

Table of Contents (Cont.)

Page

Chapter 3: Personality Aspects (Cont.)
Being Good and Enlightened 113

Chapter 4: Perceptions and Misperceptions 119
Perceptions, Trust, Love 122
Misperception Levels 127
Misperception Types 133
Misperception Cycles 139
Understanding Our Partners 140
Personal Flaws and Reactions Due to Misperceptions 143

Chapter 5: Consciousness and Communication 147
Consciousness and Personality Aspects 162
Consciousness, Communication, and Perceptions .. 165

Chapter 6: The Nature of Love 167
What Is Love/Why It Is Important to Know That 167
The Effect of Hormones on Love and Relationships 178
Love as a Reflection of Personality Aspects 181
The Outlook for Love 184
The Meaning of Love 186
The Power of M-love 190
Reasons for People's Impressions of Love 192

Chapter 7: The Nature of Relationships 193
A Definition of Relationships 197
The Transition 198
Objectives of a Relationship Framework: 201
A. To Enforce Teamwork 202
B. To Bring Objectivity Back into Relationships 209
C. To Increase the Effectiveness of Communications 210
D. To Reduce our Expectations from Relationships 210
E. To Overhaul our Mentality and Social Mechanisms .. 213

Table of Contents (Cont.)

Page

Chapter 7: **The Nature of Relationships** (Cont.)
Myths and Misperceptions about Relationships: 213
- Misperception about the Longevity of Relationships 213
- Misperception about the Role of Love 216
- Misperceptions about Happiness and Human Nature 222

PART II: Relationship Structure for the New Era

Chapter 8: **Relationship Expectations—Old versus New** ... 235
   Social Implications of Relationships 237
   Successful Relationships 240
   A Review of Relationship Expectations 241

Chapter 9: **Relationship Framework** 265
   Components of a 'Relationship Framework' 271
- R-entity 271
- Commitment to Teamwork 277
- Relationship Expectations 278
- Relationship Models 280
- Relationship Principles—GARP 281
- Relationship Needs (Success Factors) 281

   The Ultimate Objective of the Relationship Framework . 283
   Need for a Fresh Mentality 288
   How Partners Can 'Relate' 290

Chapter 10: **Relationship Principles (GARP)** 295
   Can GARP Solve Our Relationship Problems? 297
   List of GARP's Objectives 298
   GARP's Main Challenge 306
   Is Developing GARP Feasible? 309
   How Can GARP Be Developed and Propagated? .. 311
   A Replica of GARP 313

Table of Contents (Cont.)

	Page
Chapter 11: **Radical Solutions**	321
Adjustments to Couples' Mentality	327
Adjustments to Social Mechanisms	328
Chapter 12: **Relationship Needs Hierarchy**	357
Relationship Models	360
Personal Needs versus Relationship Needs	364
The Interpretation of Relationship Needs Hierarchy	366
Need Urgency Implications	374
The Impact of Need Urgency on Relationships	379
The Impact of Instinctual Needs	382
The Impact of Need Urgency on Need Setback Hysteria	383
Chapter 13: **Compatibility Measures**	385
Type One Measures: Partners' Personality	388
Personality Factors	389
Type Two Measures: Partners' Needs	399
Type Three Measures: Partners' Perceptions	402

PART III: Final Observations and Recap

Chapter 14: **The Destiny of Relationships**	407
Is Year 2115 a Good Target?	408
Facts and Trends Regarding Relationships	411
Emerging Relationship Circumstances	415
The Timetable to Implement Radical Remedies	447
Chapter 15: **Gender Differences**	451
Chapter 16: **Summary and Conclusions**	469
Epilogue: **The Mystery of Love**	543

List of Diagrams and Tables

Diag.	Table	Description	Page
1.1		Maslow's personal needs hierarchy	31
1.2		Three pillars of relationships	33
1.3		Companionship needs vs. personal needs	35
3.1		A simple model of mental structure and behaviour	90
	3.1	Descriptions of numbered arrows in Diagram 3.1	91
3.1		Personality ABC (measured by its three aspects)	100
3.1		Two examples of personality based on the lengths and angles of X, Y, and Z	100
3.1		One's perception of oneself	102
4.1		Our partners' perception of our personality	120
	4.1	Each partners' perceptions of each other and their relationship.	131
	4.2	Partners' common misperceptions	132
5.1		The basic cognition model	148
5.2		The cognition model	149
5.3		The Self with three levels of consciousness	151
5.4		The impact of consciousness, perceptions, and communications on behaviour (reactions)	166
	7.1	The basic nature of relationships (emerging trends)	194
	8.1	A preliminary list of relationship expectations	242
	8.2	The updated list of relationship expectations	263
	9.1	Components of a 'relationship framework'	271
	9.2	The proposed list of relationship expectations	278
	9.3	The list of invalid relationship expectations	279
	9.1	Parameters of a successful relationship/ Relationship needs	282
	11.1	Realistic relationship expectations	324
	11.2	Unrealistic relationship expectations	324
	11.3	Main Adjustments to couples' mentality	327
	11.4	Adjustments to social mechanisms	328
12.1		Relationship needs hierarchy	358
12.2		Relationship needs hierarchy shown as a social need	364
12.3		Relationship needs hierarchy shown as a basic need	365

List of Diagrams and Tables (Cont.)

Diag.	Table	Description	Page
	12.1	Main relationship models	371
13.1		Personality chart	389
13.2		Need urgencies of partners A & B versus C & D	400
13.3		An example of perception measurement	403
15.1		Gender Differences	452

Foreword

I was facing a crisis fifteen years ago when my marriage was breaking down and I couldn't do anything about it. For many years, my wife and I made the best of the bad situation while our kids were growing up and we felt the need to keep the family together. We sacrificed ourselves, while the initial love that had brought us together kept fading away.

Out of desperation, I began my research about relationships. I read more books every day and I did extensive analyses based on my academic background in human behaviour and relationships. Along with detailed studies of many other relationships, I thought I could find some solutions to save my marriage. The situation was depressing because I believed that both my wife and I were reasonably good human beings and we were not looking for adventures outside our marriage. We were financially successful and had fulfilling careers. We were educated and raised in progressive environments, both in terms of family and society. We *tried* to communicate our concerns intelligently and we met marriage counsellors too. On top of all this, we still sort of cared for each other and our sex was relatively good in terms of temperament and needs. So what the heck was the problem?

My research continued for fifteen years, while I was forced to look deeper and deeper into the roots of the problems. It became clear that dealing with the symptoms of relationship conundrums would only delay the separation. Nonetheless, my wife and I tried many suggestions that marriage counsellors and relationship books provided. In the end, still our marriage failed and we separated when our kids grew up and left us. But, by then, at least I was convinced that there was nothing more I could have done to save our relationship. I realized that relationship problems nowadays are too complex to be remedied easily. The only problem was that my wife and I were not prepared to face the reality of relationships in the new era and the high possibility of their failure.

I had assumed that my wife and I could learn to agree on a kind of relationship model that fitted our personalities. This happens in many relationships automatically when partners learn to accept and tolerate each other somehow. I only hoped that we could go one step further and agree on the issues we should handle personally, like making our own investments and not being accountable to each other about them. Or about the amount of time we spent on our hobbies, careers, friends, or travelling alone. There was really no point for us to constantly argue about the conflicts that could not be resolved. I really believed that it was possible to achieve this objective, if only we agreed on the relationship model suitable for us and accepted some reasonable compromises. I tried hard to implement such a model based on the main principles that we both valued. We tried it for about eight years anyway out of necessity, because we were forced into that kind of a rather passive relationship. But, at the end, she wasn't satisfied with the reduced level of expectations in our relationship. She was still attached to her all-or-nothing ideology, which eventually resulted in our separation because we couldn't change our personalities to the liking of the other person.

I don't blame my wife for her inability to lower her expectations from our relationship. It was hard for her to do so when everybody else is expecting more from their relationships and themselves. This is a difficult thing to do as will be explained in this book. To mention only one of the hundreds of hurdles, the hoopla around positive thinking in recent decades has caused disturbing consequences on our perception of life. We have lost touch with the harsh reality of life and believe that we deserve to have all the best of everything, including a flawless, loving relationship. We have all become too idealistic.

I was successful in lowering my expectations only after many years of meditation and self-awareness. Only then I learned that lowering my expectations was the best way to enjoy my marriage. I also believed in the value of living in a contained relationship to none at all. My sincere realization made the process of adjusting my needs easier. During this process, I also learned to be more humble, content, and forgiving—although not submissive. Even my wife noticed the difference in my attitude and admitted to my drastic improvement in terms of behaving and communicating. But even then, I had to maintain some level of pride, principles, and independence in order to respect myself, too, which meant I couldn't submit to my wife's desires and lifestyle preferences. So we split in the end despite my efforts to save our marriage by becoming a better human being, in the best way I could figure it out.

Anyway, the results of my long, systematic research are put together in this book for everybody's benefit. Unfortunately, the conclusions are not what most of us like to see, i.e., quick fixes for relationships. However, they might open our eyes and help us change our mindsets gradually. They could benefit us in the long run in a rather unconventional manner.

We must start by studying the obvious trends. The increasing number of divorces and endless family conflicts reflect the hectic environment of relationships. These facts also demonstrate that the existing schemes to deal with the agonizing hurdles of relationships are failing. Basically, we are ignoring the real sources of relationship problems while focusing on symptoms. So, this book is designed to analyse the roots of relationship problems in the new era. It intends to explain the high complexity of relationships in modern societies. It is also going to offer radical solutions compatible with our newer social values and expanding personal needs. To get to the roots of the problems, however, it is necessary to discuss the issues head on rather than beating around the bush to make the book appealing to everybody. So, I hope you forgive my blunt and pessimistic viewpoints once you realize my good intentions. This book is written only for the purpose of exploring the true causes of so many relationship breakdowns. I definitely have no intention to judge our social values or take side with one gender. I believe we must learn to adapt ourselves to the new realities one way or another, sooner or later. We simply cannot wait for a miracle to reverse the deteriorating trends in relationships. We must somehow help ourselves before we get hurt too much and cause more social distress for all.

This book doesn't intend to provide relationship tips, though the readers could gather many pointers from various discussions throughout the book. One purpose of the book is to suggest a framework that could assist couples assess their relationships more realistically. Nowadays, too many relationships are ruined due to partners' subjective assessments and hasty decisions. Thus, the ultimate goal of this book is to bring objectivity back into relationships. Yet it would be unrealistic to expect tangible changes in couples' mindsets and relationship approaches in the near future. So, the best this book hopes to achieve is to help people merely appreciate the *need* for changing their mindsets about relationships. In a sense, one could say that this is a futuristic book in the way its suggestions would most likely take many years to materialize, probably sometime in the 22nd century, but hopefully sooner. This outlook sounds too pessimistic. People might argue that this prediction shows no faith in society to overcome relationship problems. On the other hand, another group might find even the 22nd century an optimistic projection for reversing the deteriorating trends in relationships. Their arguments might sound quite logical indeed. They could suggest that it is too naïve to believe that people would give up their alluring lifestyles and values to rectify their relationship issues. The changes require a lot of patience and an ability to forgive our partners' flaws time and again. Developing such a humble mentality to accommodate our selfish partners sounds too unrealistic. People are normally too obsessed with their immediate personal needs and egos to feel sympathetic toward others.

Another major hurdle is that people trust each other less every day due to bad personal experiences and rampant socio-economic corruption in modern societies. Deep down, we trust each other less, but expect more love, respect, and honesty from our relationships. What a weird mentality. We are too naïve and selfish to see this obvious conflict. We simply don't pause to appreciate that these contradictory feelings (i.e., love and mistrust) cannot be easily reconciled in relationships. That is, people's expression of love cannot be sincere while they must always be cautious about the viability of their relationships and stay vigilant to prevent future disappointments. We simply cannot afford any longer to put our guards down nowadays and assume that relationships are safe the way they used to be a few decades ago. The question, then, is whether people's trust in relationships can be somehow restored, or whether we need a *framework* to help couples live together in some harmony with minimal clashes, despite their general mistrust? What kinds of relationship models might best fit human nature and our newer social values?

Nonetheless, people resist any suggestion about the need for a relationship framework and a new set of principles. They can offer a variety of legitimate reasons why this would not work. Two main reasons they might offer would be the impracticality of: 1) creating a universal relationship framework, and 2) making people pursue its guidelines by controlling their ego and temper. There are all those personal urges *(inner forces)* and many social demands *(outer forces)* that prevent this revolution from happening.

Yet I strongly believe in the need for a relationship framework and a set of principles to bring objectivity back into relationships. The simple reason is that everybody would eventually realize that relationship decisions must become less arbitrary and emotional. And the only way to achieve this is to introduce some simple principles that everybody can accept as practical social norms. This would help them assess their relationships according to reliable criteria instead of personal whims. Also, couples need some principles to make their communications more manageable instead of arguing or retaliating all the time. As mentioned before, this dream might not materialize until the next century anyway. Yet we will benefit from studying and implementing some of these ideas now, at least in terms of understanding our options about relationships. If we agree that the existing relationship environment is not functional, what other options might be out there? The most logical option, in my opinion, is the one described in this book. It is developed step by step by analysing the purposes and properties of a 'relationship framework' and assessing its usefulness.

Obviously, relationships are not similar in terms of nature and properties. Couples' unique personalities lead to a large variety of relationship types. But perhaps it is still possible for all of them to work from within a similar framework to maximize relationships' effectiveness. The framework could be logical and flexible enough to accommodate all reasonable types of relationships. The question is whether developing such a flexible framework and its corresponding principles is feasible. This book suggests that it is possible and necessary. The book actually proposes the main properties and structure of this framework.

Discussing relationships in this book has required substantial analyses of human psychology. Basically, relationships must be viewed as a challenging partnership between two individuals with unique (and peculiar) mentalities. In a sense, our discussions about relationships apply to any kind of encounter between any two human beings—same genders or not. Thus the book would be of interest to individuals who like to explore human personality and/or relationships. But it is also useful for scholars and marriage counsellors. They could critique the ideas put forward in this book, suggest more complete designs or explanations, and apply some of these techniques in their practices at least by the turn of the 22nd century.

Relationships are studied mainly in the behavioural science, as it reflects the encounters of two individuals with different psychological profiles and needs. This is a major area of psychology that requires greater attention and further research, since relationships comprise the foundation of family and personal life. But the health of relationships is enormously important for our socioeconomic welfare too. Therefore, relationships must be studied in social sciences more seriously as well. Obviously, the findings must be explained in simple words for common use purposes. I have decided to use some diagrams, however, when I felt they would assist the readers grasp some concepts better.

Trying to be scientific about relationships might appear rather absurd. But, considering the rising trend in relationship problems, the need for some form of analytical review is quite obvious. As societies become more modern and complex, we must become more conscious and rigid about our relationship needs. In recent decades, people have relied too often on their chaotic perceptions and interpretations to define their relationship needs, and they have measured the health of their relationships rather arbitrarily. It would be too risky to pursue the same approaches. The increasing complexity of relationships cannot be interpreted and treated loosely anymore. We need a more scientific understanding and a platform to explain our relationships.

There are many suggestions about relationships and human psychology in this book. They are based on direct observations, experiments, and personal experiences of the author. Nonetheless, the readers are reminded that these assertions should be viewed as working hypotheses and not ultimate theories. First of all, it is difficult to turn human behaviour and personality into pure science. Second, there are always exceptions to the rules. Nonetheless, if these suggestions sound practical and useful, we can gradually implement and refine them in order to alleviate our relationship issues. On the other hand, the author hopes that most of the hypotheses presented in this book would stand the test of time and gradually used as basic theories of relationships.

In all, the readers will find many of the ideas and discussions in this book most plausible and also verifiable by their own experiences and thoughts. Remember that even Freud and Einstein have been wrong about some of their theories. Yet their theories have made us think and find better alternatives while studying those original hypotheses. We are not looking for absolute solutions because there is none. But we can strive to find plausible approaches to make relationships more objective, endurable, and enjoyable.

For example, saying that 'humans are cruel' is a hypothesis that cannot be proven in this book. Though, it might be possible to prove this hypothesis if we took on a major research and wrote another book. Nevertheless, there are also many humans who are not cruel, but rather quite compassionate. But the general hypothesis is that humans have become too arrogant and cruel in the process of adapting to our highly competitive socioeconomic settings. They have become ruthless and egotistical even if they were not instinctually. In all, often a general concept is developed solely to study trends and explain the possible causes of individuals' behaviour. For the purpose of this book, the proposed concepts are my best judgments based on simple evidences surrounding us and in line with the existing theories as much as possible. Still, if you don't agree with some of them, that is fine too.

It is stressed again that the ideas and hypotheses offered in this book are developed by the author for the sole purpose of clarifying the hurdles in relationships and to achieve the sacred objectives enumerated in this book. They are expressed in the simplest forms in order to maximize their usefulness to the general public. If similar theories by other scholars are printed somewhere prior to this publication, then, of course, they should get all the credit that they duly deserve.

This book is not going to solve relationship problems. It will, however, help couples appreciate some basic facts about their own personalities as well as their relationships. Then they should decide whether they can find ways of relating to one another effectively or whether separation feels like a better alternative to them. Even these preliminary steps could help reduce marital hassles and breakdowns a little. Meanwhile, we look forward to the eventual implementation of the radical suggestions offered in this book. If there are even a few good points coming out of this book for couples, I consider my efforts a major accomplishment. I always welcome your comments and advice.

Tom Omidi, Ph.D.
Vancouver, BC, November 2011

PART I

Personal Issues
in Relationships

Introduction
Relationship Obstacles

This book is not about finding love or a companion. Rather, its objective is to clarify the true nature of love and relationships, so that we may come to terms with ourselves at a personal level for a more tranquil life. Once we learn to live without expecting love and relationships bringing us that elusive happiness, we might begin to enjoy our relationships too. The discussions in this book demonstrate the wide range of relationship obstacles that infect love and partners' ability to relate. In particular, Chapter Seven focuses on the nature of relationships in the new era and explains why a new relationship framework is needed.

Three Cautionary Points

1. The discussions and analyses presented in this book are straightforward and easy to follow. Yet some parts of the book might appear a little technical for some readers. This group of readers may refer to Part III where most of the facts, analyses, and conclusions are presented in an outlined form. In this manner, the reader will understand the objectives and messages of this book rather quickly. Then he/she can read the related discussions in the chapters at leisure and in any order he/she wishes. Of course, under-

standing the process and logic used to develop the ideas in each chapter is interesting and the readers would definitely benefit from them. As the concepts are built up in the sequential order of the chapters, following the details in the order presented is recommended. Yet, in case some chapters are read out of the sequence, the essence of the discussions would not be missed. One point to note is that the simpler books that focus on quick fixes cannot really help us much. It is like building a house without a foundation. The matters of love and relationships are becoming really complex nowadays, somewhat more complex than the laws of physics!

2. All references like 'we', 'people', 'men', or 'women', throughout the book, don't mean everybody, but rather a significant portion of them.

3. The analyses and suggestions in this book may come across to some readers as naïve or maybe even offensive on a few occasions. But the only purpose of this book is to improve the state of our relationships. These solutions and approaches are probably not going to see the light of day soon anyway. But it is the author's belief that we must take serious actions now. We must start viewing relationships as a major determinant of social welfare more than what society sees it presently. With this kind of mindset, discussing ideas like the ones offered in this book can begin to prepare society and couples for a major overhaul.

The author believes that the changes might happen around the years 2115 to 2150. This is of course a ballpark, imaginary date. But the author's pessimism stems from the fact that we resist change, due to humans' personality flaws noted in this book. We are comfortable with who we are. We believe in the purity of our personalities, as we feel quite proud of ourselves the way we are. Indeed, we are too attached to our convictions, despite all the evidences about the ways they are turning us into dogmatic, arrogant, and greedy individuals. Furthermore, we are in denial regarding the depth of relationship problems in the new era. We imagine they would go away automatically without us making any adjustments in our perceptions and behaviour. So, it would probably take more than a century until we finally appreciate the need for drastic changes, mostly in terms of revamping our mindsets. Yet there might be a miracle. We might suddenly view our relationships in a proper light and make the needed adjustments sooner.

Nonetheless, studying relationships is the most urgent matter facing civilization in the author's opinion. This book is hopefully one of many attempts to understand ourselves and our relationships.

Adjusting to the Changing World

The sad fact is that most relationships in modern societies lead to separation or couples' incessant suffering in highly complex environments. The sense of failure to find our soul mate, despite our lifelong search and struggles, causes deep psychological scars and stress. This in turn curtails our ability to deal with our socioeconomic responsibilities, and so on and so forth. A vicious cycle destroys our lives and people around us. It appears that the harder we struggle to fulfil our professional and emotional needs, the deeper we fall into despair and loneliness. Why? Why are we so incapable or unwilling to help each other suffer less?

During the last few decades, psychologists and marriage counsellors have been busy finding solutions for troubled relationships. They have written books and developed awareness methods to enhance love and communication between partners. They have offered solutions through expensive seminars and private sessions. Unfortunately, their efforts have not worked, judging by the increasing percentage of separations and the rising frustration of both married and single individuals.

Experts suggest all kinds of solutions and still relationships keep failing more than ever. The mere fact that there are so many incongruent solutions (all these variations) reflects that scholars have not developed dependable and uniform solutions. They have not even agreed upon a reliable framework to focus their research on and improve its potentials gradually. On the contrary, they keep suggesting new ideas every day. This shows that relationship studies are in disarray.

The effect of marriage counselling is tentative at best, too, especially when solutions focus on role-playing. Couples are encouraged to play phony roles and express passion or compassion to save their relationships. Obviously, role-playing is an artificial activity that causes more frustration in the end if partners are not intellectually (and emotionally) convinced about the authenticity of their own (or their partner's) feelings and words. Sometimes the argument in favour of role-playing is that partners have passion and compassion, but lack the communication skills to express them. It is assumed that role-playing can help them develop the skill for expressing their feelings. But usually this is not true. The reason people cannot express their feelings is often not due to a lack of communication skill. Usually the problem lies deep in the psyche of individuals; so deep indeed that even detailed psychotherapy might not reach the roots of the problems. Some of these psychological hurdles are discussed later. These barriers simply cripple couples to perceive and overcome their personal and relationship flaws. In these circumstances, couples feel the humiliation of role-playing. They resent the idea of behaving in certain ways just to stop their partners from nagging. All along, they are not truly committed to resolve their personal or relationship defects. Sometimes they turn into passive partners just to minimize the quarrels, and then suffer the burden of their hidden anxiety. In all, role-playing is a mentally fatiguing activity. The struggle to stay focused and playact properly might indeed add to the problems of relationships rather than solving them. Soon a small event triggers partners' inner conflicts and frustration. Or they get tired of playing those superficial roles.

The bottom line is that role-playing methods have not shown any substantial outcome. Divorces, anxiety, mistrust, and suspicions are increasing every day. The artificial quick fixes have failed to help us, because we have not tackled the increasing problems of relationships as a deep-rooted pandemic yet. So now it is time for a more comprehensive approach to study the nature of relationship problems. We must study the needs of our new society and scrutinize all the emerging facts.

A fundamental fact is that couples' personal needs, and their expectations from relationships, have increased drastically as societies have become modern and satiated with progressive philosophies. Accordingly, relationship solutions must be found by first examining the changes in society. Then we must learn how these changes have affected relationships. Finally, we must find radical mechanisms that best correspond with the new needs of individuals. Basically, we must study *what* has changed in society, *how* they are affecting relationships, and *why* radical changes are needed. Some suggestions about the nature of these radical changes will also be offered in this book.

A prominent, emerging trend is that we value our freedom and identity a lot nowadays. We are giving the highest level of emphasis to our personal need for independence (and self-worth) more than ever in human history. There are many reasons for this development. But the main reason is that women are finally given equal rights. Due to their efforts, everybody is now more aware of their personal needs for independence and identity. This major premise, i.e., the need for independence, should then be our best guide in developing the new principles of relationships.

The second development is that nowadays people are constantly playing various roles and games to portray an appealing personality, mask their idiosyncrasies, adapt to social values and demands, and manipulate (control) others. People are losing touch with their true identities more every day because of the roles and games they are forced to play to stay popular and be accepted in society. For one thing, they like to exaggerate their self-worth to themselves and others in order to prove their identity. Under this circumstance, they are not as authentic as they could be in their encounters. They have indeed become too phony compared with their true nature. This debilitating condition creates all kinds of problems for people in terms of finding the right companion, communicating, and perceiving their partners. It obviously sabotages their passionate struggle to find their identity as well. The situation gets worse when counsellors make couples play still another category of roles to solve their relationship conflicts. These new roles create even more confusion for people in terms of who they are and how they should be relating to their partners. Their own roles and games are at least familiar to them and partially justified emotionally and intellectually. But new roles often cause more anxiety, as they contradict both their existing roles and true nature.

The inconsistency of the above two emerging trends, i.e., people's strive for independence (identity) and their tendency to play phony roles to be popular, creates inner conflicts for them, because the more they try to prove their identity, the more they lose it and the phonier they become.

The third major new trend in society is that couples' personal needs supersede their relationship needs. Nowadays, we all expect our relationships to be functional (maybe even ideal), according to our subjective criteria, and also assist us in achieving our personal goals. If a relationship cannot fulfil these high expectations, we want out. We are no longer willing to tolerate mediocre relationships. We are now more important than our relationships. Some readers may wonder whether this has not been the case before. No, our old values inherently placed the needs of relationships ahead of individuals, according to tradition and religion. But we are now past those outmoded systems. Now individuals wish to be more important than their relationships. We keep insisting that life is too short and we live only once. So we wish to take advantage of life as much as possible before it is too late. In a nutshell, we can say that in the older times the emphasis was put on 'survival,' whereas nowadays the emphasis is placed on 'happiness.'

Of course, this doesn't mean that we are happier people than past generations. Rather, we just like to think (and pretend) we are happier. We want to show our resolve to find the elusive happiness. Why? There are three major reasons for our incessant quest for happiness: **First,** we have been brainwashed to believe that happiness is out there and we can easily find it by satisfying our artificial needs for wealth, power, and love. So we keep struggling to satisfy these artificial needs with no end in sight or real happiness in our hearts. In effect we are losing touch with reality every day by introducing more artificial needs in our lives and then failing to feel the expected happiness thereupon. **Second,** we have been learning and propagating a lot of philosophy about life and happiness in recent decades. We like to talk a lot about happiness and prove our ability and conviction to build a happy life. All these exaggerated ideas about positive thinking, living in the now, and similar philosophies are screwing our ability to perceive reality. **Third,** the increasing depression and suffering in society make us more eager to find happiness, and we become more susceptible to all these philosophical gimmicks too. As societies grow, we suffer more and thus seek relief (happiness) more obsessively. Actually, the above noted three reasons are interrelated. They have evolved to support (and also incite) one another: That is, we try to avoid (deny) reality by making up all kinds of philosophies in order to mitigate our suffering.

This is our new mentality. And we cannot change it. So, our challenge is to develop relationship principles that fit this new reality (perceptions). The old premise to depend on partners' romantic vows to love and cherish each other forever regardless of health and wealth is no longer helping them. Our daily experiences confirm that it is not working anymore. So let's be honest about these facts. Those good (or bad) old days are far gone.

Another major task in this book is to recommend methods and a relationship framework that might bring *objectivity* back into relationships. In recent decades, old values and relationship guidelines have been eradicated without new ones replacing them. We have only developed more unrealistic expectations for our relationships every year. And we make subjective judgments about the health of our relationships merely based on our personal perceptions and needs. To avoid these misleading approaches, we need a simple set of relationship guidelines that makes sense to everybody and fits our new social reality.

In line with the above stated objectives, this book is intended to demonstrate the following dozen facts:

A: We need to upgrade our mindset

1. Both our initial optimism about relationships (when we start one) and subsequent retaliations (when it fails) are destructive.
2. Our perspective of relationships is too naïve, unrealistic, and incompatible with the format of modern society. Basically, we must learn to lower our expectations from relationships in order to attend to our increasing personal needs independently.

3. We must prepare ourselves, both emotionally and financially, to deal with the high possibility of failure in our marriages and relationships.
4. We must appreciate that only by conscious efforts and major personal sacrifices a relationship can be sustained on a long-term basis. Our present mindset (personal priorities) and social values make the job of prolonging our relationships extremely difficult, if not impossible altogether.

B. We must understand human limitations
5. The complexity of human cognition and behaviour, driven by a variety of personal needs, traits, and perceptions, causes all kinds of relationship problems.
6. The underlying causes of relationship failures remain beyond partners' control. In other words, partners cannot help the situation. They are helpless due to human's psychological defects and genetic built.
7. Our faultfinding attitude toward our partners is a futile exercise. Also our efforts to change others (our partners) are absurd, especially when the matter is pursued through retaliation and intimidation.

C. We urgently need new solutions and guidelines
8. Dynamic relationship principles are needed to reflect the realities of the modern world.
9. New guidelines are needed to facilitate individuals' strive to be independent, assertive, proactive, and make the best use of their lives.

10. Revolutionary social mechanisms and norms are needed to help us manage our relationships and possibly reduce the chances of failure.
11. Revolutionary laws must be devised to make separations easy.
12. Revolutionary social mechanisms and education are needed to prepare couples for the psychological effects of relationships, especially separation.

Traditionally, we have viewed relationships as a manageable, sweet arrangement that can satisfy many of our personal needs, including companionship. But, nowadays, the likelihood of any relationship failing is much higher than succeeding. This is an obvious observation judging by the percentage of divorces and the turmoil of dragging relationships. This means that, as logical people, we should make major adjustments in our mentality to suddenly view relationships as a temporary arrangement, unless partners in a particular relationship are smart and lucky enough to make it work on a long-term basis. That is, couples must be able to prove that they deserve to stay in their relationships. Now couples should carry a high burden of proof (by demonstrating their aptitude) for prolonging their relationships past the initial romance and as partners' patience begin to falter.

Naturally, this condition (to view relationships as a temporary arrangement) appears like a major setback in terms of relationships' success. The readers might ask, "How could this seemingly negative mindset lead to the success of relationships?" This is a good point that will be clarified later in this book. Of course, making such a harsh mental adjustment—to view relationships as a temporary arrangement—would be difficult for people. So it will take time to get there. But, at the end, this mental adjustment is necessary (and extremely important) for so many reasons that are discussed in the book. One objective is to make people more conscious and careful about the true nature of relationships in the new era. They should become more realistic and view relationships with open eyes and minds—not by the way they feel and hope for. Most people are actually doing this already, though in an incomplete way. They furtively assess the financial prospects of their relationships, but don't wish to admit its importance or express it openly. They don't want to be accused of being calculating and unromantic when they are starting a relationship. Nonetheless, we must act according to the statistics and vivid experiences around us. They all indicate that marriage is a temporary arrangement unless partners are lucky and conscious about the real needs of relationships. We must now admit this fact openly and prepare ourselves for it (both financially and emotionally). In all, the concept might appear too radical, if not vulgar, and it may turn off many readers already. But by the time we reach the end of this book, the readers may feel more supportive of this and other radical points offered in Chapter Eleven. But please don't jump to Chapter Eleven before reading the discussions and analyses in the earlier chapters. They explain the need for introducing radical solutions.

Obviously, it is unromantic and depressing to start our relationships on a seemingly wrong foot, with a seemingly negative attitude. But being realistic at the outset may save us nervous breakdowns and separation hassles. The challenges of separation seem inevitable for a majority of relationships and it pays off to be prepared for them. Learning about the deep roots of relationship failures would also help us realize that they are basically the symptoms of social changes that we have not adapted ourselves to. So partners' retaliation out of spite cannot correct anything. Retaliating to make our partners change is not going to work either. It merely reflects our own utmost immaturity and wishful thinking.

As noted before, one objective of this book is to pinpoint the high vulnerability of relationships in modern societies. Low longevity is one of its obvious vulnerabilities. Yet, with a more realistic perception about the most likely outcome of relationships, we would have a more rational state of mind when things start going wrong and react more constructively. On the other hand, this heightened awareness might actually provide enough incentives and sincere efforts by us to save our relationships. Learning about the inherent causes of relationship problems might help those who are smart and humble to adopt a constructive role for managing their relationships. Adopting some relationship principles, as suggested in this book, is also for the same purpose, i.e., to make couples relate more effectively.

Knowing about the complexity of human behaviour and its adverse effects on their relationships is the only remedy left to save couples. We should reconsider our view of relationships, redefine our expectations realistically, and be prepared for the worst scenario, i.e., separation.

The Book Structure

This book has three parts. Part I will explain the causes of relationship problems. Part II will offer some plausible solutions to keep relationships manageable. It will explain why we need a 'relationship framework' and a variety of radical solutions. These steps are necessary since our existing methods of solving relationship problems have failed. Part III will provide an outline of all the main points addressed in the previous chapters, plus some final observations about relationships.

Each chapter in Part I is devoted to a specific dimension of the human psyche in the way they drive our thoughts and actions, as follows:

Chapter One will explore the types of *human needs* and explain how they impact people as an individual and in their relationships. This will also help later when 'personal needs' of partners are compared with the 'relationship needs' in order to pinpoint the sources of conflicts.

Chapter Two will provide a list of personal *inner forces* such as instincts, and *outer forces* like culture and family. The role of these forces in personal behaviour and in relationships will be explained.

Chapter Three will attempt to dissect the *personality components* of a person. A simple personality model will show how people's *three aspects of personality* interact and result in the way they conceive things and others. These aspects of human personality influence our thoughts and actions. They make us behave in certain detrimental ways that affect us personally and hurt our partners too.

Chapter Four will focus on our perceptions of ourselves and others, especially our partners. It will show the complexity of perceptions in general. And it will show the high degree of misperceptions, which lead to relationship problems.

Chapter Five will discuss the role of mental consciousness in the effectiveness of partners' communication.

Chapter Six will discuss the nature of love and the effects of human hormones on love and relationships.

Chapter Seven will discuss the nature of relationships in the new era. What does it really take to build and enjoy good relationships?

Part II will study the concept and components of relationships. It will suggest a relationship framework and a list of principles that can benefit couples in the new era. The following topics are covered:

Chapter Eight will review relationship expectations with the aim of identifying the ones that are realistic in the new era.

Chapter Nine will review relationships as an independent entity with specific needs. A relationship framework is developed as well.

Chapter Ten will propose a tentative set of Generally Acceptable Relationship Principles (GARP). The objectives of GARP and how they could be propagated in societies are discussed in this chapter.

Chapter Eleven will recommend some radical changes that might help us view and implement the needs of relationships in modern societies. It is argued that a major overhaul of social mechanisms is required to accommodate the newer relationship needs.

Chapter Twelve will discuss the concept of 'need urgency' and compares it with the personal needs hierarchy of Maslow. Even though we usually follow the needs hierarchy to fulfil our personal needs, need urgency plays a higher role in relationships. This is because our need for a companion could in essence be considered a *basic* need rather than a social need per se.

Chapter Thirteen will review the factors and methods of measuring partners' compatibility in the new era. The old process of measuring compatibility cannot be applied to our new relationship framework as suggested in this book.

Part III has three chapters. The final observations about relationships and gender differences are discussed in this part. Then the highlights and main issues raised throughout the book are outlined for the readers' convenience and future reference. These chapters cover the following topics:

Chapter Fourteen will provide the author's rudimentary account of why relationships' deteriorating trends might not reverse until 2115. The facts and conclusions of this book are outlined here to support the author's pessimism about the lengthy struggle ahead.

Chapter Fifteen will provide a list of major personality differences between the genders. It will be shown how these differences and priorities hinder the process of reconciliation in relationships.

Chapter Sixteen will provide the highlights of Chapters One through Thirteen in a recap format for ease of reference.

Chapter One
Personal Needs versus Relationship Needs

Ibrahim Maslow theorized that humans are driven by a set of hierarchical needs. Basic needs, such as food and shelter, are at the bottom of this hierarchy. Our needs for social interaction and recognition stand in the middle. And, the higher needs consist of self-esteem and actualization. According to this theory, people move up the needs hierarchy as their lower needs are satisfied. Diagram 1.1 is a simple presentation of Maslow's personal needs hierarchy.

↑ Self-actualization/Spirituality
Status/Recognition
Social
Security
Shelter & Food

Diagram 1.1: Maslow's Personal Needs Hierarchy

Fortunately we satisfy our basic needs for food and shelter rather easily in modern societies. But we usually have major difficulty satisfying our middle range needs, including relationships and recognition. Then we rarely find the opportunity to strive for our higher needs. We are so consumed by our middle range needs we hardly get a chance to attend to the higher ones. In particular, our struggle to find and keep a suitable companion proves too frustrating and time-consuming. Yet, despite our relentless efforts, this need (for a companion) remains substantially unfulfilled for most of us. Some of the reasons are: Couples' excessive expectations from relationships, the complexity and ambiguity of values in modern societies, and occupational stress.

Our personal needs dictate our priorities, thoughts, and actions. Accordingly, they impact our relationships in major ways. So learning about the nature and authenticity of our personal needs, and motivations behind them, can help us at many levels: We learn about ourselves better. We might even find the needed enlightenment to figure out 'who we really are.' Also, we learn more about our partners, who are driven by similar needs. And then we can hopefully learn how couples' specific personal needs clash in their relationships. This book will emphasize mainly on that group of personal needs that impact relationships directly.

In relationships, partners try to help each other achieve their medium range personal needs, such as security and compassion, better. But in reality, these personal needs prove too difficult to understand and satisfy. Contrary to our naïve presumptions, our personal needs usually get frustrated instead of fulfilled in relationships, which then lead to partners' clashes. In particular, the need for compassion is the one that couples seek the most and the one that remains most often unfulfilled in relationships. Why? (This conundrum will be studied later in this book too.)

'Seeking a companion' is a medium range need if it is considered an extension of our social need according to Maslow's model. But, as argued in Chapter Twelve, perhaps the 'need for a companion' should be viewed as a basic need due to its significance and urgency. Anyway, we seek a companion to satisfy three major personal needs: Sex, compassion, and love. They are the three pillars of relationships. By the way, using diagrams throughout this book is only for facilitating our discussions. Hopefully they will help the readers without making this book look too technical.

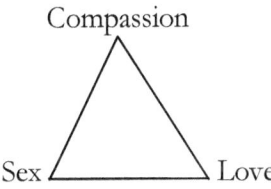

Diagram 1.2: Three Pillars of Relationships

An ideal relationship satisfies our needs for sex, compassion, and love:

Sex—and the urge for procreation—is obviously a strong, instinctual need. It is a *basic* personal need and a *basic* purpose of relationships. But the role of sex has become complex and controversial in relationships, as explained in the following pages. By the way, a main reason that sex must be considered a basic purpose (or outcome) of relationships is because partners' basic need for sex becomes ethically restricted, i.e., it becomes solely dependent upon their relationship; all based on the major assumption that relationships could and would satisfy this need.

Compassion contains a wide range of personal needs depending on partners' circumstances and maturity. They consist of security, sympathy, socializing, respect, recognition, and similar ones.

Love is the need most misunderstood. The meaning of the word 'love' has gradually become too ambiguous. Its commonplace usage nowadays is quite different from the selfless love that we usually imagine and expect. Sometimes we witness selfless love between partners. But the 'love' we often express to many individuals nowadays is a new phenomenon. It is what Maslow refers to as D-love (deficiency love), which is a possessive, selfish kind of love. Basically we want somebody to love us. We want to possess our lover and pamper our own insecurities, often without a capacity to show sympathy, sentiments, or sensitivity ourselves. D-love's characteristic is that it creates anxiety and hostility. The real love within the context of Maslow's hierarchy is B-love (love for the *being* of another person). It is a mystical and spiritual experience. It is unselfish, unconditional, anxiety-free, highly fulfilling—a kind of self-actualization. In B-love, partners are independent, but capable of giving love without worrying about getting it back in return. B-love is a symptom of needlessness compared to D-love that craves attention.

Nowadays we are mostly using the word 'love' to satisfy our need for D-love. We want to draw our partners' affection and attention, and also ascertain their level of commitment and loyalty to us. So, D-love is at best another kind of 'need for compassion.' Consequently, while we exchange love with each other to fulfil our complex need for 'compassion,' our true need for B-love remains unfulfilled, but a lifelong dream.

Overall, people's complex 'need for a companion' contains many personal needs that extend over the full spectrum of Maslow's needs hierarchy. Sex is a basic need. Compassion contains many of our medium range needs. And B-love is a spiritual sensation at the highest level in Maslow's model. The following diagrams show that the three pillars of relationships in the triangle (a) fall on a straight (hierarchical) line (b) when we stretch the baseline, as if setting 'sex' and 'B-love' apart.

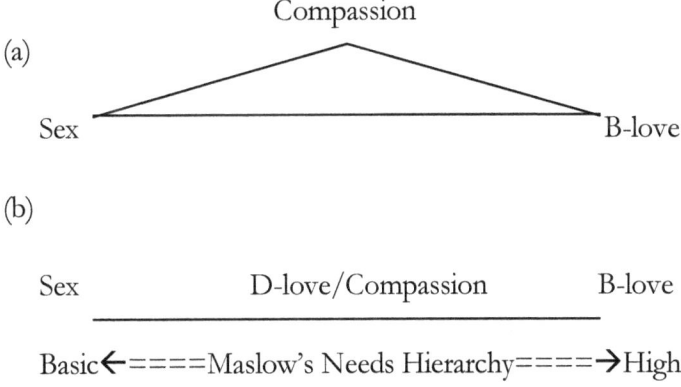

Diagram 1.3: Companionship Needs vs. Maslow's Personal Needs Hierarchy

Thus an ideal relationship can *potentially* cover many of our basic, medium, and high level needs. This is exactly why we *perceive* the 'relationship needs' as a natural extension of our 'personal needs.' But placing such an extreme demand on relationships, to fulfil so many of our personal needs at all levels, is unrealistic. Especially, our new social order cannot deal with this huge demand, as will be discussed throughout this book. There are other implications to notice as well. First, these facts emphasize the psychological significance of having a companion. An ideal companion can seemingly solve almost all of our problems and needs. Second, this significance (and urgency) suggests that companionship must be viewed as a *basic* personal need, and not merely an extension of social (medium range) need. This important viewpoint, and its impact on relationships, will be elaborated further in Chapter Twelve.

The above points also show our naivety to perceive love as the main factor for the success of relationships. We like to believe that love can empower relationships to satisfy a large variety of partners' personal needs, including B-love, sex, and compassion (mostly D-love). But since most relationships cannot fulfil so many of partners' personal needs, their love and relationship collapse too. Satisfying any of our own or our partners' needs is a horrendous job, let alone the whole collection of them.

Especially for compassion and B-love, the amount of self-sacrifice and selflessness required is beyond the patience and ability of most of us. B-love reflects our romantic nature and instinctual search for spirituality. Yet seldom does a person reach the level of wisdom and selflessness needed for B-love. As a start, he must be self-reliant and not obsessed with his/her lower level needs for sex and D-love. Only a superhuman might achieve this! It would be even less conceivable that both partners attain such high qualities and maturity. And yet, in relationships, we seek love (both B-love and D-love). Consequently, we are ignoring the task of defining and sustaining relationships in a practical manner.

Everybody has a personal impression of love that is influenced partly by their instinctual need for B-love, but mainly by their fantasies, wishful thinking, and a variety of psychological urges. Studying the true nature of love will help us understand the forces behind our naïve impression of love. Only then we might adopt a new mindset about the role of love in relationships. Only then we might realize that the viability of relationships depends on partners' capacity to relate effectively instead of expressing hollow love, which is mostly driven by D-love anyway. A variety of motivations behind love are listed on page 22 and an in-depth analysis of love is provided in Chapter Six.

'Sex' has also become a major source of conflict in relationships, because it is treated nowadays as a regulating tool instead of a basic need. Unlike the situation in the older times, couples abuse 'sex' as a bargaining chip to satisfy their D-love and ego. They make sex conditional upon the satisfaction of their higher needs and expectations, which are often not logical anyway. Instead of satisfying the 'basic' need for sex before moving on to the higher levels of relationship needs (i.e., true compassion and love) naturally, couples approach it the other way around. They use sex to tame each other. They use it as a potent tool to play their games.

This manner of treating our personal needs—in reverse order—is a rather new trend in society. It is not necessarily wrong or right. But it is different from what it used to be and it is contrary to Maslow's needs hierarchy too. This condition has emerged in line with new social values, especially partners' search for equality and independence—while they also play all kinds of games to manipulate each other (for increasing their partners' dependency on them). The relationship processes, including our routine retaliations and games, appear natural to everybody, of course. This is because we have been raised in environments satiated with all sorts of vague perceptions about the purpose of relationships and how to make them work. Thus all these games and manipulations feel quite ordinary to most of us. We are conditioned to take them as an inevitable part of relationships. We don't see the shallowness of our expectations and our rising neediness in general. Obviously, we cannot do much about this situation (including the role of *sex as a basic relationship need*) until our mindset is modified in some radical ways in the far future.

Sex is one of many ways in which partners withdraw their support of each other's needs. But sex deprivation causes more harm in relationships than other marital deprivations, because sex is a basic and authentic need. It is a tangible activity with a higher urgency compared to unfulfilled D-love. Sex also reflects compassion and love to some extent, but not conversely. No amount of compassion and love can mitigate the sexual needs of partners. So when retaliation for unfulfilled D-love hinders sex, it leads to partners' severe inner conflicts and harsh reactions, including adultery. These are only a few basic examples of 'relationship needs' clashing with 'personal needs' and causing stress and confusion for couples. More complex examples will be forthcoming in the future chapters.

Personal Needs (Motives) behind Love

As noted before, we exchange love (mostly D-love) to satisfy a large variety of personal needs. Some of these motives are mentioned below:

- To *communicate* with our partners. Showing passion may be only a means of striking a conversation with our partners for a variety of reasons, maybe for measuring some aspects of the relationship, or possibly even for manipulating our partners.
- To express our basic *feelings*. We may show passion to draw our partners' attention to our urgent needs and feelings. We may feel happy, fulfilled, depressed, lonely, lost, etc. We like to share any kind of feelings with out partners and hope to receive their sympathy too.
- To release *psychological* pressures. We may show passion in order to satisfy our needs for acceptance and dependence. Insecurity and need for continuous recognition motivate a partner to use D-love as a mechanism to enforce his/her dependency on his/her partner.
- To mimic our *spiritual* needs. We have an instinctual urge for B-love. Although our medium range needs prevent us from acting on this high-level need, B-love is triggered subconsciously now and then, e.g., when we hear a romantic tune or watch a drama. For a moment, we get in touch with this obscure feeling, i.e.-love. We may eventually act upon it, but usually these spiritual experiences are fleeting moments that we cannot internalize and apply regularly. As noted before, we can truly reach B-love only after fulfilling (or containing) our basic and medium needs and becoming a needless and selfless person. This spiri-

tual love requires these levels of maturity and enlightenment.
- To *control* our partners. An inconspicuous, but common, purpose of love is to satisfy one's need for control. That is, often, a person's urge for love is for the purpose of controlling his/her partner somewhat easier. People exchange love phrases, hoping to enhance their partners' love for them, so that they can live within certain boundaries agreeable to one or both partners, depending on who loves the other more and who is setting the boundaries. People's rising urge for control is not always out of malice. They do it because that is the only method they know for managing their relationships and for prolonging them. Another reason for partners' 'need for control' is that they trust each other less every day and thus get an urge to impose controls on each other.
- To *manipulate (abuse)* our partners. Sometimes a partner expresses love or attachment in order to use his/her partner only for her personal needs—mostly financial and sexual needs—with the least amount of sincerity in her words or attitude.

A side comment worth making, based on the above discussions, is that both our basic need for sex (including the urge for reproduction, especially for women) and our high-level need for love (B-love) are instinctual needs. So, it appears that we have created most of the medium-range personal needs through evolution and according to cultural conditions. As we have felt psychologically weaker and more vulnerable within new environments, we have developed all types of superficial needs to soothe our suffering and deal with our dependencies on others. We have also introduced new social values and personal games to satisfy our urgent need for a companion. This is another clue that the faster our societies grow, the more superficial needs we impose on ourselves and our relationships, and the more complex the relationship environment gets.

Satisfying our Needs in Relationships

We assume that relationships can magically fulfil our most prominent personal needs. We also assume that relationships can somehow deal with all the idiosyncrasies that partners bring to this environment. In reality, however, relationships only place more demands on partners. Instead of helping, relationships cause more frustrations for couples by restricting their means of achieving their personal needs individually. We assume that our partners can (and must) respond to our personal needs, while we selfishly believe that those needs are sensible too. We also imagine that our partners are psychologically equipped to respond to our particular needs at the exact time and manner we desire. Basically, we assume that our partners are capable of making us happy. This is a common mistake that couples make when they start a relationship.

We have not been able to be happy as individuals and we don't know anything about the path to happiness either, so we look for a relationship to do it for us. But a 'relationship' is not a happiness-generating machine. Thus we end up placing high expectations on our partners to make the relationship work and make us happy. We make our partners accountable for the happiness that a relationship is supposed to provide. Since our partners are looking for the same thing, our relationships begin to face a great deal of pressure quickly. Instead of getting the kind of happiness we desire, we face our partners' demands to focus on making them happy—a total contrast to what we had initially assumed! Even when both partners have good intentions, are good-natured, and realize that give and take in a relationship may provide a relative sense of comfort (not necessarily happiness) for both partners, they still don't know how to do it fairly. So we need a relationship framework and a set of principles to show us how to achieve this task.

Nowadays, the first sign of disagreement leads to partners' power struggles to establish their territories and inform each other of their urgent personal needs. Soon, partners engage in all kinds of destructive schemes, supposedly to make the relationship work. They play games and resort to retaliation even when their intentions might be unselfish. They do so because they don't know of any better method to curb their frustration and deal with relationship conflicts that keep growing every day. They often play these games merely for the sake of forcing a solution. They sincerely feel they are helping their partner and their relationship. But usually these games and retaliations end in disaster. Even the most civilized games, such as a temporary withdrawal, could lead to a long-term confusion and an irreversible alienation process. A partner may simply withdraw his/her compassion until a solution for their relationship is found. Then the other partner reacts in a retaliatory way as well. For example, he/she doesn't feel or wish to have sex until the other partner responds to his/her D-love needs. Meanwhile, partners find each other's demands unrealistic. They find each other's retaliations a kind of blackmail. So the game heats up. A partner's decent objective for a temporary withdrawal—to signal his/her partner about the existence of a conflict between them—is not perceived the same way by his/her partner. In the process, the mental or sexual deprivation puts added pressure on both partners. They take the threat to their needs for compassion and sex seriously. They get hostile. All along, the point ignored by both partners is that their partners might have had good intentions, at least initially. Both partners might have in fact been genuinely trying to salvage their relationship. Albeit they don't know how to make their points clear to one another. And this is not necessarily a matter of bad communication either. They are living in such an imaginary world they don't even understand the nature of problems, even though they insist that they do. More importantly, they ignore that often it is their own personal needs and expectations that require adjusting; and not the attitude of their partners. As stated before, most of our personal needs in new societies are artificial anyway. Our needs for more things and more compassion are what we have imposed upon ourselves by habit and imitation. We have become too demanding because we believe we deserve better. We have become too ambitious and spoiled. Our phony social values have made us too needy and desperate. So, in most cases, it is our needs that must be adjusted if we really were interested in the health of our relationships. We simply must learn to look at the bigger picture and stop fussing about our long list of artificial needs. We must find ways of fulfilling our personal needs independently so that the burden on relationships is reduced.

People are normally better in retaliation than finding a means of reconciliation. This is human nature. It shows humans' inherent limitations, as will be discussed in the future chapters. We are unwilling to accept that our spouses often cannot fulfil our personal needs merely due to their unique characteristics and not necessarily out of spite. So, in the end, partners' honourable intentions get lost amidst their psychological deprivations and clashes. Soon both partners face major catastrophes: Their personal needs are not satisfied, and they must face their partner's retaliations too. Things get out of control. Relationships fall apart.

We must then either submit to our partner's demands, which are normally outside our means and beliefs, or prepare ourselves for further struggles and alienation. In either case, we introduce more destructive games and retaliations into our relationships. Thus the war of nerves continues until our relationships are out of control. This is an obvious scenario that we are all familiar with. But the main reason it is explained here is to draw the following conclusions:

People assume that relationships can fulfil their personal needs, or empower them to do so personally. But instead they find more restrictions in achieving them. Each partner gets frustrated because:

- Fulfilling even his/her basic needs, including sex, is suddenly at the mercy of someone else.
- The cost of satisfying his/her needs often seems to be too high and against his/her convictions, integrity, and sense of independence. The cost mostly entails some type of humiliation he/she must bear to accommodate his/her partner.
- He/she cannot seek relief anywhere else because of his/her commitment to their relationship. For example, if he/she seeks sex outside of this failing relationship,

he/she faces the charge of adultery. It would be a taboo to satisfy a strong natural urge, a basic need that he/she could satisfy almost at will prior to entering a relationship.
- The situation spins out of control, because his/her partner's unending demands are unrealistic and it is not easy to abandon the relationship either. The relationship stays in a stalemate indefinitely.

In this frustrating environment, partners' needs for sex and compassion are jeopardized and they face mental and physical hardship. Those who insist on finding 'love' in a relationship, too, are in an even tougher position, because their expectation is beyond the limits of a normal relationship to begin with.

Yet, often, neither partner is at fault in these situations. They are both victims of their *complex needs* and irreversible idiosyncrasies. They have been conditioned in society to set high expectations for relationships. 'Complex needs' is meant here to reflect both our instinctual needs such as sex and those artificial ones, such as need for more things and more compassion. After all, these artificial needs are the symptoms of new lifestyles in modern society and we are helplessly obsessed by them. Our personal needs are becoming too complex because the authentic and artificial ones are getting mixed up and creating new meanings and expectations beyond our apprehension and ability to satisfy. Yet we must somehow learn to deal with all these needs, whether authentic or artificial.

Even partners' retaliations, when their complex needs are ignored, might be considered natural if we accept them as defence mechanisms. It will be discussed in the future chapters that partners' many personality flaws force them to react irrationally. To them, reacting or retaliating is their only tool to survive in this chaotic society. Their only guilt is that they have naively believed that they would get their needs satisfied faster in a relationship. They have naively ignored the fact that their partners are entering relationships with many urgent needs and demands of their own. They also have naively believed that they can convince their partners better through retaliation and by playing games. Retaliation and playing games are all they know for controlling their relationships and partners.

We ignore the high likelihood that our partners haven't been able to make themselves happy (even though nowadays everybody likes to shout how happy and mature they are and how beautiful life is). So how can we expect them to make us happy? Are we naïve, or selfishly assume we can tame them to serve us? Of course, sometimes, one partner submits to the whims of the other partner eventually, because he/she gets tired of fighting or playing games, or whatever. But this type of relationship is doomed and unacceptable in our modern societies anyway. Our faulty assumption is that happiness is something that someone else can bring to us in a relationship. With this kind of mindset, we should expect only more headaches in our relationships and life in general.

It can be counter-argued that relationship inconveniences are a reasonable price to pay for its advantages. Considering the benefits and the joy of relationships, we will continue to get ourselves into this difficult conundrum time and again regardless of all the warnings. Especially for younger people with all kinds of hopes and urges, relationships will continue to appear a safe haven despite all the daunting evidences in society. We ignore the high likelihood of future agony for the sake of the immediate pleasure of someone's company *now*—another major repercussion of living in the now. We cannot avoid the temptation of getting into relationships, but we must become more conscious about its devastating pitfalls too. We must be better equipped to deal with its inevitable hardships, and know how to get out of it—which most likely becomes necessary—with the least amount of damage.

Nonetheless, each partner in a relationship feels the burden of unfulfilled personal needs, plus the added demands of his/her partner to make him/her happy. Moreover, a 'relationship' creates a variety of needs of its own, as will be shown in the upcoming chapters. Most often these needs remain unrecognized and unfulfilled, which then cause added confusion for partners personally and in terms of relating to one another. The most obvious ones are created once children are brought into the equation. Parents, already burdened by unfulfilled personal needs and their partners' demands, suddenly have to deal with the needs of the children too. Furthermore, they usually have conflicting strategies for satisfying their children's needs as well. On top of all this, children's needs are getting too complex and irrational these days anyhow. We are allowing, actually encouraging, this to happen without proper justification. This is all part of social pressure to give children more every day, and because partners like to satisfy their own egos and their need for the love of their children. The children's needs also limit partners' time and ability to attend to their own personal needs. Thus they get edgy and blame their partners for all these inconveniences, at least subconsciously. A symptom of partners' deprivation (for compassion) emerges when parents begin to compete and fight for the love of their children. Each parent tries to prove his/her love to the children by spoiling them more, and sometimes badmouthing or humiliating his/her partner. They do all these ridiculous crimes with the aim of satisfying their own personal need for compassion, which now they hope to satisfy partially through their children at least.

So, in every relationship, three sets of unfulfilled needs (personal needs, their partners' demands, and relationship needs) place unmanageable pressures on both partners. And, then, these subdued needs and demands keep piling up and causing more tension, clashes, and retaliations.

Relationship Needs

We all have similar needs in terms of companionship, but, oddly enough, we cannot help each other achieve them. It is depressing to see that finding a suitable companion has become such a challenging and frustrating task despite the increasing number of matchmaking services and meeting places. Maintaining a decent relationship has proven even more difficult. Aside from the high divorce rate in modern societies, many married couples are only tolerating their substandard relationships. They cannot find a way out of the mess they have been trapped into. They feel helpless while striving to save their marriages by visiting counsellors and psychologists. No wonder antidepressant is the most widely prescribed drug in the United States and probably in all other modern societies too.

We witness these facts around us, feel the heavy toll this situation is taking on our health, and still continue with our present approaches and mentality. Why are we, as partners in this common cause, incapable of agreeing on a solution? Why do we actually sabotage the process of achieving our common goal, i.e., a manageable relationship, by humiliating and traumatizing our partners? Is it because we soon get tired of a relationship we had so eagerly tried to get into? Is it because partners' personal needs suffocate their relationship? Are our personal idiosyncrasies and insecurities getting out of control? Aren't we intelligent enough? Are too many philosophical slogans obscuring our sense of reality? Is our ego and impatience stopping us from reaching a decent compromise? Is our sense of romanticism preventing us from assessing relationship hurdles practically before marriage? Are we hoping for miracles to save our relationships instead of relying on proper principles to keep it together? Or is our legal system, which must strengthen the foundation of family life, in fact hurting the situation? The answer is: All of the above.

Nowadays, nobody really has a good idea about the relationship needs. At best, people list some vague objectives, such as love, security, family, etc. When looking for a companion, however, most people have a long, fanciful agenda, which contains both their personal problems and personal needs. They imagine that their relationships can solve a large variety of their financial and emotional problems. Without any knowledge of 'relationship needs,' each partner creates an absurd personal perception about their relationship's potentials and what they must get out of it. In this kind of environment, obviously partners cannot relate effectively.

Soon, their misperceptions and miscommunications engulf their relationship, while the relationships' unique needs remain unfulfilled too. Making the matter worse, partners' needs and priorities also keep changing over the years. As our societies progress, people's problems and needs seem to be increasing out of proportion. The agenda is getting longer every year, and people get more frustrated as their partners fail to fulfil those expectations. In all, relationships are getting more instable due to partners' lack of objectivity, the absence of an independent platform to measure the state of their relationship, and the fact that relationship conflicts are assessed according to partners' own personal interpretations and egotistical needs.

These agonizing symptoms reveal two simple facts: 1) Partners' naïve (and random) expectations cannot coincide with the relationships' concrete needs. And 2) there is no definition of the 'relationship needs' to prepare couples for the challenges of companionship nowadays amidst all other pressing life demands. No uniform set of objectives is available for relationships to provide a clearer picture to couples; to tame their wild perceptions. Hence, couples have no standards for setting their personal priorities and plans in line with the relationship needs. They cannot even envisage the necessity of containing their personal needs in order to pinpoint, and focus on, the relationship needs. Instead, they put more demands on their relationships and partners inadvertently or selfishly, simply because they are convinced that their needs are logical and justified.

So, the first step is to find those *specific needs of relationships* in order to bring some form of harmony into relationships. The second step is to enhance partners' willingness and patience to learn these needs. They should understand how relationship needs may clash with their personal needs. Furthermore, they must curb their egos to stay objective. A lot of issues must be sorted out to make a relationship work, eh? Absolutely! Nonetheless, we should learn to view 'relationships' as a unique entity with specific needs, which are totally different from the conflicting needs of the partners in it. It is a pity that our educational systems, especially at senior high school, do not devote a good portion of its required curriculum to this essential real life subject.

Part II of this book is devoted to the task of defining relationship needs and comparing them with personal needs of partners.

Compatibility Limitations

Another faulty assumption nowadays is that some type of partners' compatibility can guarantee the success of relationships. Some compatibility tests are designed to measure couples' background and personality. They are supposedly compatible if they have similar traits and needs. The first problem with this approach is that it emphasizes on partners and ignores the specific needs of relationships. It assumes that relationships could have different forms, meanings, and objectives according to couples' personalities. It assumes that the sets of factors contributing to the success of relationships could be as varied as personalities are.

Of course, as noted before, every relationship has its unique characteristics and setting. And of course, there should be some level of flexibility in relationships to accommodate all personalities. But relationship formats that can support partners, to relate to each other effectively, are limited. It will be discussed in Chapter Twelve that only a handful of relationship models is available for couples to adopt. That is, all relationships should operate from within a certain model, because there cannot be infinite models for the infinite types of personalities. This fact also indicates that not all couples need (or should seek) the most ideal model of relationship. A handful relationship models can help almost all couples build and maintain a good joint life together without obsessing themselves with the myths and impracticalities of an imaginary, ideal relationship. At the same time, couples can introduce a lot of flexibility into their relationships if only they agree on the type of relationship (model) most suitable for them. In a sense, they must evaluate their personal needs in comparison to relationship needs objectively, in line with the relationship model that best fits their personalities. The model chosen should be suitable for both partners and not forced by one on the other. In case none of the models suits both partners, it is the best indication that this couple is not fit to be in a relationship. They must each find the right partner with whom they agree about the specific relationship model for them. Of course, these relationship models all work from within the overall 'relationship framework' that will be discussed in Part II as well.

Another problem with the existing compatibility approach is that it ignores the fact that partners' needs and expectations hardly remain consistent, compatible, and achievable. When their personal needs change, they usually proceed to redefine their expectations from their relationship. Still another problem with the existing approach is that it assumes that partners at least know the basic requirements of relationships intuitively. This bare minimum of knowledge is required so that couples can relate and communicate effectively. But no longer do people know these basic needs due to drastic cultural changes and migrations. Furthermore, partners' preliminary compatibilities no longer help when the relationship environment does not develop according to their expectations. External forces and partners' personalities can change everything quickly. Another major problem with present compatibility tests is that, regardless of a couple's initial seeming compatibility, it takes a long time, perhaps years, for them to really begin to relate to one another, if at all. Their real personalities and perceptions of each other emerge based on their natural encounters during a lengthy period, probably two years of co-habiting at least. If the same compatibility tests were applied at the beginning and the end of let's say two years of co-habitation, the results would be quite different. The longer a couple lives together, the more the results of the initial compatibility test would fall off the chart. The reason is that compatibility is mostly a function of partners' perceptions that keep growing and stabilizing only after lengthy interactions and once the initial over-optimism about relationships is replaced by reality. So in a sense, the value of compatibility tests for match making is quite minimal. They are probably more useful in diagnosing the problem areas at any particular point in a relationship.

Even two compatible partners with reasonable expectations still find themselves in conflict regularly. This is because they judge the health of their relationship too emotionally, still based on their unfulfilled personal desires and demands. Their deprived needs lead to gross misperceptions about the health of their relationship and their partner's intentions. And then these misperceptions (mistrusts) further complicate their means of communicating and relating to one another. This is a most likely scenario even for two compatible partners with moderate expectations from their relationship. Now just imagine the level of conflicts and stress when partners' expectations have been set too high unrealistically at the outset due to their initial eagerness, ego, optimism, or silly promises.

The point here is not to undermine the value of partners' compatibility. Obviously, some measure of couples' compatibility can help partners to a large extent, especially when some acceptable relationship norms or guidelines are hopefully available. But without guidelines, even compatible couples are subject to loose interpretations about the state of their relationships and there are high chances of misperceptions and clashes. A new kind of compatibility measures is needed for the new era anyway. They should determine whether two individuals are capable of living together within a specific relationship model. The tests should measure partners' aptitude and personalities in relation to the factors applicable to various relationship models and determine whether they fit in one of those models. They can, of course, decide to adopt a different model later, if necessary. The factors and methods used for the new compatibility tests are suggested in Chapter Thirteen.

One might argue that allowing people define their own meaning of a relationship better reflects our quest for freedom and independence. But this book advocates the opposite: that enhancing awareness about the needs and traps of relationships can save people and society a lot of financial and emotional hassle. Actually, the lack of a uniform relationship framework and global principles is jeopardizing our need for independence and freedom. This is because we end up spending a great deal of time arguing with our partners on all sorts of marital issues to no avail. Our freedom and individuality are tainted in the process of never-ending conflict resolutions and games. The intention is not to regulate relationships or restrict individuals' freedom of choice or behaviour. On the contrary, devising some relationship principles will promote the idea of individuals' independence both in and out of a relationship. But, at the same time, depicting a picture of a successful relationship, and the essential factors needed for achieving it, can benefit couples and society in general. The objective is to minimize the effects of partners' hasty perceptions and subjective judgments. These anomalies are currently misleading couples and driving society away from the main purposes of modernization and true civilization. The couples' lack of knowledge about the specific demands of relationships has caused many of the problems they are witnessing nowadays. And pursuing the same approach is a disservice to individuals and society.

In any contract negotiation, in business or otherwise, the chances of success depend on the objectivity of the parties and the initial rules of engagement. These rules are set before the parties even begin discussing specific issues. Similar principles are needed for relationships even more seriously considering couples' limited expertise in negotiating.

The Forces of Evil

Partners' compatibility obviously improves their chances of communicating and relating to one another. Objectivity is introduced in their relationships at many levels when they share certain values and have compatible mentalities. In reality, however, even this basic tool for introducing objectivity is constantly sabotaged by partners. That is, not only we don't know how to measure compatibility, but also ignore the signs of incompatibility when they are clearly in front of us. For example, when we are in love or need a companion urgently, we ignore all the potential hassles of incompatibility. It seems as if some evil forces are at work to make us choose the wrong partners for ourselves. Sometimes we go out of our ways to ignore compatible partners in favour of incompatible ones. Sometimes we prefer jerks because they seem to challenge us. There are many reasons for this behaviour. They all relate to the effects of inner forces and outer forces that make us jump into relationships prematurely. The initial chemistry that partners feel toward each other often obscures their objectivity. And quite often, we don't get the opportunity to be choosy. When someone shows compassion and love, we stop worrying about the consequences of gross incompatibility. This is true especially since the hassles of relationships are not felt until we get involved in one. Or we always believe that the next partner and the next relationship would be different, i.e., it would be manageable and nice!

So, the value of compatibility tests is low at the present time also because couples depend mostly on their intuition, chemistry, and arbitrary values that society and parents have injected into their minds about relationships' success factors. Sometime in the far future, people may finally find access to reliable compatibility tests to understand where they stand and what kind of a relationship they might be able to build together. Meanwhile, even basic compatibility tests, which may be developed quickly based on the models suggested in Chapter Thirteen, can help couples pinpoint their incompatibilities and potential problem areas.

In a group therapy session with divorced men and women, they were asked to mention the main reason for choosing their spouses. The answers were quite informative. The typical answers were as follows:
- Mother figure
- Out of pity, I felt sorry for her/him
- Lifestyle change
- To stabilize my life
- To have a home
- I loved him/her (the most popular answer)

Obviously, when the initial purpose of a relationship is not valid or solid, the chances of bringing objectivity into it would be slim. After a while, couples realize their mistakes and begin to resent their partners and themselves for being dragged into a relationship incapable of satisfying their needs (which are superficial most often anyway). Some other reasons for couples choosing the wrong partners are: physical attraction, lust, age, social/family pressure, psychological dysfunction, misperceptions, E-love, obsessions, material issues, security/insecurity, lack of meaningful criteria to use, loneliness.

Based on limited (unscientific) findings, the author has developed a cynical hypothesis that explains so many of relationship problems. That is, the author believes that people usually feel chemistry toward individuals whom they are not compatible with in any justifiable measure (if we used the relationship success criteria suggested mostly in Part II). The hypothesis stipulates the opposite as well: Compatible individuals normally feel little or no chemistry toward one another. Still the latter group has a better chance of managing a good relationship for themselves compared with the first group, i.e., incompatible lovers.

Need Setback Hysteria

Maslow's needs hierarchy implies that people go about satisfying their needs in a civilized, orderly manner. They are content with the level of personal needs they have satisfied so far, while looking forward to the next level in the hierarchy with patience and objectivity. But, in reality, the atmosphere for need fulfilment is no longer calm and logical. In particular, with all the hoopla in society nowadays for people to get rich and famous quickly, the price of not satisfying personal needs has grown too high. People set unrealistic goals for themselves and treat them as legitimate needs. Society pushes the idea that everybody can become whoever they want to be and have everything they wish if they put their minds into it. So people have become too obsessive with their goals and needs. Everybody is looking for a shortcut to have more things with less work, and to get a lot of sympathy when they are too arrogant themselves. Since a large portion of people cannot achieve their exaggerated plans and whims, they feel frustrated and unappreciated. The need to prove one's individuality, nowadays, is further pushing people to set unrealistic goals. They are hoping to make their so-called individuality manifest through fame, wealth, and recognition. In all, people just keep creating more artificial needs for themselves. Their needs for identity and success have combined and turned into an epidemic obsession for many people.

When these artificial needs, these naïve fantasies, are not fulfilled, people don't take their failures lightly. They feel incomplete and a total failure if they don't become somebody special. They store deep inner hurts and conflicts. They get hysterical. The level of frustration and anger in society is increasing because of people's rising inner conflicts. So the kind of graceful content and orderly progression of personal needs, as is somehow suggested by Maslow's needs hierarchy, is no longer prevalent. On the contrary, we witness people's major hysteria for not succeeding to climb up the needs hierarchy quickly enough. The author likes to refer to this emerging epidemic as Need Setback Hysteria—NSH.

NSH is particularly evident and harmful in relationships. Couples start with high expectations, to be magically fulfilled through their magnificent relationships, by their faithful partners' devotion. When they face the reality and their partners' inability to respond to their high expectations, they react hysterically and make life miserable for themselves and their partners. Furthermore, everybody feels some kind of urgency to fulfil their personal needs and attain the happiness they believe they deserve. Need Urgency—NU—is further discussed in Chapter Twelve.

In all, people are getting less patient while expecting a larger number of their needs getting satisfied quickly. So while couples' seemingly urgent (fanciful) needs are increasing constantly, NSH has aggravated the stress level in relationships.

NU + NSH = Rising chaos and stress in society and relationships.

Chapter Two
Inner and Outer Forces Affecting Personality

Chapter One explained the hierarchy of personal needs and their impact on relationships. Personal needs affect individuals' perceptions of the world, their desires and behaviour, and thus their personalities. On the other hand, personal needs are themselves developed and triggered by a wide range of inner and outer forces, which are discussed in this chapter. Understanding these forces can help us manage our personal needs better, improve our personalities, and reduce relationship clashes. The question is whether we can learn to manage our needs better or would like to allow our untamed needs keep destroying our relationships forever.

Obviously, everybody is ultimately responsible for his/her actions and attitude regardless of the forces making him/her behave irrationally. Couples must act smartly and decisively for their welfare if their partners' attitude is offensive or when personality clashes become unbearable. The only question is whether they have been objective enough in judging their partners. Do they realize that certain inner forces within them prevent them from being objective? So, another purpose of studying these inner forces is to increase self-awareness and thus stir objectivity into relationships. Objectivity is further increased when couples realize that their partners' personalities are also developed by forces beyond their control. This awareness might increase their sympathy toward their partners. After all, everybody is often paralysed by his/her flaws and cannot see the harm he/she is inflicting upon him/herself and others. Even if he/she were humble enough to acknowledge his/her flaws, still he/she can do very little to change him/herself. In all, awareness about the destructive forces behind personalities might make couples more flexible instead of letting their arrogance infect their judgments and relationships. They could cooperate to find solutions for controlling their flaws instead of retaliating and demanding personality changes too much.

Two big misperceptions in relationships are that i) our partners are in control of their personalities and ii) they can change themselves easily. Thus we rush to retaliate in our own ways in order to teach them a lesson. We ignore the fact that retaliations only add more barriers for couples to assess the viability of their relationships objectively. The idea is by no means to advocate tolerance against aggression or irrational attitude in relationships. Not at all. But instead of judging our partners naively and hastily, it would help to remember that they behave irrationally because their defence mechanisms are triggered by our comments and attitude. There are debilitating forces behind their actions. Equally important is partners' ability to act civilly and end their irreconcilable relationships without causing each other too much harm.

I. Inner Forces of Personality

Inner forces basically refer to our inherent or rooted characteristics. We hardly have any control over them since they mostly operate from within our unconscious and subconscious mind. Their influence over our behaviour is quite substantial, though, without us even realizing it. We don't know why we do certain things or think in certain ways. In all, four types of **inner forces instigate our thoughts, urges, needs, and actions:**

Instincts: The primitive urges that all humans share.
Genetics: Specific family genes that affect people's thinking and behaviour.
Habits: Idiosyncrasies and conditioning caused by rearing experiences.
Reactions: Defence mechanisms, impulses, and progressively developed schemes (games and roles) to sustain ourselves.

These four highly potent forces control our wellbeing and behaving, but also impose major limitations on us in terms of becoming who we would like to be. We have difficulty mitigating their effects regardless of the incentives to do so. They generate both positive and negative outcomes for us and others. They cause happiness or frustration. So, as intelligent beings, we try to reward positive attitudes and punish malice in order to tame ourselves and the negative forces within us. This is one intention of civilization. We have developed laws, ethics, and etiquettes because we believe that people's urges and actions are often fuelled by erratic forces mostly beyond their control. Accordingly, society in general, and legal system in particular, show tolerance when they deal with people's inherent flaws. Our laws take into account the effects of psychological disturbances behind personal behaviour, especially when there is a clear sign of mental disorder. But, as individuals, most of us have not learned to make similar adjustments in our thoughts about our partners when they seemingly make a mistake. We don't give our partners enough slack for their weaknesses. We have little patience for imperfections because we arrogantly assume that we are perfect ourselves. We expect others to be perfect, too, according to our image of perfection, of course. These two terribly erroneous presumptions are by themselves the symptoms of inner forces dictating our judgment and dulling our objectivity.

People usually pretend to be in control of their personalities and behave appealingly, out of etiquette, to keep others happy. But, deep down, the inner forces remain in control and then suddenly resurface with great vengeance at the worst possible time. Especially in relationships, partners' attempt to tame each other aggravates these inner forces regularly. With our arrogance and demands, we fuel our partners' defence mechanisms and they retaliate in their own destructive ways. We simply forget about these untameable, explosive forces within humans. So we expect our partners to be in full control of their personalities. In addition, we expect them to think and behave in certain ways, simply because we like them better that way. Both of these expectations are absurd, of course.

Discussing the variety and impact of inner forces is beyond the scope of this book. But some of them will be reviewed briefly in the remainder of this chapter under each of the four above stated categories.

A. Instinctual Forces

Some inert urges are common amongst humans. They consist of the simple urge to breathe all the way to our complex urge for spirituality. Yet, individuals' level of self-awareness determines how closely they might access and utilize these forces. For example, some people learn better means of breathing by taking yoga lessons. And many people adopt religion to soothe their spirituality needs. Of course, true spirituality can materialize only through meditation and self-awareness and gaining selflessness. Tapping the power of the unconscious through self-awareness has an impact on individuals' personality and will be reviewed in Chapter Five. But for the purposes of this chapter, only four types of instinctual forces are reviewed due to their immediate impact on relationships.

i) Needs for Dependence and Independence

At adolescence, we face many inner conflicts as we try to develop our character. These conflicts make us think and behave in certain bizarre ways. We learn how to deal with many of these conflicts eventually. Some of them become irrelevant when we move on to the next stages of our lives. But one particular conflict stays with us for the rest of our lives. This persistent conflict arises when our two fundamental needs for dependence and independence keep clashing constantly in our mind. These inherent needs play a major role in our lives, probably more prominently than any single hierarchical need defined by Maslow does. In fact, any one of Maslow's hierarchical needs is often at the mercy of our needs for dependence and independence. Our other needs are substantiated or dampened only based on our prominent need for independence (or dependence) regardless of the consequences. For example, our pride (a symptom of independence) often defies any single need, even the need for food or survival. We go on hunger strike sometimes. In this sense, pride finds urgency even ahead of our basic needs. On the other hand, our need for dependence, e.g., the need for passion and a companion, might supersede our need for food or even breathing. We might prefer to die when loneliness is crippling our existence and mind. Need urgency concept, in Chapter Twelve, will discuss these points further. The point of interest here is that our personal needs for dependence and independence create deep conflicts for us individually. But more importantly, partners' conflicts due to these needs affect their relationship quite adversely.

At adolescence, we get ready to announce our independence from family and their lifestyle. We begin to develop our own thoughts and preferences. We strive to show off our independence and freedom by adhering to all types of rebellion and exaggerated expression of opinions, including our appearance and attire. Meanwhile, some weird feelings for dependence begin to creep into our heads sneakily. We feel the need to belong to groups of friends, be accepted by others, be loved by a girlfriend or boyfriend (not to mention drugs, alcohol, and cigarettes). As we proceed through life, the number of dependencies piles up, while, at the same time, we struggle to develop our unique identity and independence. We get frustrated when our independence is constantly threatened by our need for dependence on other people and society. We feel our independence invaded and we hate those who are doing it.

When we face the opportunity of entering a relationship, we realize the need to give up some of our autonomy for the benefits of companionship. We may find this trade-off equitable initially. But we find it humiliating when even small conflicts make us doubt our identity, the purpose of our relationships, and the value of our sacrifices. We hate the way our partner is squashing our independence. The longer we stay in a relationship, the larger the level of personal conflict between dependence and independence gets, and the more pressure is put on the relationship.

Especially, with the added emphasis on individualism and independence nowadays, personal conflict due to the inner needs for both dependence and independence has become too prominent and more prevalent. We try to create some level of balance between our needs for dependence and independence in order to make our relationships manageable in societies that are satiated with slogans of personal identity and individualism. Creating and maintaining this balance is tough, even if such a balance could be found. Most couples have difficulty in this area.

Yet a tougher personal conflict resides even deeper in our psyche. This conflict stems from the fact that many people seek dependence obsessively because of their prominent insecurities and need for a companion. As discussed in Chapter One, 'need for a companion' is a strong, complex personal need that expands across Maslow's needs hierarchy. Companionship satisfies our basic, medium, and high level needs. Most of us seek compassion and a companion almost more than anything else. Although we acknowledge the need for creating a practical balance between independence and dependence, we might be a very needy person inherently. We might prefer to depend totally on our partners. We want to depend on her/him to provide the compassion and passion that we crave. We might even need someone to lead us through life. This is a much higher level of dependence than a normal person with some hypothetical balance (between dependence and independence) needs. Meanwhile, we don't want to show our neediness to our partner, especially if he/she is not as needy as we are. So, while one partner insists on creating a workable balance for partners' independence, the other partner hides his/her need for more (or total) dependence. And yet, he/she hopes all along that his/her obsessive (but unexpressed) need for dependence is understood. Another way of stating this condition is that most individuals' need for D-love has increased irrationally in recent decades, but they hate to admit it. Their ego stops them from expressing their true need for all that extra compassion, mostly because it is not fashionable to show their vulnerabilities and inability to be independent.

In general, true independence requires (and leads to) a lot of isolation and self-reliance. Dependence, on the other hand, is mostly synonymous with compassion and a willingness to pay a price for it. We all value compassion a lot. We feel the need for dependence on another individual and society, because we doubt our ability to survive as an independent person. Some of us need dependency to another person—a lover perhaps—more urgently in order to validate our identity and existence. Yet our partners and society do not have the capacity to cope with our need for dependence. In most cases, they actually ridicule and take advantage of our perceived weakness, i.e., our inability to be independent. But even for people seeking dependence obsessively, their need for independence emerges quite regularly too. Even this group's need for dependence isn't absolute and permanent. It continues to remain an unmanageable urge.

The matter gets really out of hand when we pretend to be more independent than we really feel we are, or can handle. Most of us are trained nowadays to insist on our individuality and independence. That is how we believe we can assert ourselves and show our identity. We learn to play all kinds of roles and games to prove our independence and strong identity. But, as we engage in these types of exaggerations, to prove our needlessness, we place a higher pressure on our psyche to set a fake balance between our needs for dependence and independence. We lose touch with reality and our true needs. We are in effect imposing another set of artificial needs on ourselves that are unachievable. At the same time, we are depriving ourselves from fulfilling our need for dependence. These artificial needs and situations cause more inner conflicts and psychological damages. They lead to futile clashes with our partners too. We become aggressive in order to show assertiveness, mostly because we don't know the delicate art of assertiveness. In most situations, assertiveness might not even be in our nature anyway. We are fighting our own natural urges to become somebody else. We play the role of an independent person with some imaginary identity, but yet unfulfilled. This kind of confusion causes identity crisis, of course, and often we feel this deficiency ourselves too. Yet we keep seeking independence, anyway, because we are brainwashed to play those roles; to fight for our individuality and identity no matter what. Our artificial need to show off our independence, as a symbol of freedom and identity, has in effect become counter productive for both our individuality and relationships.

At the other extreme, many people have become too submissive and dependent on their relationships and accept all kinds of humiliations and intimidation, including their partners' infidelity. Only a few decades ago, infidelity was a taboo and led to an automatic divorce. But not anymore. Yet, even these people, with high dependence orientation and a submissive attitude, have difficulty sustaining their relationships. Their sacrifices go unnoticed and they lose their relationships unexpectedly. Some of these people might eventually learn that it is impossible to depend on others, even their partners. To survive in their relationships without getting hurt too much, they eventually learn to play the role of an independent person with a strong identity. They just have to. They are forced to behave that way. The bottom line is that partners' need for dependence is undervalued at so many levels by our new lifestyles, values, and social pressures. It is trendy to show one's aptitude for individualism. So people pretend to be independent in order to fit and survive. They are forced into this position (seeking independence) to defend themselves and fit. But, of course, they remain inherently a dependent, depressed person.

Obviously, the smart thing nowadays is to not depend on others or their words. They simply cannot deliver because of the limitations in their own lives and psyche, and not necessarily out of spite. So, beyond people's *instinctual urge* for independence, three other reasons make them struggle for independence: (1) because they have become too obsessed with the idea of individualism and asserting their identity, (2) just for the sake of coping with social norms and being accepted, (3) because they eventually learn they cannot depend on others.

Another paradox related to dependence-independence needs is also emerging in relationships. That is, while partners try to acquire more independence for themselves, they want to maximize their partners' neediness to them. They strive to gain more power in their relationships by dominating their partners. So there is an ongoing struggle between partners to maintain a balance of power in order to stop the other from dominating them. Everybody likes more independence for themselves but much less for their partners. Men were more domineering in the past, but the trend is reversing in the new era due to women's struggle to assert themselves. Nonetheless, the power struggle for domination is causing major conflicts in relationships nowadays. Instead of creating a relaxed relationship environment, partners' quarrels to maintain 'the needed balance' lead to frictions, mistrust, miscommunications, and misperceptions, as discussed in Chapters Four and Five.

In all, a bizarre trend is emerging as a result of couples' struggle to cope with their needs for dependence and independence: Some couples seek separation with the slightest inconvenience in their relationships (high need for independence and individualism); and some couples accept abuse and adultery as they are too apprehensive about loneliness and isolation (high need for dependence and compassion). These prevalent extremes show the extent of value changes in new societies. They show the extreme imbalance between our needs for independence and dependence, and a general confusion about the role of relationships as an important social concept. A major conclusion is that we are not as strong as we often wish, or pretend, to be in our exaggerated show of independence and individualism. We are not equipped to create a reasonable balance between our needs for dependence and independence in our relationships either. So, the question is whether a framework can be developed and used by couples to reconcile their conflicting urges for dependence and independence in relationships.

The contentious issues in regard to our personal needs for dependence and independence are summarized below:
1. We are not quite conscious of our conflicting needs for dependence and independence. Nor are we aware of the high repercussions of this conflict for us, our relationships, and society in general.
2. We don't know how to define or judge our personal needs for independence and dependence. We don't know how to be independent or dependent when we go about satisfying these needs alternately on a regular basis. Some people pretend to be independent and needless when deep down their need for dependence is overwhelming. And some people damage their identity when they become submissive.
3. We play the kind of roles that others suggest, usually with the highest emphasis on independence, since we don't know how to set and keep a practical balance between our conflicting needs for independence and dependence. Yet everybody has a different balance of needs for independence and dependence according to his/her personal-

ity. Ignoring one's particular needs (for dependence and independence) and sticking to some fake balance creates confusion and frustration.
4. Partners don't know how to discuss and match their needs for dependence and independence—mostly because it might require some kind of compromise, which would be against their presumed identity and independence. So they end up arguing about every detail or decision.
5. Without knowing about our needs for independence and dependence and the balance most suitable for us, we expect our partners to behave as if they did know what the right balance should be. For example, we expect them to respect our independence when we suddenly feel it is time for us to be independent; we ask for a vaster boundary. And then we expect them to be compassionate and caring as soon as we need their attention to satisfy our need for dependence (D-love).
6. We turn off our partners with our exaggerated show of independence and needlessness. And we confuse them with our silly roles and games to enforce our alternating needs for dependence and independence. These erratic interactions make it difficult for partners to relate to each other. Meanwhile, power struggles to dominate our partners, and enforce our gender identities, postpone the matter of finding the right balance (between dependence and independence). Only arrogance and phoniness prevail in this kind of environment. All these conditions hinder the task of bringing objectivity and peace into relationships.
7. As social complexity and the general public's intelligence increase every year, people's demands for both independ-

ence and dependence will rise. They seek more independence because society pushes them to express themselves, and prove their identity, more explicitly. But they also seek more dependence (need for a compassionate companion) because of the increased level of stress in their daily lives and the overall sense of loneliness. So instead of balancing their needs for dependence and independence, people struggle even more with their anxiety and inner conflicts. The topics covered in this book demonstrate how this increased imbalance (between our needs for independence and dependence) is forced upon us due to our lifestyles and mentalities. Relationships will become more instable in the future and their longevity will continue to decline. Considering this inevitable prospect, implementing the messages of this book, especially in terms of the 'radical changes,' suggested in Chapter Eleven, seems very crucial.

The inner conflict due to dependence/independence imbalance affects our moods randomly, usually at worst situations, e.g., when our partner is angry and pushing our nerves. We react harshly because the balance we had presumably imposed for our needs for independence and dependence is threatened. Our partners react harshly, too, for the same reasons—not out of spite perhaps, but only as a by-product of chemical and mental reactions in their bodies. This inner conflict seems to be triggered when we get into arguments with our partners. But, in reality, it is an ongoing struggle within us causing all sorts of insecurity and doubts about our identity. To mitigate this inner conflict, each partner in a relationship should deal with their dilemma of de-

pendence versus independence in three distinct ways as follows:
1. He/she should initially try to establish his/her realistic needs for dependence and independence, based on his/her personality alone, without taking into consideration any compromises necessary for being in any serious relationship with a partner. The idea is to establish one's true temperament and needs regardless of social pressures for independence or the level of compromise needed in a relationship.
2. He/she should establish the levels of dependency/independency that he/she can envision for his/her partner. Usually people dislike partners who seek too much independence. But more crucial than this case is when a person is unprepared (perhaps psychologically) or unwilling to be responsible for a partner who requires too much dependence (emotionally or financially). So he/she should figure out his/her potential partner's inclination for dependence/independence realistically before committing him/herself to any partnership.
3. Together with his/her potential partner, they should establish the kind of dependency/independency balance they require in their relationship. This balance should fit the other two above decisions that each partner must make personally, then they choose the right relationship model.

By the way, a person's needs for dependence/independence are not complementary (or contradictory). It is quite likely that his/her needs for both dependence and independence are high or low. In such cases, creating a balance between partners' dependence/independence is even more difficult. They are usually less-balanced persons to begin with.

ii) Need for Control

We have a strong urge to control our surroundings to maintain order in our lives. We wish to minimize unexpected threats by foreseeing events or obstacles. The more complex our societies and interactions become, the more we feel a need to control the sources of potential threats to our physical and mental welfare. This is particularly true because nowadays we trust people much less than we did a few decades ago. We know that crooks are everywhere, trying to take advantage of our naïveté. Accordingly, our defence mechanisms and need for control are further developed to survive in this environment. Even banks, stock brokers, mortgage brokers, and other supposedly government-controlled entities could lure us into bad decisions and losing our life savings. Hardly do governments step in to support citizens because capitalism gives a higher priority to free enterprise than individuals. So we feel the pressure to control our lives better and make sure we are not victimized. When we get into relationships, the need for control becomes even more necessary. We have to protect ourselves and our partners. But we must also be careful about our partners' intentions and possible hidden agendas. Unfortunately, the more society advances, the less it appears that we can trust our partners in relationships. So we try to control them in order to minimize the possibility of getting hurt by them. But we also wish to control them with the assumption that this would be the best way to protect and prolong our relationships. Naturally, the result of all this controlling is that couples hate, and stress out, each other. Couples' need for independence is challenged when partners try to control each other in hopes of making their relationship last longer.

Even love is often abused to satisfy one's need for control. One reason for 'love' being in such demand, nowadays, is that a person can supposedly control his/her partner better if that partner is in love with him/her. We yearn for B-love to fulfil our need for self-gratification and spirituality. But in reality, nowadays, we mostly end up seeking D-love for compassion and/or controlling our partners. We crave love, even though we are often not capable of giving love in return. We want to be loved for several reasons mentioned in this book, but also for controlling our partner through love dependency.

A lot of personal spirit and potentialities are dampened in relationships due to partners' urge to control each other, sometimes even through (real or fake) love. Both partners lose the opportunity for full growth and self-actualization when even one partner is a control freak.

iii) Need for Sex

As noted in Chapter One, sex is a *basic* relationship need as much as it is a *basic* personal need. So conflicts arise when couples' higher needs (e.g., compassion or D-love) hinder the satisfaction of their instinctual need for sex. Sex has become conditional upon satisfying many higher personal needs of partners, especially love and compassion that partners are normally least capable of delivering. Under this circumstance, the basic sexual need of partners is constantly under threat when some other aspects of their relationship are not perfect, which is usually too often.

The strong urge to procreate encourages women to seek a companion more actively. Men usually play a lesser role in pursuing this heavenly purpose (the reproductive aspect of sex, of course). So, while both genders have huge sexual drives, they have different motives (and biological clocks) for acting upon it. These differences lead to clashes, especially after children are born. Women focus more on the welfare of children and become too possessive of them. Sometimes it seems absurd the way they try to protect their children even from their husbands. Accordingly, men feel abandoned and neglected sexually and emotionally. They might also face occasional hostility if their interference or means of child rearing doesn't coincide with their wives'. On the other hand, men are often accused of their shallow pursuit of sex, although women are catching up in this regard too. The need to experiment with our sexuality is now in full force by both genders.

Anyway, nobody can be blamed for the way their sexual instincts dictate their behaviour and priorities in life, or when their lifestyles jeopardize the satisfaction of a basic need like sex. Sex has turned into a potent parameter for partners to play their games and tame each other. These are irreversible facts of life. But it is important to acknowledge their true sources instead of denying (or arguing about) them tenaciously.

iv) Need for Love

We seek love intuitively to satisfy many of our personal needs as explained especially on page 39 and Chapter Six. Aside from our selfish need for D-love, we also seek love because we sincerely believe it can bring us that ultimate happiness. We see happiness only in the arms of that special person who fits the image of a perfect soul mate. We hope to complete our existence by finding him/her. This reflects our strong instinctual need for spiritual love (B-love). On the other hand, D-love causes negative feelings, such as jealousy, loneliness, depression, and possessiveness; and there is usually nothing we can do about this demon.

B. Genetic Forces

We are somewhat programmed by our genes. It appears that our destinies are largely mapped for us in our genes. We think and act in unique ways that eventually lead to a certain destiny. It is impossible to guess how freewill, luck, instincts, and environment work along with genes to determine the final outcome of our lives. The level of self-awareness and access to our unconscious and subconscious obviously make an impact on our personality too. But it is safe to assume that a good portion of our traits is hereditary. They push us to follow a certain path in our lives or we feel miserable all the time, unless we learn to correct the nature of our thoughts and deeds through self-awareness. Genetics determine whether we are a happy or depressed person. Genetics, of course, determine our potentialities in terms of professions we pursue and in terms of how much we can discover about ourselves, including our aptitude for spirituality and artistry. And genetics affect our level of paranoia and phobias. Accordingly, we are bound to develop a perception of life consistent with these pre-determined mental properties.

In all, genetics formulate a good portion of our personality and destiny. Even our conscious attempts to adjust our personality cannot override the effect of genetics easily. We can't repair our genetic defects, not yet at least. But we can hide them cleverly in order to achieve our goals, the main one being to find a nice companion. After a while, once we relax or don't care anymore, we stop spending such an enormous level of energy to hide our defects from our companions. Even if we do, our idiosyncrasies emerge unexpectedly, usually at the worst time and to the surprise of our partners. They get disgusted by our defects. And they feel sorry for themselves for wasting many precious years of their lives on us and not noticing our defects earlier. Nowadays, couples, especially women, tell their spouses that they have wasted their youth and beauty on them, as if their partners have gotten any younger or prettier themselves.

Anyway, it is often too late when we discover our companions' flaws. More importantly, seldom we become aware of our own genetic defects. We never recognize the source of our crooked behaviour, or we deny its destructive force and impact on our relationships. But, even if we accept our flaws, we can hardly do much about them. The best we can hope for is to try to be aware of them and contain them as much as possible.

C. Conditional Forces (Habits)

Our personality reflects the influence of environments too. The scars, hurt feelings, and bad experiences cannot be forgotten easily. We may be able to mitigate their impacts on our daily encounters and ourselves partially. But their profound effect can always be traced in our psyche and unexpected aggression, hatred, and self-pity.

Our beliefs and convictions, e.g., religion, play a strong role in our behaviour too. Throughout the history, we can trace the immensity of human folly as a result of fanatic beliefs and strong personal convictions of conquerors and anarchists. We become helpless by our ideologies, quite willing to die and kill for them. In relationships, similar types of fanaticism or personal convictions can drive partners to act irrationally without realizing the impact of their actions and beliefs over the lives of others.

Conditional forces are those habits and values that we have adopted wholeheartedly. They are the absorbed effects of *outer forces,* which mainly include our daily contacts and experiences. Conditional forces are the consequences of parental and societal rewards and retributions now turned into strong convictions by us. But conditional forces also entail our doubts, eccentricities, and insecurities. We are conditioned by our experiences to perform within certain boundaries in order to safeguard our welfare and sanity. We have become this way because society and our parents have infused those values in our heads. Their teachings affect our perceptions of the world and the reality of life. The impact of genes and instincts is, of course, always felt. They sometimes make us overrule some of these conditional forces when our need for independence grows stronger with maturity. Sometimes we have enough willpower to revolt against these conditional forces to liberate our souls, e.g., from the rules of society or family.

We are all damaged by traumas during life stages. Personal hurts due to relationships are quite substantial too. They stay with us for the rest of our lives. We are confused after experiencing life's harsh realities and noticing their major discrepancies with our initial imaginations about life. We learn valuable lessons too. All these hurts and lessons turn into conditional forces that affect our behaviour and mentality in strange ways.

Nonetheless, these conditional forces impact couples' perceptions and priorities in relationships. Partners' unique backgrounds and genetics make the likelihood of their compatibility very remote. Some partners start a relationship while they are still a prisoner of their family values. They are addicted to the methods of doing even simple things based on their parents' preferences. They resent the idea of testing new options for completing certain tasks or for making decisions. This condition also hinders their ability for teamwork.

D. Reactional Forces (Impulses)

Reactional forces refer to the way we react to various stimuli, such as other people's comments or behaviour, or any kind of threat in our surroundings. These reactional forces (impulses) reside in our unconscious and subconscious minds and then activate our personality and nervous system fervidly. They are developed throughout our lives as a consequence of other inner forces as well as a person's past experiences and perceptions. They are, in a sense, a kind of impulse to different stimulus due to the effect of all other inner and outer forces. That is, reactional forces are the optimal way we choose to react under the combined influence of instincts, genetics, and conditional forces. Reactional forces reflect, to a great extent, what we normally refer to as *defence mechanisms*—reactions to other people's aggression toward us.

To use a simple metaphor, reactional forces resemble pressing any particular key on a piano. A specific tune is triggered in people when they feel a special stimulus. The significant difference with a piano is that everybody has a unique keyboard with weird tunes attached to each key. Everybody is a unique piano. So when you press a similar key on them, usually different tunes are played. The good thing about this situation is that we might finally learn the kind of sound we can expect to hear from a special key on our partner's piano. But then we continue to wonder why he/she sounds so weird (illogical) when we hear such a nice tune when we press the same key on our own piano. Even other pianos sometimes sound better than our partner's, when we happen to press the keys on strangers' pianos. Why would our partner insist to sound that way when we keep pressing the right key? Why would he/she resist learning the right tune that might be played on that piano of his/hers?

The confusion due to unfamiliar sounds and reactions in relationships leads to retaliations and games. But, at the same time, we might have some level of control over reactional forces. This is the opportunity we almost never have with all the other inner forces discussed above. So, for serious partners who wish to improve the chances of prolonging their relationship, reactional forces could be somehow tamed through awareness. Actually reactional forces are not always negative. That is, partners might learn to show positive reactions in their encounters in order to enhance the quality of their relationships by simple gestures. Learning social rules, ethics, and etiquettes is for the purpose of containing our impulses and maybe even turning them into positive stimuli.

II. Outer Forces

The above four inner forces (A to D) work from within each individual. They build our personalities and affect our relationships. But there are many external (outer) forces, too, that impact our mood and reaction to events constantly. Thus they impact our long-term view of life and our relationships. Family finance, work environment, role-playing, power games, and our daily struggles to survive make a profound impact on the health of relationships. Social issues and injustice lead to personal and relationship problems. The level of work-related stress in society has at least doubled in recent decades. One reason is that more women work in organizations. They must handle all kinds of stressful activities at work, and they face a time shortage to deal with their children and household affairs the way they like. Besides this added stress on relationships, the side-effect of women's role outside the house manifests in their higher expectations at many other levels. Women feel that they deserve more appreciation considering all their extra work and responsibilities. But men have proven unable to respond to this demand properly because they don't know how, or even why. They themselves are already under similar pressures at work anyway. So, the stress due to the lack of full recognition for women in organizations, and at home by their passive husbands, is fuelling the overall level of stress in society. Nonetheless, couples' stress and deprivations (both in society and in their relationships) quickly translate into more personal and relationship dilemmas, which in turn lead to further increase of overall social stress. It is quite likely that women's life expectancy decline and get closer to men's due to their larger role in social life, work stress, and insecure marriages.

Another outer force affecting our relationships adversely without anyone's fault is that women are in a state of transition in terms of the progressive role they like to play in society and relationships. The social changes and the women's new role are obviously necessary. But the process is not still complete, and, even worse, it hasn't been smooth from the start. The means and the format of women's new role are not grasped even by the majority of women, let alone by men who are expected to know what the new format should be and how to behave. Nobody seems to know, let alone agree, where the boundaries must be in order to facilitate this transition without now putting men under undue pressure. Women wish to be assertive and open up about their personal needs. But implementing or enforcing this new role smoothly has not been successful yet, simply because of the four inner forces that are still ruling people's personalities and hindering their communication.

Women's transition from submissiveness to assertiveness surely requires a long period of trials and errors to reach a steady state. But the present generation has no time and patience to let the genders' historical predispositions get adjusted smoothly. And to make the matter worse, the old wounds have not still had a chance to heal. So, a special situation has emerged: Women find it necessary to become aggressive in order to attain the assertiveness they need urgently. Especially for some women, who do not quite understand the meaning and the mode of practicing assertiveness, the only practical approach appears to be retaliation (inner force D above) and by resorting to aggression to make their points clear. For men, the new demands are not only threatening their identities, but also confusing them (again considering the power of inner forces A to D ruling their minds). Women's expectation from men—to overcome the inner forces that shape their (men's) identity—is unrealistic. They are ignoring the fact that men can't readily revamp all those inner forces built within them. Making the required changes is an extremely difficult task, even in a timelier manner, even if they agreed with the changes women are expecting of them. But women can't wait for history to take its course. They cannot struggle forever to prove their points of view rationally to stubborn men. So, they must put their feet down to get things done; what other option do they have? They live only one short life. They cannot wait for decades and centuries for men to gradually understand and acknowledge the validity of the new roles for both men and women. They are tired of waiting for a miracle to clarify the new gender roles in relationships. They must take this crucial matter in their own hands.

Within this confusing situation, both genders' destructive aggressions are complicating the transition process. Instead of progress, we witness sabotages and retaliation, more games, more divorces, and family murder suicides. The bottom line is that men have lost their identities (whatever it was, good or bad) and don't understand the sensibility of what is expected of them. Women are frustrated, too, because they can't enforce their new identity, which they believe they know what it is—an identity they believe they deserve. To women, it appears that men are resisting or careless at best. So everybody is drowning in despair during this transition process. We can only hope that we eventually emerge out of this chaotic situation with a new workable identity. It might be a wishful thinking, though, when nobody even knows what these identities should look like. We don't even know how the transition process may evolve without too much agony and more divorces. We haven't even clarified the genders' new roles or the format of their interactions in that supposedly innovative setting. The only obvious fact is that change, if possible at all, can't happen overnight, especially when no one knows how this transition and affirmation of the new roles should happen. The result of the current confusion is that partners finally get fed up with their struggles to convince each other about their self-conceived new roles and imaginary relationship rules. So they try to dominate one another or resort to divorce. Some may just give up and play only a passive role. Meanwhile, we are all stuck and our relationships remain in limbo; a bunch of men and women without clear identities, put under relentless pressure by both inner and outer forces. Under the hostile environment of relationships, we have actually turned into another destructive *outer force* for our partners. And we are facing a global identity crisis too. With no clear gender identities in our modern societies, we have been importing our vague values to less modernized nations as well!

A few other types of outer forces are quickly mentioned below before we complete this chapter:
- Environment and various forces of the universe impact our lives in substantial ways nowadays. We have created a

lot of pollution. Global warming is causing natural disasters in all forms, including devastating and costly hurricanes, floods, food shortages, etc.
- Our economic systems are collapsing all around us while arrogant, incompetent, and greedy politicians and business leaders rule the world. We wonder who is going to save us. We are personally responsible for these problems by the way we allow our immediate personal needs (e.g., greed or ego) affect our way of choosing our leaders. The democratic processes are ridiculously flawed when a group of people buy our votes by their misleading ads and negative propagandas.
- Our erratic thoughts, feelings, concerns, and doubts are unsettling forces, as they have not yet turned into our personal convictions and beliefs. So they can be viewed as outer forces bombarding our minds constantly and affecting our personal mood, needs, and relationships.
- The pressures to cope with our surroundings for social acceptance and success are major outer forces causing stress for individuals and relationships.
- Our daily interactions have become too complicated and artificial. We must regularly deal with a variety of harmful values, games, personalities, perceptions, doubts, encounters, reactions, pleasures, hatred, suffering, hypocrisy, random noises, theories, stressful lifestyles, philosophies, slogans, propagandas, unemployment, uncertainties, etc.

Chapter Three
Personality Aspects

The inner and outer forces (as explained in Chapter Two) develop our urges, view of the world, and a perception of our personal needs. These *perceived* personal needs could be authentic, like the need for food and sex. Or they could be artificial (or auxiliary), such as our needs for luxury, power, and D-love. Together, all these needs reflect our values, outlook on life, and strive for happiness—our personality. So, how needy we are shows who we are.

On the other hand, it is the way we go about satisfying our personal needs that portrays our unique 'personality' most clearly. In this sense, personality mostly demonstrates, i) our *efforts to relate* to the world (which consist largely of roles and games we play), and ii) other people's *perceptions of our efforts* to relate to the world (which are usually biased). Therefore, 'our calculated efforts' and 'people's biased perceptions' are the main factors that manifest personality. As a result, who we really are, or are capable of being, remains largely hidden from us and others. Ideally, we expect our inherent characteristics to emerge and present our true personality, and we expect our personality to reflect our intrinsic characteristics in return. But in reality this is hardly the case. The reason is that we have difficulty understanding and demonstrating those innate characteristics and obviously others can see only a snapshot of us in our encounters. Furthermore, we are too engaged with our role-playing and games to allow our inherent characteristics surface even if we understood them. Even couples living together for many years still don't appreciate the depth of each other's personalities. By this definition alone 'personality' turns into an abstract concept, because it is only a reflection of who we want to be or try to be, not the true person we are. And also because personality remains largely a matter of judgment by others about who we are, again not the person that we really are. As a whole, 'personality' remains an obscure, complex dimension of human with very peculiar characteristics that are hard to pinpoint or predict, let alone manage. It is easier to talk about the human body and mind than to explain human personality. Diagram 3.1 depicts the concepts and factors that affect personality and Table 3.1 explains the meaning of the numbered arrows in Diagram 3.1.

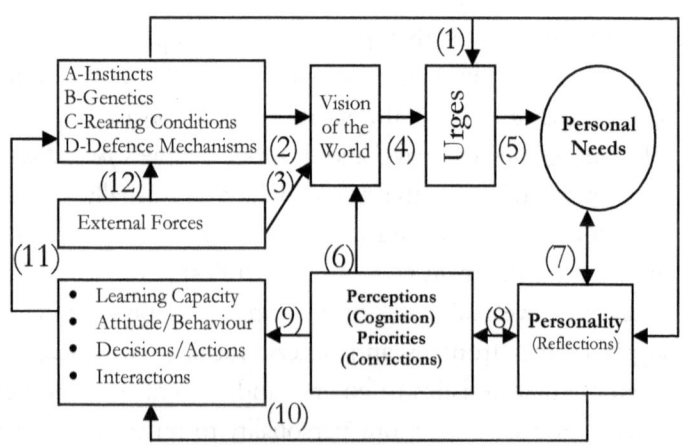

Diagram 3.1: A Simple Model of Mental Structure and Behaviour

Table 3.1: Descriptions of Numbered Arrows in Diagram 3.1

1. The inner forces A to D create our urges and personality.
2. The inner forces A to D create our vision of the world.
3. The outer forces, including our interactions with people, also contribute to our vision of the world.
4. Our vision of the world impacts our urges.
5. Our urges incite our perception of personal needs, and vice versa.
6. Our vision of the world helps our cognition and perceptions about life. It also affects the way we set our priorities and convictions.
7. Our personal needs impact our personality, and vice versa. Basically, personality (reflections) is a manifestation of who we think we are or have learnt to be. It is only partially self-controlled, as it is mainly a manifestation of inner forces and deep convictions.
8. Our personality affects our perceptions and priorities. It also dictates the way our cognition and convictions are developed. Our convictions and cognition, in return, impact our personality.
9. Our perceptions (cognition) and priorities (convictions) determine our learning capacity, attitude, decisions, etc.
10. Our personality affects our learning capacity, attitude, decisions, and interactions.
11. Our learning ability, attitude, decisions, and interactions influence our inner forces A to D.
12. External forces influence inner forces A to D as well.

Personality reflects our perceptions, motivations, and priorities. But it is also a tool that can be somewhat developed to help us attain our needs easier. Overachievers' unique personality, for example, helps them pursue their goals obsessively in order to fulfil their complex needs. On the other hand, stoics and pacifists limit their personal needs in order to devote themselves to larger causes and personal growth.

Some people might feel incapable of fulfilling their higher level needs, e.g., social, or don't believe in burdening themselves physically or mentally for such intangible objectives. Our unique personalities goad us in making these judgments and decisions about our personal needs. At the same time, personality dictates the level of risk we take. It empowers us to overcome the hurdles and proceed at the speed our stamina allows.

Obviously, personality contains a large inventory of emotions and cognition. Thus studying our 'personality' and its role in fulfilling our needs could have enormous impact on the quality of our lives, i.e., happiness and tranquility. It can help us learn about the authenticity of our needs and urges. This could lead to our understanding and removal of the sources of our agony. But understanding our personality is difficult, mostly because we resist learning about ourselves. We also abhor changing it. We love *who we believe we are* and thus avoid any advice or clues about the way our personality is hurting us or people around us. So we seldom give ourselves a chance to really find out *who we are*. Accordingly, we have difficulty understanding the true characteristics of human beings in general. We keep making hasty judgments. This is a major bottleneck, especially considering the vast changes in social values and our desire to develop good relationships at work and home. Studying human personality is becoming quite urgent also because we are all striving to assert our identities individually and in relationships. Unfortunately, we hate to agree that our new values, and our personalities forming around those values, are too ambiguous and rather phony as well. We just continue seeking happiness in places and values that would harm us more than helping us, e.g., consumerism and D-love. Our needs and personalities are becoming detrimental to our happiness and health. What a weird approach we have chosen for ourselves as human beings. Greed and wealth have destroyed the mentality of not only rich, but more so the mentality of common people who are trying to imitate rich. In this environment, personalities are deranged drastically very rapidly.

Personality is a complex subject that has been studied seriously in psychology for many decades, yet our knowledge is still primitive. More disappointing, of course, is our resistance to use the limited knowledge that is out there anyway. We have not learned about the mechanism of self-awareness. We don't know how to pinpoint our personality flaws to improve our relationships and personal lives.

Research about personality has taken many approaches. In its simplest form, we believe that humans have a good and an evil side. They emerge alternately from time to time and they are responsible for our thoughts and actions. Ethics and religions are invented to help us resist devilish deeds and thus become a better person. But those guidelines have not helped us, either, going by all the facts enumerated in this book. So perhaps we could benefit from a simple personality model that could guide us on a daily basis, to help us enhance our awareness about ourselves and assess our flaws and strengths objectively.

Personality Model

Beyond the general distinction of 'good' versus 'evil' aspects of one's personality, it is more useful to learn about one's *motives* to be evil or good. Why are people good or bad always or on certain occasions? The personality model explained in this chapter is developed by the author only to demonstrate *how personality works*. The intention is to explain 'personality' for practical application in our daily lives. Hopefully the model would prove comprehensive as well for wider purposes too. The model is somewhat different from general discussions, including Freud's, about *how personality develops*. Although related, the immediate use of the term 'personality' in this book is to reveal, i) how we go about satisfying our personal needs, and ii) how we perceive, and react to, other people's attitude and messages. The objective is to learn why we act or react in certain ways (according to some personality factors). Consequently, we may be able to discern our personality weaknesses and strengths more accurately. Also, we might decide to improve our personality once we acknowledge the need for it.

To develop a simple model of personality, we can actually expand the traditional model of 'good vs. evil' to explain human nature. After all, the end result of our actions and behaviour is either good or evil for others and us. The personality model must only explain why we do good or evil things. Of course, one problem with this approach is that nowadays the distinction between good and evil is getting too subjective. We are depending on authorities, celebrities, and propagandas to decide about good and bad. This issue deserves separate analyses in some other document.

Obviously, our inner needs (A to D) instigate our thoughts and actions. The perceived outcome is then assessed by others and us (usually differently) to make judgments about our personality. We usually justify our actions, even when they appear evil in the eyes of others. In return we judge others harshly too. We criticize others quickly even for convictions they believe in so faithfully. We might even condemn their supposedly noble beliefs and sacred ideologies. So what may appear logical and good by some people could be seen as evil by another group. A superpower invades a country under wrong pretences and half of the world agrees with this aggression under the auspices of humanity, while the other half of the world finds the aggression the ultimate show of evil and insanity. So we live in a world where the distinction between good and bad has become a blur. This is true even at the highest levels of authority for social justice and humanity. This shows how susceptible we are to propagandas and how partial our mentalities are. Logic seems nonexistent as long as we continue to disagree about even the most fundamental social issues, like the effect of free enterprise, consumerism, humanity, and environment. Meanwhile, the widespread misuse of communication and world-wide hypocrisies are destroying the chances of establishing reliable social values.

If we analyse people's actions and thoughts and compare their logic, ideologies and convictions, we recognize the vast diversity of people's way of thinking in line with the complexity of their personalities. They might even seem to have similar needs, motives, humanitarian ideologies, and goodwill. But very seldom even two individuals are capable of agreeing on fundamentals or building a mature relationship. Why is this? Why are our personalities so controversial and incapable of reconciling? The personality model presented in the following pages might shed some light on this question.

The model suggests that personality has three components. A part of our personality exerts our self-centredness and assertiveness, which we may refer to as 'ego' aspect of personality, or Ego-P for short. This personality aspect reflects (and drives) our desires, ambitions, sense of responsibility, defence mechanisms, and all other traits that enable us assert ourselves and protect our lives. Depending on the social environment and values we embrace, Ego-P develops a set of conditional traits, such as jealousy, competitiveness, greed. It also learns tactics and tools, such as aggression and deceit, to achieve its selfish objectives. While Ego-P has positive attributes that instigate our ambitions and growth, it has become the main source of our personal evil. Our needs for power, success, identity, and wealth, as influenced by the norms and values of society, reinforce Ego-P. An Ego-P dominated person is highly self-centred, needs to control everything and everyone, and imposes unrealistic expectations on others and the world. His/her need for dominance causes problems and anxiety for him/her and others due to unfulfilled expectations, anger, and retributions. Ego-P is mostly driven by our conditional urges, although instinctual urges and genetics play a role too, especially when people use Ego-P to defend themselves or exert supremacy.

On the other hand, the aspect of our personality that reflects humans' soul and vulnerability is mainly driven by our instinctual needs. It contains our inner urges, love, integrity, inquisitiveness, potentialities, creativity and spirituality. What we refer to as an individual's psyche or 'self' is basically an image of a pure spirit that can think clearly outside the rules and norms of social living. So we may refer to this aspect of personality as Self-P. It is the venue connecting us to the spirituality realms that we all try to grasp intuitively. Obviously, the religious beliefs and superstitions, which might be erroneously associated with spirituality, are merely other forms of social conditioning, and created for manipulating human soul. Spirituality is beyond these superficial beliefs and gestures. It may emerge only from within us when we learn about our connectedness to the universe through our psyche and full consciousness. (This author prefers to see 'psyche' mainly as the inherent, pure part of personality (the self) and not the whole personality. But this is not an important issue for this book anyway.) 'Self' reflects the nucleus of an individual's existence and total cognition, as explained in Chapter Five. Many of us have little faith in the intrinsic power of the self, since it appears intangible and irrelevant in the context of social values we are accustomed to. With our greed, and our strive for power and social rewards, we neglect to unleash the abundant potentialities that reside within us and instead waste our time on trivialities. Our potentialities are vast not only in terms of creativity and character, but also in terms of spirituality, which can open our minds to spheres beyond worldly dogmas and enigmas.

The third component of this simple personality model is driven mainly by our conditional and adaptation needs. Living in society makes us alert about certain roles we must play. It teaches us special behaviour that can help us get ahead and be popular in as many fronts as possible. So, this aspect of personality—let's call it Model-P—is basically the most practical aspect of our personality in the way it helps us adapt to social norms and get accepted and admired if possible. Model-P may be partially influenced by our instinctual needs, too, since socializing may be considered an instinctual urge. This aspect of personality reflects a person's charisma, playfulness, and adaptability. But Model-P is also responsible for manipulating others by devising cunning plans and playing all kinds of games.

So, in a general and crude way, personality may be conceived to contain three main components. Depending upon genetics—our inherent nature—and life experiences, each individual's personality manifests by a different degree of Ego-P, Model-P, and Self-P.

In a nutshell, Ego-P accounts for a person's strive for security and fulfilling his/her aspirations, Model-P mostly reflects his charisma and adaptation ability, and Self-P is the level of love and spirituality he can access in the depth of his being.

The overall strength of these personality aspects for each person is obviously different. The more complex a person, the higher would be the ratings of his/her personality components. For a passive or subdued person, all three aspects of his/her personality are most likely low. But usually an individual's personality evolves in a direction dictated, and strengthened, by one, or seldom two, personality aspects at a time. For example, a person with high Self-P has somehow subdued his/her Model-P and Ego-P, especially the latter. On the other hand, a person empowering his/her Ego-P, and maybe Model-P, is not interested in enhancing his/her Self-P.

The three personality aspects are mutually exclusive (complementary and contradictory) in some respects, while they also co-mingle constantly to create a certain personality balance for an individual. So, in a sense, there is a balance among the three aspects of personality within each individual. This implies that when one of them intensifies in a person, it would be at the expense of the other two aspects of personality. For example, when Ego-P dominates in a special circumstance, the levels of Model-P and Self-P decline. Our personal experiences can verify this observation. For example, anger, as a by-product of Ego-P, allows neither compassion, which is the symptom of Self-P, nor tactfulness that is the symbol of Model-P. This applies to single incidents when one aspect of personality suddenly overwhelms the other two aspects. But it also applies to general conditions and long-term behaviour of a person. That is, although we may apply any combination of the personality aspects in a special instance for a particular purpose, we usually adopt a relatively fix personality profile that reflects a certain proportion of each aspect of our personality. Egoists obviously use their Ego-P more extensively than a normal person. People seeking social acceptance and approval depend heavily on Model-P. And those who find their own niche and depend on themselves for self-actualization are basically driven by their Self-P.

The Personality Model can be depicted nicely in a diagram too. We can do so by projecting the three aspects of personality on three axes of a sphere as shown in Diagram 3.2. The three aspects of personality reflect the following:

A. Self-P reflects the way **one is meant to be**. The human soul.
B. Ego-P reflects the way **one has become**. The effect of nurture.
C. Model-P reflects the way **one likes to be**. The adaptation force.

    Triangle ABC: reflects what **one is.** One's personality.
    Point O: reflects how **one perceives oneself**.
    Axis X: reflects **one's perception of one's Self-P**.
    Axis Y: reflects **one's perception of one's Ego-P**.
    Axis Z: reflects **one's perception of one's Model-P**.

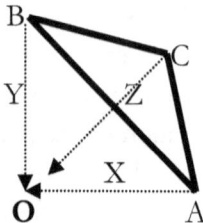

**Diagram 3.2: Personality ABC
(measured by its three aspects)**

The triangle ABC reflects the unique personality of a person. The shape and size of the triangle vary when the lengths and angles of axes X, Y, Z change; when one axis (e.g.) moves closer to the other axes (e.g. or Y), as shown in the two examples in Diagram 3.3. This reflects nicely the infinite number of personalities that exist in the world. The lengths and angles of axes reflect each aspect of personality and how they interact in general and within certain circumstances.

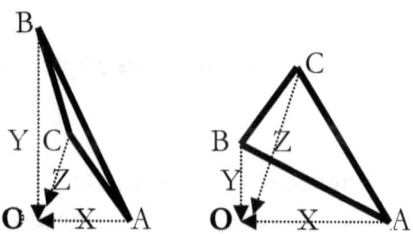

**Diagram 3.3: Examples of Personalities Based on
Lengths and Angles of X, Y, and Z**

The triangles, one for each person on the globe, reside in a universal sphere where the position of ABC within that sphere has a unique coordinates and significance. But this universal dimension is not included here for the sake of simplicity and because it doesn't impact the scope of our discussions in this book significantly.

Although each individual's personality can be depicted by the shape of triangle ABC, there are minor changes regularly in his/her personality (and the shape of ABC) when he matures or when he/she is affected by some significant incidents. The changes could be temporary or permanent.

Point O in the diagram reflects a person's accurate perception of his/her true personality, in case he/she was capable of doing so. It reflects an accurate measurement of the three aspects of his/her personality, i.e., Self-P, Ego-P, and Model-P at points A, B, and C respectively. In reality, however, we almost never stand at Point O when we assess ourselves. We are biased by many factors (including our own personality aspects) and we are not objective enough. So, it means that when we perceive our personality, we are making this observation not from Point O. We perceive ourselves from any other infinite possibilities, such as Point P as shown in Diagram 3.4. This is a fact, even though we always believe that we are perfect in terms of personality and we sincerely believe that we know who we are. Diagram 3.4 shows that although the personality ABC is the exact copy of the diagram in 3.2, (reflecting the true representation of one's personality), the way one observes oneself from point P is skewed (crooked) because one is not objective in assessing oneself. A person's perception of himself is represented by the information imparted to him by X, Y, Z axes. He doesn't see ABC properly, because of the crooked feedbacks by X, Y, Z axes.

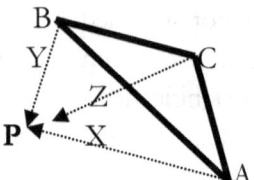

Diagram 3.4: One's Perception of Oneself

The following hypotheses also seem reasonable:
- Self-P is driven mostly by the inner force A (instincts and spirit).
- Ego-P is driven mostly by the inner force B (genetics, chemistry, and nervous system). But Ego-P is also affected by the inner forces C and D (conditioning and defence mechanisms).
- Model-P is driven mostly by the inner forces C and D as well as the external forces.
- 'Human nature' is mostly a combination of Self-P and that part of Ego-P that is driven by the inner force B.

Interactions of Personality Aspects

Our actions and attitude reflect some degree of all the three aspects of our unique personalities. However, every one of our daily interactions can be noted to have a tone particular to one aspect of our personality. Sometimes we may combine two aspects of our personality to interact. For example, Ego-P might use the charm of Model-P to manipulate another person for its selfish purposes. Usually, our intentions, our perception of the person we are communicating with, the topic of discussion, and our general mood trigger a particular personality aspect at every instance or timeframe. For example, we might get angry with another person when our Ego-P is triggered by jealousy. Depending on the perception and objectives of the other person, he/she would react also according to a specific aspect of his/her personality. He/she may decide to use his/her Self-P, which means he/she would try to tolerate the situation or walk away. Or he/she might use his/her Ego-P to confront us in an equally hostile manner. Or he/she might use Model-P to calm us down and reason with us diplomatically.

Every individual gradually develops a personality that is dominant by one of these aspects of personality. Other aspects of the personality manifest from time to time in his/her actions and attitude. But usually he/she behaves under the influence of a main personality aspect. For example, the interactions of an Ego-P dominated person are usually self-centred and biased. People usually perceive him/her in light of his/her domineering (aggressive) personality, especially after they have had enough contacts with him/her. But it is also likely that other people's perceptions are inaccurate. It is normally difficult to understand the intentions of others. Some people become experts at hiding their true personalities, by using Model-P, to deceive us. On the other hand, a person's Model-P might not be developed enough to conceal the dominant aspect of his/her personality despite his/her efforts. We become experts ourselves in guessing and playing the same games in order to prevent their harmful intentions. We get suspicious and overreact quickly even to small incidents. We become paranoid and develop our crooked self-defence mechanisms, such as mistrust or even retaliation.

A major hurdle in relationships is that couples are not conscious of the way their personality aspects interact in general and how they get out of control in specific instances, e.g., when they get angry or feel betrayed. If couples paid attention to the way their personality aspects interact and damage their communication, they could eliminate a lot of misunderstandings and conflicts.

The complexity of relationships is partly due to the fact that:

a) Couples are not conscious of the ways the three aspects of their personalities instigate them personally and also their partners during their interactions.
b) Couples don't appreciate their partners' limited capacity to manage their three aspects of personalities.
c) Couples are unaware of the enormous levels of misperceptions in relationships due to the clashes amongst the three personality aspects of partners.
d) Partners are not aware of the relationship needs and instead overload their Ego-P and Model-P to interact with each other and to fulfil a large variety of their complex personal needs.
e) There are no relationship principles and framework to assist couples assess the health of their relationship. So, they depend mostly on their subjective criteria, dictated by their (emotional or egotistical) personality aspects, to make this important decision.

Ego-P is usually dominant in our interactions, because we are selfish by nature and give the highest priority to our personal needs. Model-P is the second most widely used aspect of personality because it helps us adapt to our environments and/or manipulate others. Most people use Self-P much less than the other aspects of personality, because it mostly has private and personal implications and it is difficult to comprehend or apply. Thus, a prominent type of personality, i.e., a combination of Ego-P and Model-P, dominates and corrupts relationships most often. It causes too many conflicts and clashes. At every instance, one of the more dominant aspects of personality, i.e., Ego-P or Model-P, of one partner challenges the similar personality aspects of his/her partner. Very seldom one partner draws on Self-P to respond to an Ego-P or Model-P message by his/her partner. Even when he/she seems to be tolerating the situation, he/she is mostly drawing on Model-P to adapt tentatively with an eye on the opportunity to retaliate with his/her Ego-P later. Obviously, only interactions at Self-P level can be friction free and productive. And we know that it is very rare for one or both partners to interact at that level.

To make the matter worse, partners' messages are often misperceived not only in terms of their contents, but also regarding their intentions. Because of our own personality flaws, we often misunderstand an innocent message and consider it hostile prematurely. We may perceive it to be driven by our partner's Ego-P or Model-P due to our own predisposed Ego-P or Model-P. In that case, we retaliate with a harsh message through Ego-P or design a plot through Model-P for eventual reprisal, which would then result in subsequent reactions and clashes. We can seldom predict which personality aspect of our partner would be triggered by our messages. So we are shocked by our partners' seemingly absurd reactions. Also, we believe that our partners cannot detect the personality aspect hidden behind our supposedly calculated and controlled attitude or message. We assume that the roles and games we play remain undetected by our partners. Furthermore, in relationships we soon develop an impression that our partners have a rigid personality that receives our messages with bias all the time anyway. Thus we assume that he/she processes our messages and responds uniformly, all the time, according to his/her Ego-P or Model-P. This assumption, although correct in most cases, stirs more mistrust during communication and leads to relationship hurdles. One way to correct the situation is by partners making a small effort to pay attention to their own personality aspects as they send and receive messages. The important point to remember is that our personality aspects could cause misperceptions in both situations: when we are sending a message and when we are receiving a message.

As a whole, the complexity of relationship interactions and communications is due to the way different personality aspects of partners react to one another in every situation without proper attention or intention. The irony is that we believe or pretend to be communicating with total honesty and integrity. We believe we are communicating with our Self-P. But in reality almost all communications are contaminated by Ego-P and Model-P. Our normal belief that we are communicating naturally through Self-P is just another example of our Ego-P limiting our objectivity.

People who depend on their Self-P to communicate with others are not immune from the hassles of relationships either. Their submissive attitude is taken as weakness and a lack of leadership ability. So they either must bear the consequences of being a 'good' person, or learn to become assertive and use Ego-P and Model-P to a large extent as well. It is becoming more difficult every day to be a good person in our crooked societies. The worst part of it is that not even our spouses or children take us seriously or respect us enough when we are Self-P oriented persons. Anyway, we are never aware how the three different aspects of our personality are contaminating our communications and relationships. We are not particularly aware which one of our personality aspects is sending a message. We are not used to thinking that there is more than one way to deal with each situation.

Another dimension of the personality aspects is worth mentioning. That is, in many situations, we subconsciously engage some aspect(s) of our personality to deal with, and account for, the actions of the other personality aspect(s). For example, our conscience, which resides in Self-P, questions the actions of Ego-P and Model-P during our interactions with our partners. By doing so, it causes inner turmoil that is sometimes even more difficult to bear than the consequences of our partners' adversarial reactions. Dealing with our conscience, ego, and the sense of etiquettes (the three symbols of the three personality aspects) is not always easy. As a general rule, every message sent under the influence of a particular personality aspect, is internally contemplated and judged by the other two personality aspects eventually, if not instantaneously. We may be aware of this process quite consciously or we might have learned to subdue all these conflicting messages in our subconscious. Nevertheless, the damage to our psyche is certain whether we keep the idiotic actions of our personality aspects in our conscious or try to deny them.

Learning about our Personality Aspects

The three aspects of personality drive partners' communications without their adequate awareness and sensitivity and thus they both get offended during this process quite often. So, it may help our relationships, and life as a whole, if we learn to gauge and adjust the volume of these personality aspects regularly. We can make a habit of monitoring and distinguishing the personality aspects in our encounters. We can be the best judge as to which one of our personality aspects is in control during an event or communication. We sometimes do this assessment after the communication is completed. Sometimes we feel sorry for what we said. We might go back and at least try to correct our past mistakes. Often, however, Ego-P stops us even from correcting our mistakes, i.e., by apologizing at least. Nonetheless, the most effective method would be to assess the tone and content of our message before it is communicated.

Especially, we can make an effort to use Self-P more often to soothe someone's hurt feelings. We know how to do this and probably do it occasionally. So it is possible to use Self-P if we just push ourselves to be a little more conscious of the personality aspect that is trying to dominate a message. After we do this simple exercise for a while, we begin to notice our awareness level enhancing gradually. This awareness helps us notice and improve our habits, and attain the tranquility we crave all our lives. Of course, changing our habits and personality is not a straightforward matter. It doesn't happen easily and quickly. Still the mere sense of committing to a self-awareness regimen is crucial for overcoming the difficulties of changing ourselves and perhaps the people around us. Keeping track of the interworking and manifestation of our personality aspects is the most important step toward self-awareness.

Committing oneself to such a noble regimen is difficult because we must keep fighting our ego without any tangible incentive. Attaining tranquility is the only incentive for self-awareness and personality change. This is a major incentive, though, if we really wish to find peace and happiness. This is the best way to enjoy a sense of relative freedom from social burdens and we might even start to enjoy our relationships. Obviously, breaking the rules of social belonging to build Self-P appears too naïve and ridiculous. How can we ignore the tangible rewards of social compliance like wealth, sex, and power, all in pursuit of tranquility and freedom? These states appear to be abstract concepts and wishful thinking after all. For all these reasons, a person must truly feel the need to change the direction of his/her life, and then gain the needed courage and commitment for pursuing the path of self-awareness. Some people come to this realization when they face life hurdles and hit the tall wall of disappointments, especially in their relationships. Even then, they require special wisdom to realize the need for an alternative lifestyle. Only this wisdom and their devotion might help them learn about Self-P and move on the path to self-awareness.

As noted before, all the three personality aspects have both good and bad qualities. It is true that Ego-P causes more trouble and leads to badness more often than the other personality aspects. But Ego-P contributes highly to our welfare in so many ways, too, especially for boosting our confidence and managing our defence mechanisms. On the other hand, Self-P could cause trouble and badness too. For example, instincts make us believe in certain ways or beliefs that are no longer applicable in our complex society. For example, imagine making investments based on trust or intuition rather than doing due diligence and studying all the risks and alternatives before committing ourselves. Marriages in the past worked nicely simply based on couples' trust and traditional habits. But society is now too complex to choose a spouse and live with him/her before years of searching and contemplating. It is not necessarily a good thing that we have been forced to be analytical and indecisive, but we have reached this point by the force of history. Our sense of spirituality, which is a pure symbol of Self-P, is nowadays tainted, too, by all kinds of religious fanaticism and major corruption of clergies. So, Self-P has its weaknesses for adapting to the newer social needs and survival.

The problems with Model-P are numerous, too, and beyond the scope of our discussions in this book. For one thing, Model-P has made people phony and calculating and we have a hard job separating true compassion from fake ones. The manipulating power of Model-P is infecting our lives and minds. We don't even believe the words of our leaders in politics, economics, or religion. They keep disappointing us out of stupidity, sheer arrogance, and hypocrisy. Even in smaller scales, the problem with Model-P is that people can read our fake pretences if we are not good at playing the role. This causes more mistrust, frictions, and resistance because people want to challenge our phony personality. Although many gullible people buy phony pretences, the task of making Model-P to look convincing is tough nowadays. Everybody is becoming more sceptical about other people's attitudes and words. Instead of trust, we now mistrust one another unless proven otherwise.

Model-P is too prevalent in modern societies, which means people are manipulating or cheating one another more than ever. Everybody is trying to show-off and portray an image of themselves that is quite unauthentic. But, at the same time, they must try hard to be convincing too. Their lies and deceits must remain hidden. This is hard, though, since everybody is learning to discount people's pretences, and the trust level is declining fast in society.

Relationship problems are particularly attributed to personality clashes between partners. But most people are unaware of the roots of personality clashes. They are insensitive about the interworking of their personality aspects. And of course they ignore the fact that they and their partners cannot change their personalities at will. People's unique personalities cannot be changed easily. Only awareness, partners' goodwill, and gradual modifications through Self-P and Model-P may help them save their relationships. Using Model-P might resemble the role-playing methods prescribed by relationship counsellors. But there is a fundamental difference between these two approaches. Using Model-P, for improving ourselves, would be based on partners' true conviction to learn about, and manage, their personality aspects. The idea is not to express love or behave in certain ways artificially just to satisfy one's partner. Rather, the idea is to learn about (and manage) one's personality flaws. Model-P is used to play artificial roles or authentic ones, of course. Model-P may cause damage if it plays artificial roles, but it becomes useful when it is used to reinforce our authentic needs.

A useful process of self-awareness and also minimizing relationship clashes is to pursue the following steps:

1. Monitor your behaviour in terms of personality aspects regularly. Learn how each aspect of your personality is driven by some motives or impulses and then find out what they are. You may use the list of the motives on page 39 as a general guide.
2. Assess the integrity of your motives and decide if they are suitable for an enlightened person who doesn't need to play games or retaliate. Apply Self-P and Model-P to curb your selfish motives and improve your tactics for managing your daily routines.
3. After gaining enough self-awareness, monitor your partner's behaviour in terms of his/her personality aspects. The objective is to see how your partner is helpless in the face of his/her forceful personality aspects. Note his/her helplessness to change his/her behaviour. Remember that personality aspects, e.g., Ego-P, are triggered by inner forces (A to D) and external forces. Instead of criticizing him/her for his/her flaws, see if you can help him/her follow a self-awareness routine too (mainly by observing his/her own personality aspects).
4. If impossible to tolerate your partner, or if you are unable to convince him/her to pursue a self-awareness approach, stop your useless struggles to save an irreconcil-

able relationship. Either learn to live with his/her imperfections or get out of the relationship in a most civilized and hassle-free manner. Stop retaliating and arguing.
5. Even when both partners have some level of self-awareness and knowledge of the personality aspects, building relationships requires a continuous monitoring of the 'personality aspect clashes' during partners' encounters, and then making proper modifications along the way. Furthermore, couples must satisfy all the other needs of relationships, too, mainly the matter of choosing the right relationship model for them. An important role of a proper relationship model is to minimize the frequency of clashes between partners' two sets of personality aspects.

Being Good and Enlightened

The conclusion is simple and obvious: For building an *ideal* relationship, partners should be *good and enlightened* persons first. Naturally, a definition for an 'ideal relationship' is needed to measure partners' success in achieving its standards. This task is pursued in Chapter Nine where a tentative list of relationship success factors is provided in Table 9.4.

Obviously, becoming a good and enlightened person would be the most natural approach for building a good relationship (and life), if partners could suppress their Ego-P and become humble humans. Actually, the incentives for becoming better humans are substantial, considering our eagerness to find happiness and an ideal companion. One thing is certain though: Our conventional use of Ego-P or Model-P to find our soul mate is definitely doomed. It has failed all along in recent decades. It has brought us only more loneliness and frustrations and it would never get us the spiritual love that we seek. But, becoming a good and enlightened person is a difficult task too.

Being a 'good' person mostly refers to an individual's personality dominance, with an emphasis on Self-P, and the least amount of Ego-P. This person has a higher chance of building an ideal relationship, because he/she has more control over his/her attitude and expectations, and also because he/she believes in the value of a good relationship that is driven by unselfish standards. Model-P dominance mainly involves phoniness and game playing, which hinder the goodness and naturalness of a person. Yet Model-P dominance is somewhat less destructive than Ego-P domination for building relationships. As noted before, both Model-P and Ego-P have some positive attributes as well, which, in moderate dosage, might help in building a good relationship. Especially Model-P can be quite useful in exchanging complimentary gestures and empowering partners' positive interactions when it is done properly.

Assuming that we can learn to become a bit less selfish, the next step to being a better person is to become as natural as possible by getting rid of all those layers of phoniness, pretensions, neediness, and games. We must really believe that arrogance and game-playing only create more obstacles for building healthy relationships and finding happiness. But becoming natural is a tough task even if we knew how to do it. For one thing, we cannot overcome our habits and conditional forces. Our modern societies advocate only more superficiality, greed, and games. To some extent, even marriage counsellors are making couples more unnatural when they encourage them to play phony roles. To become natural, we must understand who we are, which starts by assessing our needs and the authenticity of the motives behind them. We must value our independence and integrity more than anything else. We must find our purpose in life instead of only imitating others and accepting their values blindly. While respecting others and their choices, we must curb our desire for their approval of who we are. Most people would have difficulty accepting a simple and needless individual in their close circles, and we should learn to live with that without any grudges.

For building successful relationships, partners must be *enlightened* too. 'Enlightened' mainly means that partners are aware of humans' inherent limitations. Accordingly, they have higher sympathy toward each other and also keep their expectations from relationships low. They realize their own flaws and appreciate that their partners often behave according to some inner and outer forces beyond their control too; so their behaviour should not be considered utter malice all the time. A major implication of being *enlightened* is that partners are wise and patient. They know how to apply their goodness effectively in their relationships despite the inevitable disappointments and even occasional hostility between partners.

Only a small group of people has genetic superiority, grows up in enriching environments, or automatically turns into good-natured and enlightened humans. For the rest of us, with mediocre genes and meagre rearing conditions, becoming a good, enlightened person requires major motivation and effort. We must first learn to overcome so many of our idiosyncrasies and personality flaws through self-awareness. It takes special courage, talent, and conviction to acknowledge one's deficiencies and pursue a path of self-awareness. The learning process is long and painful, as it requires new convictions that contradict our phony values and lifestyle. Through awareness, we must learn about ourselves, the interworking of our personality aspects, relationship standards and objectives, and authentic life values. We must be able to forego some of our habits, greed, and jealousy.

The concept of being *good* and *enlightened* is a noble and popular principle in our minds. We know intuitively that, for building an ideal relationship, partners should be good and enlightened individuals who know themselves as well as their relationship needs. But the problem is that intuitively we also always blame others and justify ourselves. We are not objective. Our logic is not strong enough to realize that relationship conflicts cannot always be the fault of our partners. Our crooked logic and Ego-P have convinced us of our flawlessness. Some of us actually believe to be saints. Some believe to know it all. So we react negatively toward other individuals' points of view and logic relentlessly. We strongly believe that our relationship problems are due to the badness and stupidity of our partners. So, the depth of relationship problems clearly lies in our hasty judgments about, and misperception of, our partners, instead of realizing our own imperfections. In order to see even the scope of the problems, we must sincerely try to scrap our Ego-P tendencies and focus on self-awareness rather than passing judgment on our partners. This is almost as hard as asking a swimmer to unlearn swimming.

Nonetheless, seldom both partners can be good and Self-P dominated, which means most of us must find a way to relate by maintaining a good balance of all the three aspects of personality—with Ego-P contained as much as possible. Ego-P's force and motives should be somehow controlled through constant improvements in Self-P and Model-P, but more importantly, we need a relationship framework to help partners maintain an effective balance among the personality aspects of partners.

Chapter Four
Perceptions and Misperceptions

People's unique needs and personalities cause havoc in relationships, as discussed in the previous chapters. Furthermore, people's *perceptions* have a permanent effect on their personalities, outlook on life, and relationships. 'Perception' basically refers to our ability to observe, analyse, assess, and judge a person or event. Usually our ability to accurately perform all these steps, from observation to judgment, is limited. Aside from the technical difficulty of completing these steps, we are too biased and impatient to perceive a person or event properly. We just make a quick decision and move on. Thus, most of our perceptions are inaccurate. They are merely misperceptions

Misperceptions obviously cause communication barriers for partners. But they also confuse people about who they are, what they need, what they should expect from a relationship, and what may really make them happy. Delusion and anxiety result from people's misperceptions about themselves, others, and the world. In relationships, the increasing level of misperceptions often leads to misunderstandings, gross misjudgments, and hasty decisions. For one thing, people cannot decide whether they prefer to be in a relationship or live alone. This has become a major dilemma for most people in the 21st century because both options of living alone and being in a relationship really suck nowadays.

Diagram 3.4 showed a person's perception of his/her personality. In Diagram 4.1, point Q is added to show his/her partner's perception of his/her personality ABC.

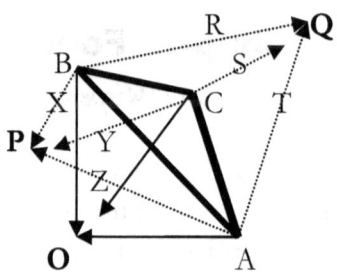

Diagram 4.1: Our Partners' Perception of Our Personality from Point Q.

- Point O reflects an accurate picture of our personality ABC, based on the weightings of Ego-P, Model-P, and Self-P. The axes OA, OB, and OC depict the correct impressions of personality.
- Point P reflects our *typical* (biased) perception of our personality, based on the information gathered through axes X, Y, and Z.
- Point Q reflects our partner's (biased) perception of our personality, based on the information he/she gathers through axes R, S, T.
- So while people's true personalities remain undiscovered, both partners in a relationship keep making erroneous judgments about each other and themselves based on biased perceptions.

Diagram 4.1 shows that our partner's perception at point Q is grossly biased, and also too different from how we see ourselves at point P, as if we had arrived from two different planets. In addition to people's inherent capacity for misperceptions, the discussions in Chapter Fifteen about gender differences suggest that men and women have substantial differences in terms of perceiving events and people. They have unique capacities in seeing and interpreting the world. They also have drastically different priorities and values, which make it more difficult for couples to understand each other, even beyond the regular 'misperception hurdles' that people have in general.

We perceive ourselves from a biased perspective. We see an image quite different from our real personality. **We don't know who we are.** But we usually assume and insist that we *do* know ourselves. Furthermore, we are absolutely happy with who we are. We are inherently convinced about these conclusions. Furthermore, we insist that we know our partners too. These two assumptions prevent us from understanding who we are and how to relate to our partners. They create more obstacles for building our relationships. But the main point here is that we, including our partners, cannot abandon our perceptions and assumptions readily, due to our deep psychological constructs. Our resistance usually has instinctual and genetic sources too. These deep-rooted defence mechanisms drive our Ego-P and prevent us from grasping our personality defects. Even when we seem to be aware of some of them, we readily discount them, or perhaps even cherish them privately. Only when Self-P subdues the other aspects of our personality, we might be able to explore who we are and who our partners are.

The bottom line is that we judge one another based on bad communications, hurt feelings, and our own personal needs—a bunch of misperceptions. Nowadays, another major obstacle is that we like to prove our individuality by winning all the arguments with our partners. Common sense and logic don't seem to matter anymore when we must win at all cost. We think we know better than our partners and we should be the master of our lives. We have become the most snobbish people on earth during the entire history of mankind. Nowadays, it has become difficult not to be arrogant when everybody else is. It has become a way of communication even though sometimes we try to conceal our smugness partially through Model-P.

We never get a chance to understand ourselves and our partners because of our hasty judgments and misperceptions. By the way, Diagram 4.1 shows only the first level of misperceptions. Our partner, standing at point Q, is trying to make a judgment about our personality based on the feedback he/she receives through R, S, and T axes. Other levels of misperceptions occur regularly between partners in relationships, as noted later in this chapter. But first, the effect of perceptions on the most contentious issues in relationships, i.e., trust and love, is briefly discussed.

Perceptions, Trust, Love

We usually have difficulty loving, or living with, someone we don't trust. But mistrust is often the result of our own perceptions tainted by personal biases, idiosyncrasies, oversensitivity, impatience, or communication hurdles. The high level of deceit, duplicity, and phoniness in society is also responsible for our cynicism and a kind of logical mistrust (as a means of self-defence).

In relationships, partners' initial attraction is usually infected by new perceptions rather quickly—in three or four years maximum. This occurs because partners' flaws become more apparent in time, or they start misjudging each other as their cynical misperceptions keep rising. Anyway, we usually lose our trust in others rather quickly, though we do not show it. At the same time, we get annoyed if we sense our partners' loss of trust in us. We feel betrayed if we aren't trusted fully. And we feel betrayed, too, when we lose our trust in them. We blame them for it. We take it personal when they don't understand us, while we assume naively that we understand them perfectly ourselves. Not only we see ourselves as a trustworthy, open person, but also believe that our partners should see us the same way. We forget that we all have difficulty knowing who we are, and our partners have even more difficulty knowing us. Our ego and poor logic prevent us from seeing all these facts.

Our perceptions are the product of our lifelong experiences, education, and psychological constructs, including our idiosyncrasies and defence mechanisms. According to our perceptions (and misperceptions), we eventually learn to keep our guards in society, especially in relationships, because there are lots of bad experiences out there. The need for sharpening our defence mechanisms has become particularly important in the new era, because of the rising expectations and hassles in relationships. This logical tendency, to keep our guards, obviously lowers the possibility of trusting others totally. In particular, men and women mistrust the opposite gender much more than their own. Another factor is that people have different capacities for trusting others based on their backgrounds. This doesn't mean that they are flawed or guilty for not trusting others as much as we think they should.

Overall, trust and love are quickly diluted in relationships due to all types of misperceptions. Love and trust are unstable perceptions to begin with, after all. We fall out of love or lose our trust due to our oversensitivity and misperceptions. This condition cannot be remedied, but knowing the causes of mistrust might enhance our awareness. We may learn that trust is a complex concept and condition. It covers many areas, especially when it comes to relationships. Trusting someone usually means having faith in his/her fidelity, integrity, words, promises, emotions, stability, character, wisdom, devotion, hardworking, judgment, and basically everything else about that person. We must trust him/her in all respects. If we suddenly dislike something about a person, we lose our trust in him/her. In the new era, especially, we lose our trust more often and faster, because we have set such high expectations for our relationships and companions. We are all looking for an ideal, imaginary, soul mate. So, even small disappointments turn us off. In all, trust is a loaded word we conceive when we find our relationships less favourable than we had initially perceived.

While we usually lose our trust in our partners after a few years of cohabiting, we are willing (or pretending) to trust them totally at the outset. This exaggerated trust is another extreme that usually leads to disappointments too. In fact, our exaggerated initial trust (wishful thinking) leads to a faster and deeper disappointment, and loss of trust, even based on simple disagreements. Obviously, the level of trust must be a function of risk. That is, the potential repercussions of trusting someone must dictate the level of caution we exercise when dealing with him/her. For example, trusting a gardener to do a good job is less risky than trusting someone to do electrical work in our house. The high likelihood and repercussions of marriage breakdowns simply make relationships quite risky nowadays. Thus, absolute caution regarding the words and promises of our prospective partners is necessary. Simply because we can never know who other people are, or even who we are ourselves, we must remain conservative and maintain our guards, especially when we fall in love or start a serious relationship. Instead, couples try to show their goodwill by naively exaggerating their trust in their partners.

On the other hand, we must learn to work around some level of mistrust in relationships without making a big fuss about it or using it as an excuse to end our relationships. Nowadays, we must be more cautious (especially when getting into relationships), but also more flexible, open-minded, and forgiving. To say it bluntly, we must be prepared to handle some level of mistrust in our relationships because total trust is as obsolete in relationships as B-love. The following conclusions can be drawn:

1. Our accurate perceptions of corruption and duplicity in society cause cynicism about people's truthfulness and authenticity. This personal wisdom and warranted defence mechanism might inadvertently lead to a large level of misperceptions in relationships. A lot of misperceptions

are also caused by our idiosyncrasies or communication hurdles.
2. The high percentage and repercussions of marriage breakdowns simply make relationships too risky in the new era. Thus, absolute caution regarding the words and promises of our partners is warranted.
3. Mistrust is a natural (and often necessary) condition in relationships in the new era. This is a logical consequence of social life and not a sign of a person's weakness or selfishness. But partners' mistrust is often caused by their own oversensitivity and misperceptions, too, which then affects their behaviour and their partner's added mistrust in them. In all, partners must remain conscious of the high possibility and many causes of misjudging each other.
4. We must stop expecting our partners to trust us completely, especially when we honestly feel the difficulty of doing the same thing ourselves.
5. We can never know *who we are* or *who they are* and they can never know *who they are* or *who we are*. We must honour this fact with an open mind. We struggle all our lives to find ourselves and happiness, to no avail. So how can we expect others to know us and trust us when even we don't? It is simply impossible to build complete trust based on our doubtful perceptions of ourselves and others.
6. We shouldn't consider love and trust as the main factors of relationships' health anymore. This is a misleading, illogical yardstick. People often lie about their love or trust to avoid confrontations, or to be tactful and wise. Expecting trust or love beyond people's natural capacity would

only bring more duplicity and phoniness into relationships.
7. We must come to terms with two major facts in the new era: 1) it is natural that couples lose trust in each other to some extent eventually, and 2) we should learn to live in relationships with imperfect trust levels instead of making a big issue out of it. We should be ultra cautious at the time of starting our relationships, but then remain flexible about inevitable mistrust and disappointments later on.

Misperception Levels

The rather confusing tables and discussions in this section are presented **only** for the purpose of demonstrating the complexity of misperceptions. This complexity cannot be truly described or appreciated by words alone, so including the following presentation was necessary. Yet the idea is not to overwhelm the readers by these tables and discussions. So please read this section very lightly just to grasp the enormity of the problems caused by misperceptions. Or simply accept the author's word about it and continue reading on page 133. Only the patient and adventurous readers are advised to read the next five pages and challenge themselves. You have been forewarned enough!

Table 4.1, on pages 131 and 132, describes the perceptions of two partners A (male) and B (female). R denotes their relationship. The table shows several levels of perceptions that each partner, A or B, has of:

1. him/herself,
2. his/her partner, and
3. their relationship.

Perceptions and Misperceptions

A large variety of perceptions constantly occupies partners' minds and impacts their relationship, as shown in Table 4.1. The corresponding perceptions between the two partners are then listed in Table 4.2. These tables are hopefully clear and self-explanatory, yet reading them could be somewhat awkward as already noted above. So, some readers might find it easier to read the meaning of these comparisons in the narrative form presented in the list below. It reflects the gist of the most common misperceptions according to the cases listed in Table 4.2: (Even reading the following narrative could become overwhelming, so read it only lightly.)

A list of common misperceptions based on the cases shown in Table 4.2:

Case   Common Misperceptions

1. How A sees himself is different from how his partner B sees him.
2. How A sees his partner B is different from how B sees herself.
3. How A believes B sees him is different from how B really sees him.
4. How A sees his partner B is different from how B believes A sees her.
5. How A believes B sees him is different from how B believes A sees himself.
6. How A believes B sees herself is different from how B believes A sees her.
7. How A perceives his role in the relationship is different from the way B sees his role in the relationship.

8   How A perceives B's role in the relationship is different from the way B sees her role in the relationship.
9   How A perceives his expectations from their relationship is different from the way B perceives her expectations from their relationship.
10 How A perceives B's expectations from their relationship is different from the way B perceives A's expectations from their relationship.
11 How A believes B perceives their relationship is different from the way B believes A perceives their relationship.
12 How A perceives their relationship is different from the way B sees it.
13 How A perceives himself is different from his true personality.
14 How B perceives herself is different from her true personality.

The last two items in the above list reflect the simple, but important, fact that partners' perceptions of themselves are different from their real personalities anyway. If we start to compare each partner's perceptions with the true personality of his/her partner, the list of common misperceptions becomes three times longer and more difficult for this book.

According to the basic comparisons in Table 4.1, each partner is struggling with at least seven different perceptions about him/herself, about his/her partner, and about their relationship at every moment. And these perceptions are different from the perceptions of his/her partner about the same matters. So, between the two partners, A and B, there are at least fourteen conflicting perceptions that might cause clashes in their relationship at any moment. Most often, not even two of these perceptions match when partners A and B are communicating or thinking about each other and their relationship. These are, by the way, still the primary levels of misperceptions. We are not even going to discuss the secondary set of misperceptions caused during subsequent communications after initial misperceptions. Misperceptions build up exponentially when conflicts are not corrected quickly. In all, the levels of misperceptions increase and troubles mount as relationships prolong. Then retaliations begin to create additional levels of misperceptions too.

A potential for more conflicts between partners arises when any pair of the corresponding perceptions, as noted in Table 4.2, doesn't coincide. Which is almost all the time! For example, looking at the first pair, i.e., when our partner perceives us differently from how we perceive ourselves in a relationship, the means of communication between us becomes limited, if not hindered altogether. We would like to be understood and respected in the way we perceive ourselves, but our partner shows a different kind of sentiment, and sometimes even retaliates, because of his/her misperceptions. We expect respect but get humiliation, which comes across as our partners' insensitivity if not deliberate instigation. As more pairs of perceptions between partners stop coinciding, the level of frustration, mistrust, and miscommunication rises rapidly.

It is not really necessary to spend too much time to figure out the following tables, and even the narrative in the list on page 128. They could become overwhelming, which is contrary to the author's intention. The idea of presenting these tables is only to demonstrate the horrendous levels of misperceptions in our relationships. The intention is only to raise couples' awareness about the enormity of misperceptions and their impact on relationships. As noted before, there are a dozen or more ways of comparing the variety of perceptions that occur between couples beyond the basic ones shown in Table 4.2. The irony is that we are not even conscious of the basic misperceptions affecting our brains in any instant. This is because we judge every piece of information hastily and accept them as facts rather than interpretable perceptions. This is odd because we feel the burdens of our mental struggles and the ensuing depression and fatigue. But let's move on.

Table 4.1: Each Partner's Perceptions of Each Other and their Relationship

Partner A's perceptions:

+	+	=	=
A thinks of A A's perception of himself and their relationship. **AAA**	**A thinks B thinks of A** A's perception of B's view of him. **ABA**	**Partner A's total perception** of self in the relationship. **AAR**	Partner A's overall perception of the relationship. **ATR**
A thinks of B A's perception of his partner and relationship. **AAB**	**A thinks B thinks of B** A's perception of B's view of herself. **ABB**	**Partner A's total perception** of B in the relationship. **ABR**	

Partner B's perceptions:

+	+	=	=
B thinks of B B's perception of herself (and their relationship). **BBB**	**B thinks A thinks of B** B's perception of A's view of her. **BAB**	**Partner B's total perception** of self in the relationship. **BBR**	Partner B's overall perception of the relationship **BTR**
B thinks of A B's perception of her partner (and relationship). **BBA**	**B thinks A thinks of A** B's perception of A's view of himself. **BAA**	**Partner B's total perception** of A in the relationship. **BAR**	

Table 4.2: Partners' Common Misperceptions

Case	How partner A		Compared with	How partner B	
1	Sees himself	AAA	↔	Sees A	BBA
2	Sees her partner B	AAB	↔	Sees herself	BBB
3	Thinks B sees him	ABA	↔	Sees A	BBA
4	Sees her partner B	AAB	↔	Thinks A sees her	BAB
5	Thinks B sees him	ABA	↔	Thinks A sees himself	BAA
6	Thinks B sees herself	ABB	↔	Thinks A sees her	BAB
7	Perceives his role in their Relationship	ARA	↔	Perceives his role in their relationship	BRA
8	Perceives her role in their Relationship	ARB	↔	Perceives her role in their relationship	BRB
9	Perceives his expectations from their relationship	AXR	↔	Perceives her expectations from their relationship	BXR
10	Perceives B's expectations from their relationship	AXB	↔	Perceives A's expectations from their relationship	BXA
11	Thinks B perceives their relationship	ABR	↔	Thinks A perceives their Relationship	BAR
12	Perceives the relationship	ATR	↔	Perceives the relationship	BTR

Misperception Types

The topic of misperceptions is complex enough even if judged only by the preliminary levels presented in the last three pages. In the already dense presentation in Tables 4.1 and 4.2, we are assuming that partners are expressing themselves clearly and openly. Just imagine the amount of misperceptions and frustrations when partners deliberately try to remain vague about their messages. It would become too overwhelming and awkward to discuss all these other levels of misperceptions in this book. But it is necessary to briefly mention a few other levels and causes of misperceptions, such as:

1. Equivocation
2. Misrepresentation
3. Transference
4. Apprehension
5. Identity

1. Equivocation

A major cause of misperceptions is when partners behave in a certain way, or say something, but they mean something different. They keep beating around the bush. In a way, they are expecting their partner to be a mind reader and guess accurately what they are implying by their words or behaviour. In his bestseller, *Men are from Mars, Women are from Venus*, Dr. John Gray devotes a great portion of the book to this concept. He has suggested some plausible translations of a large variety of scenarios and phrases communicated between partners. These are real situations in relationships that happen all the time. Our sentimental tendencies may be blamed for some of this abnormality. We think that our partner should be sensitive enough about our needs and feelings to grasp the meaning of our words and behaviour without us being clear and open about them. We feel that sentimentality and fun would be lost if we were clear. But these are only romantic gestures and assumptions. Not only partners' needs and messages are not understood, but the way they go about expressing them actually causes further confusion, frustration, and misperceptions. In all, we have been spoiled not only in terms of setting high expectations for relationships, but also in the way we go about expressing and negotiating our needs, which are usually unrealistic anyway. Romanticism and arrogance are obviously causing many additional misperceptions in relationships.

2. Misrepresentation

Often misperceptions occur in relationships when partners try to portray a false personality of themselves. Model-P is used extensively these days to portray a kind of personality we like others to see in us. Couples do this to impress or deceive their partners for some reason. Obviously, when they are deliberately lying and playacting a false personality, the intensity and complications of misperceptions heighten drastically. On the other hand, our partners often try to read between the lines about who we are, mostly according to their misperceptions, regardless of our efforts to show a flattering picture of ourselves to them. The level of frustration due to these futile encounters and gross misperceptions can break the strength of our relationships quickly.

Sometimes couples misrepresent (hide) their feelings or thoughts with good intentions. They are trying to be tactful, flatter their partners, or avoid arguments. Yet, if this becomes a habit, it would erode partners' objectivity and ability to assess themselves and the state of their relationship. Moreover, partners will eventually lose trust in each other's integrity and words. Expressing opinions objectively, yet tactfully, is not hard if couples stay calm and stop their Ego-P from interfering.

3. Transference

The concept of transference refers to our tendency to see the world according to our needs and insecurities. Consequently, we judge our partners and our relationships based on this illusion. Our desires or hatred blind us and we see our partners according to an image that fulfils (or obstructs) our needs at a particular time. For example, we could see a person as a prince or princess, an image of perfection, when we are seeking B-love with spiritual sensations. But the same person could be viewed as a witch or devil when our needs are redirected to something or someone else, or when our quest for D-love is unanswered by our partner. We all suffer from this tendency to some extent. But some people are obsessed by their illusions and artificial needs. Their fundamental misperceptions about life make their relationships too difficult to manage. Anyway, transference refers to misperceptions about the world out there, including our partners. This is different from the case of 'identity,' discussed below, where misperceptions are about our own personalities. This is one distinction we can draw between transference and identity.

Often we *project* our flaws onto our partners and other people. For example, we may think that our partner is a big liar because we have always lied ourselves and thus believe everybody is a liar. We tend to blame others, especially our partners, for the same faults we have, sometimes as part of our subconscious efforts to deny or hide our own shortfalls. We accuse others of the same offence we often commit ourselves.

4. Apprehension

Often partners are apprehensive about revealing their true personality and needs because they believe that their partners would detect their vulnerabilities and take advantage of them. This is a somewhat legitimate concern because nowadays people indeed use their partners' vulnerabilities to strengthen their superiority in their relationship. When a person realizes that his/her partner is attached to him/her or needs him/her, he/she feels superior and uses this information to dominate his/her partner more. Because many of us are not good humans, we get caught in silly games to prove that our partner needs us more than we need him/her. The minute this balance is tilted even slightly, the pressures begin to mount. This is another reason for mistrust between partners. This apprehension in relationships also leads to misperceptions, miscommunications, and power struggles. By the way, this could be another cause for people's phoniness, because they are afraid to show who they are. Naturally, relationship environments are contaminated in many ways when partners are scared of each other. They don't dare to relax and be natural until the time comes when they get fed up and no longer care about playing certain roles to keep their relationship.

5. Identity

It has been repeated throughout this book that the main theme of modern society is 'individuality and identity.' We all like to find and establish our identity. But it appears that the more we struggle to do so, the less we succeed, and the more frustrated we get. We try to convince others about who we are and they don't buy it. This makes us angry. Often, even we, ourselves, do not buy the image that we are trying to create of us; it is just too unauthentic and insincere. Many of us have turned into phony people in order to become popular or adaptable.

As mentioned before, we lose our identity when our perceptions of our personality and the world contradict reality to a large extent. We face an identity crisis that causes its own anxieties. In addition, the lack of identity causes more confusion and misperceptions. It makes the job of adapting to our environment difficult and frustrating. This vicious cycle continues until we are totally out of touch with reality and our purpose of living. Our expectations and needs remain unrealistic, but we keep struggling to attain them. Then we keep suffering because of our unfulfilled dreams. The basic truth is that we can never know who we are despite our lifelong struggle to establish our identity. The reason is that we perceive ourselves and our personality according to bogus social standards and the inner forces A to D, which offer a biased perception of the world. We judge ourselves based on preconceived criteria and logic, through Ego-P, none of which are objective enough for the purpose of knowing who we are. Neither our perception of ourselves, nor our partners' perception of us, is correct. So we have no access to objective input, either, to contemplate and perhaps establish our true identity.

At the same time, being in a relationship imposes a new identity for each partner just for the sake of making the best of the situation. If they insist on sticking only to their personal identities and preferences, the chances for compromise and reconciliation would become minimal and the relationship would fail too quickly. The point is that, in relationships, the task of finding and maintaining our identity faces even a tougher challenge. Some people might finally give up and become passive altogether, because fighting with all these forces and misperceptions about their identity could cause extreme frustration.

When a person says, "I want to discover WHO I AM," he/she is hoping to go beyond his/her superficial and tainted perception of him/herself, bypass the effects of the inner forces (A to D), ignore all the feedback people give him/her, and reach his most inner instincts and unconscious. This is such a horrendous task! Aside from its spiritual connotation, 'Who am I?', as a philosophical question, reflects the complexity of our personality and perceptions. We have all realized the difficulty of answering this question. But the question 'Who am I?' also reflects the existence of another dimension of us, the self, which is unknown to us. The self, we agree, is different from either our perceptions of ourselves or other people's perceptions of us. Occasionally we find the opportunity to learn something about the 'self'—like the time we feel B-love when our child is born or when we stand in awe in nature. But soon we doubt or forget what we learned or at least observed deeply. Occasionally, we use this awareness to question our crooked perceptions and personality. This rudimentary awareness can by itself induce additional confusions within us, until we learn to internalize this knowledge and override the effects of the inner forces (A to D), partially perhaps.

Misperception Cycles

Overall, we perceive the world according to our superficial standards and act based on our crooked motives, all in an attempt to fit in society. Furthermore, we are forced to play various games and roles against our true nature in order to find a good companion or manage our relationships. We feel our inner conflicts from behaving so unnaturally. But we are simply afraid to show our real (vulnerable) self in a society where arrogance and showing off have become the main standards of success and survival. As a result, the whole society is becoming less natural every day, which in turn reduces the chances of relationship success. The artificiality of relationships makes it difficult to get to know ourselves and relate to our partners. Unfortunately, there is no way out of this catastrophic situation.

All along, the three aspects of our personality, i.e., Ego-P, Model-P, and Self-P, are constantly clashing within us. The resulting inner conflicts, along with the stress of dashed ambitions, confuse us about our identity. We question who we are and the purpose of our lives. Often we suffer from our doubts about our identity. But usually we try to ignore it and move on. Ego-P tries to hide all those doubts and questions in our subconscious, which is of great help to maintain our sanity.

Without clear identities, we lose ourselves even more in relationships and thus keep increasing the possibility and level of misperceiving both ourselves and our partners. We want to know what we are doing in this relationship and why we are staying in it, especially when things are not working out. With our confusion, we confuse and frustrate our partners, too, more than they already are by themselves.

Since we are not aware of the true sources of our frustration in relationships, we invent still more phony means of relating to each other (e.g., more role-playing) to make up for our inability to relate to one another naturally. We usually believe that we have an authentic and functional identity, so perfect we can even brag about it openly. Most of us believe we know who we are and we are quite proud of it too. This is, of course, Ego-P pushing us to feel so confident about our identity. By hiding our doubts about our identity, Ego-P is actually serving us, because questioning our identity without promptly following an awareness path to find it would hurt us even more than living with a phony identity. We have enough doubts in our lives to deal with already. If we don't have some type of confidence at least about who we are (even as a phony person) we can't function. Nonetheless, a vicious cycle of misperceptions empowers itself and ruins our relationships as well as our spirit.

Understanding Our Partners

The high potential for confusion in relationships is evident from the above discussions of misperceptions. Accordingly, the absurdity of our expectation from our partners to 'know who we are'—to understand us—is clear. Of course, this is a legitimate expectation with the intention of reducing the gap between AAA and BBA (see Table 4.1), i.e., how we see ourselves and how our partners see us. We hope that if they understood us they would stop nagging and hurting us. We believe that only if they realized the purity of our intentions, they would sympathize with us instead of showing resistance. But, in reality, how can we expect our partners to know who we are if we don't know who we are ourselves? We now know that our perceptions of ourselves are incorrect, because the four inner forces (A to D) distort our ability to know our personality, not to mention the added effects of our misperceptions caused by environment and our partners. Thus, the reflections of our personality, i.e., the way we see it, the way others see it, and what it really is, remain incongruent to a great degree in relationships. We behave in certain ways to portray a strong and reliable personality to others. But others refuse to see it that way. How successful we are in portraying a phony personality of ourselves depends on so many factors, but nonetheless we are hiding, and overriding, our real personality even from ourselves by our attempts to fit within society.

Equally frustrating is our partners' expectation of us to *know who they are*, when even they themselves don't know *who they are*. Their expectation seems unrealistic and silly when our knowledge of who they are is only based on the level of our observations of their highly Model-P driven personality. We can see the role they are playing to come across as civilized and compassionate individuals. But we know that it is not their true personality. We try hard to read between the lines or wait until they make a mistake and suddenly reveal their true personality temporarily. But they would, of course, deny the critical observation of their personality when we find the courage to mention it. And thus we fight over these disagreements too. Obviously, for entering into a relationship, or dealing with an existing one, we can't wait forever until our partners find out who they are or until they decide to relax—put down their guards—and let us see their personality. We usually don't have enough patience to deal with our partners' idiosyncrasies in the hope that conflicts would be resolved someday by some stroke of luck. Life is precious. So it is completely justified to make a decision based on what we see, i.e., our present (flawed) perceptions. After all, the possibility that our partners' personality change or we change our perceptions of them later is minimal. So realistically, we must act based on the available knowledge—the unfortunate misperceptions, while staying aware of the points discussed here about misperceptions and their potential for causing big problems.

We must remain vigilant of *our own* misperceptions and hasty judgments. The question is how much our partners are misrepresenting themselves and how much we are misperceiving them. It shows that when we assume, under the influence of the inner forces (A to D), that *we know ourselves* and remain stubborn about it, we may be doing ourselves a disservice and imposing more pressures on our relationships. Continuing with the same mentality and attitude would only reflect the power of the inner forces (A to D) in defining our superficial personality. In the final analysis, we are responsible for misperceptions between us and our partners when we keep insisting that we know who we are instead of trying to learn more about ourselves through self-awareness. We are responsible for the way we allow our misperceptions cripple our understanding of our partners, the means of communicating, and our ability to solve our conflicts.

The discussions in the next section also provide many other reasons for partners' difficulty to understand each other.

Personal Flaws and Reactions Due to Misperceptions

We can conclude that relationship problems emerge because of our limited awareness of who we are and our stubbornness to insist otherwise. Despite our intelligence, we have not yet learned to do self-analysis for understanding the extent of our defects and faulty perceptions. Our ego simply prevents us from being objective, especially when it comes to gauging our own shortfalls. This lack of intuitive objectivity makes us perceive ourselves very close to perfection. And then we use our erroneous perceptions of ourselves as a yardstick to judge everybody else too. As a result, when we perceive ourselves as a symbol of human perfection, everybody else's attitude appears quite offensive, or at least inadequate, compared to ours. This is true even when we love someone, though we are usually more forgiving and tolerant at the beginning and harsher later.

The lack of objectivity also makes us rigid. For example, we assume and insist that we know who we are, and that our partners are fully aware of who they are too (as we perceive them). Our persistence about these two erroneous assumptions makes relationship problems hardly reconcilable. Of course, the first mistake is that we believe that we are a perfect person. And then we also believe that our partners are capable of being perfect like us if only they begin to listen to what we tell them to do. What they are now—their personality—is obviously inadequate and unacceptable. But, the fact that they are, in our opinion, aware of their flaws, and are deliberately resisting our reasoning about changing themselves, seems most ridiculous and offensive to us.

The most common struggle in relationships is partners' attempt to change each other. For this purpose, we believe with great certainty that we know who they (our partners) are. Not only do we assume that we know ourselves and they know themselves, but also believe that our perceptions of our partners are accurate. Furthermore, we expect them to perceive themselves exactly as we perceive them, i.e., with all the flaws we have detected in them according to our biased standards. We expect them to agree with our demented perceptions of them. We insist on judging our partners quickly based on our rigid opinion of who they are, and then get upset when they disagree with our perceptions of who they are. Once we set our minds about *who they are*, positively or negatively, it becomes close to impossible to accept any counter argument about the validity of our opinions and perceptions. When we are in love, our partners appear flawless and compatible with our needs—we are so sure of that. And when we face problems and their resistance, we emphasize mostly on negative images of that person just for the sake of strengthening our new antagonistic perception of them.

To make the problem even more complicated, we also assume and insist that *they (our partners) know who we are*. We don't know *who we are*, but naively expect our partners to know *who we are*. And further, we expect them to see us exactly the way we want them to see us, which by the way could be how we truly see ourselves, too, or not. We want them to see us according to the role we play by our Model-

P. We want them to accept the role we like to play as a legitimate personality. We hate it when they are not fooled by our Model-P. Of course, we all have difficulty expressing ourselves properly even on those occasions when we want to be sincere and honest. Even if we could do so, the chances that others really believe us or perceive us correctly are slim. Their past experiences with us and their demented general perceptions still make the job of knowing us impossible. Anyway, we are often offended by the fact that our partners have not still figured out our sentiments, desires, and expectations. We expect them to have learned by now the legitimacy of all of our peculiar demands. In addition, we expect them to accept our viewpoints and sentiments as proper standards for our relationship.

If only we realize that our partners cannot learn what we insist they should learn, we may be able to better manage our relationships and assess our options realistically. But the problem is that our Ego-P won't let us learn this simple lesson. We keep insisting that our partners can learn what we are asking them to learn, especially about *who we insist we are or they are*. We insist that problems will be solved if only they stopped being so stubborn. Both partners feel the same way. What an irony!

So, almost all relationships suffer from a multitude of erroneous assumptions. We are caught in a web of huge misperceptions about our personalities, the appropriateness of our attitudes and standards, knowing our partners, our partners knowing themselves, us, and our expectations, etc. These assumptions have misled us about the potentials and purposes of relationships too. We have become totally self-centred not only in terms of focusing on some phony personal needs, but also in terms of imposing all those needs on our relationships. When things don't work, we blame our partners for everything. We believe we understand their intentions and know the meaning of their antagonistic behaviour. We assume they know (or must know) our personal needs and stubbornly refuse to consider them legitimate.

Conflicts are inevitable as long as relationships are viewed and evaluated according to partners' misperceptions of themselves and their partners. Conflicts are due to self-centredness of human beings in general, obviously. But the drastic increase in relationship conflicts in the new era is due to couples' misperceptions about *who they are and who they can be*. They just keep portraying a pompous identity to prove their strong individuality. Thus they confuse themselves and others.

Chapter Five
Consciousness and Communication

Communication hurdles have always been blamed for relationship breakdowns. As noted in the previous chapters, couples' personal needs, misperceptions, and excessive Ego-P affect their behaviour and damage their communication. What they witness, often, is mutual resistance and frustration when they try, in their minds, to communicate logically and calmly. In addition to these common obstacles, many other psychological factors affect partners' communication, as discussed in this chapter.

A prominent factor in communications is the level of consciousness. The question is, 'How much of our communication is driven by our conscious mind and how much by our subconscious or even unconscious motives.' To study this topic, some basic principles must be initially introduced. First, it is common knowledge that a person's cognition and behaviour are influenced by his/her genes and upbringing environment. While nature (genetics) is probably most instrumental in one's development and behaviour, nurture (environment) plays a major role as well. Nature and nurture contribute to the development of mind, which, in turn, directs our urges, feelings, thinking, and actions. The health and capacity of the brain are therefore crucial for one's level of cognition too. This simple concept is shown in Diagram 5.1, where:

A: Denotes Nature (biological construct/genetics).
B: Denotes Nurture (environment, including family and society).
C: Denotes Mind (logic and analytical capacity).
ABC: Denotes Cognition, i.e., one's ability to understand and process data.

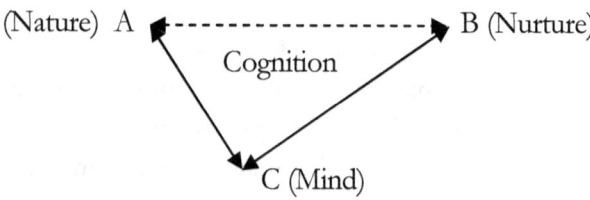

Diagram 5.1: The Basic Cognition Model

The area ABC, one's cognition, is constantly influenced by one's biological and environmental variables, as well as one's mental ability to receive and utilize various stimuli. The mind, a tool developed by A and B, in turn assists one's 'cognition,' to serve A and B. That is, by developing a strong cognition, the mind serves A and B to maintain a person's biological needs and face environmental issues, including relationships, more effectively and efficiently. The notion of 'healthy mind in healthy body, and conversely' reflects this principle.

In Diagram 5.1, line AB is shown as broken to indicate that A and B are semi-independent sources of mental development. The former (nature) is an inherent aspect of man, while the latter (nurture) contains a set of external forces affecting his identity. Yet A and B impact each other to some degree, too, directly or indirectly. For example, anger, caused by somebody or an event, changes the biology and chemical reactions in our body. Our reaction may change B—the person or event—too.

When we talk about the environment (nurture) affecting individuals' development, we mean *physical* environments and interactions. Aside from this physical world, man has always believed in, and pondered, metaphysics in the context of religion, supernatural, and myths. Regardless of the level of our beliefs and meditations, metaphysical concepts and connections affect our minds. Although metaphysics is scientifically intangible and beyond our physical realm, many evidences point to some kind of connection between our physical existence and the rest of the universe. Nonetheless, this class of thoughts also contributes to our cognition. It adds another dimension to the cognition model, as shown in Diagram 5.2, where:

D: denotes metaphysical realm.

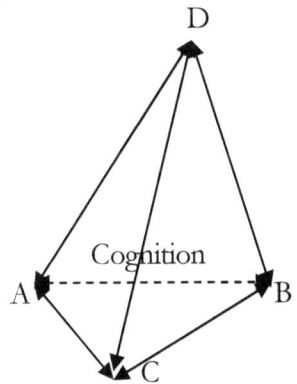

Diagram 5.2: The Cognition Model, ABCD

As the arrows in Diagram 5.2 show, D is a person's mental perception of the universe by using his/her capacities in terms of A, B, and C. Meanwhile, it is plausible that D in turn impacts our biological and mental health (A and C), as well as our social behaviour (B). D reflects intangible thoughts and realities beyond our routine encounters and experiences. Our instincts (from A), perceptions (from B), and logic (from C) are supplemented by myths (from D). Together they create a vague level of cognition that operates mainly within subconscious and unconscious domains. Basically, what D says is that there is much more to man than is obvious to him and people around him. This includes his spirituality aspects too. Even though he attempts to develop ideas and visions about these additional aspects of man, he would remain mostly unaware of them and thus he is unconscious about their true existence and meaning. In daily routines, we assume that we are always operating at a conscious level, but there are subconscious and unconscious urges and information that trigger our behaviour and thoughts. For example, it is claimed that each person processes 40,000 thoughts every single day. Obviously we don't recall even a dozen thoughts in a particular day, let alone 40,000. The findings suggest that we make 200 decisions alone every day about what to eat. Obviously many of these thoughts and decisions happen at some level of consciousness beyond our control and awareness. Before we spend any time to review these points further, explaining what ABCD represents can help.

The triangular pyramid ABCD reflects 'self,' a concept we often have difficulty envisioning. 'Self' is the complete picture of man containing all his intrinsic potentialities, although in reality he never gets a chance to grasp or use them. While 'identity' mostly reflects the known (conscious) aspect of man, 'self' contains all levels of consciousness, particularly the unconscious and subconscious, which he neglects to access or draw upon. Of course, as the level of self-awareness increases, one's 'identity' approaches one's 'self.' So, 'self' is the essence of man and contains all the three levels of consciousness as shown in Diagram 5.4, where:

ABCEFG: Denotes one's level of 'conscious' cognition
EFGHIJ: Denotes one's level of 'subconscious' cognition
DHIJ: Denotes one's level of 'unconscious' cognition
ABCD: Denotes 'self' and total cognition

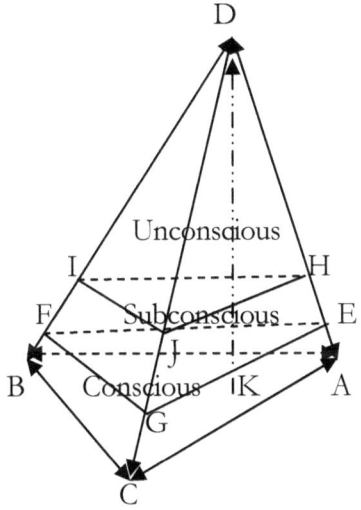

Diagram 5.3: The Self with Three Levels of Consciousness

While ABCD reflects a person's total cognition at three levels of consciousness, we mostly depend on the conscious level of cognition to communicate and understand the world. The cognition at subconscious and unconscious levels is mostly abstract since our chances to delve into those territories in isolation from social norms and conditioning are quite remote. Nonetheless, cognition reflects the level of our awareness about the metaphysical aspects of the universe, the self, and their ultimate links according to many philosophies. The higher our awareness, the higher would be our chance to learn about the self—for a fuller cognition. In Diagram 5.3, 'awareness' is represented by the perpendicular line DK.

Another principle suggested by the model in Diagram 5.3 is that the subconscious and unconscious minds, for each person, are developed by different levels of biology, environment, and mental capacity. (The positions of triangles EFG and HIJ are quite flexible, and their planes are not necessarily parallel to one another or to ABC.) That is, our subconscious and unconscious are the by-products of our genes, social encounters, the power of our minds, as well as the degree of our self-awareness. Their format and capacity change from person to person too.

So what is the significance of these assertions about one's cognition and the three levels of consciousness? The answer lies in the fact that cognition and consciousness are the locus of our attributes, behaviour, and decisions. Our genetic characteristics, natural instincts, and social learning are stored within, and disseminated through, individual's cognition at various levels of consciousness. Everybody has a body and a mind. We associate the body with the heart and emotions. And we associate mind with brain and logic. We say, for example, that he let his heart take over his brain. Or we say that her logic superseded her emotions. So the question is, 'Whether there is a higher entity in humans that allows body or mind to supersede in a particular situation or for a decision.' On the surface, brain seems to be responsible for all our decisions and actions. But the reality is a little bit more complex.

Statements like, "Try not to think about it", "Try to forget her", "Go with your heart", or situations when we concentrate on our body to reach a state of thoughtlessness, during meditation for example, are only some examples that show our brain is not the organ in charge of our lives, but rather it is a tool we use to store, manipulate, and apply the information and experiences we have accumulated. The notions of body-mind coordination and consciousness also reflect that both our brain and body are tools that work together to serve a higher entity responsible for running the affairs of a person. This higher entity can be envisioned for our purpose to be the 'cognition' as demonstrated in Diagram 5.3. In fact, cognition, consciousness, and the self are used interchangeably to imply the same thing in this book. Although understanding the nature of cognition, consciousness, or the self is not easy, this book attempts to explain it as best it can. But beyond any academic explanation, each one of us has had a private sense of cognition. We have felt how our spirit improves or depletes according to special experiences (due to changes in brain chemicals of course). We recall the ways we use our willpower, spiritual strength and other instinctual forces to control our affairs, make decent decisions, or stop our devilish thoughts. In all, cognition can be thought of as an inherent entity (maybe our soul) that makes the final conscious decisions about our welfare based on our level of awareness, i.e., the strength of the self.

Our weaknesses and strengths are stored at all levels of consciousness. They affect us and people around us positively or negatively depending on our awareness. Awareness is simply the level of our cognition we have learned to master—how effectively we tap the power within us. The importance of self-awareness becomes evident when we consider its objective to dig into our subconscious and unconscious territories and gradually explore the causes of our deep-rooted behaviour. The more our conscious thinking and activities are sensitized by these explorations and realizations, the purer our behaviour and judgments would become. We would learn which ones of our needs are authentic and which ones are the symptoms of our addictions to consumerism and competition. We would understand how so many of our legitimate instincts, such as urges for independence and individuality, have been gradually undermined due to the social pressures for compliance. And then we understand how we have developed phony identities to pretend independence and individuality. Somehow it appears funny that society is abolishing people's chances to develop and keep their true identities, and instead encourages them to develop phony identities in order to pretend independence and individuality. What a sarcastic concept and remark, some readers might say. But if we look around carefully, we might arrive at these conclusions easily. We seek D-love relentlessly to satiate our hunger for compassion instead of digging into our potentialities to embrace B-love. We struggle to be accepted by a society which we abhor for its phony values and hypocrisy. We like to own more things instead of learning more about ourselves and humanity. We see how love deficiency causes frustration and hardship, but we keep increasing our expectations from relationships and end up living alone most of our lives. We realize how our encounters with people are contaminated by some preconceived rules of success in society, but we don't care about changing our values. We judge the success of our relationships based on the same superficial values too. We assess our partners based on their ability to think and act competitively and aggressively instead of valuing their integrity and needlessness.

A philosophical question we may ask is, 'How conscious our actions or decisions are when we are so helplessly influenced by all the inner and outer forces?' Can we really say that our actions are truly conscious, while these forces and compulsions contaminate our perceptions and judgments? Saying 'no' would sound like an extreme definition for our level of consciousness. Though, we are partially accepting this position in reality. We excuse a criminal due to his insanity. We say that he has not been *conscious* of his actions. In our modern societies, psychiatrists have drawn a line to define some actions conscious and some others unconscious. But this line is somewhat arbitrary when we are all driven by the same types of inner and outer forces at some level. If these forces can make someone unconscious of his behaviour, then they can have the same effect on everybody else at some degree too. The level or definition of clinical insanity is not the point here. The point is that the inner and outer forces make us somewhat unconscious of our deeds and thoughts. Obviously, this is an extreme viewpoint about consciousness. And there is no need to quarrel about this simple observation. The only question is, 'How often even supposedly sane people might not be truly conscious and responsible for their actions?' One implication of this viewpoint is for couples to remember that some of their own and their partner's behaviour are influenced by their unconscious or subconscious urges. So showing sympathy is more logical than retaliation when partners are unable to act and think according to each other's liking.

At its most ideal level, consciousness could reflect the degree of purity of our thoughts and actions outside our egotistical urges, free from greed and self-interest. Only at full consciousness our deeds would be unselfish. This is, of course, the definition of conscientiousness, where our conscious actions and thoughts are authentic and useful for approaching our true identity as a human (if we assume that human is capable of being pure, of course).

Becoming a better human was considered the best way for building sustainable relationships in Chapter Three. And for becoming a better human, it is suggested here that we must find some access to our subconscious and unconscious to behold man's essence of life—the self. We might be able to cleanse our conscious mind by drawing on the power of unconscious and subconscious (through self-awareness) and become a conscientious person. Meanwhile, couples must appreciate the difficulty of relating to each other as long as their conscious activities and thoughts are contaminated by personal inner forces and social values.

Yet the idea of accessing our unconscious to enhance the quality of our conscious actions is mostly a philosophical reflection. Self-awareness is not an easy process to pursue, nor is it a subject for discussion in this book. Realistically, the possibility of becoming an enlightened person and finding our true identity is low for most of us. We don't even have the time and patience to explore the means of getting there, let alone the conviction and courage to actually follow the formidable path of self-awareness. We are too deeply sunk in the norms of society and we are softened too much. We lack the stamina and devotion to free ourselves from the life of luxury, greed and superficial needs. The naivety of positive thinking schemes lies in the fact that they assume cognition can be explored and manipulated easily. They assume that our unconscious and subconscious minds can be penetrated by a superficial modification of thoughts or actions. It is odd how so many people believe in quick fixes to attain an everlasting life of prosperity and tranquility. Even for talented people who can endure a path of wisdom, the amount of needed work and devotion is quite horrendous and lengthy. How can one become a new person, a pure man, just by willing it or attempting to change one's way of thinking and playacting? It sounds absurd to some of us.

Just a quick note about positive thinking: Its only possible effect is in assisting a person discover and apply his/her potentialities beyond what he has commanded previously. It is one of many devices that can guide a person realize his/her hidden potentialities, e.g., turning a talented musician into a virtuoso. But for the rest of us, no amount of positive thinking and practice can help us achieve beyond our capabilities, e.g., to become a virtuoso. So, the idea of positive thinking helping everybody is ludicrous, except for keeping their hopes alive a bit longer. Positive thinking and similar schemes might benefit a small minority, but they should not be propagated for their universal effect and thus causing deeper disappointments and depression for people. People's ability to change themselves follows a similar argument. A few might change only if they have an inherent capacity for grasping the benefits of change and have the stamina to implement it over a long period. Some of us succeed to change for a while, too, but we normally revert back to our previous positions, where we feel most comfortable, and not the ones that make sense even to us.

An evidence of the unconscious mind is offered by people who dream deeply and remember them later. Occasionally, their dreams reveal their hidden desires and characters and help their self-awareness efforts when they try to understand the clues. There is no need for interpreting dreams, but only sensing them naturally. Obviously, the more complicated social life gets, the less we find access to deeper knowledge in our cognition. Still, once we finally go to sleep and our minds get a chance to relax, the unconscious mind might spill some clues about the self and one's real character. This is the same principle followed in meditation. Many creative ideas and artistic notions could potentially reach us in our dreams or through meditation when the unconscious mind operates somewhat freer. People who have reported 'near death experience,' NDE, suddenly change their lifestyles and become more spiritual. They usually abandon their routine, useless life activities with a plan to learn more about themselves and the universe. A plausible explanation about this turnaround in their way of thinking is that they have spent a great deal of time within the domain of their unconscious minds during an NDE.

While unconscious (the self) remains an untapped resource that contains one's essence, signs of its existence show in our actions and behaviour regularly. Obviously, an enormous level of human potentialities is neglected as they remain buried in people's unconscious. A more important implication of using the term 'unconscious,' however, is that we insist on keeping many useful and relevant information in our *unconscious* instead of facing them and using them. We seem to hate the idea of being a more conscious and conscientious person. With our superficial lifestyles, we insist on ignoring the urges, forces, and symptoms that emerge unexpectedly from our unconscious and give us clues about the meaning of our existence. We usually push those clues back into our unconscious mind even when the information seems helpful to improve our lives.

Granted, all these ideas about awareness and consciousness appear to be outside our existing comprehension and social norms. Reaching such a level of enlightenment, while we struggle with our rampant desires and expectations, would be difficult. We dislike learning about ourselves, especially our defects. We hate to explore, or acknowledge, the motives behind our thoughts and actions, because they reveal our wickedness. We justify our bad habits and cruelty instead of paying attention to the nagging voices in our conscience. We avoid self-awareness, because we believe we already know everything that is necessary to know. And we do not want to waste time or energy to learn about others either, except for the kind of information that would help us exploit or manipulate them. We do not have the patience, or stamina, to go through the agony of learning about ourselves and others. We do not want to be bothered or add to our problems. Obviously, this resistance to learn about oneself or others is a major cause of misperceptions in relationships. 'What you don't know won't hurt you,' is an infantile slogan we have developed to relieve our conscience when we find it to our advantage. This slogan, however, can never be justified for our reluctance to pursue self-awareness or the means of boosting our compassion toward others.

Despite the difficulty of pursuing a self-awareness path, learning about the natural obstacles of our encounters and communications, including the role of consciousness, can help our relationships. We should not bypass the opportunity of being a more conscious and conscientious human, a process that begins simply by remembering that a great majority of our thoughts and decisions is processed outside of our control. How often some incriminating or offensive words have jumped out of our big mouths unconsciously, before we got a chance to censor them? Those experiences are clear clues about the interworking of our subconscious and unconscious minds—our cognition. This is a fact that most of us believe or at least heard before. Yet the concept of self-awareness and tapping the power of the unconscious mind to improve our lives and relationships appear illusory to many people.

We may eventually realize that we have become lazy, selfish, and unrealistic about the purpose of life and relationships. We may admit that our desire for wealth and power has diminished our capacity to entertain our very basic need for true independence. We simply cannot free ourselves from people and symbols that constrict our ability to think straight and unselfishly. As mentioned in Chapter Three, the best option for developing a successful relationship is to become an enlightened person, capable of feeling and giving love unselfishly. On the other hand, Part II of this book will discuss other options for creating relatively successful relationships when they are fitted within the requirements of our freakish modern societies. Since we resist living in a simple environment to attain a fuller cognition, the second best option for building our relationships is to adapt ourselves to the requirements of new lifestyles. Presently we are following neither of these paths and thus our relationships are becoming increasingly dysfunctional.

Our perceptions (misperceptions) are mostly created by our conscious (active) mind, although the information stored in subconscious and unconscious occasionally interfere too. But, in general, perceptions and the conscious mind are the cause and effect of each other and they are both contaminated by rearing and conditioning effects. Together, they keep us circling in some narrow domain of thoughts and cognition. They systematically stop us from accessing the power that is buried in our unconscious mind. They make us dogmatic and stubborn about our vision of life, events, and other people. Accordingly, our communications, knowledge about ourselves and others, and judgments about our relationships remain biased and shallow. One obvious symptom of this condition is that couples and society refuse to acknowledge that the existing manner of running our relationships has failed. We continue to depend on luck and court systems to manage our relationships and to impose justice as needed—to protect us against the prevalent agony of relationships (which we have brought upon ourselves). Instead of understanding the roots of relationship problems, we increase our expectations from our partners and we assume that they can understand our and we assume that they can understand our needs and must comply too. We have lost touch with reality and still believe that our relationships can fit our fantasies and survive the hectic environment we have invented.

Consciousness and Personality Aspects

The three personality aspects coincide with the three levels of consciousness very nicely. This reflects the perfect correlation of a person's level of consciousness with his/her personality and behaviour. It also enhances the validity of both models that relate in the following manner:

The Model-P aspect of personality mostly operates from within the conscious level of one's mind. We use mostly our conscious mind for interacting with others and for making decisions. With Model-P, we try to behave logically and tactfully, based on our conscious access to valid information. We do so in order to maximize our chances of success in our interactions or actions. The more we attempt to impress a person or make a better judgment, the more we depend on our Model-P to help us perform this task. We become ultra conscious of our behaviour too. We have developed Model-P to become charming and successful with others and in our businesses. Model-P is most representative of our conscious mind and together they fulfil our immediate social needs. Model-P draws heavily on the tangible knowledge and logic we have accumulated in our conscious mind (perceptions).

The Ego-P aspect of personality represents our subconscious mind, which reflects mostly our rather private and selfish traits and motives. The ego, greed, jealousy, and many other of our unflattering urges are hidden in our subconscious. We deny our shortfalls and destructive urges that often interfere with our decisions and interactions. Whenever our conscience tries to warn us about our malice and egotistical behaviour, we quickly dismiss it by justifying ourselves and pushing those ethical flashes deep into subconscious. Subconscious mostly stores unpopular urges, defence mechanisms, and bad memories that we like to hide from others (and from ourselves, too, to a great extent). Nonetheless, they have become part of our personality and manifest as Ego-P.

The Self-P aspect of personality represents mostly our unconscious urges, instincts, potentialities, and spirituality inclinations. Depending on our level of awareness about the self, we may access and apply the energy and knowledge hidden in this part of our mind. Wisdom, as we call it, is the amount of pure knowledge that is dug out of our essence as a human free from social values and people's influence. Social values are imposed on a person and they impact his/her Ego-P and Model-P. In this sense, unconscious refers to that part of mind that has remained mostly unaffected by social values. Since we spend our lives working within the primary levels of mind, i.e., conscious and maybe subconscious, we never find an opportunity to explore unconscious. It is argued that the unconscious holds those unflattering personal experiences that have been buried deep in one's mind to mitigate one's suffering. It is not essential to argue whether all of our experiences are stored in subconscious or partly sipped through to the unconscious as well. Whether this precious resource (the unconscious mind) is infected by our unfavourable life experiences should not constitute a ground for argument. Nonetheless, unconscious resembles a gold mine buried underneath many layers of solid barriers. In the final analysis, the unconscious is the only source of pure knowledge about the essence of man. The ultimate objective is to access the unconscious to improve the Self-P aspect of personality. Using our inherent potentiality and spirituality would make us a better person.

The models and hypotheses presented in this book are for the purpose of presenting a simple picture and framework for the general public about the complexity of mind, personality, and perceptions. The ultimate goal is, of course, to explain the true sources of our behaviour and motives. This knowledge might mitigate our eagerness to judge others hastily. The hypothesis in this part of the book, by paralleling the three aspects of personality with the three levels of consciousness, is aimed at presenting a plausible picture of our thought processes and behaviour. In reality, however, it is very likely that personality aspects move within the boundaries of consciousness not as cleanly as presented above. For example, our conscious mind may in some instances reflect our Ego-P, too, instead of only supporting our Model-P—for example, when a man is aware how selfishly he is attempting to lure a woman by lying and flattery. As another example, arrogance, which is usually perceived as a manifestation of Ego-P, could manifest partially or totally in a person's Model-P. This is due to the fact that arrogance has become a means of intimidating others, to portray a particular tough image of oneself. Under the disguise of assertiveness or boosted self-image, arrogance has become an epidemically popular development in the new era. People have learned that arrogance gives them an edge in their dealings and negotiations with others. So they have incorporated arrogance in their Model-P, and use it consciously, in order to enhance their dominance over others.

It is clear now why it is so difficult to develop our Self-P. The difficultly lies, obviously, in the fact that Self-P is mostly hidden in our unconscious beneath many solid barriers of social conditioning. Model-P and Ego-P prevent us from accessing Self-P as much as we like. Hundreds of reasons have been offered throughout this book why we personally sabotage the possibility of accessing our subconscious and unconscious to find more about ourselves.

Consciousness, Communication, and Perceptions

Plenty of reasons exist for miscommunication between partners. But basically the five main causes of misperceptions, as discussed in the previous chapter, page 133, are also responsible for miscommunication. They are: 1) Equivocation, 2) Misrepresentation, 3) Transference, 4) Apprehension, and 5) Identity.

A simple fact is that miscommunications and misperceptions keep impacting each other and piling up dangerously in the early stages of relationships. Initial communications set permanent images and perceptions in couples' subconscious. Many types of misperceptions are deposited in various levels of couples' consciousness too. Within a short period of time, a large volume of misperceptions and miscommunications eventually lead to partners' negative views of each other and about their relationship.

In all, our communications (both verbal and oral), perceptions, and consciousness (including the three personality aspects) are highly interrelated impulses. Collectively, they instigate our reactions and behaviour in any waking moment of our lives and during our encounters. This concept is shown in the oversimplified Diagram 5.4.

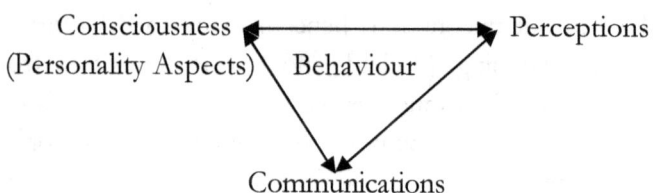

Diagram 5.4: The Impact of Consciousness, Perceptions, and Communications on Behaviour (Reactions)

Chapter Six
The Nature of Love

Since love has become the locus of relationships in modern societies, we must at least know what it is and understand the role it can realistically play in relationships. This chapter explains the nature of love in order to remove some of the ambiguities clouding its meaning.

What Is Love and Why It Is Important to Know That

Chapter One highlighted two crucial points: (a) a good companion can *potentially* satisfy a wide range of our personal needs, and (b) we are programmed, instinctually and culturally, to look for a soul mate because we believe he/she can relieve our loneliness and satisfy our personal needs. In a sense, we intuitively put too much faith in the potentials of companionship. And we spend a lot of time and energy, all our lives, to find that special person who matches our image of a soul mate. Anytime we meet someone resembling that image, we begin to fantasise about him/her in a 'love routine' to test our luck with this new candidate.

Accordingly, the word 'love,' in the context used nowadays, basically consists of people's impression (and expression) of their 1) urges, 2) feelings, and 3) moods during their search for a companion.

The **Urges** that drive humans to find a mate, as noted in Chapter One, are Sex, Compassion, and B-love. Compassion is meant to include other urges such as D-love, security, dependence, respect, recognition, etc.

The **Feelings** related to humans' search for a mate are numerous, including delight, elation, lust, jealousy, possessiveness, hatred, anger, and almost all other feelings that humans face while chasing any desire. A variety of feelings emerge during couples' love affairs and separations.

The **Moods** that emerge during humans' search for a companion are comprised of: Attraction, Romance, and Attachment. They are fed by a mix of urges and feelings, but also by conscious assessments. That is, we use both our instinctual and logical attributes to manage these moods (processes or modes) successfully. These three moods, i.e., attraction, romance, and attachment, are close reflections of our urges for sex, B-love, and compassion respectively and they are satiated with a huge amount of feelings too. We also use our logical and calculating minds when we are in one or more of these moods. These moods reflect a person's state of mind and the progress of a love affair (all for the purpose of fulfilling his/her need for a mate).

Attraction is triggered by physical appeal, lust, but also our careful evaluation of a person's attributes and resources. Our instinctual criteria for selecting a mate, mostly for the purpose of bearing a child with this person, often play its role too. People (and love literatures) usually confuse attraction with love. The minute they are attracted to someone, they believe they are in love.

Romance is our innate impression of B-love and our calculating expressions of passion in order to lure in our beloved. So, again, we are using both our instinctual and logical assets to find a companion.

Attachment is the effect of closeness to a person and enjoying the compassion satisfied by this union.

A lot of feelings, including elation, lust, hope, security, dependency, etc. are stirred up when a person's urges (sex, compassion, B-love) push him/her to find a companion. As love moods progress successfully, or when they face disappointments, more feelings are still brought into this situation, such as the feelings of possessiveness, jealousy, hatred, anger, depression, suicide, etc. We have historically combined all these urges, feelings, and moods and called it love. Not only we confuse love with attraction, but also attach a large assortment of feelings, urges, and moods to this initial attraction and call the whole mix 'love.' That is why love has always been a vague definition and too difficult to deal with. People suffer because of love for two main reasons: First, the forces behind their love urges, feelings, and moods are not clear to them in order to deal with the sources of their anxieties directly. Second, they assume love is a lasting condition. Consequently, they feel miserably defeated once they face the natural downfall of love. They take it too personal, while cursing their beloved too.

Understanding the true meaning and implications of love might help us curb our initial unwarranted enthusiasm and prepare ourselves better for its heartbreaking consequences. So, the moods, urges, and feelings related to love would be studied briefly in this chapter.

The first thing to agree on is that the customary method of combining all the *urges, moods, and feelings* related to 'finding a companion' and calling this overwhelming mix 'love' is confusing, but also untrue. The *urges, moods, and feelings* related to 'finding a companion' should be studied as psychological reactions—symptoms of love—but not love itself. They are the same symptoms that manifest at lower intensity when we have any desire, e.g., for a car or a pair of shoes, especially when satisfying it falls outside our means. This is a fine distinction, which its usefulness will be explained shortly.

So what is true love? True love is that unique instinctual urge that we have identified as B-love. Love, in its purest sense, is just a simple, selfless appreciation for the mere 'being' of another person without having any selfish urges to own, control, or impose one's needs upon that person. Just pure B-love as a unique state of mind. Most people have experienced B-love temporarily when they have been affected by music, nature, their children, some kind of passion, or during self-actualization. This pure feeling of B-love, which is engraved in our unconscious, is occasionally directed toward our beloved, too, but usually for a short period. We fail because we cannot internalize B-love unless we learn to become a selfless individual. Anyway, in real life, we create all kinds of images and love moods (attraction, romance, and attachment) in our minds when some flickers of B-love strike us. But these love moods are only the outcome of our pressing urges for 'sex' and 'compassion,' while we struggle to find a companion. We encounter all kinds of feelings, including sexual attraction, security or insecurity, dependency, passion, jealousy, possessiveness, attachment, ecstasy, etc. The minute these varied emotions are introduced in any love affair, B-love loses its inherent property and love becomes something totally different. It mainly turns into D-love.

Basically, it is our strong 'need for a companion' (once directed toward a particular person) that creates all those urges, feelings, and moods that we customarily (and wrongly) attribute to love. It is not 'love' that creates all those (good and bad) feelings and usually leads to enormous suffering (despite the initial elation and hope). "So don't blame love," is one important conclusion to draw here. It is our deprived 'need for a companion' that causes pain all our lives. This simple and subtle distinction is important because it makes us reflect inwardly to put our love related urges and feelings into a proper perspective. It would help us remember that our powerful 'need for a companion' and 'sense of loneliness' often make us behave in strange ways. The induced symptoms are unrelated to love or our beloved. The real cause of our restlessness and loneliness is not love (or a lack of it), either, although we crave more love the lonelier we get. The real cause of our loneliness is our increasing inability nowadays to *relate* to one another, while our obsession to find a soul mate keeps growing at the same time. This awareness might help us redirect our focus to ourselves and become more objective. Instead of self-pity, we could act smarter about our need for a companion. We might decide to adopt a new mentality: to either give less importance to having a companion, or go about finding him/her in a more honest and productive manner—unlike the approach at the present time, especially the emphasis on love and game-playing. We would also learn about the true meaning of love

(B-love), compared with the selfish manner that we have come to define love nowadays.

Our 'need for a companion' is actually so strong it has turned into *'desperation* for a companion' in recent decades. As noted before, a companion can *potentially* satisfy a large number of our personal needs, ranging from sex to compassion and B-love. Our instincts and social conditioning make us see these deceiving potentialities as real possibilities. That is, we remain hopeful all our lives to find a soul mate who would fulfil most of our personal needs. But our chances for actually finding a soul mate is quite remote, and then realizing the 'potentialities' of a companion is even smaller for all the reasons explained in this book. Nowadays, partners have difficulty even fulfilling each other's basic need for sex on a long-term basis, let alone all those more complex needs for D-love, compassion, and B-love. Therefore, while people never give up their optimism about realizing the potentialities of relationships, their real experiences keep leading to failures, frustration, desperation, and anger. People's chronic optimism is admirable but corny.

Overall, our 'desperation for a companion' would keep rising in the years to come, because we cannot find or keep a partner or trust him/her in the long run. Obviously, this critical state is the outcome of drastic social changes and our rising idealism. Instead of understanding the roots of relationship problems and our role in causing many of them, we keep dreaming about a soul mate and an ideal relationship with another partner. We do not see the futility of our search for love or a soul mate. With more relationships failing every year, the more desperate we all get, which, ironically, only heightens our craving for passion even more. In all, our obsession for love nowadays is a reflection of our increasing loneliness and desperation for a companion, but our exaggerated expectations (including love) ruin our relationships and we become even more desperate and lonely. This vicious cycle is destroying people's trust in each other and their expressions of love.

If we look inwardly to review our personal needs and relationship expectations objectively, we can find the roots of relationship issues and see how they are causing havoc in society. Then, instead of blaming love or a lover, we might focus on changing our mentalities about love and relationships. We would understand why finding or keeping a companion has become so difficult nowadays. We would then realize that love cannot be the success factor for relationships and thus redirect our focus to our own personalities, lifestyles, needs, demands, and methods of finding a companion. The way we have become—so haughty and needy—is to be blamed for the failure of relationships, not the lack of love or couple's inability to be romantic.

'Attraction' has always been an instinctual mood (process) for selecting a mate throughout the evolution. But it has been a temporary mood just to bring two naturally suitable couples together. Nowadays we get, or pretend to be, attracted to someone based on many unnatural factors, too, such as his/her wealth, status, or our own personal insecurities. So attraction nowadays has become even less stable.

'Romance' has always existed in nature in some form, too, although its role has been tentative for animals and humans. Nowadays, however, we humans like to have a lot of it. And since romance is only partially intuitive (the impression of B-love), we have to fake a lot of emotions not only to impress our beloved, but also keep them impressed enough to stay with us. This is an added pressure on relationships in the new era—a naive demand that is raising couples' expectations and tension.

With respect to 'attachment', scholars believe that it has evolved in humans as the need for support to raise offspring emerged for our ancestors several million years ago. It was mostly a temporary arrangement, too, and then partners went their own ways when children could live on their own. But nowadays we have got used to the idea of having a long-term commitment with a partner. This mentality has grown stronger as a result of humans becoming more insecure, religious, and needy for love and compassion in recent decades. Of course, we have at the same time become more arrogant and choosy and thus sabotage our chances to sustain long-term commitments with anybody. Nonetheless, our yearning for both romance and attachment appears to be largely self-imposed moods and also a reflection of humans' insecurities as well as struggle for social morality. The upcoming discussion of love-related human hormones will show that we are not built to be romantic or stay attached to one another for too long.

Love has always been studied as a combination of many feelings, urges, and moods related to humans' search for a companion. Following some rudimentary methods, scholars have defined many types of love based on the categories of those feelings and urges. It is true that love leads to, and stirs up, a mix of all those urges and feelings, but it doesn't mean that love is all (or a portion) of those feelings and urges. The way various types of love were defined two millenniums ago, based on the symptoms or the object of love, is still pursued by some scholars at the present time. If the ancient Greek had defined ten different kinds of love, now psychologist come up with six or eight types again based on its symptoms. For example, psychologist Robert Sternberg suggests that love has three ingredients, i.e.) passion, 2) intimacy, and 3) decision and commitment. Then he defines seven types of love based on a mix of these ingredients. For example, he suggests that *romantic love* is a mix of the ingredients 1 and 2. *Infatuation* is 1 alone. *Empty love* is 3 alone. The other types of love are *consummate love* (1 + 2 + 3), *compassionate love* (2 + 3), *liking* (only 2), and *fatuous love* (1 + 3). Now perhaps the next question is the proportion of each ingredient in each mix! (Also notice that love and relationships are used synonymously in his method, as evident by the definition of *empty love*.)

Dividing love into certain categories according to certain feelings would not help the chaos in relationships. It would only convolute the meaning of a simple concept like love. For example, identifying *romantic love* as if its true nature were different from other kinds of love (if it contains any real love at all) has very little practical implication. The only important question is whether this romantic love has any sense of B-love (selflessness) in it or not. If yes, how? And if not, should it be even considered love, romantic or otherwise? In the final analyses, the essence of love is always that notion of selflessness toward another being regardless of all the feelings and urges that are exerted in that particular case, e.g., love toward our children, parents, a person, or even objects such as nature, an artistic passion, etc. Love is always the unique feeling of B-love regardless of all the emotions that get attached to it. Having (or showing) compassion is noble and perhaps even more precious than love, but it is not love in its true sense; it is compassion. More importantly, the symptoms of love should not change the nature of love, if it were true love. There are hundreds of love symptoms that emerge in different situations according to people's personalities. Bringing them into a definition of love causes only ambiguity about the meaning of love.

We make a big fuss about the way a lover becomes restless, jealous, depressed, sleepless, etc. But these symptoms are common in many other situations, too, when any particular plan or desire of a person is threatened. People lose sleep or become restless about any matter that occupies their minds, e.g., a project, a catastrophe, etc., or get jealous if a job promotion is given to another person. Of course, love-related symptoms are usually more intense than other cases—only because of our 'desperation for a companion.' But those symptoms do not define love.

In the end, there is only one kind of love (B-love) that can be directed to any person or object when it is sincere and true. For practical purposes, we must then focus on approaches that can help us find and relate to our partners easier and build manageable relationships. One objective of this book is to switch our focus from 'love' to 'need for a companion,' which is a term more akin to 'relationships' than 'love.'

It is acknowledged here and in other parts of this book that getting hit by love is an extremely powerful experience and dealing with its symptoms is very difficult. We feel all those mind-blowing urges, moods, and feelings related to this so-called love. We cannot change the fact that we keep falling in love and we must deal with its symptoms. So one could argue that maybe it is easier to attribute all these symptoms to one simple concept, i.e., love, for our common communication. This might sound like a reasonable proposal to people. They would probably prefer to view love that way: surrounded by all those ambiguities. That is fine, if they really prefer it that way. But it is essential to recognize that none of those symptoms (urges, feelings, moods) have anything to do with pure love.

Pure, unselfish B-love satisfies some peaceful emotions and urges of humans, but it doesn't lead to self-destruction or war with our beloved. This would be the simple definition of love that would be adopted in this book. Hatred, retaliation, and rage, when love fails, clearly show that our perception of 'love' hadn't been pure (B-love). Obviously, many of our selfish and destructive urges and feelings get attached to our *impression and expression* of love. And it helps to know the real motives behind these urges and feelings.

In all, people's sense of love nowadays consists of their mixed urges for sex, compassion, and B-love. Then they express some feelings and moods while pursuing their goal to find a companion. Research has shown that people's sense of love might last maybe up to two years, but it is usually shorter. Also, research indicates that humans' mating moods, e.g., sexual attraction, romance, and attachment are not necessarily directed toward the same individual constantly. We are chemically (instinctually) built to connect to different people for satisfying different urges. Various hormones that drive our moods for love affect one another to a large degree as shown in the next section, but often they work independently to allow humans to be in several relationships at a time. We are already witnessing the outcome of humans' true nature (especially sexuality) as it is manifesting freely in our modern societies. This is not a very comforting situation for building long-term relationships. But this is the reality of life, at least for the time being.

The Effect of Human Hormones on Love and Relationships

The hormones that rule human urges do not seem to support people's excessive expectations from love and relationships. The recap presented below is the author's overall understanding of various research findings in the field of human hormones. These findings can hopefully help us more in the future for building relationships. Meanwhile, they reveal some interesting points about the effect of human hormones on love and relationships. These findings are not absolute, but seem to match our daily experiences, too:

1. Testosterone is the hormone that increases the urge for sex.
2. Vasopressin and oxytocin are hormones believed to cause the urge for attachment.
3. Testosterone, vasopressin and oxytocin are found in both genders.
4. During orgasm, vasopressin increases in men and oxytocin increases in women. Therefore, **sexual activity seems to increase partners' urge for attachment.** Especially, after-sex cuddling seems to be the result of these hormones' activities.
5. Vasopressin and oxytocin also trigger testosterone. This implies that these **attachment hormones could enhance sexual urges.**

6. However, if the dosage of vasopressin (and possibly oxytocin) is increased, the level of testosterone is reduced. This implies that **prolonged attachment might reduce partners' desire for sex.**
7. Testosterone can trigger vasopressin and oxytocin in animals and most likely in humans too.
8. However, increasing testosterone dosage would reduce vasopressin and oxytocin and thus dampen the urge for attachment. This implies that **too much sex might diminish partners' desire for attachment.**
9. Dopamine is the chemistry for romance. It is the hormone that triggers passion, attraction, and ecstasy.
10. Dopamine and norepinephrine might stimulate oxytocin and stir attachment under certain conditions. This implies that **romance sometimes leads to attachment.**
11. On the other hand, no definite relationship has been established between neurotransmitters of romance and the hormones of attachment (vasopressin and oxytocin). Thus **romance and attachment are not proven to be related**.
12. Oxytocin interferes with dopamine and reduces its effect. That is, the **attachment hormones can suppress the romance hormones**.
13. Furthermore, increasing dopamine reduces the level of testosterone. This implies that **romance diminishes the urge for sex.**
14. Some DNA of a gene causes monogamy in some animals and also in the laboratory tests on mice. Some people have a trace of this DNA, but not all humans. Therefore, **no chemistry or evidence has been found in**

humans to suggest they are built to be monogamous.
15. Various studies have shown that **love usually dies between six months to about two years.** Of course, some people have continued their love under certain conditions based on their unique personalities and definition of love.
16. Research indicates that **humans' mating moods, e.g., sexual attraction, romance, and attachment are not necessarily directed toward the same individual constantly.**

To summarize the above findings, we can safely blame human hormones for the following facts:
- Sexual activity triggers the mood for cuddling and attachment, but the increased sex might erode the sense of attachment in the long run.
- Although attachment might increase sexual urge initially, prolonged attachment might eventually dampen the urge for sex.
- Romance and attachment are not proven to be related.
- Attachment might erode romance.
- Romance might kill sex.
- Humans are not built to be monogamous, unlike some animals that have the right chemistry for it.
- Love most likely dies within six months to about two years.
- Humans are chemically (instinctually) built to connect to different people for satisfying different urges (romance, sex, attachment).

The effect of human hormones and mood changes, especially for women during childbirth, menstrual cycle, and menopause, contribute largely to gender differences, which are discussed in Chapter Fifteen.

Love as a Reflection of Personality Aspects

People's three personality aspects perceive, and react to, 'love' differently. The spiritual love (B-love) that we often perceive and long for arises from Self-P. We have this instinctual desire to love an idol that we imagine in our minds. This is usually the basic force that instigates our search for a soul mate. We remain optimistic all our lives to find such a person despite our negative experiences in relationships. Our initial attraction to someone triggers our Self-P and we feel romantic and hopeful about his/her attributes. As a naïve, optimistic creature, we simply see perfection and find many reasons for adoring him/her unconditionally. Then our actual experiences and interactions with our partners begin to disprove our initial perceptions and hopes. So we begin to impose our desires and fantasies upon our partners and demand that they behave in the way we had mentally pictured them. When they don't—because they can't—we get mad at them and ourselves and show our frustration even more. We continue pushing them to become the idol we want them to be, or we decide to abandon (maybe even hurt or kill) them for their imperfection and disobedience. In either case, it is our Ego-P that makes these love related decisions. It acts with utter arrogance, despite Self-P's struggle to maintain the initial love image and to continue satisfying its thirst for B-love. Ego-P is the personality aspect that is now *demanding* love. We just want to feel loved because of our Ego-P. When neither Self-P nor Ego-P can succeed, eventually Model-P emerges to put a stop to the inner fight between Ego-P and Self-P. It tries to impose equilibrium. But eventually we get tired of our efforts to change our partners or stabilize the relationship. Some of us might finally give up our dream of finding (or creating) a soul mate, or even maintaining a friendly relationship with that particular partner. We submit to our doomed destiny. We might continue to live with a person we no longer love. We have no stamina or motivation to fight anymore. Model-P, as the adapting agent, takes over to a large degree. Some sentiments of Self-P and anger of Ego-P continue to distort the equilibrium that Model-P is trying so hard to maintain. Eventually, we often learn to adapt and live through our Model-P. It can help us cope with bad situations and learn tolerance.

In general, our Self-P needs, especially B-love, are seldom satisfied in relationships, although our Ego-P and Model-P often make us believe otherwise. For example, some people believe that they are happy and loved in their relationships, because their Ego-P and Model-P give them that impression. Another group is aware of humans' true nature and thus keeps their expectations from their partners in check. Some people are too self-absorbed to care about their Self-P needs or their partners' love for them. Many people try to satisfy their Self-P needs in other passions outside of their relationships, e.g., in art or nature. In all, most people don't find B-love in their relationships, so they either begin to validate their relationships in more practical ways without B-love or keep looking for love elsewhere.

With Model-P, we hide our true emotions and anger about our partners. Sometimes Model-P helps us show love, too, which, despite its artificiality, feels pleasant to our partners at times. Sometimes it even feels satisfying to us. We begin to perceive and enforce an illusion of love in our minds in hopes of mitigating our need for B-love. This delusion helps us carry on with our lives, while deep down we might feel awful for being illusive. Nonetheless, our culture advocates the use of illusive love to sustain our sanity and our relationships. We try to pretend love through Model-P to remain tactful and to validate our relationships. This is a practical approach simply because finding B-love is a rather unrealistic goal for most people.

Overall, it appears that relationships might thrive better if we stop considering B-love an important factor. That is, maybe we could allow a more practical definition of love be driven by Model-P instead of Self-P. We don't need to see love a selfless and exaggerated devotion, but rather a means of respect and harmony. This would be a practical definition of love for the new era, which is driven by Model-P. It might actually work. This point will be further discussed below under the heading of *The Power of M-love*.

Based on these discussions, we can define three types of love, each satisfying one aspect of our personality. B-love satisfies Self-P, D-love satisfies Ego-P. And then there is this most practical kind of love that we portray regularly through Model-P. Let's call this kind of love M-love.

Since this new model (three kinds of love) fits so nicely with the personality aspects, we will change the notations to make them consistent: That is, we change B-love to S-love, and we change D-love to E-love. So now we have the following types of love:

- **S-love** is Self-P driven and reflects the most **spiritual** and selfless way of loving someone. This is what Maslow refers to as B-love.
- **E-love** is Ego-P driven and reflects our **deficiency** need for love and attention. This is what Maslow refers to as D-love.
- **M-love** is Model-P driven and reflects our most **practical** way of communicating our passion to another person.

These new notations for love are used in the remainder of this book.

The Outlook for Love

Love has always been a mysterious and thought-provoking topic for humans. During the last five or six decades, however, its ambiguous meaning and exaggerated role in relationships have caused a lot of complications for people and society.

In the past, love played a small role in relationships, while poets and philosophers kept people amused with their speculations about it. It had little impact on people's daily lives and their relationships, simply because people didn't read many books and were not exposed to such relentless amount of misleading propaganda about love. They had real life hardships to worry about. They were not so obsessed about expressing themselves as much as people in the new era are either. Due to all the new exposures and brainwashing, people have made love the locus of relationships. Love has become confused with attraction and mixed up with many other urges and feelings of humans. The objectives of love and relationships are also muddled up in people's minds. Love and relationships are mostly perceived, even by some scholars, to be synonymous. But love (S-love) is maybe only 5% of all the urges and activities that go into a relationship. The other urges (sex and compassion) and moods (attraction, romance, and attachment) provide another 45% of the ingredients useful for running a relationship. But the main ingredient of relationships (around 50%) simply relates to its own specific needs and structure, which has been neglected to a large extent in recent decades. We have lost sight of the relationship needs while emphasizing on love (mostly E-love) as the main criterion for starting a relationship and for measuring its health. This and other problems related to our common misuse of the word 'love' are discussed throughout this book. Overall, the destiny of love doesn't look very bright because:

1. The meaning of love is getting more vague and useless, especially for building relationships. But, at the same time, we usually like to make a big deal about the phrase "I love you." In effect, the use of the word 'love' has become too hypocritical considering that people have a variety of purposes for, and understanding of, love. Their low capacity for love ruins all their love affairs sooner or later anyway.
2. The general increase in social complexity, sexuality, and corruption makes people less and less trustful of one another and their expressions of love. But, at the same time, people insist that relationships and love must be built on absolute trust and honesty.

Under this circumstance, couples continue to get hurt because of their wrong impressions of love, and because they annoy each other with their exaggerated expectations for love and attention. People destroy not only their chance for building manageable relationships, but also the opportunity of understanding the meaning of S-love. Our limited options to face the reality of love and relationships are:

- To become selfless and internalize S-love, which is a hard task for most of us.
- To pursue love affairs here and there if we are lucky, while the state of our relationships grows more chaotic and instable.
- To live alone while waiting for love (and not knowing how to build relationships).
- To use M-love to instil mutual respect and civility in relationships by overcoming our present craving for E-love and S-love.

The Meaning of Love

How does the commonplace expression of love fit the model suggested above in terms of S-love, E-love, and M-love? Basically, it can be theorized that the commonplace love consists of i) attraction, and ii) a mix of S-love, M-love, and E-love. This theory confirms the following facts:

- A person's 'need for a companion' is driven by all the three aspects of his/ her personality, and each personality aspect plays a special role when he/she expresses love to another person.
- Seeking love reflects both our instinctual and conditional urges.

- Each person is driven by various levels of S-love, M-love, and E-love when expressing passion. Thus, the meaning of love is different for each person depending on the level of each personality aspect he/she has applied to perceive love. The intensity of love also varies based on his/her insecurities, needs, and the prominence of each personality aspect. Moreover, his/her level and meaning of love change rapidly, too, in different circumstances, even toward the same individual.
- Inventing an imaginary meaning for love (anything other than for defining S-love, E-love, and M-love) and spreading it for common use is pointless—except for writing fiction and making movies.

Overall, when we fall in love, all aspects of our personality exert a type of love that we wish to fulfil. If someone is totally selfless and willing to give love without condition, his/her S-love is most prominent. But for most people, their urges for romanticism and spirituality are only partially triggered by some perception of S-love and physical attraction. Behind their idealism for S-love lies their need to fulfil their love deficiencies, i.e.-love. They also play the role of a good lover by applying the charm of Model-P to impress their partners through tender expressions of M-love. Usually, their initial impression of S-love fades away after they get into relationships. The reason is very simple: People who are not driven mostly by Self-P aspect of their personality cannot maintain S-love. S-love and Self-P go hand in hand.

S-love also diminishes when new perceptions about our partners soon override the initial ones. So, the majority of us end up perceiving love and handling it in a personal, and unique (non S-love) manner. If we are patient and properly trained, we might be able to bolster our relationships by using only M-love. In most cases, however, we end up nurturing E-love in our relationships and put unreasonable demands on our partners. Meanwhile, we expect our partner to love us with his/her power of S-love. We want him/her to keep proving his/her selfless love. What an ego!

The inherent nature of love, particularly the effect of human hormones, shows that love doesn't survive too long in relationships in the form we had initially perceived it. What we call love nowadays is often only a combination of lust, possessiveness, and insecurities we have compiled through social interactions and imitations. Accordingly, love cannot be a main success factor for relationships either—not even S-love. Only couples' ability to relate and their capacity for compassion, comradeship, integrity, teamwork, as well as their knowledge of the relationships' specific needs can stir sincere passion and prolong their relationships. Successful couples eventually learn to create that sense of attachment and compassion without depending on S-love or E-love. With people's increasing need to be self-reliant, couples would gradually adjust their mentality about the limited role of love in relationships. Then they can seek both love and relationships realistically without assuming that they are necessarily the same or the cause and effect of each other.

Couples may even wish to substitute the word 'love' with some other word that conveys their commitment and understanding of relationship responsibilities better. We could actually create a word to express love in relationships, such as M-love, e.g., by saying: "I mlove you." It means, 'I like to cherish you realistically based on mutual respect and teamwork, and I will try to respond to your needs for compassion the best I can.' It doesn't sound too awkward to pronounce 'mlove' either. If a person were certain and courageous enough to say I slove (S-love) you, it means that he/she is willing to devote him/herself to his/her partner and he/she doesn't even look for love in return necessarily. He/she doesn't even mind being a slave for his/her slove.

Now we can be clear about the meaning of 'I love you.' Although most loves are E-love in relationships, nobody would admit it. Also, only a few people may have the courage and conviction to admit that they S-love their partners. It would be such a big commitment. They cannot take it back lightly if they say to their partners that they slove them like a slave. So the most likely type of love people would express to one another would be M-love. Very clear. They stay practical by expressing a kind of love that is conditional on partners' attitude and sharing M-love. But the good thing about M-love is that both partners realize that their love expressions aren't exaggerated emotions, but rather a conditional and calculated message of affection. Couples could actually express their attraction to each other most often by using the phrase, 'I'm attracted to you' instead of using the word 'love.' And when they wish to use the word 'love', they might like to be specific that it is only M-love. Hopefully, we might eventually minimize the need for E-love in modern societies. If we can at least eliminate the ambiguity of love from relationships, we would be taking a giant step in the right direction.

Of course, there is no harm in using the word 'love' as an expression of intimacy as long as we remember its true meaning. Indeed, with the frequency we express love to one another all the time, it is losing its traditional inclination gradually anyway. We are learning that it should not be taken seriously. Anyway, it will help couples to distinguish the three types of love as noted above and understand that we usually express E-love, or at best M-love, to each other to fulfil our need for compassion.

Somehow many people imagine that their partners have really meant S-love when they expressed love and maybe even cried for each other. This misperception causes confusion and places unreasonable expectations on relationships. Almost always, a person's emotional expressions, including crying, are only the symptoms of his/her 'desperation for a companion' and a reaction to the existing environment of relationships. He/she is tired of looking for the right match and someone to soothe his/her agonies. Don't take it as S-love.

The Power of M-love

Using M-love in relationships actually has many advantages. First of all, it provides a venue for partners to be romantic without raising relationship expectations or creating misunderstandings about their love expressions. The fact that they can remain open and honest about the intention of their love expressions eliminates the need for phoniness and increases the chances of bringing more foreplay into relationships without the fear of creating unsustainable commitments. Within a few decades, the flow of communication would improve, as couples eventually learn to apply M-love properly in their relationships. Using a new term, such as M-love, can overcome the cynicism about the phrase 'I love you,' which is losing its value fast.

The next advantage of M-love is that expressing one's feelings through M-love would partially respond to partners' need for S-love. Their deep need for S-love is tentatively satisfied through M-love, which would help them psychologically and physiologically. Although M-love might appear like a kind of role-playing, partners are doing it wholeheartedly in order to simulate S-love. Thus, it is not a forced role-playing, but rather a pleasant expression of the self.

Another advantage of M-love is that it might also fulfil some of partners' E-love needs. This happens because people's *subconscious* easily substitutes M-love for E-love, while their *conscious* minds remember the purpose of M-love. Therefore, M-love can indirectly satisfy partners' needs for both S-love and E-love, at least partially, while preventing those love expressions from being misinterpreted. In all, partners wouldn't build up too many unwarranted expectations in their relationships simply because they have been expressing nice words (with M-love) to each other. Contrary to cases where one partner keeps giving E-love to the other in order to feed the latter's ego and spoil him/her further, M-love only fills the gap for E-love without increasing partners' expectations from each other.

One important point about M-love is that it is a voluntary and possibly periodical gesture by one or both partners. It could be withdrawn and re-introduced, off and on, in a relationship by one or both partners only at their discretions. Therefore, it shouldn't be turned into an expectation by one or both partners, otherwise it would be E-love and not M-love anymore.

Reasons for People's Impressions and Expressions of Love

As noted before, people seek love (mostly E-love) to satisfy a large variety of their personal needs. They have some impressions about the meaning of love, and they have a variety of motives that they try to satisfy by their expressions of love. These motives are listed below without repeating the explanations that can be found on page 39:

- To *communicate* with their partners.
- To express their basic *feelings*.
- To release *psychological* pressures.
- To mimic their *spiritual* needs.
- To *control* their partners.
- To *manipulate (abuse)* their partners.

The above noted motives drive us to use the word 'love' rather sloppily. In the absence of a better word to express our exact motives (or just for hiding them), using the word 'love' for so many purposes has become customary. But it is important to keep our expectations from exchanging 'love' phrases in proper perspective. Obviously, the word 'love' covers a large variety of meanings and none of them really reflects true love (S-love). Also, note that love is perceived and applied differently by each individual according to his/her psychological and circumstantial needs. It has no definite meaning to draw upon or set expectations for. We can apply it arbitrarily only to soothe our need for compassion without making an issue out of it or expecting long-term commitment on that basis. "You said you loved me!" is a common complaint when couples interpret love according to their arbitrary and ambiguous perceptions.

Chapter Seven
The Nature of Relationships

As social values and personal needs of couples change during the course of history, the meaning, purpose, and format of their relationships should be reassessed and redefined as well. The reason is that the personal needs of individuals dictate the kind of relationships they are willing to accept for their lifestyle. Obviously, the changes in lifestyle and personal needs in the last few decades have been enormous. Yet we have not developed a reasonably compatible framework for our relationships, hence the hectic situation we are facing. Part II of this book will suggest a relationship framework more suitable for the new era. But let's review the nature of relationships briefly in this chapter and assess the need for a new relationship format. Basically, we have three options:

A. **Continue with the status quo**, hoping that nature will take its course and eventually a format will emerge for relationships. Meanwhile, there will be more separations, conflicts, and paranoia about relationships. And there is no way to predict the outcome. The chance that a logical and efficient framework evolves out of this chaos is terribly slim.

B. **Hope that one gender will eventually dominate the other** so that order may return to relationships. It is a fact that humans have difficulty relating to one another, and to work as a team in the long run, especially the opposite sexes. This is truer nowadays with individualism, arrogance, and greed satiating our mentality and social values. But the option of one gender taking the superior role in relationships would not work in the long run either. Chaos and equality struggles would continue to overwhelm relationships.

C. **Create and propagate a relationship framework** to guide couples run their relationships smoothly and relate efficiently. With the increasing complexity of society, the longevity of relationships might be doomed anyway. But a flexible and modern relationship framework could at least anticipate, and prepare couples for, the high likelihood that relationships in the new era would fail.

Hopefully the third option would appeal to most of us. It would minimize the amount of frictions between partners. Also, couples would be better prepared to deal with the reality of separation and living independently. Anyway, this book advocates the third option, as the author believes it would provide the only solution for relationships.

This entire book explores the nature of relationships in the new era, but this chapter specifically focuses on this topic, starting with a recap of the emerging trends as shown in Table 7.1 on the next two page.

Table 7.1
The Basic Nature of Relationships (Emerging Trends)

1. Nowadays, most people do not look for a partner to merely satisfy their basic companionship need. Rather, they want their relationships make them happy and also satisfy a host of their personal needs and/or solve their personal problems. Accordingly, they blame their relationships for their personal failure to figure out life or find happiness.
2. Greed and ego don't disappear even when couples happen to be in love. In fact, greed and ego reinforce all their other pressing needs in relationships, including their needs for identity, control, recognition, love, and retaliation. The point is that love would not eliminate greed and ego and all the subsequent problems they create in relationships.
3. People are forced to play games and roles all their lives. They are dragged into situations beyond their control to play along with others and assert themselves. This condition infects relationships, too, as partners constantly play games and roles—out of necessity unfortunately. Hardly anybody is natural these days.
4. Couples play games and roles to: 1) impress (charm), 2) flatter, 3) intimidate, or 4) snub someone. So the amount of time they are natural and sincere is too little.
5. Personal idiosyncrasies and insecurities keep rising as social values keep deteriorating, and vice versa. This is another vicious cycle that would continue to spin out of control and make the success of relationships less likely every year.
6. The probability of finding our soul mate is extremely slim. But we all have difficulty accepting this fact, as we want to stay positive. Our romantic search for a soul mate is preventing us from perceiving relationships realistically.

7. For keeping an acceptable companion (let alone a soul mate) partners must have many common interests and compatibility, be good humans, and know how to work on their relationships continuously. But human nature does not support these requirements.
8. Most often, partners actually destroy each other's lives instead of enriching it. This is because life is getting more complex and stressful every year and people have more difficulty coping with social pressures while they live longer too. The main outcome of this condition is that people are too disturbed and impatient to deal with their excessive relationship demands effectively.
9. Considering the above facts and hundreds of other reasons explained in this book, marriage must be viewed as a temporary arrangement, unless both partners gain all the high qualities required for building an effective relationship.
10. To attain relative tranquility, we must know the art of living independently instead of looking for a soul mate to bring us happiness. For all practical purposes, we must learn to live alone instead of looking for relief in relationships.
11. We would always face a major trade off in relationships: They always bring us major headaches, whereas for tranquility, we must deal with loneliness and be self-reliant. The dilemma is to make a right decision according to one's personality.
12. A question is whether we can develop relationship models that fit couples' personalities and provide an atmosphere for a relatively tranquil and effective companionship. This book suggests that only a relationship framework and its corresponding principles can bring objectivity back into relationships.

A Definition of Relationships

We can say that, a relationship is mainly a collection of activities and feelings shared by partners. But a relationship must also be viewed as a system or atmosphere for facilitating partners' cooperation to achieve certain goals. These goals are of two kinds: First, the goals that fulfil the realistic personal and common needs of partners. Second, the goals that help maintain the health of the relationship itself.

Thus a comprehensive definition is: *a relationship is a system or atmosphere with specific needs and goals to sustain itself, which only then might fulfil partners' realistic goals too.* This definition places the emphasis on relationship needs and goals before it can be of any use to couples. Obviously, a relationship dies, like any entity, if its needs are ignored. Accordingly, we can make the following observations:

1. Relationships get into trouble when partners are not conscious of its needs and goals or when they find them in major conflict with their personal goals.
2. Couples should learn to view relationships as an independent entity with specific needs and goals of its own, which are different from partners' personal objectives and needs.
3. Boundaries should be set between partners' personal needs (or goals) and the relationship needs in order to minimize conflicts.
4. A theoretical framework may be developed to define the needs, objectives, and boundaries of relationships.
5. This relationship framework must also define the characteristics of a successful relationship.

6. As a major role of a relationship framework, it must enforce teamwork and increase the effectiveness of partners' communication.
7. As personal needs change in society, the relationship framework must be adjusted accordingly in order to reduce frictions.
8. Partners' need for independence and individuality should be given the highest priority in developing this relationship framework.
9. The main tool to achieve a balance between personal needs and relationship needs is to reduce couples' expectations from relationships.
10. Like any kind of machinery or system, relationships require routine checks and balances, too, to sustain its functionality.
11. The main challenge for partners is to find the right relationship model for their combined personalities and to function within its parameters. They must stop guessing what a relationship is or what they like it to be.
12. The onus is placed on partners to stay objective and fair by respecting the relationship boundaries in order to prolong their relationship.

The Transition

We consider older cultures outmoded mainly in terms of men's treatment of women. Obviously, abuse is intolerable. But our modern approaches have been unproductive as well. The stress caused by new lifestyles is crippling a good majority of relationships and also threatening the foundation of our societies. The situation is only going to get worse if new solutions and a framework for relationships are not found soon.

Developing a relationship framework would be a difficult task. Even defining its parameters would be gruelling since such a framework must be quite flexible to accommodate a large variety of couples' personalities. Furthermore, it must be justifiable as a new approach to relationships. It must make sense to people around the world, especially to those living in modern societies. It sounds like an impossible job, and the author is the first person to admit that. But without a framework, the state of relationships would deteriorate beyond control very soon. It will reach a highly explosive and unmanageable level. Sooner or later, we will be forced to acknowledge that some kind of a framework is needed, so that we can assess and manage our relationships more objectively. So, if we begin working on it now, we may have a reasonably useful framework in place within the next century or so. But we must first believe in the need for such a framework and then continue to work on its development seriously and systematically. Part II of this book is devoted to this task.

The first step is to imagine and agree that: A relationship is an *independent* setting, and not a collection of partners' untamed expectations (from relationships). Then a framework can be developed to define the properties and boundaries of this independent entity—relationships. The idea is that working from within this framework gives partners a better chance to relate. This implies that partners can learn to follow some specific guidelines to *relate* to each other, instead of hoping for it to happen automatically or by a lifelong trial and error. An ideal is to bring all the effective ideas that experts are using nowadays for helping relationships be brought together into one comprehensive, easy to understand document. As long as we cannot do this, it simply implies that none of the ideas that experts and marriage counsellors use presently are effective and universally acceptable. The new framework must help couples set their objectives and expectations from relationships more realistically. The framework would also provide couples with the opportunity of settling their conflicts objectively. Another purpose of the relationship framework is to identify a handful relationship models that can fit a large variety of individuals' personalities, while each model provides the fundamental advantages of being in a relationship. The ultimate goal is to minimize arguments about every task or issue and to reduce couples' urge for aggressive behaviour when they feel some kind of unfairness. Everybody is paranoid about fairness these days. So, the framework should replace the need for couples' constant struggle for equality. By insisting on *equality* in all aspects of relationships, couples are wasting energy on measuring every activity or incident subjectively instead of focusing on teamwork objectively. The flexibility of a universal framework could replace the rigidity of equality approach.

Relationships are supposed to create synergy when couples combine their resources, especially their brains, effectively. Often, however, the opposite happens when retaliations bring their lives to a halt. Instead of empowering each other, couples often compete and retaliate. A reason for conflicts in relationships is that couples keep arguing about the roles they would like to play, either independently or jointly. Each partner likes to set the rules for their relationship. This decision is often based on his/her rotating and abrupt preference to push his/her *need for independence*, (e.g., making investment or some family decisions alone,) or *need for dependence*, (e.g., seeking support and attention.) One objective of a relationship framework is to eliminate conflicts caused by these extreme need changes of partners or equality arguments. The reasonable guidelines of a framework could replace couples' arbitrary decision processes in relationships. Obviously, synergy is achieved better, usually, when partners work together to fulfil certain tasks or share decision-making needs of a relationship. But synergy can be achieved also if couples support each other to perform their roles separately with real independence.

Usually relationships thrive when couples adopt complementary roles while giving each other room to act independently. They don't need to fight for inequality, unfairness, lack of independence, etc. A relationship framework would facilitate both teamwork and partners' independence. While men and women have the same rights and acknowledge each other's contributions, they need not share the same tasks and roles to ensure equality. This is an obvious concept, but in reality a lot of energy is wasted by couples nowadays, consciously or subconsciously, on measuring the difficulty of various responsibilities and quarrelling about them.

Objectives of a Relationship Framework

The main objectives of a relationship framework are:
 A. To enforce teamwork,
 B. To bring objectivity back into relationships,
 C. To increase the effectiveness of communications,

D. To reduce partners' expectations from relationships as much as necessary in order to create the right balance between their personal needs and the relationship needs, and
E. To overhaul individuals' mentality and social mechanisms regarding relationships.

Discussing the merits and objectives of a relationship framework without knowing what a 'relationship framework' looks like might annoy some readers. So, a couple of points must be made before we proceed. First, although a preliminary format for a relationship framework will be suggested in Part II, developing its final form is not a task for this book. It will take many years before such a framework can be fully developed. Second, a relationship framework has many components, as discussed in the upcoming chapters. It is better to define these components first and then let the model evolve by itself through these discussions. At least, this is the approach taken in this book. Nonetheless, convincing the readers about the *need* for a relationship framework—*why* and *how* it can help couples—is the most important task. Modifying people's mentality about relationships is the most significant step. So, this chapter will provide more details about the objectives of a relationship framework and then Part II will explain its format, components, and characteristics.

Objective A: To enforce teamwork

Teamwork is not a revolutionary idea or a concept forgotten by couples. But knowing about teamwork and actually being committed to it, as the only solution for relationships, are two different things. Commitment to teamwork is, in particular, difficult while couples strive so obsessively for individualism and independence. Indeed, partners often perceive teamwork and individualism as two contradictory concepts. They often find 'compromising' an infringement on their individualism. Their partners' suggestions come across as a deliberate opposition or an intrusion of their independence. This is how our Ego-P regularly operates. So, a relationship framework must somehow overcome all these obstacles and prove the merits of real teamwork. The challenge is to invent the means of enforcing teamwork principles without threatening partners' individuality. The radical solutions explained in Chapter Eleven would accomplish this objective to a great extent, where partners would find it to their advantage to participate in teamwork naturally. A major hurdle nowadays is that couples often don't know the meaning of compromise, or the method or timing to make one. Sometimes partners compromise just to show their sense of cooperation. They usually do this at the wrong time and for the wrong reasons. For example, a person is seeking his/her partner's objective and honest opinion to make the best decision together, but his/her partner simply agrees with him/her carelessly or maybe even callously. This partner is unaware of, or ignores, the process of reaching a compromise. He/she only pretends to do it just to show his/her cooperation, or simply because he/she has no guts to take a risk by expressing his/her opinion, e.g., about certain investment. And then this same partner makes a big fuss if the outcome of that decision (or compromise) turns out unsatisfactory. He/she tries to dissociate him/herself from the wrong decision. He/she declares his/her initial input only a simple gesture of support, and not a real consent. In all, partners often lose the opportunity of benefiting from each other's wisdom because they are incapable of discussing the merits and demerits of their plans through teamwork. Other times, couples compromise simply because their partners are showing a lot of sensitivity (or resistance) toward a specific suggestion just out of spite or narrow-mindedness. So, one partner gives in because reasoning stops working.

The ever-increasing need for individuality is a given fact in relationships. Accordingly, teamwork is facing the highest level of resistance by partners, due to their obsession for independence. They don't realize that teamwork is actually the only tool that can guarantee their independence, not arguments and retaliations. Enforcing such mentality in relationships would not be easy. And that is exactly why 'teamwork' is considered a main parameter of a relationship framework. It will take many decades for couples to change their mindsets and accept teamwork as a major requirement for maintaining both their independence and relationships. Yet it must happen sooner or later to minimize havoc in relationships.

Obviously, there is no need to emphasize on the merits of teamwork in any environment. Rather, the idea is to stress that, for the mere reason that individuality is becoming the most important requirement of relationships, creating new methods of teamwork is imperative more than ever. New methods of teamwork might depend on a variety of tools, including a simple agreement about sharing family responsibilities and finances and sticking to the plan.

Another role of teamwork would be to keep the balance between the personal needs of partners and the needs of their relationship, according to the relationship model they have chosen. It will be explained, in the future chapters, why couples' expectations from relationships must be reduced in order to exert a balance between their personal needs and relationship needs. To maintain this balance, and stay within the boundaries of their chosen relationship model, more teamwork is required.

Still another role of teamwork would be to abolish the need for equality struggles. Nowadays, we have oversimplified, perhaps even abused, the interworking of relationships by pushing the concept of equality and assuming that all the problems would be solved automatically. We attempted to solve women's personal problems and reduce the amount of intimidation and control by men. But we have not solved the problems of relationships. In fact, it appears that relationship conflicts have increased dramatically in society the more this concept of equality has been emphasized and enforced. Even worse, women's frustration has increased due to their unfulfilled expectations. The more they have expected from their relationships, the less they have actually ended up receiving (again judging by divorce rates and increasing family conflicts).

Often, women's expectations for equality appear vague, sounding more like whining, with devastating effect on their relationships. Some women's exaggerated strive for equality sometimes looks more like a quest for superiority. Initially, the equality movement sounded logical for overcoming men's superiority. But now everything appears to be turning around. That is, men feel unequal in a world where women set most standards of equality, which appear one-sided or arbitrary. They often feel intimidated by their partners' ambiguous expectations. Many of them have adopted a passive role in their relationships due to the severity of their spouses' view of equality. The problem is that, nowadays, 'equality bargaining' is infected by partners' Ego-P.

Equality expectations are often driven by partners' urge to control one another. The concept of equality is psychologically absurd anyway. This is because everyone inherently believes that his/her logic is superior to other people's, including his/her criteria for defining equality. We strongly believe that we know about everything better than anybody else regardless of their genders. A strong tendency exists in most humans to feel superior to others, not equal, although they might pretend to be fair and humble. In modern societies, almost everybody believes in gender equality, but not intellectual equality. By default, our Ego-P forces us to feel almost perfect in terms of logic, intelligence, cognition and all the rest of the good stuff. The gender equality issue is resolved for the most part, but the inherent sense of superiority can never be erased from people's minds—due to their innate perception of their intellectual superiority. This is the source of all the inequalities nowadays. They are not gender driven but rather Ego-P driven for both genders. Gender equality is a hot issue nowadays due to the relationships' rising importance and troubles in society, and because everybody (men and women) feels special and superior and not equal.

Once partners learn to focus on teamwork, their obsession for *equality* subsides. Instead of depending on equality, or superiority, the success of relationships would be measured only by the smooth operation and outcome of teamwork—not the level of one partner's influence over the other. Equality is, by the way, perceived and measured differently by people according to their subjective criteria and emotional maturity. Teamwork enables couples to contribute to major decisions and feel active in their relationships. But it doesn't deprive partners from doing most tasks independently based on their expertise or merely for creating synergy. Partners should be able to decide independently, instead of doubting their authority or identity all the time. They shouldn't lose their confidence and the control of their lives in fear of retaliation.

Indeed, the strength of teamwork lies on its emphasis on partners' independence and objectivity. Their independent (yet objective) opinions are needed for important decisions of the family. This is more in line with the trend in society to promote individualism. But it also gives partners a chance to use their unique expertise for the benefit of their relationship without being constantly second-guessed by their partners. In teamwork, partners' roles are clear. This is contrary to the existing approach where partners are confused or depressed about their roles because they are mostly preoccupied by equality games. It is indeed too difficult to understand the equality rules, since we haven't yet established the objectives and means of *family equality*. Equality, and measuring it, remains at best ambiguous and arbitrary. It lives only in people's imaginations and it manifests in the form of immature games of resistance and confrontation with no definite purpose or guideline.

The concept of 'equality' has initially emerged out of a sense of desperation, but is now being driven mostly by

Ego-P—the urge for superiority. Teamwork, on the other hand, is Self-P and Model-P driven. So it isn't too difficult to decide which approach could have a better chance of success in the long run. Couples' confrontations to exert equality would only reinforce the Ego-P of both partners, which would only lead to more clashes. Besides, as said before, the concept of equality is psychologically flawed anyway, because our prominent Ego-P absolutely abhors equality. People are psychologically incapable of handling equality because they feel superior in their deepest level of consciousness.

The best test of equality in terms of partners' decision making or sharing household affairs is to see how well those activities and processes fit within the guidelines of teamwork. If they don't fit, then they are biased, Ego-P driven, and futile. Conversely, understanding the guidelines of teamwork and implementing them in relationships would enhance partners' Self-P and Model-P at the expense Ego-P—thus more effective relationships. In all, teamwork guidelines would inherently ensure couples' fairer treatment of each other, which is the objective of equality struggles theoretically. By adhering to some basic guidelines for relationships (and teamwork), partners' rights would be best served in an environment built for coexistence. So the question is, if any standards can be invented what would they look like? We will tackle this question in the future chapters of this book.

Considering the power of teamwork, it is amazing how our Ego-P prevents Self-P and Model-P to play a more prominent role in relationships and make teamwork a more successful mechanism. So, an important objective of the relationship framework is to *enforce* teamwork. The format of the relationship framework is such that teamwork cannot be bypassed.

Objective B: To bring objectivity back into relationships

Objectivity has been eroded in relationships nowadays due to couples' rising Ego-P and expectations. Relationships are erroneously perceived as a mechanism to fulfil a large variety of partners' personal needs.

In the author's opinion, objectivity was more defined and achievable a few decades ago because the goals of relationships were limited, manageable, and better understood. Those objectives fell more in line with the traditional and instinctual needs of humans to cooperate for building a family. But now, with all the demands for love, compassion, independence, and extravagant lifestyles, relationships are burdened by a large collection of artificial expectations. In line with our personal obsession for more things and more affection, we have reduced the capacity of our relationships to be objective. Furthermore, partners have different ideas about the type and level of personal needs that their relationship should satisfy. In all, couples' subjective perceptions of relationships and their unrealistic demands have made the task of managing relationships quite difficult for couples. Therefore, to reduce family clashes, we must somehow bring objectivity back into relationships. This can be achieved by creating a manageable relationship framework and by viewing relationships as an independent entity separate from couples' personalities. Couples' personalities must not overwhelm their relationships constantly.

Objective C: To increase the effectiveness of communications

Partners' communications have become too emotional, subjective, Ego-P driven, and destructive. This is obviously causing a lot of relationship conflicts. The situation will continue to worsen unless couples are given better tools for communicating and relating more effectively. The objective is to minimize the effect of partners' Ego-P during family discussions. This is a rather unrealistic expectation. But a relationship framework might achieve this important task to some extent. It would give partners an opportunity to make their communications less egotistical and more goal-oriented. It would also reduce arguments altogether by giving partners more autonomy. We can never eliminate arguments and bad communications, especially when one or both partners are Ego-P oriented or mentally sick. But, for reasonably logical couples, a relationship framework provides enough guidelines to negotiate within certain boundaries and thus minimize the chances of miscommunication.

Objective D: To reduce our expectations from relationships

The fourth objective of a relationship framework is to keep partners' expectations low. Basically, they should reduce their expectations as much as necessary until a balance between their personal needs and relationship needs is created. They must understand and respect the set boundaries. Nowadays, we value our individuality and independence more than we value our relationships. But, at the same time, we have been placing more demands on relationships. For example, we expect our partners and relationships to bring us ultimate happiness and a lot of compassion. This is an unrealistic expectation, because the logic dictates that the more we seek independence, the less we like to depend on others, and the less we should expect from our relationships too. We must become more self-reliant to maintain our independence and individuality.

Couples must learn that personal needs and relationship needs are not the same or coincidental. Basically, every relationship consists of two individuals with different personalities and perceptions. Thus, their conflicting personal needs cause relationship clashes. Especially, while both partners are hung up on individualism, the areas of common interest between them are automatically reduced. Each partner gives priority to his/her personal needs and his/her perceived expectations from a relationship. So they cannot comply with the particular needs of a relationship, even if they knew what they were. At best, if they really wanted to be in this relationship, they must decide how to reduce their expectations from their relationship. In practice, however, it is hard to expect this kind of understanding and sacrifice, especially from young couples. Thus a relationship framework is needed to do it for them, i.e., reconcile couples' personal needs with the relationship needs in a logical manner.

A useful relationship framework must have a flexible structure to somehow accommodate a large variety of personalities, while attempting to modify partners' perceptions of relationships too. Obviously, this framework wouldn't fulfil all the personal needs and objectives of couples. It can fulfil only a bunch of global needs that are most commonly agreeable to the general public. These global needs would not necessarily include enough personal needs of all couples, e.g.-love or happiness. The relationship framework cannot bring happiness to partners. It only provides the right atmosphere for smart partners to find happiness individually first and then possibly in their relationship too. Couples thus learn that they cannot depend on their relationships to fulfil all their personal needs, especially happiness.

The relationship framework would be incapable of responding to partners' subjective preferences for their relationship. Yet partners learn gradually that observing the general guidelines of a framework would potentially give their relationship a better chance to survive. They may not like all the features of this framework, but it would be better than arguing with their partners all the time or living alone. Since all relationships would be following the same guidelines, no one would feel oppressed in a particular relationship. They also know that going to a different relationship would not change the rules of the game. People would judge all relationships and their success based on couples' ability to adhere to the general guidelines of the relationship framework. Partners get into relationships with advance knowledge of the rules of the game. If they don't like the framework, they shouldn't start a relationship, unless both partners agree to have a relationship outside this framework. So, couples would still have a choice to set their relationships outside the norms of a relationship framework if they desired to do so. But, for the majority of us, sticking to a general framework would prove more practical and effective in the long run.

A major purpose of developing a framework is to discuss and eliminate some of the existing misperceptions about relationships. Once we have a better appreciation of what doesn't work anymore in the new era, we can set out to create the new framework. Next chapter will outline couples' unrealistic expectations from relationships in modern societies. It will then suggest how they should be modified in order to arrive at a set of realistic expectations.

Objective E: To overhaul couples' mentality and social mechanisms

As evident from the discussions in this chapter, a great deal of soul searching and mental adjustments is needed in order to adapt our relationships to the new social framework. We need radical changes in our mentality, and we must change social mechanisms, especially the legal system, to fit our new personal needs and lifestyles. These topics, as well as some suggested solutions, are discussed in Chapter Eleven.

Myths and Misperceptions about Relationships

A few misperceptions and myths about relationships are reviewed below as they relate to the development of a new framework for relationships.

Misperception about the Longevity of Relationships

One major misperception in society and people's minds is that relationships should last forever. This misperception comes from our traditional mentality. Nowadays, however, this is the least likely scenario considering the statistics on divorce, family problems, strive for individualism, sexuality, and the increasing level of stress in society. So now it is time to perceive relationships more in terms of an open-ended arrangement rather than a long-term commitment. In the author's opinion, we should indeed look forward with great excitement to implement this approach. The reason is that the advantages of such a relationship arrangement might amaze us in the end. This would prove to be one of those unique instances where reverse psychology would prove to work extremely well. The couples' knowledge that their relationship would terminate *automatically*, at a certain point, would make them stay together much longer than would be under the present circumstance. They simply stay vigilant and protect their relationship in a constructive, teamwork environment. They realize that they must work on their relationship regularly to maintain it instead of taking it for granted and letting it expire at a preset date. This reverse psychology would definitely help our societies in at least four ways:

- Couples get into their relationships more carefully based on intelligent analyses of their needs, compatibility, and the suitability of a particular relationship model for them.
- Couples work harder and more consciously to prolong their relationships instead of allowing it to expire. This would most likely increase the longevity of most relationships that are worth saving.
- Couples are mentally prepared to leave their relationships with the least amount of shock and hassle when a relationship is not working. They know from the beginning that, if necessary, separation is a good and acceptable possibility.
- Ending relationships is automatic and hassle free.

The point is that we need modern thinking and principles for relationships to match the modern life we are so eagerly embracing. Along with our new lifestyles and thirst for individualism, we would also behave more in line with the humans' innate sexual tendencies and hormones, as were listed on pages 178-180. We are addressing our sexuality more liberally every day with lesser concern about social ethics. So, viewing relationships as a temporary arrangement may be the only logical solution for the dilemma of relationships considering the rate of relationship failures, our sizzling sexuality, and our eagerness to have a companion, too, anyway. If we learn to perceive relationships *only* as a conditional companionship, which might entail a family too, then we can possibly define a set of relationship principles more appropriate for the modern life and then set our expectations accordingly.

Some people have already reached similar conclusions and are building their relationships more freely. They are not concerned about marriage formalities, such as a license or a church wedding. In another type of relationships, mostly prevalent in developing societies (where romantic imaginations have not corrupted partners' cultural view of relationships), couples still depend on tradition or religious principles to maintain their relationships. But the rest of us believe that neither of these kinds of relationships is appropriate. We disapprove these approaches since partners are not bound by official documents or they are not marrying based on love. We perceive these relationships valueless, because in our modern thinking we have learned to focus on relationships as a love-union. Yet, at the same time, we insist on legal documents and court system to protect us when love erodes. We all know that our naive love has a good chance of faltering sooner or later. But we insist on ignoring this information at the outset. It is a big irony that we wish to base our marriages on love and trust, but in fact don't trust each other's promise to live together merely on the strength of the presumed love. We want a marriage license and legal protection. Love without trust! This is hypocritical but also an obvious contradiction. We insist on legal protection for the possibility of the marriage breakdown, but we are too shy and romantic to sign a contract that dictates partners' rights upon their marriage breakdown without any need to go to court.

Misperception about the Role of Love

In the recent decades, couples have suddenly become too romantic, but also too antagonistic. Everyone believes that love should be the foundation of relationships. In this sense, life has become a big theatre. Everybody tries to be romantic. And they expect their partners to be equally good in romance, too, as a test of their commitment. But then they retaliate harshly, and show their evil side, when love fades away—which happens regularly in most relationships. They turn separation into such a calamity when they realize that their supposedly initial love had been a farce. They make life hell for themselves and their partners because love has evaporated (if there was any real love to begin with). Now couples turn into ferocious adversaries accusing each other of lying about their love promises at the outset. They curse their partners for not loving them anymore, as if love were something to force upon oneself and not a natural phenomenon. They find their partners responsible for the lost love, even if they are the ones feeling out of love. Actually, they often blame their partners for making them fall out of love. They accuse their partners of having killed their love. They also blame them for their loss of youth. These past lovers now suddenly view each other as criminals deserving a severe punishment, including a difficult and costly separation. The penalty for falling out of love is too horrendous nowadays. So some people continue to play the role of a romantic fool to keep the situation under control. They accept the humiliation of submitting to the whims of their spouses to stop their whining, and because the penalties, financially and emotionally, for ending relationships are too high.

On the one hand, getting out of relationships proves excruciating, in terms of the hardships imposed by our partners and society (the judicial system in particular). On the other hand, many couples are frustrated and confused, nowadays, because they feel trapped in their loveless (usually hostile) relationships. The situation is in particular stressful for persons who really believe that love is the essence of relationships. Even worse, many couples have to continue playing some phony roles that marriage counsellors tell them to play in order to save their relationships.

Almost everybody finally admits that love, in the sense they had initially imagined it, is a transitory state. Then they may decide that the option of staying in loveless relationships, against their convictions, is preferable to loneliness or high penalties of separation. But now they don't know how to handle a relationship that is not defined by love. They believe their relationship has failed and has no value. Some may seek love in another person's arms; to find the love they believe they deserve.

Everybody believes they deserve love and must find it somehow. But we all ignore a simple fact about the meaning of love: That the more one seeks S-love, the more one must be honest and sincere in character. And yet it is becoming more difficult to be honest and sincere nowadays, because of all the games introduced in relationships. Of course, we imagine that we can hide our insincerity, mistrust, and dishonesty from the rest of the world. But this mentality only shows our arrogance and trust in Model-P to bail us out. The good news is that people can largely see each other's true nature despite all the elaborate games they play to portray a false personality of themselves and to conceal their calculating nature. In all, the games and retaliation schemes in relationships show how ridiculous the idea of measuring the strength of our relationships by love is. We just ignore all these contradictions and keep looking for S-love in such a contaminated environment.

Our present mindset reflects our lack of clarity about the nature of love and its role in relationships. Basically, we insist that relationships, and its survival, must be justified and driven by love. In the contemporary definition of relationships, our culture permeates many invalid myths. We believe that:

- Love is the test of success for relationships.
- Love lasts forever.
- Love makes a relationship last forever.
- Relationships must be validated by love.
- Relationships thrive on love.

- Anybody considering a serious relationship should and would find a person to exchange love with each other.
- Expressing love regularly guarantees the success of relationships.
- Love is a common phenomenon that everyone understands and is capable of delivering.
- Love is a common commodity that everyone must find and enjoy in his/her life.
- When there is love, relationship problems are rare and manageable.
- Love overcomes all the relationship problems.
- Partners have control over their feelings to love each other forever.

These myths are furthest from the nature of relationships in the new era. Love doesn't have the meaning or the power stipulated in the above myths. Nor do relationships necessarily last longer if partners start their relationships with love. We are not learning any lesson from the fact that almost all relationships in the modern world have started based on *some kind of love* and they still keep failing miserably. It is amazing.

Maybe it is all right to seek love so eagerly. But we should also remember the nature of love in general—as outlined in Chapter Six—as well as the chaotic nature of relationships in the new era. We should do so to be prepared for the consequences of our futile search for love or even finding it. We should indeed concentrate on developing our Self-P (selflessness) instead of indulging ourselves with more E-love and phony lovers. Besides, S-love happens by accident and not active search.

Another cause for misperception in relationships is that partners use love as another yardstick for measuring equality. That is, they expect their partners to love them as much as they think (or pretend) they love their partners. They demand love-equality to ensure the fairness of their relationships. Obviously, love-equality is a symptom of the general equality craze in society. People believe that love is a spiritual feeling (Self-P driven), but then make it totally conditional on their partners' ability to love them equally. With their demands for E-love and equality, they simply expose their selfishness (instead of selflessness) and destroy their chances to relax and relate naturally.

Couples' perception and expression of love are obviously not S-love as long as they insist on love equality. It is even more bizarre when they often retaliate harshly when they don't perceive the love they get adequate. How can this attitude have any trace of S-love in it? It is at best only a Model-P driven love (where partners try to play the role of lovers), without any sense of selflessness (needlessness for equality). This is clearly an example of partners' increasing confusion every day about their perceptions of love, which then leads to more expectations from relationships. The need for equality has become such an imposing social phenomenon that it has even infected our love affairs. We are less interested in figuring out how our partners' integrity may qualify them as our soul mates. Nobody knows what the characteristics of a soul mate should be. Rather, we insist on measuring, in greatest accuracy, the equality (as well as the intensity) of the love our partners can show, which we continue to doubt anyway.

While equality, in the sense of *fairness*, is the foundation of our democratic society, it has turned into a socio-political platform to further spread our demented social values. The term 'equality' is somewhat misused inadvertently to express our repressed anxieties, which then leads to creation of new expectations and headaches. Unfortunately, the meaning and implication of equality are often exaggerated, so much so it has ruined the structure of relationships altogether.

Obviously, relationships' chances of survival have declined drastically with love becoming the main success factor—because love itself cannot survive in relationships. In fact, a cynical interpretation of *love* implies that it flourishes only by deprivation and not through a relationship. Perhaps believing that relationships (marriage) kill(s) love is cynical. But we can safely say that after the initial stages of companionship, couples encounter a special atmosphere dissimilar to their initial perceptions of *love*. The new atmosphere is shaped according to the peculiar personal needs and personality aspects of partners, which is hardly ever spiritual or logical. So, in light of all these clues, both a more meaningful view of love and a better perspective of relationships are essential. The question is why shouldn't our culture focus on factors that are effective in prolonging relationships without depending on love too much? And the question is why we cannot identify these relevant factors of success for relationships? The answer is that we really don't appreciate the true nature of love and relationships in the present era. And we have not yet realized the importance of developing a relationship framework.

Many of us might realize eventually that our perceptions of an ideal relationship are unrealistic and then lower our expectations. We may end up thinking *practical* at the end, but not before hurting ourselves and our partners for a long time with our misperceptions. Often it would be too late anyway. 'Practical' is mostly a reference to a type of submission, 'a sense of resignation and disappointment,' that eventually prevails in relationships nowadays. Most relationships contain good doses of resignation and disappointment. On the other hand, many people may lose good companionship opportunities due to their unrealistic demands. They destroy their marriages or look for an idol until most of their useful lives are wasted on dreams. Some of them might then further damage their pride, integrity, and convictions when they keep downgrading their expectations drastically for the sake of getting into a relationship quickly despite its obvious flaws and predictable headaches.

Misperceptions about Happiness and Human Nature

Happiness is a myth all by itself, but finding it in relationships is plain utopian. We have difficulty even defining happiness because it is not a stable state or experience. We only perceive it as an everlasting state of joy and tranquility, which we also expect to result from our endless materialistic desires, greed, and competition. This is a fundamental contradiction already. We want happiness to fit our contaminated lifestyles, instead of a lifestyle that could induce peace of mind as the closest state of happiness. We forget that any chance for happiness requires a drastic change of personal lifestyle (mainly toward selflessness), which only a few of us might eventually find the courage to effect.

Unfortunately, human nature does not support happiness and tranquility because of innate human urges for challenge, controversy, power, domination, competition, greed, struggle for survival, etc. Anger, hatred, jealousy, spite, and aggressiveness come to us so naturally, but we must try really hard to be honest, compassionate, sincere, and all the other good stuff. Life is not a happy journey either. Our occasional taste of happiness and tranquility soon faces new dilemmas and disappointments. So, as the first step toward tranquility, we must actually learn that happiness is a myth and not a stable state.

In relationships, the notion of happiness becomes even more idealistic because partners expect each other and their relationship to satisfy their illusory perceptions of happiness, including their egotistical and materialistic needs, pleasure, sexuality, and everlasting tranquility. This expectation is actually one major cause of relationship breakdowns. Partners deprive themselves from the basic privileges of relationships because they believe relationships are meant to bring them happiness. They cause themselves more suffering with their obsession for happiness. This is an ironic condition we have brought upon ourselves in recent decades. Instead of learning selflessness and contentment, partners try to strengthen their identities in relationships through arrogance, and then expect happiness too.

Furthermore, most of us mistake pleasures (especially sexuality) with happiness, or assume that more pleasures lead to happiness. So, most relationships become instable soon enough, only because they fail to satisfy our fantastic appetite for happiness and sexuality. Of course, we cannot avoid the impression that companionship can fulfil a large number of our personal needs. But depending on others or relationships to satisfy our personal needs and bring us happiness is naïve and the leading cause of our suffering. Any chance for tasting this elusive happiness is to seek it within ourselves according to our mental capacity and awareness.

Happiness is a complex topic for discussion, especially within the context of our crooked social values. Many books are written on this topic and maybe another one is due to explain the connection between happiness and relationships in more details than are possible in this book. The natural conclusion in most 'happiness' books is that it may be found only inside a person and he/she needs a special mindset to understand and effect this state. This is what this book advocates as well with an emphasis on becoming better humans through personal awareness, to contact our spirit and become needless about many artificial facets of life in the new era. But this book also emphasizes on staying practical and understanding our humanistic limitations, which hinder our efforts to be content and a better person. A great collection of happiness definitions can be found in *Happiness*, Perennial Books, 2014.

Some books (quoting philosophers, Buddhism, and the Dalai Lama) suggest that the purpose of life is to find happiness. This is a notion that this author has some reservations about, because he believes that life doesn't have a purpose by itself and humans have many other ambitions besides happiness. The purpose of life (in the context of creation) is neither to spread happiness nor to create good human beings. Happiness is not even the purpose of one's life (regardless of the purpose of the universe). Life is merely a collection of events and moments that transpires in people's lives according to natural laws and chances and affects them based on their cognition (i.e., beliefs, awareness, intelligence, etc.). We all prefer happiness because suffering hurts, and not because it is the purpose of life. We have many higher ambitions in life that we often pursue with greater passion than our desire for happiness or even pleasures, e.g., need for love, power, or recognition. Most of us just cannot sit idle and be happy with our contentment. We resent boredom and we want more adventures even if they cause suffering. We want to be loved even though it often leads to disappointment and pain. The point is that we are not born to be happy or good humans and these are not the purposes of life. We want to become better human beings to soothe our hurts, release tension, or because we sometimes prefer (or like to pretend) to be at peace with ourselves and our surroundings. Happiness and goodness are the probable outcomes of our personal choices to set the right balance between our ambitions and contentment. Life doesn't have any particular meaning, nor is it about anything in particular. Even if life is about something or has a meaning, God has not yet revealed it to us through His prophets, nor has He given us enough intelligence to figure it out.

The slogan 'life is for the purpose of happiness' is in fact causing more suffering than guiding people toward happiness. The reason is that it makes people believe that such a myth (happiness) actually exists, and that the reason they cannot find it is due to their stupidity or relationships. They feel incompetent and frustrated. They leave their relationships prematurely or seek all kinds of pleasures and sexuality to attain the purpose of life, i.e., happiness. But then they feel even more empty and lost.

Most importantly, life is not for the purpose of getting hung up over a mythical concept like happiness and causing extra suffering for ourselves. Ninety-nine percent of us cannot find that elusive happiness. The one percent who claims to have found it, like monks and priests, must make many sacrifices, limit their social activities, and accept celibacy and suffering in order to maintain their state of contentment, which they call happiness. It seems that happiness has a lot to do with selflessness, meditation, celibacy, and absorbing sufferings. But, by nature, most of us are selfish, and like our sexuality and pleasures a lot, which would accordingly lead to unhappiness. How many of us are willing to be celibate, limit our pleasures and social lives, and welcome sufferings to reach the height of enlightenment (for happiness)? We have to really force ourselves to fulfil most of these requirements, which shows happiness can never be a natural pursuit of humans, especially in our materialistic world. Accordingly, the purpose of our existence is not to seek happiness, as the Dalai Lama says, because we humans are not prepared to pay the price for it and we are not made for it. We must think and act within our natural capacities, while aiming to be better human beings too.

The fact that we have to try so hard to become better human beings and find happiness shows that humans are not pure by nature. On the other hand, acknowledging our impurity should motivate us to overcome our egos and try harder to understand the meaning and process of becoming a better human; not merely because it would be a social ideal, but because it would make us happier at the end. The simple fact that the ego is an inherent part of the human psyche is enough to cause human bias, selfishness, hypocrisy, and hundreds of other flaws. The fact that we are so greedy and competitive, and the way we love capitalism, materialism, and pleasures show that we are impure by nature. The fact that Christians believe Jesus died because of their sins—and similar beliefs in other religions—shows humans' tendency to sin. The fact that so many relationships fail nowadays, and the way partners treat each other at the time of separation, show their impurity; it also shows people's inability to get along and show compassion. The fact that we must constantly go for confessions and repentance, to cleanse our souls, is another clue about our impurity. The fact that we do good things and charity as well (often for self-serving purposes, to clean our conscience, or for pretension) doesn't wash all other negative tendencies that exist in human nature. Purity is not a matter of comparing the number of good deeds versus bad ones either, even if people did more good than bad. Purity is an absolute fact and not an algebraic equation. It either exists or not. Even doing one bad thing indicates the impurity of human nature. We must be blind not to see it at such a high dosage. The only question is how often humans' impurity reaches evilness. Too often and globally, it usually feels!

The groups and individuals who like to insist that humans are pure and compassionate by nature argue that adopting this positive perspective would at least encourage us build a kinder and gentler society eventually. Such optimism! They have good intentions, but chosen an erroneous logic and approach to achieve their goal. Propagating that humans are good by nature would only create a false expectation in society, and people get even more disappointed and frustrated all the time when dealing with reality. The more we consider people's malice unnatural, the more deliberate their actions appear. People get angrier every day and struggle harder to change one another instead of their own stubborn, selfish mentality. On the other hand, if we accept that humans are flawed and impure by nature, we would develop more tolerance and compassion because we understand that human actions are mostly beyond their control (i.e., genetic) or are pushed by greed and social corruption. They are mainly trying to adapt themselves to the environment as their instincts tell them that only the fittest would prosper and survive. We would try to find solutions to circumvent the repercussions of people's natural impurity instead of fighting amongst ourselves even about the purity of human nature. We might smarten up and correct the social causes of human corruption. In reality, we get surprised when someone says that he is happy or when people attest to his goodness. It sounds so magical and unnatural. He comes across to us as a superhuman. Indeed, it is such a huge exception we remain sceptical about his claim of happiness or people's judgment about his purity. Our reaction to people's claims of purity and happiness shows our major scepticism. We need a lot of evidence to believe in even one person's goodness and happiness.

Once we accept that human nature is impure, we also learn to keep our expectations from people and relationships low. We get less surprised and angry while we develop some form of understanding and compassion toward our partners and helpless humanity.

The historical evidence indicates that impure humans have always had a better chance of survival than the men of integrity and simplicity. It appears that nature has been rewarding power and domination. The greedy, egotistical, aggressive, hypocrites, and illogical humans seem to have an upper hand on our planet. Luck seems to be on their side more often. So who wants to be a loser or be associated with losers? The aggressors and hypocrites have gained the supremacy even more in our civilized societies. They know better how to conspire and consolidate their powers to exploit naïve populations and nations. They know how to manipulate the public. The losers may insist that they have a more tranquil life. But if they are about to perish in the history sooner or later, why would one wish to pursue the path that has the least chance of survival? A stoic individual is perceived as weak and passive in our culture because he refuses to compete or struggle for values and things that the whole world is killing one another over. He is not taken seriously, and he is not respected or supported. Thus he would soon be secluded from the domineering circle of social structure.

All these observations seem to contradict the wishful philosophy about the purity of man. The puzzle is, 'Why would nature support the survival of impure humans if the essence of man was supposed to be heavenly?' A plausible answer is that human purity is only a myth. Why should humans' nature be purer than all other animals?—a cliché asked often. So far we haven't been able to prove it anyway. Actually we have historically behaved much worse than the fiercest animals. We kill each other not even for survival, but only out of sheer greed, dogmatism, and spite. We keep choosing and voting for leaders who are proven to be corrupt and criminals. Overall, this theory (i.e., human impurity) seems to better fit the scientific inclination about the 'survival of the fittest.' The idea of the search for tranquility and purity has possibly emerged out of humans' struggle to escape constant suffering and stress. Then religions and gods were created to speculate about the path of enlightenment. People needed some relief. So, finding the path of tranquility and purity seemed like a good device to deal with the chaotic surroundings they had created for themselves. We are still struggling, however, despite all the religions around us. We actually fight even more because of these religions. There are too many of them and most of them are condemned by the others. Now we have psychologists and human behaviourists, too, who try to invent positive thinking methods and means of taming our thoughts so that we can reach tranquility. In this context, we are trying to invent a pure man or at least an image of his characteristics.

The success of a relationship depends on the goodness of its partners. But individuals' characteristics, actions, and nature indicate that the chances of creating even a small society of pure humans are slim, because they would not be left alone to choose as they like. In fact, it might be easier to prove that humans become more arrogant and unreliable as time goes by. Developing a pure man within the crooked value systems of modern society simply appears like a funny concept. It sounds like a plan to nurture edible fish in a contaminated swamp. With the speed we are destroying the environment, where nature is supposed to flourish itself and embrace us too, how could a puritan emerge?

These conclusions are again depressing in terms of human relationships. They only confirm the earlier assertions about humans' limitations to understand the requirements of relationships and coping with them. Obviously, it may benefit us psychologically to assume that we can try to become better human beings than we have so far been. We know that we have spiritual tendencies. We know that with meditation we can find some level of awareness and thus tranquility. But are we made to be a peaceful and logical species? Do we really understand 'logic'? Does our logic and common sense have any meaning or significance? It is hard to judge. But I doubt it personally. We have not yet been able to demonstrate such capacity. But since human is not inherently pure, perhaps we should strive even harder, against our nature, to become a bit purer in order to serve ourselves in such a harsh social environment.

PART II

Relationship Structure
for the New Era

Chapter Eight
Relationship Expectations—Old versus New

The discussions in Part I suggested that an ideal relationship develops when both partners are *good* and *enlightened*. 'Good' refers to partners' ability to be natural, rely more on their Self-P, and less on Ego-P, to relate to one another. 'Enlightened' means that partners are aware of humans' inherent limitations and thus have low expectations from relationships. They realize their own flaws and sympathize with their partners for being run by the same inner and outer forces beyond their control.

Obviously, these tough conditions drastically restrict the opportunity for building good relationships nowadays, considering the difficulty of being good and enlightened individuals. The possibility of both partners being good and enlightened is even more remote. Just the opposite: Our genetic defects, sexuality, and the negative impacts of social and family environments, make us rigid with huge egos. We are crippled by our grave misperceptions about life values and who we are. So, we seldom give ourselves a chance to learn about some of the finer means of thinking and living. Even when we do, we have extreme difficulty staying on a path of awareness when people around us are consumed with superficial needs and spread phony values. For example, it is too difficult to resist the niceties of 'consumerism' when the whole world is embracing it so dearly. It is hard to overcome one's obsession for 'equality' and show enough patience for teamwork. How could one not adopt these progressive and seemingly rational ideologies? How could one explain one's passivity and modesty to one's obsessed friends? One's Model-P would not allow it. These examples are not meant to undermine the need for 'equality' or to criticize consumerism. Rather they reflect that, in most instances, social trends usually override even our purest personal beliefs or logic. Thus we have to find relationship solutions that fit the irreversible course of history.

We must now view relationships in a new light. We need new approaches to empower relationships. The new objectives must correspond with our new social structure and our increasing demand for independence and individuality. Instead of looking for an ideal, imaginary relationship environment, our new goal should be to make relationships only manageable and tolerable. It is time to lower our expectations and define new objectives for our relationships. Finding a workable framework is an ambitious goal, but if we are lucky and lucid we may be able to create a balance between our personal needs and relationship needs.

A major source of relationship conflicts is that couples perceive and define their relationship needs as an extension of their personal needs. Most of us assume that personal needs and relationship needs are the same, or they should coincide. Some people are even more selfish and insist that their personal needs must supersede relationship needs and their partners' needs. They try to dominate their partners and set crooked guidelines for their relationships. These misperceptions and assumptions have gradually contaminated relationships. The objective of this book is to identify the relationship needs and explain how they usually compete with partners' personal needs.

Social Implications of Relationships

Social evolution has changed the nature and format of relationships in the new era quite carelessly, to the point where now society itself is threatened by the poor health of relationships. For one thing, the increasing relationship conflicts can be blamed for the rising stress in society, which in turn affects the economy too. The question is how societies can survive if relationships continue to cause so much havoc and the situation keeps getting worse every day. This is a serious matter that makes the task of finding new approaches for relationships even more urgent.

At two extremes, a relationship may be viewed as a spiritual connection between partners, or as a boring repetition of some mundane activities and interactions between them. We may perceive relationships as a sacred experience in beauty and selflessness, or only a means of social adaptation and self-gratification. While the latter position appears closer to reality, the former reflects our instinctual search for perfection and spirituality. In new societies, people's perceptions of relationships cover both of these extremes and everything else between these two realms. In particular, more people strive nowadays to find their soul mates, while at the same time they are unable to cope even with the basic needs of their relationships. Under this circumstance, we have no clear picture of what relationships are supposed to be (or can actually be). In general, we try to bring some degree of both practicality and romance to our relationships. Yet we often fail to use common sense when it is wise to be practical, and we don't know how to express emotions when it can sweeten a relationship. We haven't captured the right sense about relationships or the right balance between practicality and romance. The reason is that social changes have been too drastic and misleading in recent decades. They have tainted our personalities, our perceptions of the world, and our relationships. We have become too spoiled, needy, and impatient. Meanwhile, our relentless search for a reliable companion, usually with negative experiences and outcomes, is causing confusion and depression.

In all, we seem helpless to create a balance between practicality and romance. For example, most people have realized that signing a prenuptial agreement is necessary as a practical measure, but doing so still appears businesslike and unromantic. We believe that relationships should begin with romance and trust. Our need for a companion is so strong we commit ourselves prematurely and set high expectations for the success of our relationships too. Ironically, most of us keep thinking all along about the financial consequences of our relationships too. Especially nowadays, we are too calculating and businesslike about relationships. But we shyly (or slyly) hide those unromantic thoughts, in order to ease into a relationship that could soothe our mental burdens and insecurities. Deliberately, we ignore the high possibility of separation and all the added pain that relationships usually bring to couples' lives anyway. The truth is that our *urgent* emotional *needs* (e.g., need for sex and E-love) overpower our ability to think practically about the potential catastrophes of relationships. This is particularly true because our spirit is usually weakened by other harsh realities of modern lifestyles. We have become too soft and lonely. We also believe that luring in a companion requires a lot of romance, which shouldn't be tainted with matters of practicality. Only afterwards we become logical (calculating) in running our relationships, while losing sight of all the romance we had felt before. But, all evidences about relationship calamities indicate that we must be doing exactly the opposite, i.e., to be practical first and romantic later.

In all, our tainted social norms are responsible for relationship failures, which in turn damage society altogether. The only way out of this vicious cycle is to review our vision of relationships and reset it gradually to avoid further social downfall. Basically, our *personal mentality* has to change in order to fit our newer social structure. The *social mentality* about relationships and the government's role must be modified, too, as explained in Chapter Eleven. The required changes in terms of personal mentality are tackled in this and forthcoming chapters.

It must be reiterated that some relationships thrive merely based on partners' stoic personalities. Sometimes one partner may be so enlightened he/she can single-handedly make the relationship flourish. Sometimes one enlightened partner can bring out the good in his/her partner too. And, of course, sometimes he/she might face the harshest resistance by his/her partner and actually receive malice despite his/her good intentions. Anyway, the number of relationships flourishing based on partners' goodness is quite small. Thus, the objective in this book is to suggest solutions useful for the large majority of relationships in the new era.

Successful Relationships

No one really knows the parameters of a successful relationship due to rapid social changes that have tainted most people's personalities and their relationships. So we usually list out some relationship objectives, such as love, security, longevity, and wealth, as indicators of its success. We also consider 'communication' an important factor for the success of relationships. Those who have had bad experiences in relationships are quite cynical about the possibility of building successful relationships. To them, relationships can be nothing but hell.

So we create our own subjective perceptions about the purpose and potentials of relationships based on our personal needs and superficial values around us. We create a fantasy in our heads about the nature of relationships and their success indicators. Thus, we set ourselves up for disappointment, because our naïve expectations cannot be fulfilled. The bottom line is that we (as a society) no longer have a common understanding of relationships and its purposes, let alone a grasp of the factors making them successful. Our educational systems, especially at senior high school, have failed to teach this essential real life subject to the group of people who need this knowledge so urgently. It is a pity that such an important matter, with such grave effect on our social wellbeing, is left to personal interpretations instead of being researched for everybody's benefit.

Obviously, to deal with the existing chaos, couples must also show willingness and patience to learn about the relationships' special needs. They must view 'relationships' as a unique entity with specific needs. For sure, the process of acknowledging and applying this principle to relationships would be gradual, because couples must learn to reduce their expectations from relationships and attend to their personal needs more independently. So, the first thing we must study is the viability of people's expectations from relationships in the new era.

A Review of Relationship Expectations

To develop a realistic list of relationship expectations for the new era, we can start by creating an ideal list of expectations from relationships. On this list, we include all the common expectations that couples could desire. Then we eliminate the ones that are too conflicting with partners' personal needs. The main premise is that relationships in the new era should accommodate couples and promote their craving for independence and individuality. So, as a starting point, Table 8.1 (next page) presents a preliminary list of general expectations from relationships.

An ideal relationship would satisfy all the expectations in Table 8.1 and more. But we must aim only for the ones that can fit the majority of relationships according to our present lifestyles. The discussions in the following pages will show why many of these expectations are hard to achieve nowadays; and thus the need to exclude them in order to minimize disappointments in relationships. This would be contrary to what couples are in fact doing nowadays, due to their erroneous assumption that relationship expectations can be a natural extension of their rising personal needs. As society promotes phonier lifestyles, the level and complexity of partners' expectations keep rising. Everybody believes they deserve to live like movie stars. But the reality is just the opposite. That is, the level of expectations from relationships must be reduced to compensate for the growing pressures that society is placing on the personal lives of people already. They have enough headaches outside the house without the need for more pressures from their relationships too. In some special cases, all the expectations in Table 8.1 may be fulfilled in a relationship. But, as a rule, we must satisfy most of our personal needs independently. Now let's review the expectations listed in Table 8.1 and pinpoint the unrealistic ones.

Table 8.1: A Preliminary List of General Expectations from Relationships

1. Sex
2. Dependence- support
3. Financial Security
4. Communication
5. Compassion
6. Companionship
7. Teamwork
8. Love: S-love, E-love, M-love
9. Trust
10. Happiness – Peace of mind, tranquility, joy
11. Friendship – Loyalty, honesty, etc.
12. Respect- Social acceptance
13. Personal Success
14. Commitment
15. Longevity

1. Sex: This is the most reasonable expectation from relationships. Since couples don't wish to look outside their relationships to fulfil this urge, they must depend on their relationships to satisfy this essential need. In reality, however, partners sometimes use sex as a tool for emotional blackmail or retaliation. Also, sometimes partners cannot cooperate in this regard and thus look for sex elsewhere. Nonetheless, nothing can be done about this need beyond what everybody already knows and practices the best way they can. This is a legitimate expectation from relationships. All other dramas surrounding sex cannot be helped either. Most of them are psychologically explainable and rather inevitable.

2. Dependence: Our conflicting personal needs for dependence and independence were discussed in Chapter Two. We get into relationships in most cases for relieving our loneliness. But, in reality, many relationships make partners feel the ultimate sense of loneliness. Maybe the sense of physical loneliness is remedied somewhat by living under the same roof with a partner. But psychological loneliness reaches its height when partners fail to relate and communicate. Relationships enhance our sense of loneliness many folds, because we feel the difficulty of relating to another person tangibly, and because we had imagined we could do all that rather easily, mostly on the power of love alone. Most of us had never felt so desperate and lonely psychologically when we were living alone. We are terribly disappointed after all those years of daydreaming about finding a partner to relieve our loneliness. So, depending on our partners to cure our psychological loneliness is an unreasonable expectation.

Another hurdle is that even if our partners were capable of satisfying our need for dependence, we personally sabotage their willingness by our constant expressions of individualism and independence. Our false pride prevents us from expressing our need for dependence and their moral support directly. Instead we pretend quite strongly to be emotionally self-reliant. Showing our neediness could tilt the balance of power after all. Meanwhile, we strive to fulfil both our dependence and independence needs just by playing some superficial roles and expecting our partners to understand their meanings and also respond favourably. But these conflicting (unexpressed) expectations and role-playing only frustrate our partners. They recall our previous shows of independence, especially when we suddenly play the role of a vulnerable partner seeking dependence. Showing the right balance of dependence and independence and clarifying the timing and areas we need our partners' support is difficult. We might imagine that we are doing a good job of it, but that is only another selfish assumption and gross misperception.

Partners' erratic attempts to be dependent or independent confuse them, especially when they don't get the responses they expect. Relationship mechanisms, including communication, stop working. So what is the solution? Since our emphasis nowadays is placed on independence, we must adjust our expectations from relationships accordingly. That is, **we should stick to independence and assume that relationships are no longer capable of satisfying our need for dependence at the desired level.** We must also prepare ourselves to deal with our inner conflicts (caused by inadequate dependence) without blaming our partners. Many readers might object: 'What is the point of being in a relationship if partners cannot depend on each other?' This is a valid question that is answered in the future chapters. But the bottom line is that we cannot really demand independence so strongly and also seek dependence. This doesn't make sense. Analysing this impossible puzzle is what this book is all about. We may still count on our partners' integrity, cooperation, support, and teamwork, but not total dependence.

Our struggle for independence and dependence makes us jittery regularly. Thus we react unfavourably toward our partners, unjustifiably, especially when we assume they are refusing to understand our needs intentionally. Naturally, when a partner seeks independence and finds the other partner a hurdle in achieving it, he/she feels frustrated and resentful toward his/her partner. And he/she gets frustrated, too, when he/she needs attention and dependence and the partner is not available or capable of providing it. The situation gets out of hand as relationships remain undefined in terms of dependency and independency needs of partners.

Of course, showing compassion with Model-P and M-love would help the health of relationships when couples notice their partners' need for dependence despite their arrogant show of independence. It is a good gesture by partners to stay civilized toward each other in those circumstances. But when we keep switching between our independence and dependence urges and roles in relationships, we should also expect that our partners lose their sensitivity and true sympathy about our needs. Obviously, partners' personal tension heightens while they are unaware of the ongoing competition between their conflicting needs for independence and dependence. They sense only their partners' indifference toward their needs even when they continue to play a variety of idiotic roles to draw their attention.

Overall, each partner has difficulty understanding and responding to his/her partner's incongruent expectations for dependence and independence. He/she is also frustrated when his/her own needs for dependence and independence are not satisfied. These dual deprivations lead to many personal (inner) conflicts for him/her already, as noted in Chapter Two. But partners' inner conflicts heighten when their needs for dependence and independence don't coincide in terms of timing and partners' mood fluctuations. It hurts them deeply, since their natural (instinctual) personal needs for dependence and independence are badly imbalanced and ignored. This gross incongruity causes constant frictions between partners while they criticize each other's erratic needs, too. All along, partners' rotating struggles for more freedom or more attention come across as unnatural and sinister. The situation makes both partners believe that his/her partner is instable or neurotic. They also feel that their partners are placing these expectations on their relationship illogically or even out of spite. So instead of understanding and *dealing with it logically*, they react negatively by retaliation and confrontation.

Nonetheless, it is difficult to deal with the unrealistic expectations of our partners for dependence and independence; especially in the eyes of an impatient partner who is unwilling or unable to cope with such conflicting needs so frequently. The irony is that people's needs for both dependence and independence are increasing simultaneously every day. As noted before, people are getting too spoiled and needy due to the effect of complex social values. They ask for more compassion (dependence) while also demand more freedom and identity (independence). Of course, when partners accuse each other of behaving erratically, they face only more arguments and frustrations. So, instead of discussing their relationship dilemma calmly and objectively, they focus only on dominating the situation and each other, or opt for separation. They see no option other than either adapting to this confusing environment or getting out of the relationship altogether. Both options are obviously destructive.

In our modern way of thinking, we accept open-mindedly that both dependence and independence are essential needs, and we naively believe we can cope with this major dilemma in our relationships. We might even assume that by some magical power we would find the right balance (between our needs for dependence and independence). We assume we can make compromises so that both partners can fulfil their rotating needs for independence and dependence by common sense. This is an unrealistic expectation. Nonetheless, the options are clear: We could either keep looking for magical compromises, or agree on a set of principles that best fits the mentality of couples in modern societies. These principles, of course, lean toward partners' higher independence. The new trends show that couples consider independence their most urgent personal need, and give it the highest priority in their relationships too. So, based on the strong trends evident in society, we can say that:

"Since we humans are usually unable to respond to the rotating demands of our partners for independence and dependence, we must adopt a relationship model to deal with the situation consistently. The existing social fervour for independence suggests that, as a general rule, couples should place emphasis on a relationship model that has the highest potential for guaranteeing partners' independence. Accordingly, partners should reduce their expectations from relationships in terms of satisfying their dependence needs as well."

Relationship Expectations-Old versus New

Advocating independence in relationships might appear inconsistent with the objective of 'enforcing teamwork.' But 'teamwork' is an objective negotiation process between two independent partners, and not a sign of partners' dependence on each other.

Whether we like it or not, it is now time to refine our assumptions about the conflicting needs of partners for both dependence and independence. It is time to stop the negative impact of these useless struggles on relationships. These facts should be clear to couples at the outset. This is necessary because, nowadays, the idea of 'dependence' has been losing its practicality in relationships. Therefore, couples must think through and plan their relationships based on the assumption that they must remain independent in all respects regardless of the outcome of their relationships. Hopefully, partners learn teamwork and compromise, too, to make their relationships manageable. But starting on the wrong foot, i.e., hoping that their need for dependency can be satisfied in a relationship, is simply opening the door for major disappointments.

The relationship success factors discussed in the next chapter gives the highest score to partners' degree of independence. In fact, it would be the basis for setting all the other expectations defined in Table 8.1. Our personal need for independence has become the locus of all other relationship expectations. Our urge for independence has affected all the expectations we traditionally had from relationships, especially financial security, i.e., the expectation number 3. Simply, partners nowadays (must) get into relationships with confidence in their ability to support themselves financially if their relationships don't work out. It seems silly in this day and age to envision that couples get into relationships for financial security. In the past it worked. But this concept feels increasingly more incongruent with the values of equality, which is so seriously pursued, particularly by women. Obviously, many couples would continue to prefer dependency on their partners. It would be difficult to draw the lines so rigidly (about independence). But here we are talking about *setting mindsets* that are realistic and congruent with other aspects of our desires. Relationships would continue to fail because of so many factors. Only one of them would be partners' reluctance to be self-sufficient and competent, and hoping that a relationship would rectify their financial insecurity.

As noted before, the worst case is when a partner is really craving security and dependence upon his/her partner, but keeps playing the role of an independent person forcefully, while also nagging about his/her partner's insensitivity. He/she doesn't admit that he/she is the one restricting his/her partner's ability to feel his/her need for dependence. He/she doesn't realize that his/her sudden need for attention (and expecting his/her partner to sense it automatically too) is frustrating his/her partner.

3. Financial Security is on its route to becoming an obsolete concept, although many relationships are still based on one member of the family being the main breadwinner. The point is that financial security is no longer an automatic arrangement like the old times. People aren't getting into relationships for the sake of financial security anymore. Or at least they shouldn't when society is revolving around 'independence.' Now, financial security in relationships, when it happens, is mainly by accident or some kind of agreement between partners. It is an exception, not an expectation. Financial security is no longer a norm, but rather a possible by-product of being in a relationship and only in the spirit of teamwork. Nowadays, partners should somehow understand and agree on the mechanism of their household finance before they commit themselves to a relationship. Accordingly, the more relevant topic that has emerged is 'financial control' and not 'financial security.'

In terms of financial control, also, the trend is changing. In the recent past, financial control referred to situations where one or both partners insisted on (or fought about) controlling the whole financial affair, even if the other partner made all the money. Even though both partners sort of discussed some aspects of financial decisions, usually one partner ended up being in control of financial issues and bank accounts (although they usually shared the accounts). Nowadays, partners must be responsible for their own share of the pie, whether they have earned it themselves or is allotted to them through some type of family budget. Financial autonomy is now an essential factor that partners must discuss and plan at the outset. So the phrase 'Financial Control' is now more appropriately referring to the fact that each partner should keep financial control over his/her own financial affair. The other partner should not expect otherwise. The matter of sharing income, and any type of joint investments, is a reasonable arrangement when it is done voluntarily and through cooperation and teamwork, but never as an expectation anymore. Those of us who are still in the transition process must overhaul our mentality.

4. **Communication:** This is still a major expectation from relationships. Effective communication is obviously the essence of successful relationships, especially for enforcing teamwork. But many good relationships are ruined because of simple misperceptions and miscommunications. Partners' oversensitivity, arrogance, and false pride usually obstruct even common dialogues. Effective communication is nowadays also essential for implementing a process of hassle-free separation when necessary. Instead of spending time and money on lawyers, a prenuptial contract, as well as partners' objectivity, can enhance communication when separation seems inevitable. Nonetheless, effective communication is the most difficult expectation from relationships, because most often partners are not properly trained to communicate, or because retaliation and Ego-P make the process extremely hard to manage.

5. **Compassion:** Our ability to give and receive compassion is a direct function of our humanness and humility, which are becoming scarcer every year. Compassion depends on how good and enlightened a person is. Expecting compassion in relationships is a logical expectation. But in reality it seldom materializes at the desired level. This is because everybody seeks more compassion every day while the number of humble and patient people in society is shrinking. Our superficial gestures of compassion, mostly through role-playing or even submission, cannot fill the gap for real compassion either. People often detect our hypocrisy and resent it, mostly because our Model-P is not well-developed to play a natural role. So it is wise to set our expectations rather low for receiving real compassion in relationships nowadays. But if relationships cannot fulfil our thirst for

compassion, the question is whether we can fill this gap in our lives in some other way? Need for compassion is too strong and urgent to ignore, after all. The answer is that we may in fact learn to play a major role personally in this matter, as will be suggested shortly.

The problem is that we always crave sympathy, but have difficulty expressing it ourselves. Often we feel that our partners' needs are too superfluous and selfish, i.e., driven by E-love. It is demanded too often or the nature of their expectations seems unreasonable to us. Sympathizing sincerely is difficult, anyway, even when we feel that our partners' need for compassion is genuine. This is because most humans are inherently more selfish than compassionate. Overall, people's need for sympathy is tremendously higher than we, as humans, are capable of delivering, especially in the new era. So, the supply and demand for compassion are drastically unbalanced in societies and across the nations. Yet, instead of understanding this general shortfall of human nature, we take the matter personally and turn against our partners when they cannot give us as much compassion as we seek. We don't notice our own inability to offer genuine sympathy often enough, but we are needy for it so relentlessly.

The complexity of modern life is creating additional mayhem and stress for everybody. Accordingly, demand for sympathy has increased astronomically. This is happening at the time when people are more egotistical, impatient, and mentally unprepared (because of their own problems and stress) to provide sympathy to others. A person under constant pressure at work and from life issues is really too preoccupied and exhausted to provide sympathy to others (including his/her spouse). This is especially true if his/her partner's demands are only for satisfying her/his deficiency need for attention—E-love. Partners are playing enough games outside the house. And then expecting them to use their exhausted Model-P to play similar games at home is simply impractical. Despite this obviously persistent problem, marriage counsellors keep advocating artificial means of expressing compassion in order to satiate the needs of partners. But aside from the points expressed above, the problem with this approach is that it wouldn't be perceived genuine often enough by the receiver, and the giver loses the patience and interest to play games.

In all, couples should realize that expecting sympathy is unrealistic in a modern society where the supply and demand for compassion are unbalanced—mostly due to inherent human nature. The increased level of stress in society has simply made us vulnerable and too needy for sympathy, but there is nobody out there to give it to us. So, expecting it on a regular basis is both selfish and a definite cause for disappointment. The bottom line is that everybody is alone in this world—an old saying that makes more sense every day as we constantly adopt more egotistical values. So, we must define our lives personally and live it the best way we can within the stressful routines of modern society. Sympathy and compassion would be exchanged naturally when people are capable and ready to express it. But it would lead to further alienation and resistance if it is demanded or even perceived as an expectation. Receiving sympathy (and giving it) is a fringe benefit and not a right. Exchanging compassion is nice and must be encouraged and appreciated. But its inadequacy mustn't cause additional stress in relationships. Our partners might not be good in expressing compassion even if they genuinely mean to provide it. Conversely, learning to mimic compassion by reading a few books or attending seminars would never make people more compassionate. If we are looking for phony compliments to satisfy our need for compassion, we will never reach satisfaction in relationships. We just keep asking for more E-love to feed our addiction.

Yet compassion is a reasonable expectation from relationships—with a major reservation in terms of its nature and source. A more realistic definition for compassion nowadays should mostly emphasize on our personal ability to generate it instead of craving it. The best way to achieve this is by supplying more compassion to others than demanding it. We must realize that we should expect compassion only if we are good at generating it ourselves. Just needing something doesn't give us an entitlement to get it. The irony is that the more we learn to give compassion sincerely, the more we receive it from others naturally, and the less we feel the need for phony sympathies. By learning to become a compassionate person in a real sense, we become self-sufficient to a large extent and get a lot in return too. So, in a sense, we can generate the compassion that we need personally. Only this mentality can reduce our depression and dependence on psychiatrists to manage our lives.

6. Companionship: This is an automatic outcome of relationships. We all prefer to have a companion, and relationships make this dream come true. The only question is whether we prefer a lousy companion to loneliness. Conversely, finding an ideal companion is a matter of luck and usually a doomed expectation too. Our initial perceptions of our companion usually prove to be erroneous later on anyway.

We all seek high-quality companions to get love and compassion. A companion must be like this or that, we imagine, while we strive to satisfy our need for E-love. So, the comments made before about the supply and demand for compassion and love, apply to companionship too.

7. Teamwork: Couples' ability for teamwork is a major requirement for relationships. As we insist on more independence and individualism, the need for teamwork becomes greater in order to keep our egos under a leash. Obviously, for teamwork, partners must have some genuine qualities, including modesty and objectivity. Yet we nowadays face more *obsessions for individualism* instead of *modesty*. So, finding partners of such quality and implementing teamwork in relationships would be a major challenge. Nonetheless, teamwork is an absolute necessity.

For managing the 'relationship needs' and responding to at least some of our partners' personal needs, we must commit ourselves to teamwork and learn about the means of compromising. Teamwork is the only tool available to couples to coordinate and monitor the needs of their relationships. The urgency for teamwork is not still appreciated, since couples consider it a threat to their sense of independence and authority. But it should become a major expectation soon, with some training to go along with it. The methods of family teamwork must be developed soon too.

8. Love: We have talked about love in several parts of this book. It is a tool that makes couples' communication more effective. It helps them satisfy their need for compassion.

But love does not qualify as a legitimate expectation from relationships, due to its illusive nature. We all like to taste love at least for starting a relationship, and love is a good gauge for measuring the degree of partners' attraction and success in satisfying their sexual need. But we should not consider love a reliable factor to keep partners together. Love is not an objective measure for assessing relationships either. The reason is obvious. As noted before, when we express love, we are influenced by a perception of S-love while we are driven mostly by E-love. We all have this spiritual need, S-love, to love someone or something passionately. When we meet a person who can stir this feeling in us, we consume ourselves with a perception of S-love. This individual becomes a mirage that satiates our need for S-love. At the same time, our need for E-love (ego-ridden deficiency love) further encourages us to identify this person as our soul mate. We are suddenly in love. This is great for bringing couples together. But true S-love happens only rarely and only when partners are needless and enlightened persons. So our perception of S-love is only a transitory 'perception' and not a reality. E-love, on the other hand, is an absolute reality and not a perception. So E-love continues to place more demands on partners every day, because its only purpose is to feed partners' selfish need for attention. It creates possessiveness, jealousy, and frustration.

M-love helps us express our emotions and sweeten our relationships. So, maybe M-love should be listed as an expectation from relationships, with some reservation. The reservation relates to a point raised before about the nature of M-love, when it is not genuine enough to count on its continual effectiveness. M-love contains role-playing and it lacks authenticity at some degree. Its effect depends on the strength of a person's Model-P. Not everybody can be good at it. On the other hand, M-love can help a lot to keep romance alive in relationships.

Many radical ideas have been proposed in this book. They make the nature of our relationships appear too dry and impersonal. This picture of pessimism might prove to be the reality that we must eventually face based on the values and the culture we are embracing so fast, most often inadvertently. So M-love is a helpful and relatively realistic expectation to induce passion in relationships. It reminds partners of the need to keep working on their relationship and communication.

In general, however, love, as we express it so readily nowadays, is not going to help relationships. Therefore, **we must remove love as a legitimate expectation from relationships.** (Except for M-love.) We can use 'love' as a gauge for attraction and for facilitating communication, but not as a factor of relationship success.

The arguments presented before regarding 'compassion' apply here too. We all seek love but don't know how to give love. We think we do, but, for the reasons noted throughout this book, we are only assuming to know what love is and how we can offer it to others. Again, the supply and demand for love are unbalanced and causing undue pressure on our lives and society in general. We have become too needy for love since everything else in society sucks. And we assume that by stating love to someone, he/she gains the power or expertise to provide the genuine sympathy we need to mitigate social pressures.

9. Trust: The discussions on page 122 suggest that while mistrust is becoming a general condition nowadays, partners should stop fussing about it and instead live with some level of it as long as the integrity of their relationship is not jeopardized. Trust cannot be a legitimate expectation.

10. Happiness: We expect relationships and our partners to bring us happiness. We expect joy and tranquility as a result of finding a companion. We discussed happiness in Chapters One and Seven. Basically, neither our partners nor our relationships are capable of providing happiness. Whether we can find happiness in relationships or not depends on a large number of factors, but mainly our mental capacity to interpret, absorb, and reflect happiness. In all, happiness is more a subjective perception than a tangible commodity to expect from relationships. If anything, relationship environments are normally too complex and demanding to exert direct happiness. It is our responsibility and art to enjoy our companion and explore the merits of being in a relationship. Usually, if we are a happy person, we know how to generate our happiness with or without a relationship. The opposite is even truer. If we have no capacity for being happy, relationships normally make us unhappier. So, in all cases, expecting happiness from our relationships or partners is unrealistic. Couples should accept that the only source of happiness that could be expected from relationships is the mere presence of a companion in their lives. If a partner's presence alone doesn't cause happiness automatically, then the relationship has no other source of happiness to offer. Under this circumstance, the couple must either learn to relate passively or opt for separation, but not nagging and demanding.

We usually think that relationships can bring us happiness because it can solve our personal problems. This is a false assumption and an unrealistic expectation too. In fact this mentality is destroying relationships and further reducing its capacity to cause even a slight measure of peace and comfort. As a whole, expecting relationships to solve our problems is a damned expectation. A good relationship helps us mentally to deal with our personal problems more effectively, if we were smart and humble. A bad relationship, on the other hand, destroys our ability to even take care of our basic needs, let alone solve the complicated problems of life and the relationship itself. Judging by the statistics, more relationships fail than succeed. So instead of expecting relationships to solve our problems, we should expect and prepare ourselves to deal with the hardships of relationships and the high likelihood of separation. Relationships become the source of new problems instead of solving our existing problems. This is what this book is all about—trying to prepare the readers for the headaches of relationships.

Playing more roles and games to exert happiness wouldn't work either. Although many experts advocate this method to make couples release their tensions and express the sources of their anxiety, this author believes that couples can decide about the viability of their relationships only by understanding the deep-rooted causes of relationship obstacles in the new era. Relying on the intelligence of partners to learn the sad truth about relationships works better than keeping them hopeful by playing some artificial roles. This is especially true when they are already under pressure mentally and physically. Role-playing causes more stress and frustration when partners feel the futility of their efforts deep down. Why they feel this way? From experience we know that once the process of alienation between partners begins, it is almost impossible to return it to its initial state of moderate tranquility. The only thing that can save relationships is learning the truth about the real causes of problems, which often relate to partners' own irreparable idiosyncrasies.

11. Friendship: A good test of 'relationship success' is partners' ability to enhance their friendship. But this idea has never been promoted as an expectation. Often couples actually prove their inability to be friends, but still insist naively to build a relationship. The main feature of successful friendships, which is missing in relationships, is that friends' limited expectations are set gradually and naturally without pressure or demand. Then even if those expectations are not fulfilled, they seldom argue or fight over them. They only moderate (realign) their own expectations to keep their friendship. They value their friendship so much, they willingly reduce their expectations. This is indeed the strength of good friendships and a main reason for their success. This is exactly an opposite mentality we see in relationships. In relationships, couples set high expectations immediately and don't appreciate the value of what they have like the way friends do. In fact, couples keep increasing their demands and expectations, and nag all the time, too, until their relationship falls apart. So, a new expectation that should be promoted and analysed more actively in relationships is partners' aptitude for friendship. A relationship should be expected to be based more on friendship than love.

12. Respect/Social Acceptance: As part of our struggle for equality, independence, and identity, couples nowadays demand total respect from their partners. This is in line with social trends and thus an absolutely acceptable expectation from relationships. But partners should not only expect respect. Rather, they should really learn how to respect their partners despite their obvious idiosyncrasies and personality weaknesses.

Society gives a higher status to family than individuals. We personally value our relationships highly for many reasons, too, but mainly because we expect them to help us fit better within the society. This is an automatic by-product and expectation from relationships.

13. Personal Success: A relationship is expected nowadays to facilitate partners' personal success and independence. There is a positive consequence for this seemingly selfish need of partners for personal success. That is, with the emphasis on the personal success, partners need only look for the appropriate relationship model that can best fulfil the range of their personal needs. Otherwise they should not even bother getting into a relationship. After all, if partners feel successful and fulfilled individually, their relationship would be a success too. It makes total sense.

Partners' cooperation is expected to give them a higher chance for success in social and personal endeavours. Synergy and moral support are the expected benefits of companionship. In all, personal success is a reasonable and helpful criterion to include in the list of realistic relationship expectations. Unfortunately, in reality, the very sense of individualism and independence forces partners to compete with each other. Their unrelenting urges for recognition and showing off their independence and identity make them too arrogant at the cost of losing their relationship. So couples must not only choose the right relationship model based on their personalities and need for achievement, but also keep their egos under a leash.

14. Commitment: We have traditionally expected relationships to enforce some form of commitment for partners to stick together even when some aspects of their relationship are not ideal. Maybe 'commitment' was a useful tool in the past and even now. But, as a practical step, partners should begin to realize that nowadays the sense of commitment is vastly eroded by the need for individualism. Nowadays, couples insist on enjoying their lives at the highest level possible. They get out of their relationships sometimes even based on childish reasons or their perceptions of a better life with a different partner. So the bottom line is that commitment can no longer be considered a reasonable expectation from relationships in the new era. Period.

15. Longevity: The arguments used for 'commitment' applies to longevity too. It was a practical expectation in the past but not anymore. Point 7 (page 73) also explains why longevity erodes due to people's inability to balance their rising needs for independence and dependence.

Using the above analyses, and doing all the additions and deletions, the last column in Table 8.2 shows the updated list of realistic relationship expectations for the new era. So, out of the seventeen general expectations from relationships, we can realistically consider only nine of them still relevant and practical in the new era. Those are the ones marked by (X) in the right-hand-side column. In the following chapters, we will use this new set of expectations to develop a relationship framework and a set of relationship principles.

Table 8.2: The Updated List of Relationship Expectations

Type of Expectation	Delete Old	Add or Emphasize New	Updated List
1. Sex			X
2. Dependence	X		
3. Financial Security	X		
4. Communication		X	X
5. Compassion			X
6. Companionship			X
7. Teamwork		X	X
8. S-love	X		
9. E-love	X		
10. M-love		X	X
11. Trust	X		
12. Happiness	X		
13. Friendship		X	X
14. Respect-Social acceptance		X	X
15. Personal Success		X	X
16. Commitment	X		
17. Longevity	X		

Chapter Nine
Relationship Framework

We usually examine a relationship only when it is in trouble. Otherwise it is taken for granted the way our ancestors did intuitively. Driven by our traditional mindset, we still assume (and expect) that relationships would continue to work smoothly as a routine social arrangement. But, then, relationships were defined by simple cultural rules and they remained inherently safe. In new societies, however, relationships are extremely vulnerable from day one, because a lot of complexities and expectations have complicated the interworking of relationships. Accordingly, partners cannot comprehend or respond to relationship needs intuitively. In fact, they cannot detect the real causes of relationship problems even when they attempt to explore them actively. Not even relationship experts and counsellors can help couples in most cases. The irony is that most often the problems are simply due to partners' naïveté about the purpose and potentials of relationships, as their criteria is gravely tainted by artificial values and imitation. Most relationships would have been considered acceptable if couples were not misled by phony lifestyles and misperceptions. For this reason alone, unfortunately, couples' struggle to salvage their relationships usually proves futile, despite all the efforts that partners and marriage counsellors put into them.

We can no longer pursue a passive approach in our relationships and then suddenly become serious and react when problems are out of control and partners feel defeated. A few decades ago, this reactive approach might have been justifiable when the potential for, and the types of, relationship problems were limited. Nowadays, however, with the overwhelming variety of relationship conflicts, a proactive approach is needed. We now need to foresee and prevent relationship conflicts as much as possible. The new approach must be a preventative one. It should emphasize on educating couples in advance about relationship needs and principles. They should then be expected to monitor their relationships continuously for signs of trouble. And they should be trained to expect separation as a most likely outcome of relationships in the new era anyway.

Couples should monitor the relationship success factors that will be identified in this book. But more importantly, they must learn to disallow superficial criteria (their subjective judgments) obscure their view of their relationships. It means no more imposing of their personal needs on their relationships and measuring their partners' compliance with their crooked expectations. Chapter Seven discussed the need for a relationship framework to create a balance between our personal needs and relationship needs. Chapter Eight developed a list of *acceptable* relationship expectations for the new era. This chapter will bring these concepts together to develop the preliminary factors of relationship success.

A more complete list of 'relationship success factors' should be developed soon after deeper analyses and contributions of scholars. But in this book, we will try to identify some of the main parameters that can measure the health of relationships objectively. These basic parameters (success factors) would be applicable to the majority of relationships in the new era. A relationship framework can thus be developed to help couples monitor the state of their relationships regularly and realistically. They would no longer guess the purpose or the health of their relationships arbitrarily based on partners' sloppy interpretations. Instead of guessing (and constantly increasing) their level of expectations from relationships, couples would tame their perceptions about the objectives of relationships. They would try to focus only on those limited factors that are important and practical for the success of relationships. At least partners would know that expectations beyond certain limits are bound to cause relationship conflicts and a breakdown. So they are aware of the risks they are taking if they insist on following their personal whims instead of staying within the boundaries of the relationship framework.

Initially, we must agree that some special factors can guarantee the success of relationships. This means that we can view relationships as an *entity* with specific characteristics. This also means that, instead of relying on random criteria of couples or their in-laws, an objective set of modest criteria defines the success of relationships in modern societies. In this sense, 'relationships' is viewed as an independent entity free from random judgments and perceptions. The factors measuring the success of relationships are independent from the subjective views of partners.

At the present time, relationships' success is determined only by partners' feelings. Although the feelings and impressions of partners matter a lot, they don't reflect whether the relationship failed due to the exaggerated expectations of partners or their real lack of compatibility. Nowadays we rely on partners to assess their relationship because there is no definition for a successful relationship. Two partners in a particular relationship might actually rate the success of their relationship quite differently. This is because they are biased and mostly act based on their emotions. Furthermore, this type of assessment lacks any basis to compare different relationships against one another and find universally agreeable anomalies. Couples' assessment of their own relationships would reveal one interesting fact, though: that almost all relationships are failures if we asked couples to rate it. This is because almost nobody is quite happy these days with their relationships. Seldom would both partners consider their relationship a success. And even then they are probably using wrong or biased criteria for measuring its success.

Another problem with the existing loose definition for 'relationship success' is that our expectations from relationships are expanding rapidly. This situation cannot be sustained forever. As noted repeatedly, relationship expectations are increasing due to the rampant increase in couples' personal needs and social extravaganzas. Everybody is imagining some phony lifestyle or ideals that they impose on their relationships too. This selfish attitude is raising the bar for relationship success beyond all reasonable limits. The list of relationship expectations has become larger than the sum of all the expectations that people have imitated from one another and the movies. That is, everybody likes to have everything that all other couples have in their relationships plus everything else that their imaginations tell them. Instead of measuring the success of relationships objectively, we let the selfishness and neediness of partners make this critical judgment. It is only their arrogance that is being measured then, and not the success of their relationship. Surely, this open-ended level of expectations from relationships cannot prevail forever. The faster these expectations rise, the less successful relationships become.

With our rampant needs for things, sympathy, and security, we are placing a lot of pressure on society and limiting the chances of relationships to follow a practical path. And the impact of the failing relationships is depressing individuals and society as a whole, too, which then again stirs up people's urge for more compassion. This vicious cycle is feeding and forcing itself out of control. We must somehow deal with this situation before the time comes when everybody needs antidepressants in order to go through a day. We must redefine relationships as an independent entity with unique needs. We must agree that relationship expectations beyond some modest, humanistic level are artificial and imposed by psychologically distressed and deprived people.

We make statements like, "They have a good relationship; they can relate; or this relationship is doomed, etc." On these occasions, we somehow perceive a 'relationship' as a setting, with particular characteristics and needs. Obviously, the health of any relationship depends on couples' capacities and personalities. But we perceive 'relationships' as a state of affairs between partners, which could be good, bad, or whatever based on measurable factors. For example, if partners argue a lot or are depressed about the way things are going in their personal or joint life, then their relationship is rated low. So the question is, "What factors make a relationship successful or a failure?"

The outcome of any relationship depends on many personal factors, including partners' personality, their ability to relate to one another, their ability to cope with the relationship needs, etc. So the obvious first step for assessing relationship conflicts is to establish whether the problems are genuine or only the figments of partners' exaggerated expectations, unfulfilled personal needs, or idiosyncrasies. The outcome may not change if partners cannot live together for whatever reasons. But at least we would know whether the problems are within or without the boundaries of a normal relationship. We would know whether those problems are real or imaginary, based on partners' erroneous assumptions or even illness in some respect. Many relationships are destroyed nowadays simply because one or both partners underestimate the value of their relationship prematurely. If they had objective criteria to measure the health of their relationship, maybe it could have been saved. They might have realized that they should face the problems realistically rather than running away to find a better relationship, or merely out of spite. The onus must be placed on partners to establish whether their expectations from relationships are normal or misled. It is time to agree that the option of allowing relationship expectations to escalate continuously in line with couples' personal needs is irrational. The present approach would only lead to major socioeconomic suffering around the globe.

An encouraging environment is obviously needed for couples to suddenly see their options more clearly and choose a proper approach for measuring the success of their relationships. This environment is basically what we have referred to throughout this book as a 'relationship framework'. So let's discuss its role and components.

Components of a 'Relationship Framework'

A 'Relationship Framework' is basically a setting for couples to relate and communicate effectively and thus reduce relationship frictions. The best way to explain this framework is to identify and review its components, as laid out below in Table 9.1:

Table 9.1: Components of a Relationship Framework

1. Relationship Attributes: **R-entity**
2. Partners' commitment to teamwork
3. Relationship expectations
4. Relationship models
5. Relationship principles—GARP
6. Relationship needs (success factors)

1. R-entity

Relationship Attributes (or R-entity for simplicity) highlights the fact that relationships must be viewed as an independent entity separate from the partners' identity and needs. R-entity is only a concept to remind couples that *relationship needs are specific and not an extension of their personal needs*. R-entity is the glue that keeps all other components of the relationship framework together. Another way to view R-entity is to consider it both the conscious and conscience of the relationship. It acts like a virtual fair referee between two independent partners, thus minimizing their need to find mediators or go to marriage counsellors to resolve their conflicts. Together with the other elements of the relationship framework, it forces partners to stay *relatively* objective and thus face much less friction. R-entity can be viewed as an important third party (the third leg of a tripod) in relationships to keep partners on alert and as stable and objective as possible. Without this third leg the other two cannot withstand the pressures of relationships. Developing this type of mentality is difficult, considering our passive and stubborn personalities. Understanding and practicing this mentality in real life sound too illusory and theoretical. But enough suggestions are included in this book to gradually get an overall feel for R-entity. Anyhow, the aim is to gradually introduce this type of mentality into our relationships and society during the next few decades.

To better grasp R-entity (relationships as an independent entity), let's view it from a different angle as well: In business partnerships, we identify the purpose of the business and means of prospering it separate from the identity of its owners. Obviously, business partners contribute to, and benefit from, the outcome of the operation. But, the vision and tools for running the business, the strategies to make it flourish, and the means of measuring its performance are all separate from partners' personality or needs. Partners' personalities and management styles impact the prosperity of their business. But we don't define the objectives and requirements of a business as the sum of the personal objectives (or needs) of its owners. For a successful business, it has to be viewed as an independent entity with specific needs and objectives of its own. Usually partners take special courses to enhance their managerial skills and learn how to plan and perform organizational and business duties. They don't change their personalities because they have to run a business, but learn about the requirements of running a business by viewing it as an important entity. Even for a simple business operation, nowadays partners must learn a lot about planning, budgeting, marketing, negotiating, accounting, decision-making process, performance measurement, etc.

Managing 'relationships' has similar, if not more, demands. Thus, it should be treated as carefully and viewed as an independent entity too. In the older societies, the expectations from relationships were not as complex and demanding as they are in the new era. So, developing a new vision and approach to run this important partnership effectively is imperative. A marital partnership is many folds more complex and demanding than any business partnership, because the cost of failure is much higher. The emotional aspect of such failure is horrendous and financial aspects might prove quite substantial, too, in most cases. So, it should be viewed with as much focus and independence as any business venture is viewed. R-entity simply provides the opportunity of bringing a similar level of discipline to the concept we call *relationships*. The objective is to specify its unique needs and operational mechanisms independent from the personal needs of partners. Nowadays, relationships are beginning to resemble a business and too calculating anyhow. Most partners are looking for more things and wealth from their relationships, and they make sure these assets are properly identified and registered, in case the likely separation happens. At the same time, they ask for unlimited compassion (and E-love), too, which usually comes across as hypocritical.

Someone may claim that the emotional aspects of marital relationships make them different from any business partnership. But the fact that 'relationships' are more emotional than business indeed imposes even more need for care. Relationships need even a more stringent process and mechanism to ensure its success amidst all other social pressures, both structural and emotional ones. Viewing 'relationships' as an independent entity wouldn't undermine the importance of its emotional aspects. But, in fact, it may generate better ideas and more time for compassion once the unreasonable needs and expectations of partners are scrapped out of it. The high emotional aspect of relationships indeed places a higher demand for effective communication schemes than it is necessary for organizations. So couples should stop taking relationships for granted, or ignore the need for special education and awareness for mastering it. Rather, they should start viewing it as a separate entity (R-entity) and focus on its unique needs instead of their own personal needs and egos.

Once the concept of R-entity finds universal appreciation, it will serve couples in a substantial way. It prevents partners from focusing on their personal needs selfishly, or even each other's needs. Instead, couples will think mostly about the welfare of *relationships* as a third entity (R-entity) that imposes a set of independent, yet modest, requirements for achieving certain common goals. Accordingly, society will begin to adopt suitable values to promote the relationship needs too. For example, society can begin discouraging too many hours of work out of greed and frown upon egotistical competitions. Family values could find a new perspective. Basically R-entity says to each partner:

> "I don't care what your personal needs are. And you can continue fulfilling your own or each other's needs as effectively as you can. But remember that you must nurture and entertain me regularly, if you're interested in keeping me alive and active. I want good nutrition and your full awareness about my needs. If your egos, idiosyncrasies, or learning disability prevent you from understanding my needs and rules, then just don't even bother coming close to me. I know I sound arrogant to expect you put my needs ahead of your own and your partners' needs, but that is the only way I can stop you two from getting on each other's nerves and destroying me in the process too."

With this approach, the less (expectations) would contribute more toward keeping a relationship healthy and together. This approach prevents partners from imposing their idiotic expectations on relationships. They understand their roles in keeping R-entity alive, while maintaining their independence and respect too. At the present time, we are only suffocating R-entity with our never-ending personal needs and expectations.

Obviously, every relationship has some unique characteristics based on personal preferences and intelligence of partners. But its general characteristics must always fall within R-entity's modest guidelines. This is the same principle that governs in business too. The general needs and processes of business are not dependent upon the type of business or its owners' personalities. Some businesses are complex and huge, and some are small. Yet the general business guidelines apply to all types of businesses. In relationships, then, each partner should honour those basic rules that are necessary for being in a relationship. These rules have nothing to do with personal needs and partners' perceptions about the meaning of relationships. In fact, partners' specific needs and preferences should not contradict the requirements of R-entity. Rather, partners' personal needs should make sense within the context of R-entity. This is because R-entity advocates the independence and individuality of partners. All the logical needs of partners are supported by R-entity. So when partners' personal needs contradict R-entity, it mostly reflects the irrationality of partners' needs. They might be too artificial or imaginary.

However, the success of a relationship requires more than partners' ability to grasp and observe R-entity. In some situations, one or both partners may get bored. Or they get fed up with the efforts required to sustain a healthy R-entity. Some people are simply not made to be in relationships, the same way that not everybody has the right temperament to be an entrepreneur. Partners might feel that they are sacrificing too much (by depressing their personal needs) in order to feed R-entity. For example, their excessive need for E-love is left unfulfilled within a relationship framework which is built around the concept of R-entity. In those situations, R-entity advocates that partners go their separate ways instead of hurting each other by more demands and nagging.

Obviously, two needy people can always start (or continue) a relationship filled with their exaggerated needs and expectations. As long as they know the risks of doing it outside the norms supported by R-entity, they are welcome to take their chance. They might even succeed in their adventurous journey. Nonetheless, those exceptions are based on partners' freewill and hopefully their full awareness of the associated risks. Knowing the risks of starting a relationship outside the R-entity boundaries might actually keep them conscious and proactive enough about their relationship to make a success out of it despite the odds.

We assume we understand our personal needs and we find them quite justified too. But how authentic they really are, and how they can satisfy us in the long run, is questionable. Fulfilling them or resisting their temptation remains partners' personal decision, though. The trick is to ensure they make sense in the context of R-entity when we want to be in a relationship. And for this, we must define the requirements of R-entity and develop a mechanism to measure the personal needs of partners against them. The main question for relationships is no longer whether its partners are compatible according to some criteria. Rather, the question is whether partners are equipped to be in an R-entity driven relationship.

2. Partners' commitment to teamwork

As emphasized in Chapters Seven and Eight, a major task of a relationship framework is to develop mechanisms that can **enforce** teamwork in relationships. Yet without the full commitment of both partners to teamwork, the objectives of the relationship framework cannot materialize. If partners' impatience and ego defy teamwork, they cannot satisfy the unique needs of relationships and their relationship is in jeopardy. The discussions at the end of this chapter about the general requirements of a successful relationship framework would explore this topic some more.

3. Relationship expectations

Table 9.2 provides the list of valid relationship expectations for the present era. This is a realistic list in the author's opinion, but scholars are encouraged to suggest their refinements. Table 9.3 presents the invalid (rather traditional) expectations. Of course, both lists must be routinely reviewed and adjusted according to the specific requirements of future generations. Scholars should monitor social changes and partners' new logical expectations from relationships. The practicality of relationship expectations should be assessed on an ongoing basis. Couples must grasp and adopt both the valid and invalid relationship expectations presented in Tables 9.2 and 9.3. They can then assess them in line with their personal needs and decide on the relationship model that best suits them.

Table 9.2

The Proposed List of Valid Expectations from Relationships

1.	Sex
2.	Communication
3.	Compassion (re-defined)
4.	Companionship
5.	Teamwork
6.	M-love
7.	Friendship
8.	Respect/Social acceptance
9.	Personal Success

Table 9.3
The List of Invalid Expectations from Relationships

1. Dependence
2. Security
3. E-love
4. S-love
5. Trust
6. Happiness
7. Commitment
8. Longevity

As mentioned in Chapter Eight, the expectations listed in Table 9.3 might materialize in some relationships automatically. But they should be taken as fringe benefits of that particular relationship. The point is that couples must not start a relationship based on these invalid expectations, as they hardly materialize and last in relationships. It does not mean that their relationship is abnormal when they face the reality. Fulfilling the expectations in Table 9.2 is a major success by itself. With this mindset, partners would not blame each other for unfulfilled expectations or fuss too much about it.

The irony is that if couples fulfil the expectations listed in Table 9.2 effectively, the expectations in Table 9.3 would most likely be fulfilled automatically as well. They evolve gradually in their relationships based on partners' maturity. Once partners learn to live in peace with each other, love, happiness, and longevity would follow. But not if they keep insisting on the invalid expectations in Table 9.3. Actually, pressing for the items in Table 9.3 hinders the fulfilment of the moderate expectations in Table 9.2, and the relationship collapses under all the pressures quickly. Enjoying someone's companionship and basic compassion should suffice without partners going overboard. That type of arrangement would prove quite fulfilling, anyway, as long as couples don't get distracted by their invalid expectations. But Ego-P and related emotions prevent people from staying content with a more realistic set of expectations. It looks bizarre when sometimes a partner starts to hate his/her partner and retaliates because he/she doesn't love him/her enough. The question is how an individual's own love turns into hatred because his/her partner cannot respond to his/her love. What kind of love he/she had for his/her partner, anyway? E-love or M-love? It definitely could not have been S-love.

4. Relationship Models

We simply cannot have infinite types of relationship models to fit the infinite types of couples' personalities. So it makes sense to identify a few models that can accommodate the majority of people as long as they believe in R-entity. Every model provides a particular setting for partners to relate and communicate according to their lifestyle priorities and their capacity to exchange passion and compassion. Relationship models are discussed in Chapter Twelve.

Having several relationship models to choose from gives partners a chance to be specific about the kind of lifestyle they wish to share with each other according to their personalities and needs. A particular model makes most sense to each couple. Yet, every model offers an effective way of relating in relationships. By choosing a particular model, couples learn to curb their exaggerated perceptions about the potentials and purposes of relationships. They stop looking for an ideal relationship or criticizing the limited features of some relationship models.

5. Relationship principles—GARP

GARP is a list of practical principles that can guide couples' activities and behaviour in their relationships. These guidelines provide certain boundaries that experts agree on as a means of maximizing the health of relationships. They would be regularly studied and revised based on social values and changes. GARP stands for Generally Acceptable Relationship Principles. This concept and an elementary list of GARP are presented in Chapter Ten.

6. Relationship needs

Relationship needs are listed in Table 9.4 (next page). They are mostly envisioned and developed around the list of valid relationship expectations (Table 9.2). Satisfying these needs enhances the favorability of relationships. Table 9.4 actually represents the 'relationship success factors' too. Of course, this list is not an ultimate or complete list of relationship needs or success factors for relationships. It is only a working document. Nonetheless, the more favourable the noted factors in Table 9.4, the more successful a relationship would be. Many other factors could be identified and added to Table 9.4 later by scholars and researchers.

Table 9.4
Relationship Needs: Parameters of a Successful Relationship

1. The relationship is driven by R-entity, instead of partners' personal needs.
2. Partners are independent financially and emotionally.
3. Partners keep their expectations within the boundary pinpointed in Table 9.2.
4. Partners know the repercussions of pushing the expectations in Table 9.3.
5. Partners are attracted to each other with good chemistry.
6. Partners have chosen the right relationship model for their personalities.
7. Partners stay within the boundaries set by their relationship model.
8. Partners can relate actively and have compatible lifestyles and preferences.
9. Partners pursue a path of self-awareness to enhance their Self-P and S-love.
10. Partners know the meaning and implications of E-love, M-love, and S-love.
11. Partners understand and negate the problems of misperceptions.
12. Partners know how everybody's personality is shaped and controlled by forces beyond their control.
13. Partners understand the flaws of human nature and how they cause companionship hurdles.
14. Partners don't criticize each other's idiosyncrasies constantly.
15. Partners don't try to change each other or push their lifestyles on each other.
16. Partners strive sincerely to develop trust between them, but don't make an issue about the level of trust between them either.
17. Partners don't try to manipulate, control, or intimidate each other.
18. Partners know how to maintain good communication between them.
19. Partners enjoy having sex together.
20. Partners run their household and family affairs mostly through teamwork.
21. Partners are compassionate and know how to show compassion.
22. Partners are good friends. They know the rules of friendship and stick to it.
23. Partners respect each other despite their partner's idiosyncrasies.
24. Partners are capable of promoting each other's pursuit of social ambitions.
25. Partners can support each other in pursuing their personal goals.
26. Partners are aware how their Ego-P, Model-P, and Self-P interfere during their encounters and watch their effects closely.
27. Partners know the concept and components of the Relationship Framework.
28. Partners actively follow the guidelines of the Relationship Framework.
29. Partners know, and actively follow, GARP, which outlines the main principles of relationships. They use GARP to stay objective in their relationship.
30. Partners seek mediation and consultation when disagreements arise.
31. Partners maintain their personal integrity.
32. Partners are mentally prepared to leave their relationship in peace when reconciliation is not possible.
33. Partners never retaliate for convincing each other about something.
34. Partners are tactful, mature, forgiving, patient, and mentally stable.
35. Partners don't play games with each other.
36. Partners don't rely on government or religion to run their relationship.
37. Partners have signed a contract at the outset to govern financial and other aspects of their relationship, especially during separation.
38. Partners consider separation a normal expectation in the new era.
39. Partners believe in terminating their relationships civilly if necessary.
40. Partners measure and discuss the state of their relationship regularly.

The Ultimate Objective of a Relationship Framework

As noted before, a Relationship Framework has five objectives:
A. To enforce teamwork,
B. To bring objectivity back into relationships,
C. To increase the effectiveness of communications,
D. To reduce couples' expectations from relationships, and
E. To overhaul individuals' mentality and social mechanisms regarding relationships.

The objectives A through E have been discussed already or will be explained in the future chapters. But it must be emphasized here that the *ultimate* objective for developing 'a relationship framework and models' is to make as many relationships *manageable* as possible. Even imperfect relationships have some merits if only couples learn to relate (at least passively). Daydreaming about an ideal relationship is only a waste of our precious lives. We must, instead, control our imagination about the potentials and purposes of relationships and find mechanisms to manage them somehow. For this sacred objective, we need a relationship framework based on the values of our modern society.

In the old times, relationships weren't particularly important, understood, or perfect. Couples had simply come to terms with the limitations of relationships and didn't jump out of them when they weren't perfect. They had more tolerance naturally because their brains were not washed with some imaginary notions about relationships. They were not obsessed with love or an idealistic perception of relationships. But now everything has changed. Relationships have become too complex, we really miss the opportunity of having a soul mate more than ever, and we have become less patient too. These clashing conditions are making life unbearable for everybody and the situation would get even worse if a solution is not found soon. We must review the real potentials of relationships in our present culture in order to cleanse our wild imaginations. It is crucial to realize that relationships are not capable of giving us all the niceties that have gradually turned into relationship expectations in recent decades. We have created only more deprivation for ourselves by our exaggerated perception of relationship potentials, especially in terms of bringing us happiness.

Obviously, we all need a companion with certain qualities and mutual attraction. The problem is not as much in finding him/her as it is in keeping them. People's traditional tolerance in relationships has been suddenly replaced by oversensitivity and edginess nowadays. The reasons behind people's chronic impatience are noted throughout this book. But basically, our increasing need for individualism, romanticism, social stress, our loss of trust, and our thirst for love and respect are to be blamed. Also we are getting more snotty, spoiled, optimistic, demanding, and ignorant about the acceptable level of tolerance in relationships.

So, another objective of a relationship framework is to gradually give us a rational measure of the acceptable level of tolerance. Couples should not depend on their subjective judgment or crooked sense of romanticism to guess the level of reasonable tolerance. Of course, each couple would be the one determining their own level of tolerance. But they should also have access to a more realistic standard to

avoid gross misperceptions. We must decide whether we prefer relationships with some imperfections to isolation, or vice versa. The question is whether we prefer to live in a fantasy world and dream about a perfect relationship or wish to learn about reducing our expectations. Our options seem to be clear. They are:
- Keep fighting with ourselves and our partners over the irreconcilable issues of relationships in the new era, or live in solitude, while sticking to some rigid perceptions of an ideal relationship.
- Learn to accept the new reality of relationships, reduce our expectations from them, fulfil as much of personal needs outside the relationship, tolerate some inevitable level of relationship hardships, and separate peacefully when it proves unmanageable.

The *ultimate* objective of a relationship framework and this book's discussions is to advocate the second option. This book is less useful to people who prefer the first option. Overall, the purpose of a relationship framework is to discourage the initiation of doomed relationships based on unrealistic expectations. It also stops couples from wasting their lives in torturous relationships if they cannot reduce their expectations. But a relationship framework can also help people overcome their fear of getting into relationships and facing its headaches, because ending it would be less hectic. The guidelines of a relationship framework can actually help those couples with unrealistic expectations too, because they get the opportunity of raising them directly at the outset and discussing them.

Another major objective of a relationship framework is to *enable partners relate to each other effectively and efficiently* even when a variety of their personal expectations cannot be fulfilled in their relationship. In that kind of environment, a high standard of behaviour and communication must help partners *relate* somehow with minimal friction and stress. The idea is to develop a self-sustaining mechanism to gauge couples' means of relating to each other on a regular basis.

The complexity of relationships is easy to grasp when we consider the complexity of human nature. It helps to know how hopelessly helpless we are due to our psychological defects. We are totally dominated by our personality aspects, our misperceptions, our conscience and desires, and our needs and deprivations. A relationship gets two times more complex if we sum up the complexity of two partners making the relationship. But in effect the complexity of relationships increases beyond the sum of the two partners' idiosyncrasies, as their interactions create many additional levels of conflicts and contradictions. In relationships, many new dimensions emerge in partners' lives beyond their personal limits and their knowledge of the self. Even their dormant idiosyncrasies pop out of nowhere. They might even get an urge to kill (themselves and others) due to their immense frustration and helplessness infesting their minds at such an extreme. In all, when couples' Ego-P and Model-P interact and incite one another, they introduce a much wider range of potential problems for themselves and others.

Considering the gloomy prospect of relationships without a 'relationship framework,' the present efforts of marriage counsellors and experts seem unproductive, if not futile altogether. The reason is that, without the proper mindset and knowledge of a reliable relationship framework, couples cannot relate to one another effectively and efficiently. To really help couples, a counsellor or a writer must show them how to relate according to certain guidelines similar to what this book is proposing for a relationship framework. He/she must first explain how couples could relate, for what objectives, and how to reduce their expectations to achieve those goals. These topics should actually be taught in high schools. Instead, most relationship experts increase couples' expectations from relationships by giving them the impression that they can rekindle romance to save their relationship through role-playing. But giving couples false hope about finding their lost loves, or overcoming mistrust, is not the best way to help them. It only delays partners' decision about the viability of their relationship. It is rather naïve to believe M-love alone can make couples relate, even if they had the talent and patience to sustain the role-playing requirements of M-love.

Relationship counsellors can instead promote the reality of relationships in the new era. They can help couples perceive and adopt one of the noted options: to stay together with lower expectations, or get out of the relationship. Counsellors and writers are trying to help couples make the best of their relationships. Yet they don't have a uniform method or model to show the requirements of relationships in the new era. They don't have access to a set of principles and a relationship framework for couples to follow.

Obviously, the successful implementation of a relationship framework depends heavily on partners' mood and personality. It depends on their ability to manage their egos and tolerate their partners'. Couples must be talented team players. But we know that human nature and their conditioned personalities cannot be readily changed. *Managing their own egos and tolerating their partners'* require a great deal of efforts, awareness, and sacrifice by both partners. Nonetheless, knowing the truth about the reality of relationships in the modern world would help partners choose a viable option for them. It would shake them out of their fantasy world about relationships and realize the naivety of their expectations. This knowledge might help them find a better way of *relating* to their partners and keeping their relationship, if it is worth keeping. They might find a different relationship model to help them relate without a need to separate.

Knowing that people have difficulty in general to refit their personalities and lower their expectations might motivate couples to think through their options about a companion more realistically. This would expedite their awareness and adaptation process. Meanwhile, they would develop a mentality to separate civilly when they can no longer relate emotionally, effectively, or efficiently—the 'three E' requirements of relating.

Need for a Fresh Mentality

Relationships would always remain a demanding and confusing aspect of our lives. Accordingly, we must begin to see and accept relationships in a different light, as a temporary union. It takes a lot of courage and effort to prepare ourselves for a possible separation. And we should also learn to become humbler humans and modify our life values. We must build objectivity to assess our relationships realistically and maybe decide to stay in it despite the emotional burdens we endure. Finding manageable mechanisms to relate (in an imperfect environment) and enhancing our tolerance level require a great deal of art and devotion. But if partners are unwilling or unable to make these efforts and sacrifices, in terms of observing the boundaries of the relationship framework, then the only possible solution is to not start one or separate quickly. Otherwise, there are no grounds for expecting things to improve and that relationships stay manageable only by chance.

Obviously, the option of not having a relationship is ridiculous, as seclusion doesn't fulfil any purpose, at least for the large majority of the population who seeks a companion as a basic need. Both our instincts and culture constantly force us to attend to this need actively. So we must modify our mindset to bear the pressures of being in a relationship. The particular relationship model that we choose should keep our affairs and communications manageable, while allowing us to deal with our personal needs individually. We either accept an imperfect situation, or we don't. Our resistance to choose either of these two logical options—i.e., live it or leave it—only reflects humans' level of stubbornness. We insist on imposing our personal needs on relationships. We wish to impose definitions on a concept that is not capable of matching our wild imaginations. In this sense, our imaginary ideals about relationships are bound to give us only agony and hardship. In the existing relationship environment, partners have no definite direction or prospect to look forward to. So something has to be done; that *something* is the ultimate objective of a relationship framework. But more importantly we must adopt a fresher mentality personally.

Sadly, despite the ongoing struggles in relationships and clues about the futility of our imaginary expectations, most of us don't seem to grasp the scope of our relationship problems and just keep increasing our demands. We just continue to torture one another until death do us part. Under this circumstance, the only chance to gain some tranquility and free our spirits is to accept the realistic (and partly sad) options of relationships (i.e., living it or leaving it). It would help to broaden our minds about what relationships can be, what we can expect from them realistically, how and why.

How Can Partners 'Relate'?

We must classify *relate* into 'active' versus 'passive' levels. A couple relates actively (or positively) when they can maintain positive emotions, effectiveness, and efficiency in their relationship. The three Es are active. This happens when partners are committed to teamwork and have chosen the relationship model that best fits their personal needs and personality. They know how to live within the parameters of the model too. On the other hand, sometimes, partners have already given up on the possibility of enjoying an ideal relationship together. So they somehow learn to relate in a passive way instead of going for the separation. The passive way means minimum expectations from relationships while it still remains manageable. In this case, one or more of the three Es are compromised—they are passive. Both types of relationships are acceptable as long as couples observe the expectations listed in Table 9.2.

It is important for partners to know about the way they are 'relating,' if at all, and acknowledge it too. Next, they must find the means of facilitating their communications to increase the effectiveness of their relationship for that type of relating, i.e., active versus passive relating. Some couples can continue to get a lot out of their relationships, even though 'passive relating' is not an ideal condition. Realizing the best option for them enhances their awareness to implement its particular requirements effectively. Of course, if one partner is trying to relate actively when the other one is happy with passive relating, their relationship gets into trouble. When partners have different perceptions of their relationship, no special model or mechanism is in place and their relationship rolls on an alienation course. Confusing messages between partners frustrate them and expedite the process of alienation. Relationship counsellors can assist couples to follow a particular option (relationship model) and understand its requirements, implications, and outcomes.

How partners relate is a complex process requiring a full book of analyses. Obviously, the more the relationship needs in Table 9.4 are satisfied, the higher would be the chances of couples *relating* to each other actively. Of course, relating and communicating are two different things. In some instances, partners might enjoy a rather good communication between them, but still cannot relate because they have different mentalities and lifestyle preferences. And sometimes they can relate, but don't have enough communication skills (or patience) to express themselves. Both situations cause problems. But 'relating' is often a more important factor for the success of relationships than 'communication.' The reason is that this couple can agree on the relationship model they choose and remain truthful to its requirements. The main factors for relating are partners' lifestyle preferences, philosophies, priorities, and intelligence. Another important factor is the proximity of their personality aspects (mostly Self-P) in their daily lives and interactions, without Ego-P playing a major role. The higher their Self-P, the better partners can relate. A modest level of Model-P can also help them express themselves better and thus relate more actively.

We can analyse 'relating,' in terms of the three Es (emotions, effectiveness, and efficiency) for both passive and active modes, as follows:

- **In terms of emotions**, partners' objective is to either enjoy each other's companionship (active relating), or tolerate each other without causing undue emotional distress or setback for one another (passive relating). While active emotions reflect a high degree of love and connectedness, passive emotions reflect partners' understanding of each other, sympathy, and compassion. Knowing about humans' limitations and our partners' helplessness to change enables couples to relate even though it might not be as active emotionally as they would like it to be.
- **In terms of effectiveness**, partners' objective is to share ideas and means of pursuing their personal and common goals instead of sabotaging each other or competing with each other. They do this in both cases of 'active' or 'passive' relating, but at different degrees. When they are eagerly supporting each other to achieve their personal goals, they are active. But when one or both partners are not showing enough interest in the affairs of the other, they still could have an effective relationship, passively.

On the other hand, the urge to sabotage or retaliate is common in relationships where partners put down each other to prove their superiority. Generally, in active relating, partners can relate effectively when they work together to establish the *right things* for their relationship and personal life in general. In 'passive' relating, they don't work much together to increase the effectiveness of their relationship, but they also don't sabotage each other or show rivalry.

- **In terms of efficiency**, partners set their goals properly and economically for achieving productive end-results and to satisfy their personal and common goals. Partners relate efficiently when they can work together to do *things right* rather than wasting each other's time and energy. They avoid wasting the emotional and financial resources that support R-entity. The importance of teamwork to maintain civility in both active and passive relationships can never be overestimated.

Some level of compatibility can help couples fulfil the relationship needs listed in Table 9.4 and relate actively. Chapter Thirteen presents some ideas regarding the methods of measuring partners' compatibility in the new era. Those compatibility factors should also determine how successfully a couple is 'relating' in a relationship. Furthermore, they should measure partners' emotional connection as well as their relationship's effectiveness and efficiency. The final score would show the degree of partners' passive or active relating and the suitability of the relationship model they have adopted.

Chapter Ten
Relationship Principles

Some implied *principles* used to help humans manage their relationships, until recently. Whether it was tribal, religious, or cultural norms, some form of ethics and etiquettes prevailed. Those values, ordinarily informal but clear, guided couples to live in some form of harmony. Obviously those outmoded types of family structures are no longer applicable or useful in new societies. But the question is whether people can live without some form of norms or principles to keep the families in a relatively coherent and manageable harmony in the new world. The answer in the author's opinion is a resounding NO. Thus the objective in Part II of this book has been to develop a means of returning order and harmony to relationships despite their gloomy prospect nowadays.

Starting perhaps only half a century ago, suddenly all the old relationship principles have gradually eroded along with the advent of so-called progressive societies and mentalities. Those old principles have become obsolete considering the emergence of new lifestyles, women's new role in organizations and society, and other symptoms of human struggle to prove his independence and spirit. Personalities have changed and people have become more complex without any expertise about dealing with one another effectively. Individuals' needs have skyrocketed and their expectations from life and relationships have increased, yet their patience and morality have declined drastically. We have propagated arrogance, extravagance, sexuality, life philosophies, and unlimited artificial needs.

Now we stand at the junction of history. We don't know how to relate to one another emotionally, effectively, and efficiently. Thus we suffer from our substandard relationships. Our agony heightens daily because we ignore the current cultural deficiencies. We are unaware of the hazards that the lack of relationship principles has caused. The aggravating hurdles of relationships, mainly due to mounting personal idiosyncrasies, are affecting all of us directly and fiercely while social complexities increase too. Human interactions, at work, at home, or with friends, have become less sincere and manageable in all respects. Family relationships, in particular, have suffered both in terms of child-rearing and couples' ability to relate in their relationships. The absence of some kind of principles to guide partners is hindering the job of relating in relationships. Partners' oversensitivity and subjectivity are shortening the longevity of relationships nowadays. In all, there are no Generally Acceptable Relationship Principles (GARP) to guide coupleRelationship problems and their sources are complex. But the basic cause of all these problems is that we lack GARP to help us understand and respect each other's boundaries according to new social values. A point emphasized in this book is that humans' inherent shortfalls, mainly their ego, hinder their ability to relate to one another without authoritative guidelines. They do not have the required objectivity to handle their relationships naturally. GARP can fill this gap and gradually turn into some truthful social norms. It can minimize power struggles (domination of one partner) and it can help couples relate more effectively. It must be developed gradually and updated regularly in line with social changes and research to i) reflect human nature and needs, and ii) provide objective guidelines for a harmonious companionship. The bottom line is that we must be willing to sacrifice in some respects to gain the tranquility of manageable relationships. And we must learn how to tame our egos to accept and honour GARP. The wedding woes we exchange superficially should be strengthened by GARP. In a sense, GARP is a refined set of etiquettes to help couples get along in their relationships.

GARP is a main component of the relationship framework (Table 9.1) that has been advocated throughout this book. It provides detailed principles to guide couples in their efforts to relate to one another. It also provides the guidelines for constructing and maintaining the 'relationship framework' itself. The following questions are tackled in this chapter:

1. Can GARP really solve our relationship problems?
2. Is developing GARP feasible?
3. How can GARP be developed and propagated?
4. What a replica of GARP looks like?

Can GARP really solve our relationship problems?

GARP will be an easy-to-read document for the general public. It will list the facts and guidelines about relationships according to the social setting of the time. The author believes that people would eventually appreciate the validity and significance of GARP's objectives. Thus, they will find it in their interest to modify their mindsets in order to make their relationships manageable and live in some form of harmony. In all, GARP is intended to become a practical Bible for relationships.

The main purpose of GARP is *to establish a platform for couples to relate emotionally, effectively, and efficiently.* In this sense, GARP will help them adjust their rampant presumptions about themselves and their partners. It will become a point of reference, a defendable social norm, to measure couples' expectations and attitude. It will pinpoint the issues causing misperceptions and marital clashes. GARP will also contain all the information and rules about the relationship framework and its components. Overall, GARP would satisfy the objectives listed below:

List of GARP's Objectives

1. *GARP can help us* **capture and propagate the main features of a successful relationship.** It can show how a relationship may thrive, what it is supposed to achieve, and what we can expect from it. GARP will provide the list of success factors in relationships too, like the ones offered in Table 9.4. Accordingly, GARP replaces the arbitrary (subjective) criteria that couples nowadays use for running their relationships or assessing its viability. This will bring objectivity back into relationships.

2. *GARP can help us* **realize our psychological limitations as human beings.** It can show how our personal limitations cause relationship problems. GARP can enhance our sensitivity toward our partners, reduce our expecta-

tions from them, and mitigate our resentment about the substandard environment of relationships.
3. *GARP can help us* **realize why individuals' psychological defects are not easily repairable.** It will emphasize that we must find the means of circumventing those defects as much as possible instead of criticizing them. Some of the ideas discussed in this book regarding human psychology can be adopted as *principles* and included in GARP. For example, we can agree that, as a plausible principle, 'People can hardly change themselves.' One reason is that for a person to change, he/she must change his/her cognition, which in return requires accessing the depth of his/her unconscious. He/she must draw upon some extraordinary energy and spirituality to become a better human. A principle in GARP may reflect that 'The positive thinking methods, which attempt to give people a power to change themselves and improve their lives, would hardly provide the deep conviction and gradual enlightenment required for change.' Only ongoing meditation and realization, to grasp our Self-P more tangibly, might help.
4. *GARP can help us* **realize that couple's need for independence cannot and shouldn't be restricted in relationships.** The new models and principles of relationships should be built around one fundamental fact: That majority of people nowadays find the highest social value in personal independence. This is a prevalent perspective after the advent of the women's lib movement and race equality struggles. Despite the inherent perception of dependence in relationships, as well as humans' instinctual need for dependence, our desire for independence is

overwhelming every thought and action we engage in nowadays. So GARP should advocate this general trend that is preoccupying people. But then, for pursuing this basic principle consistently, there is a high demand on people to plan their personal lives as independently as possible, especially in their relationships. This includes maintaining financial independence, while respecting the spirit of cooperation and teamwork in their relationships more than ever.

5. *GARP can help us* **realize that a dysfunctional relationship must be terminated civilly and easily.** To insist on correcting the inherent personality flaws of our partners, or retaliating relentlessly to make them suffer, is futile and childish. Once we believe in GARP's objectives and the other facts discussed throughout this book, we appreciate our partners' helplessness in terms of their personality flaws and perceptions. With this mindset, we might at last realize the futility of our lifelong struggle to either change our partners to suit our needs, or retaliate in order to make them suffer the way they make us suffer. Partners may realize that adhering to GARP and treating relationships objectively are beyond their patience or capacity. In that case, they must courageously submit to a friendly separation. Ending unmanageable relationships should be a natural and automatic process.

6. *GARP can help us* **realize that the focus for correcting relationship conflicts is not our partner but ourselves.** As stated repeatedly in this book, the only way to make relationships work is by having each partner work on his/her own flaws individually and honestly. They must commit themselves to become a better person regardless

of its benefits for the relationship. A partner's decision to be a better person and how to pursue this impossible mission is a personal matter and challenge. Partners should not pressure each other to become a better person to save their relationship. It would not work this way. It requires personal conviction, which cannot be forced upon someone. A decision to change lies only in the hands of each partner.

The goal of self-awareness is to prepare a partner to curb his/her ego, tolerate relationship flaws better, and accept his/her partner's shortfalls easier, unless the situation deteriorates beyond tolerance.

7. *GARP can help us* **create a means of dealing with our relationships without the need to depend on government or religious rules.** The more comprehensive GARP becomes, and the more it is universally accepted by couples, the less people need the government or religious rules to interfere with their relationships. The clarity of GARP should help couples discuss their relationship bottlenecks objectively and judge the possibility of saving it or terminating it. Relationships start based on goodwill and optimism, yet we may get tired of our partner and wish to leave him or her, which is a natural reaction and must be honoured by everybody. But the main cause of separations nowadays is the lack of principles to guide relationships and to measure their health regularly. If GARP can fill this gap, there would be no need to depend on bureaucratic, expensive, and time-consuming processes of governments to resolve our differences and facilitate separation.

8. *GARP can help us* **establish relationship norms that fit the socioeconomic profile of the new era.** It must also remain dynamic and be modified as humanity progresses into more complex environments. All the evidences indicate that life and lifestyles will get horrifically complex for so many reasons. This is true even if we adopt an optimistic viewpoint and imagine that we would not destroy humanity and the Earth altogether within a few centuries. Nonetheless, GARP should fit the requirements of the time. And it must be dynamic and progressive in order to be effective. For example, partners' need for independence is a main theme of the present era. It has been only a few decades since we, especially women, have become adamant about independence. It has now been integrated within all facets of social life, including relationships. Many other psychological developments and structural changes have occurred in society, including our expanding appetite for compassion and consumption, and children's prominent role and demands in family life. They all affect the format of GARP, but nothing overwhelms GARP's theme in the 21st century as much as partners' unrelenting demands for identity and independence do. Nobody can say with certainty that in a century or so we won't feel exactly the opposite, i.e., demand dependence more heroically. People may finally realize that for real compassion they need to establish some rules of dependence. Suddenly dependence might become the new reality as much as independence is nowadays. This would actually be a rational progression that the author believes will happen. It would reflect a higher level of human maturity, which is a possibility, although so remote.

As discussed in Chapter Two, couples are still not quite aware of the conflict that their prominent demand for individualism has brought about. They are unaware of the scope of conflict that their demand for large levels of both dependence and independence has created in their relationships. They subtly expect relationships to satisfy their need for dependency while they pretend and shout independence publicly. The implicit urge for dependence, while insisting on independence explicitly and noisily, is one of the major hurdles in relationships in the new era. The sad realization we all must face is that we cannot have it both ways; to eat our cake and have it too.

9. *GARP can help us* **provide the guidelines for couple's teamwork.** GARP must be somewhat proactive in terms of suggesting the basic models and principles of teamwork and negotiating. In fact, GARP must be developed with the intention of enforcing teamwork. Couples need tools to help them deal with a large variety of conflicts in relationships. Instead of suggesting all kinds of untested models or ideas, however, GARP's initial guidelines must remain general and flexible while more precise ones are developed and tested gradually. It would take a few decades before a well-crafted set of guidelines, especially for teamwork, is developed by experts and made available to couples.

10. *GARP can help us* **choose the right relationship model and pinpoint the factors of compatibility between couples in order to minimize mismatches.** Based on their personality and needs, partners can choose the right model of relationship for them by using GARP's guidelines. These guidelines might also pinpoint the areas of

potential conflicts between partners according to the relationship model chosen. Instead of looking for compatibility factors, as is the trend presently, GARP may suggest only those principles that can help couples *relate* effectively within the context of their relationship. Preventing mismatches in relationships and pinpointing the areas that conflicts could arise is another objective of GARP. This is different from the task of finding compatible partners. The existing compatibility tests have so far proven inadequate for developing effective relationships. Chapter Thirteen will elaborate on the compatibility topic in some detail.

11. *GARP can help us* **work within a uniform framework to assess our relationships and communicate objectively.** Psychologists and marriage counsellors can communicate amongst themselves according to these guidelines instead of offering a variety of personal or unproven methods. The existing techniques are not focused enough in terms of tackling the roots of relationship problems. So, another objective of GARP is to create a uniform framework and language for psychologists and counsellors. Uniformity would not only make the diagnosis and treatment of relationship conflicts easier and transferable amongst experts, but would also reduce the level of confusion and frustration for couples when each expert suggests something different and none of them works anyway. Couples are already suffering from their relationship conflicts and they don't need to be confused even more. They need a universally tested system to help them one way or another.

12. *GARP can help us* **view *relationships* as an independent, unique entity larger than the sum of the two individuals in it.** R-entity, as a fundamental principle by itself, has to be included in GARP. The idea is to bring objectivity into relationships instead of depending on subjective and unrealistic impressions of couples to define their relationships. Various characteristics of R-entity are listed in GARP for clarity and application. But other principles listed in GARP would support R-entity as well. Chapter Nine provided a detailed discussion about the importance of R-entity and its characteristics. R-entity is the nucleus for developing the relationship framework and related concepts. It is the conceptual platform for us to make our relationships thrive.

The main points discussed in this book, especially the summaries in Part III and the radical points raised in Chapter Eleven, can be included in different sections of GARP. To develop GARP in a logical format, we can start with the list of relationship needs in Table 9.4. Let's assume that this list is a realistic one, and in line with our social values at the present time. The list must be modified regularly, of course, in order to reflect social changes, while keeping the unrealistic expectations out. Every relationship need in Table 9.4 can be expanded into a bunch of principles, which would guide the matter of fulfilling that particular need. A replica of GARP presented at the end of this chapter is created in this manner. That is, every need in Table 9.4 is expanded into a bunch of principles in GARP. Also, the large volume of hypotheses presented in Chapters Thirteen through Sixteen can be gradually verified and included in GARP to increase couples' understanding about relationships, their hurdles, etc. In Chapter Sixteen alone, five hundred points are raised about relationships and many of them can be included in GARP.

GARP's Main Challenge

The main challenge is, obviously, to convince couples and society to adopt GARP and the 'relationship framework.' GARP should replace their personal whims and perceptions about relationships. Couples should buy into the idea of lesser expectations from relationships. They should accept the responsibility of observing the needs of their relationships despite their conflicting personal urges and egos.

In all, it is rather easy to develop a set of simple principles for couples to understand and apply in their relationships. They only have to show interest and a mental capacity to function within an objective framework. But convincing couples to replace their emotional decision processes with GARP would be difficult. The process of implementing GARP would require a lot of learning and adjusting. This would take time and patience. Meanwhile, we should keep our faith in GARP as a viable solution to our relationship problems. Actually, GARP may be the only solution, in the author's opinion, to manage our relationships better.

Nonetheless, it would also be naïve to assume that companionship needs of individuals, such a complex subject it is, can be solved by any mechanism (e.g., GARP) quickly. Those very same problems and hurdles that prevent us from finding a suitable companion or maintaining a relationship, as discussed in Part I, would also affect the implementation of new mechanisms to a great extent. Resistance to change would be a major hurdle. Mostly our Ego-P and conditioned mentality about viewing relationships in certain ways would stop us from changing our attitude. Logically, a fair and sensible GARP should be adopted quickly by everybody and pursued for their own benefit. But in reality, overcoming our old habits and urges to entertain GARP or other mechanisms would be difficult. Accountants have developed Generally Accepted Accounting Principles (GAAP) to guide them in their financial dealing and wheeling. They are supposed to use GAAP to communicate amongst themselves efficiently and ethically. They have accepted GAAP and sworn to observe it. But they often forget their commitment to GAAP when profit motives supersede their sense of obligation to a higher cause. In our crooked society, even chartered banks and certified investment managers cheat and ignore their obligations. People lose their life savings left and right. Also, we have all kinds of traffic rules and guidelines developed for the safety of the public, but our personal ego and temper make us disregard those rules even at the cost of our own lives and the risk of severe punishments. In relationships, the complex emotional issues make it even more difficult to maintain a sense of commitment to GARP easily. Nonetheless, GAAP helps accountants a lot and our traffic laws bring major order to our lives despite the drunken idiots who intentionally disobey the laws and kill people. Society is benefiting, nonetheless, from GAAP and traffic laws and all the other general rules we enforce to coordinate our thoughts and actions. It is time to benefit from GARP too. Or, at least, we must begin to envision such a mechanism so that people can benefit from it in a couple of centuries from now.

GARP might appear doomed at the outset by its attempt to generalize some ideas that touch individuals' emotions and urges. The idea of formulating some principles about relationships by pursuing logical analyses and reasoning sounds absurd already. GARP appears like a bizarre approach in a society where objectivity and logic seem to have lost their meanings. Obviously, both our personal needs and relationship expectations are extremely deep-rooted and emotional. Their psychological effects and power are controlling our mindset and faith. In all, relationships and couples' behaviour are too complex to be studied scientifically so easily. Yet the idea of introducing GARP appears to be the only option left for society to mend the chaotic state of relationships. Of course, it is clear that applying rules to relationship issues, and human behaviour in general, has its limitations. Accordingly, the development of GARP will be gradual, partially based on trial and error. GARP must remain dynamic and progressive according to new findings and research.

At the very least, GARP can help us recognize the causes of relationship problems. It can heighten our awareness about our personal flaws and limitations gradually and we may learn how they affect our relationships. It may increase our sensitivity to admit that our partners' flaws and limitations are crippling them; they are unaware of those flaws or unable to do something about them. GARP may prove a useful instrument and be accepted universally as a reasonable means of coping with our complex social settings. It may show how social changes are impacting our personal needs and perceptions about everything. It may identify the factors of success in relationships. At the very least, it may help us understand the role we are expected to play even if we are unwilling or unable to adopt it due to our stubborn personalities.

GARP can possibly help a small group of people initially until it is propagated naturally in society after its benefits are proven. Two groups of people may never need or care about GARP. The first group consists of those lucky individuals who somehow find a good companion according to their simple rules and managed expectations. We all envy these blessed couples. At the other extreme, some people are so defective psychologically that no rules or reasons can help them overcome their rampant urges and crooked personalities. Others, those falling between these two extremes, the majority of us, have manageable levels of psychological defects and destructive urges. This majority might eventually appreciate the potential of GARP, despite their inherent resistance to change.

We humans have limited ability to listen, let alone learn, about the concepts that threaten our crooked convictions and deep-rooted idiosyncrasies. So believing in GARP wouldn't be an easy task, never mind practicing it. Yet we must remain hopeful that somehow some of us will benefit from GARP sooner or later.

Is developing GARP feasible?

Developing new guidelines for relationships is a great challenge in terms of its mechanics. But getting experts' universal acceptance of its contents is the hardest part. So, the answer to the feasibility of developing GARP is a reserved yes. The reservation is about the timeframe when all the feasible principles are considered 'acceptable' as social norms and included in GARP. The other obvious reservation is the timeframe for the majority of people to develop the right mindset for adopting GARP.

Yet creating GARP is not an impossible task. It can be easily developed around the factors listed in Table 9.4—the realistic relationship needs. All we need for creating GARP is innovative ideas (e.g., the hypotheses in Chapter Sixteen) that can explain relationships in the existing social environment. We need principles that can curtail the level of relationship frictions. We know the basics already. Individualism and independence have become the dominating themes of the new society. So we have the platform to build principles around these basic needs of individuals. We have to identify a practical balance between couples' personal needs and the relationship needs in the new era and define those boundaries in GARP. Once we pinpoint the conflicts between personal needs and the relationship needs, we should be able to devise effective principles and then learn to live with our choices in harmony.

So, in the author's opinion, it is feasible to create GARP as soon as we agree that we need it. After all, we are all after the same objective: to be happier in our relationships. But again, when we examine the reality, applying GARP may not become a universal concept until the 22nd century. In this book, the author is choosing the year 2115 as a reasonable timeframe for GARP being fully developed and finding a universal acceptance. This arbitrary date may appear too optimistic or pessimistic depending on the viewpoints of various groups. The author realizes this fact as well. Chapter Fourteen addresses the barriers and a projection of socio-economic stages leading to the development of GARP.

Nonetheless, this book is suggesting some ideas about the need for relationship principles and it also provides a replica of GARP. Let's hope they will prove fruitful as stepping stones for further thoughts and discussions during the next hundred years. All this book is hoping to achieve is to spread the seeds for future thoughts.

How can GARP be developed and propagated?

Despite its low chance for universal acceptance in the immediate future, GARP must be developed and expanded continuously based on trial and error and research findings of scholars. It helps if scholars and interested groups get involved as soon as possible. The general public should recognize the benefits of GARP and ask for its development. Once a platform is defined and accepted by prominent sociologists, psychologists, and the population at large, modifying and expanding GARP would be an automatic process like all other social processes in progressive societies of the future. We just have to remain optimistic and hope that future societies are given a chance to flourish out of the chaos we have created for ourselves and our children. Hopefully a non-profit foundation can be created to oversee the development and dissemination of GARP.

The success of GARP depends on our conviction about its ability to help relationships. But, the author believes, that this task would be somehow imposed upon us, whether we like it or not, sooner or later. We will be forced eventually to do something about the agony of relationships and the lack of principles. We will soon get fed up with our arbitrary assessments of relationships and our emotional decisions about the level of tolerance needed in relationships. Our children will hopefully learn from our mistakes and shattered hopes to find a soul mate. It is just a matter of time and the level of our stubbornness to pursue idealism.

GARP will be built around the relationship needs identified in Table 9.4 or a similar list (as well as the hypotheses in Chapter Sixteen). It will be an extension of the relationship needs with more details and instructions for practical application. So every 'relationship need' is represented by a dozen or more principles to address many aspects and mechanism to fulfil those needs.

In terms of how to propagate GARP, the answer is to simply introduce it at as many public forums and social gatherings as possible. Experts must advocate the objectives of this book. They must find innovative ways of informing the public about the flaws of our existing ways. They must do more empirical research and be more proactive in terms of changing couples' mindsets about relationships. Books can help us comprehend our personality flaws in terms of dealing with others, especially our partners. They must show that animosity, arrogance, and retaliation are unproductive, because they make it more difficult for people to perceive each other's intentions correctly and react to them humanly. We may also realize that as human beings, with the objective of reaching our deep potentials, we are wasting too much time and energy on the petty problems of relationships. This is absurd and a sin.

Despite the major initial resistance, the advantages of GARP will become clear when managing relationships gets totally out of control and couples' frustration cripples society. Liberal and logical individuals begin to join in and adopt GARP in order to test new options for their relationships.

They will support the rather radical approaches with open minds. The outcome will eventually encourage sceptical individuals to join the movement, too, in order to mitigate their hardships and loneliness.

It is beyond the scope of this book to explain the mechanisms of developing GARP in detail. But the principles discussed throughout this book provide enough material to start the process.

A Replica of GARP

The following replica of GARP is presented only as an example of ideas that could be included in GARP. It is not meant to be complete or correct. It is mainly prepared by expanding the relationship needs of Table 9.4. Eventually it should be expanded to also include a large number of radical solutions like the ones proposed in Chapter Eleven as well as the hypotheses (five hundred) listed in Chapter Sixteen. The principles included in GARP can be grouped and presented in a layman format in the future to make it easy for the general public's understanding. But for this basic document, the same order of Table 9.4 is more or less followed. GARP must be organized in sections, such as the following:

Part I: Structure of GARP
Part II: Relationship Success Factors
Part III: Social Mechanisms Supporting GARP

Part I: Structure of GARP

In this part, the main structure of the 'Relationship Framework' and GARP is explained:

P1. Relationships are perceived as an independent entity, which has specific needs and priorities. This universal concept is referred to as R-entity.

    P1.1 Relationship needs are different from partners' needs.

    P1.2 R-entity is not driven by partners' personal needs or personality.

    P1.3 Relationship needs supersede partners' needs.

    P1.4 Relationship needs are developed based on social settings and trends.

    P1.5 Relationship needs are dynamic and in line with social changes.

P2. Partners in a relationship are independent financially and emotionally, though partners can agree on a different arrangement at the outset.

    P2.1 Individualism and independence are the norms of society.

    P2.2 Individualism and independence set the boundaries for partners to establish their personal expectations.

    P2.3 Exceptions to the principle P2.2 are specifically noted in a contract between partners. This refers mostly to financial independence of partners, but could apply to any other condition deemed necessary for a particular relationship.

P3. Partners are familiar with the Relationship Framework and its components in detail before entering a relationship.

    P3.1 The 'Relationship Framework' provides a setting for couples to relate and communicate effectively with minimum frictions.

P3.2 The Relationship Framework has six components as follows:
- R-entity
- Partners' commitment to teamwork
- Relationship expectations
- Relationship models
- Relationship principles—GARP
- Relationship needs (success factors)

P3.3 The above components are explained in Subsections __ thru __.

P4. Partners follow the guidelines of the Relationship Framework actively.

P5. Partners keep their expectations at the level pinpointed in the table presented in Subsection P5.1.

P5.1 The realistic relationship expectations are:

1. Sex
2. Communication
3. Compassion
4. Companionship
5. Teamwork
6. M-love
7. Friendship
8. Respect- Social acceptance
9. Personal Success

P6. Partners know the repercussions of pushing the expectations in the table presented in Subsection P6.1.

P6.1 The unrealistic relationship expectations are:

1. Dependence
2. Security
3. S-love
4. E-love
5. Trust
6. Happiness
7. Commitment
8. Longevity

Part II: Relationship Success Factors

In this part, the characteristics of a successful relationship are listed in line with the factors enumerated in Table 9.4. A relationship would be successful if:

P7. Partners are attracted to each other with good chemistry.
P8. Partners can relate actively and have compatible lifestyles and preferences.
P9. Partners strive for self-awareness to enhance their Self-P and S-love.
P10. Partners know the intensity and chaos of misperceptions and avoid its traps.
P11. Partners know how everybody's personality is shaped and controlled by forces beyond their control. They understand the flaws of human nature and companionship hurdles.
P12. Partners don't blame each other constantly for their idiosyncrasies.
P13. Partners know how to maintain good communication between them.
P14. Partners enjoy having sex together.
  14.1 Partners don't use sex as a tool for blackmailing one another.
P15. Partners are mostly engaged in teamwork to run their family affairs.
P16. Partners are compassionate and know how to show it too.
P17. Partners are good friends. They know the rules of friendship and stick to them.

- **P18.** Partners don't try to change each other or push their lifestyles on each other.
- **P19.** Partners strive sincerely to develop trust between them, but don't make too much fuss about mistrust.
- **P20.** Partners don't try to manipulate, control, or intimidate each other.
- **P21.** Partner respect each other even though they know about and tolerate each other's idiosyncrasies.
- **P22.** Partners are capable of promoting each others' pursuit of social ambitions.
- **P23.** Partners can support each other to pursue their personal goals.
- **P24.** Partners are aware of the Ego-P, Model-P, and Self-P aspects of personality and their roles in their communications. They monitor the positive or negative impacts of these personality aspects in their lives.
- **P25.** Partners know the meaning and implications of E-love, M-love, and S-love in their relationships.
- **P26.** Partners have chosen the right relationship model that best fit their personalities and personal needs.
- **P27.** Partners respect the boundaries set by their relationship model.
- **P28.** Partners are familiar with, and actively follow, GARP—as the main principles of relationships. They use GARP to stay objective in their relationship.
- **P29.** Partners seek mediation and consultation when disagreements arise.
- **P30.** Partners stay honest and maintain their integrity.
- **P31.** Partners are mentally prepared to leave their relationship in peace when reconciliation is not possible.

P32. Partners never adhere to retaliation to convince each other about something.
P33. Partners are basically tactful, mature, forgiving, patient and mentally stable.
P34. Partners don't play games with each other.
P35. Partners don't depend on the government or religion to regulate their relationship.
P36. Partners have signed a contract at the beginning of their relationship to govern the financial and other aspects of their relationship, especially for separation.
P37. Partners envision the termination of relationships as a normal incident in the new era.
P38. Partners believe that termination of relationships should be civil and quick.
P39. Partners measure the state of their relationship regularly and discuss the contentious issues calmly.

Part III: Social Mechanisms Supporting GARP

In this part, all the mechanisms to promote GARP and the 'Relationship Framework' are listed:

P40. Social systems and mechanisms are modified to support and propagate GARP.
P41. Legal systems in particular adjust their processes and laws to minimize its interference in relationships.
　P41.1 The adjustments by the legal system and laws are for promoting individuals' independence.
　P41.2 The legal system ensures that people understand that they are depending on themselves to protect their own rights in relation ships instead of relying on the government to do it for them.

P42. Educational systems teach the relationship framework and its components to the general public, especially to young individuals.

P42.1 The relationship framework, expectations, and needs should be taught to all senior high school students as required courses.

P42.2 The passing grades and requirements for completing relationship courses at high schools are set extremely high and monitored by the Board of Education regularly. The relationship courses are treated most seriously.

Chapter Eleven
Radical Solutions

The radical solutions suggested in this chapter are bound to draw a lot of criticism and controversy. They might appear absurd, against our values, and even offensive to some people. Actually, some of the ideas presented so far might have already appeared offensive or naïve to some readers. So, it is repeated that the ultimate objective of this book, including the following discussions about 'radical solutions,' is only to explore better options for our relationships. This book has little value to those readers who believe that the existing situation is fine. But for those of us who are tired of the present atmosphere, we must embrace drastic changes if we are really looking for tangible results. Many drastic changes are already happening like the idea of 'open marriage,' which many modern couples are adopting in order to cope with their relationship dilemmas. But these overly drastic, desperate changes have brought us only more depression and shame. So we need more measured changes and a framework to redefine relationships more ethically and realistically. We must reassess socioeconomic conditions in our modern society as soon as possible before the situation becomes even more ridiculous than what it has become already. Are not we supposedly the most intelligent creatures of God?

The goal is to somehow manage our relationships better and give everybody, especially our children, a healthier environment to live in. The mission is a sacred one, although some of the ideas suggested in this chapter might appear absurd initially. Unfortunately, it appears that only radical solutions might reverse the fast-deteriorating state of relationships. By the way, radical isn't meant to imply immediate. It is acknowledged that these radical solutions will take decades to reach full fruition. The solutions proposed in this chapter should be viewed as a long-term vision for the 22nd century. But we must start our discussions and studies now. With this preliminary disclaimer, hopefully the readers would ponder the ideas in this chapter with open minds.

The discussions in the previous chapters suggested the need for partners' proactive role in relationships. It was suggested that, to stay practical, one should be prepared to embrace a rather pessimistic perspective of relationships, lower one's expectations, and adopt GARP too as it becomes available. The idea is to rebuild our mindsets according to the new realities of relationships in line with the drastic social changes in the last few decades. In the present atmosphere, the first thought for any person looking for a companion should be whether they both understand the intricacies and risks of relationships, have developed the right mindsets for encountering the inevitable setbacks, and whether they are enough mature, independent, and strong to deal with both the expected headaches of being in a relationship and when it falls apart. Forget about the old mindset that relationships can solve our problems, and forget about the old mindset that relationships can bring happiness and a chance for reliance on another individual.

The relationship framework suggested in the previous chapters is a good platform for couples to develop a new mindset. Yet, for this framework to operate effectively, society as a whole, including scholars and governments must be involved as well. They must suggest and implement some mechanisms in line with the characteristics of the new framework. The old mechanisms, e.g., our legal system, cannot satisfy the requirements of the new framework and relationships. On the other hand, new social mechanisms can force couples to reassess their conflicting values in society and relationships and redefine their positions more clearly. (For example, refer to our discussions about people's struggle nowadays for both independence and dependence in Chapter Two.)

So, in line with the new mindset required for partners, social mechanisms should be revamped to support the new social mentality and relationship needs. The scholars' and governments' interest would demonstrate the urgency for a new vision of relationships to improve socioeconomic conditions in the long-run. It would also encourage a gradual interest by the general public to join in and give the new vision a universal acceptance. Obviously, individuals' mindsets and social values affect each other drastically. So they must be scrutinized simultaneously. Our coordinated efforts to propagate the new realities in relationships would expedite the process of change. And developing social mechanisms to support the new mindset and values are essential, too, of course.

The discussions in this chapter might appear more relevant to social studies and beyond the immediate interest of the general public. But people's support of these ideas is essential before governments get involved. People should in fact demand these changes. It is the task of this book, and similar discussions in the future, to convince both people and governments that the existing relationship environment is only making us suffer and it has economic repercussions too. We must all believe that a different type of setting must be developed for relationships in the new era and propagated.

To identify the needed radical solutions, we can simply draw on the lists of relationship expectations and needs, as well as GARP, which were presented in the previous chapters. Tables 11.1 and 11.2 are copied from Tables 9.2 and 9.3 respectively to help us with the discussions in this chapter. Radical solutions are basically meant to facilitate partners' understanding of their realistic versus unrealistic expectations, in line with new social values. The idea is to introduce innovative social mechanisms that support the process of partners' mental adjustment.

Table 11.1
Realistic Relationship Expectations

1. Sex
2. Communication
3. Compassion
4. Companionship
5. Teamwork
6. M-love
7. Friendship
8. Respect - Social acceptance
9. Personal Success

Table 11.2
Unrealistic Relationship Expectations

1. Dependence
2. Security
3. S-love
4. E-love
5. Trust
6. Happiness
7. Commitment
8. Longevity

The reasons why the relationship expectations in Table 11.2 are unrealistic were discussed Chapter Nine. It was also suggested that if partners could satisfy the basic expectations of Table 11.1, the expectations in Table 11.2 would be realized automatically too. But if they keep insisting on the unrealistic expectations of Table 11.2, none of the expectations in either table would be satisfied. This simple fact reveals the irony of relationships. That is, we spend our energy on wrong values and thus lose sight of the ones that could give us everything we need and more.

To identify the new social mechanisms, we must first understand the social trends and major changes in lifestyles. They reflect people's mentality regarding their personal needs, which then impact their behaviour in their relationships. The following trends are noticeable in the new era:

1. Social complexities, phony values, egotism, sexuality, and personal needs are rising as society progresses and prospers. Thus relationships are becoming too complex and difficult to define and tolerate.
2. Our expectations from relationships have risen because we consider relationship needs an extension of our personal needs.
3. People's stress level keeps rising every year due to socio-economic and career demands as well as relationship conflicts.
4. Nowadays we find our relationships less tolerable than what we had imagined them at the outset.
5. People's agony due to relationships, whether they have a partner or not, keeps increasing continuously.
6. Each partner considers his/her individuality and independence the most important needs, in and outside of

his/her relationship. We consider ourselves important and deserving to live a full and happy life. If relationships hinder these needs in some ways, we always choose our welfare above that of our partner and relationship as a whole. We want out if our high aspirations are hindered.

7. Considering the above facts, our commitment to our partner and relationship is at best only conditional. It means that we keep our commitment to stay in a relationship only if our partner and relationship fulfil our personal needs and keep us happy.
8. Often we make that determination (about the wellness of our relationship) based on our selfish perceptions and misleading values.
9. With our current approach and attitude, we will face more conflicts in relationships every year, and become more impatient too.
10. All the above conditions appear to be accelerating fast in close correlation with changes in social values and complexity.
11. The rate of relationship failures will increase as our personal needs and social complexity increase.
12. The overall trends show that we should expect more of all the above facts in the years to come.

These trends clearly demonstrate the sad fate of our relationships unless we act quickly. We must review the existing environment seriously and adjust our mentality. We also need corresponding mechanisms to both encourage and handle the new social mentality. The overall features of these needed adjustments are discussed below.

Adjustments to Couples' Mentality

All the ideas in this book, especially the outlined conclusions in Part III (over six hundred points) are essential for changing couples' mindset. Some of the more radical points are listed in Table 11.3 as examples.

Table 11.3: Main Adjustments to Couples' Mentality

1. Partners must reduce their expectations from relationships drastically.
2. Partners must know the specific relationship expectations and needs (Tables 8.2 and 9.4) before entering relationships. They must also be mentally equipped and willing to observe these relationship needs and expectations.
3. Partners must learn, and be willing, to relate to each other within the boundaries of the relationship framework (Table 9.1). They must identify the relationship model that best fits their needs and personalities (Diagram 12.3).
4. Partners should view relationships as a temporary arrangement, unless they do all the right things (which would be somewhat unlikely for most people).
5. Partners should be prepared to leave their relationships with open mind, without fuss or retaliation and before they start to hate each other.
6. Partners should view their relationship as an independent entity like a business enterprise. The concept of R-entity.
7. Couples should not look up to the government to resolve their relationship squabbles. Rather, they should depend on their initial contracts that outline their commitments to one another at the outset.
8. Couples should remember that love, ethics, and religion are not reliable mechanisms for authenticating or protecting their relationships. The vows exchanged in those settings are good only for glamorizing our feelings and ceremonies.

Adjustments to Social Mechanisms

The main adjustments required for social mechanisms are listed in Table 11.4. The concepts in Tables 11.3 and 11.4 correspond almost line by line, and together they present a new perspective for relationships. This supports the idea that new mechanisms must fit our emerging mentality.

Table 11.4: Adjustments to Social Mechanisms

1. Support and propagate the idea of partners' individuality and independence.
2. Support and propagate the idea of partners' financial responsibility.
3. Support and teach the details of the 'relationship framework' to the public.
4. Support the idea of time-bounded relationships in legal channels.
5. Support and propagate the idea of relationships being viewed as an independent entity like a business enterprise. The concept of R-entity.
6. Support and spread the idea of limiting the government role in relationships.
7. Support, and participate in, all kinds of research to enhance the quality of a universal 'relationship framework.' GARP and the relationship framework should replace the outmoded guidelines of religion and inefficient laws.

How can we achieve everything listed in Tables 11.3 and 11.4? Even the very first condition in Table 11.3 (reducing our expectations) is obviously a tough challenge for everybody. Yet couples would eventually realize that changing their mentality and reducing their expectations is the only way to strengthen their relationships and enrich their personal lives too. Many couples are already making some ultra-radical changes in their mentality, such as accepting open marriage as an option for enduring their relationships. These types of extremes are neither practical nor ethical. They would only make us sicker and more desperate.

The fact that couples go to these extremes in our so-called modern society is actually the best clue that we urgently need some kind of moderate changes in our mindset about relationships. The changes suggested in this chapter will mitigate the need for ultra radical options (e.g., open marriage). We need new mechanisms before other desperate options become an epidemic, just for tolerating our relationships. We need open-minded marriages, not open marriages.

This whole book is for the purpose of adjusting our personal mentality about relationships. Particularly, the discussions in Part I about couples' view of personality and inner forces are useful for developing a more practical (and healthier) mentality. More discussions about personal mental adjustments, as noted in Table 11.3, will come in the future chapters too. So this chapter mostly emphasizes on the items noted in Table 11.4, about the need for new social mechanisms.

It is a fact that people's real needs are undermined nowadays by the existing socioeconomic mechanisms. For example, while looking for tranquility and peace of mind, people are encouraged to pursue materialistic lifestyles. Our political and economic systems have failed us as miserably as our social systems. All the mechanisms developed within these systems have proven inept or careless, not to mention our leaders, the greedy executives of major institutions, the police, stock exchange, court system, religions, educational systems, and all the rest of them. These mechanisms bring us more stress and depression instead of tranquility. Depending on such an incompetent environment to sort out our relationship mechanisms has proven equally inefficient too. So, we should try to at least minimize our dependence on these systems for sorting out our relationship needs and emotional conundrums.

In the following, the items listed in Table 11.4 are reviewed, with the aim of developing plausible social mechanisms and radical solutions.

1. Support and propagate the idea of partners' individuality and independence.

Laws and social mechanisms are supposed to be in line with people's needs. In the last few decades, however, people's personal and relationship needs have skyrocketed without governments having an opportunity to adapt their mechanisms with these new needs. The main hurdle is that people's fast-expanding needs (e.g., for identity and independence) remain ambiguous even to them as they strive relentlessly for that elusive freedom and happiness. Too many misperceptions have infected people's minds and expectations. For example, while couples insist on independence, they still want the government to protect their rights in relationships. This might not come across as a contradiction. But it is if we examine its practical implications. First of all, we know that most relationship quarrels and breakdowns nowadays are caused by partners' obsession for individualism and materialism. We have also become too sensitive and get offended quickly when our ego is even slightly bruised. And we feel too sad and incomplete when our lifestyle is not as perfect as our daydreams. So we imagine a happier life with a different partner. We are quick to abandon our relationships because we imagine it is not giving us enough independence or luxury. Yet we play the role of compromising and modest partners at the time of starting our relationships. We hide our greed and our need for independence, because they are not such a flattering attributes to brag about. We don't want to put off our partner early on. The point is that if couples didn't rely on courts to grant them financial compensation for being in a relationship, their true mentality would have been revealed before entering their relationships and many couples wouldn't have ended up in bad relationships based on trust and goodwill.

Many individuals still view their relationships as a source of financial security and dependence on someone else's struggle for money, while at the same time they emphasize on their independence in relationships. There is definitely some kind of inconsistency in cases like these. For this group at least, the existing rule to split the assets of partners 50/50 (or something like that) after separation is hypocritical. This is only an example of governments' lack of initiative to deal with financial matters of relationships more fairly and realistically. This rule, in the author's opinion, is a major cause of so many separations in the new era. When a partner realizes the amount of money he/she can get by terminating a relationship, or just for punishing his/her crooked partner, he/she simply cannot bypass the opportunity of separating. So the government is indirectly responsible for a large number of separations. The existing asset distribution mechanism at the time of separation is a silly copout. It has evolved only because courts are not equipped to make a fair assessment of relationship variables including its financial assets. People and governments are careless about the ambiguity and damages (financial and emotional) caused by the existing social mechanisms.

In recent decades, laws and mechanisms have been modified only to deal with the *symptoms* of relationship failures and not the changes in the mentality of couples. Courts have been involved in financial settlements and child-custodies, with ineffective outcomes anyway. But these legal mechanisms have not addressed the new relationship needs and couples' expectations in new societies. The government has not yet dealt with the changes in people's mindset, which is the cause of all the existing conflicts in relationships. People's mindset, especially at the time of terminating their once precious relationships, is the matter requiring an immediate attention.

Of course, it is hard to find the right social mechanisms when citizens' needs remain cluttered even for themselves. Couples don't know how to go about figuring out their true needs in a society overwhelmed by the ideas of consumerism and phony means of happiness. Many superficial needs have tainted relationships and couples are not scientists to sort them out. They just feel those needs because everybody else around them feels the same needs and pushes the same values in their relationships. Meanwhile, the government is already too busy with so many urgent socioeconomic matters to worry about the real causes of relationship failures. So it just deals with the symptoms of this social chaos the best it can at a high cost to taxpayers. Governments are just waiting idly by for the course of history to define the relationship needs eventually. In that sense, neither governments nor couples are proactive enough in appreciating and remedying the true problems of relationships.

As a general rule, couples' need for individualism, not to mention their idiosyncrasies, would not allow them to compromise about their relationship expectations. Their greed would make them competitive and vengeful. These are the facts that couples ignore at the start of a relationship. They are rather careless initially because they are depending on the government to make up for their lack of practicality and sincerity at the outset. Their naivety about the potential niceties of relationships makes them ignore their partners' inherent greediness and ever-increasing need for independence and self-gratification.

For clarity, now let's look at this picture from the opposite angle: Let's assume that there were no courts to rule on the arguments raised in relationships. Under this circumstance, now suddenly partners realize the need to become more proactive and blunt. They would try to find ways of protecting themselves in case their relationship fails. They would now really exercise their authority as independent individuals and write a *contract* that outlines their expectations. It provides the clear terms of settlement at the time of separation. This approach and mentality have many advantages that will be explained in the upcoming pages. But the main feature of this approach is that it emphasizes on partners' true independence in setting the parameters of their future life together. It is true independence because partners would consider all the available information about each other and decide independently whether to start their partnership, and according to what logical terms. Whether their decisions would be perfect or flawed is irrelevant because they, as independent individuals, make those decisions. Of course, couples can always depend on professional advice to prepare the right contract for them. Actually, when new mechanisms are in place, so many standard documents would be out there available for couples to use for choosing a proper relationship model and the type of contract that best suits their needs. We are not still talking about the mechanisms at this point. They will be elaborated later. Here we are only trying to examine the concept.

The absence of government to meddle with relationship decisions would strengthen the concept of individualism. It would empower couples' sense of independence when the responsibility of taking care of their personal interests is left to them. They learn to scrutinize on all the potential problems and scenarios, and then plan their needs and expectations in advance. This exercise makes them more careful at the outset and less frustrated at the end when separation becomes imminent. This is what people want and that is what they should get. It is time for governments to treat people like mature, independent citizens instead of a bunch of careless, irresponsible individuals needing protection at all levels even with regard to their emotional issues. This process also would make couples more open and sincere about their needs. They would understand the implications of being independent in their decisions before entering a relationship or leaving it when they cannot tolerate it. They take charge of their own destiny. And those people who are only pretending to be independent can finally abandon their indecision and hypocrisy. They have to learn to become independent, like everybody else, instead of only pretending it with so much noise and rage. Those who prefer (or need) to depend on their partners should make it clear in their contracts.

The absence of government makes couples smarter and more cautious about their relationships. This new approach would change people's mindset and attitude. There will be less unfit relationships. And couples stay in their relationships longer, because they have initially thought through the stages of their relationships more realistically, especially the heartbreaking ending that a majority of relationships faces nowadays.

In general, partners can resolve their conflicts in five ways through:
  i. love and trust,
  ii. logic and compromise,
  iii. courts,
  iv. contract,
  v. contract plus a combination of the above methods.

Obviously, partners cannot rely on the options (i) and (ii) above to solve their conflicts or finalize their separation. It would be a waste of paper to explain why, though so much of the reasoning can be found in this book already, especially in Part III. So, nowadays, couples wait until the relationship is totally damaged and then resort to courts to make all the financial and emotional decisions for them. But if they had a contract to set the boundaries at the outset, then not only they could resolve their conflicts without hassle, they might indeed take actions to avoid conflicts and prolong their relationship. The ideal (most optimistic) method would be option (v), which depends mostly on a contract, but hopefully utilizes partners' love and logic as well. The bottom line is that having a contract is necessary in the new era for couples to manage their relationships. It should become mandatory. That is, governments must begin to minimize their role in mediation and resolving relationship issues.

Many aspects of a relationship (marriage) can be planned for efficiently in a contract. The major role of a contract is to bring total transparency into relationships, especially about the contentious areas that are so prevalent nowadays. Another major benefit of a contract is that the ambiguity of the present situation would be resolved to a great extent. Those people who count on courts' mercy to exploit their spouses would be eliminated from the process of corrupting relationships and ruining the social mentality in general. Standard contract forms can provide a variety of options for couples to choose from and to address their special needs easily. For example, the matter of child custody and support can be agreed upon at the outset by choosing one of maybe two-dozen options that can be predefined in standard contracts. Couples could agree on joint custody or one partner taking the custody of their children after separation, with certain visitation rights. The matter of child custody and child support could be also linked or not. For example, in one option, the parent taking the custody would be responsible for all or most of the expenses. It might seem reasonable to some couples that the partner having all the joy of raising a kid should pay for its expenses too. But there are many other options, of course, to choose from based on couples' preferences. The amount of child support would be easy to set up at the outset, too, in case the contract stipulates that one partner should pay child support to the other. The amount of child support could be based on a percentage of the government's child support rate every year, which is set at a reasonable cost of living index. For example, a couple may agree that child support should be at 200% or 80% of the government announced rate for the years subsequent to their separation. For these cases, if the government rate is $500 a month, the partner paying the child support would be paying $1,000 or $400 a month (i.e., 200% or 80% rates respectively). To be honest, the author cannot see why some children should be spoiled more than average children in a modern society? Why should wealth have anything to do with child support? These symptoms are all part of our crooked social values when we assume that some kids should be spoiled more than others because of their parents' wealth. Nonetheless, setting child support at a percentage of the government rate would take care of this matter anyway. Some couples may wish to negotiate at the outset to set the child support at ten or fifty times the government rate, if they really want to. Whatever! The whole point is to be clear about it at the beginning. All of these terms must be stipulated clearly in the initial contract or through future modifications made to the contract only by mutual agreement. No judge should have a right to override these contracts either.

By the way, the concept of couples signing a relationship contract is not new or unromantic. For many centuries, a form of contract has helped couples stipulate their expectations and boundaries according to cultures and religions. Only in the new cultures a preference for ambiguity has found ground, because signing a contract seems unromantic, and also because a group of people benefit from this ambiguity.

The matter of alimony follows the same logic. That is, couples must agree initially whether alimony is necessary at all. With all the push for independence in the new era, the matter of one partner paying alimony to the other sounds hypocritical. Nonetheless, it is possible to include a formula also for alimony, as a percentage of the government rate for a reasonable alimony in line with the cost of living.

The matter of having kids at all and who must accept the role of the supervising parent is becoming somewhat sensitive nowadays too. Even though many couples might use nannies, still the matter of raising children versus following one's career might cause arguments between spouses. One way to settle this issue is to make the partner who insists on having children accept the main role in raising them while the methods and degree of the other partner's involvement are also negotiated in advance and recorded in their marriage contract. Actually, the question of having kids at all would become even more crucial in the future. Partners must decide carefully whether they are prepared and capable of raising children. Sometime in the far future, people might even be given a right to sue their parents for bringing them into this chaotic world or for their way of raising them. This is a good policy for making people more responsible for creating children. Why should children suffer in this crazy world—in dysfunctional families, corrupt societies, and polluted environments? Making children should become a calculated decision by intelligent parents rather than a selfish act to enrich their own lives, or even for socioeconomic purposes of governments. We have to think more about the creatures who must face the social chaos and not their parents' happiness or manpower needs.

2. Support and spread the idea of partners' financial responsibility.

The modification of the government role in relationships has the highest impact on the financial independence of partners. Instead of courts deciding about the distribution of assets at the time of separation, partners agree at the outset, independently and objectively, on a system that fits their expectations. Most relationship quarrels are about financial issues, because partners' expectations at the time of separation are significantly different from what they had expected (or expressed) at the outset.

Each relationship has its unique characteristics and must have a specific financial format that best fits its partners' needs at the time of starting the relationship and they must document everything. Of course, partners can adopt one of the many standard formats suitable for the majority of relationships. The format of contracts is flexible enough to accommodate partners' specific needs when necessary. Nonetheless, every relationship has a financial format, in which partners contribute to the household budget based on their income. This format would accommodate the situation where one partner is not working, temporarily or permanently. But beyond their contributions to the family budget, partners keep the rest of their income. They might invest it as they wish without the need to report their dealings to their partners. Couples could invest together, too, or share information about their investments. But the old mechanism that partners should know about, and interfere, with each other's financial affair is no longer valid. Each partner has total independence to make and invest his/her money. Withholding the information about one's income or investments would not be considered rude or illegal. Partners' sense of entitlement to know everything doesn't make sense in an era where everybody advocates independence and equality. The purpose of the contract is to mitigate the effect of the contentious areas of conflict between partners. This fits nicely within the overall objective of the relationship framework. A contract forces partners to focus on teamwork, the welfare of the family, and setting a proper family budget, which includes all facets of their lives including the mortgage and other long-term financial needs of the family. What each partner does with his/her money—outside their family budget—is his/her business. Partners' attempt to control each other's financial affairs, by constant nagging or through some outmoded methods, would become unnecessary. Most of these finer points would be systematically outlined in the contracts and they would all become standard practices for rational couples.

3. Support and teach the details of the 'relationship framework' to the public.

The welfare of the public and the prosperity of society are the main objectives of any government. As such it has a vested interest in supporting a type of relationship framework that may support partners' companionship needs most effectively and efficiently. Government shouldn't leave this important task to chance and hope that things would work out nicely on their own in society. In the past, couples depended on religions and cultures to define and regulate relationships. Now that those modes are no longer functional, it is important that governments play a more prominent role in two fronts: **First,** minimize its interference with the *symp-*

toms of relationship failures. (This would make people more vigilant about the purposes and potentials of relationships and more proactive in terms of finding solutions.) **And second,** promote the guidelines of the 'relationship framework' as a fundamental social structure for couples to follow. Governments should no longer leave the future and health of society to couples' arbitrary approaches, or assume that relationships can thrive without a plausible framework. Once governments come on board and agree about the need for a framework, they should support its development and propagation in any perceivable way. Most important of all, the relationship framework, models, needs, and mechanisms must be taught in high schools, with strict rules for passing these mandatory courses. They are more important than sex education.

Family budgeting and debt management are integral parts of the 'relationship framework.' Accordingly, both the government and people must remain vigilant about family finances. Nowadays, people seem to have lost their senses about the level of debt they should carry. They are lured into credit shopping, while governments ignore the spread of highly unethical business practices that ruin families and lead to economic instability. People cannot curb their temptations and reduce their expectations. They cannot stop competing with their friends and families in terms of buying a house or other assets before the money for these purchases, as well as their jobs, are secure. Most people don't have the willpower or the financial sense to stay away from *ridiculously prevalent* marketing gimmicks. In all, the level of financial risks that people take does not fit their particular financial situation. And allowing business exploit people's weakness is governments' ultimate disregard for social welfare. Allowing consumerism push couples into depression and separation is a crime. But also, governments should become a lot more conscientious and active in teaching people how to budget and live within their means. Governments' role to push consumerism to strengthen the economy is coming at the cost of family destructions and imminent social catastrophe. Governments must change their own mentality and then teach the reality of life to people instead of allowing the existing financial chaos get even more out of hand.

Another kind of support is to give newlywed couples access to free counselling, especially during the first year. The idea is to monitor their knowledge and practice of GARP. This process can keep them on track and stop unreasonable demands building up. The process is something like giving a learning permit to couples while they are trying to get the hang of their relationships, and before problems emerge and taint their relationships. Couples must use the counselling service to learn about building their relationships and preventing problems, and much less for problem solving. We need a preventative approach.

In the next chapter, a model for creating a balance between personal needs and the relationship needs is developed. The idea of creating this balance and choosing the right relationship model is discussed in that chapter. Relationship models and success factors are good tools for both relationship planning and contract preparation. They are all topics that should be taught in high schools and during the counselling sessions.

4. Support the idea of time-bounded relationships in legal channels.

'Longevity' has been a good indicator of a successful relationship. The religious teachings, tradition, and psychological benefits of a stable relationship have had a lot to do with this mentality. Naturally, the longevity of relationships has many advantages if it could be properly mastered. But three questions must be answered:

a) Are humans instinctively equipped to live together for the length of their long lives (especially with life-expectancy rising so much)?
b) Do partners' personalities and needs support the possibility of living together forever?
c) Do our new social values and settings encourage the longevity of relationships?

(a) In terms of the role of instincts, the discussions in Chapter Six, especially 'The Effect of Human Hormones,' provided a resounding answer 'No': Humans are not instinctually equipped to live together permanently. The mere fact that we all have this doubt (i.e., humans' instinctual capacity to be monogamous) answers the question to a large extent too. It means that, at best, we are not sure. In fact, we witness how liberally humans commit adultery left and right these days. They simply cannot tame their sexual desires and adventurous minds. By definition, any instinct is absolutely explicit, permanent, collective, and it requires no deliberation regarding its existence. The monogamy or devotion among some creatures, e.g., crows or penguins, demonstrate the meaning of instinct. Playing those roles is their true nature. They don't have to argue and fight over their gender roles, equality, or infidelity either. They know and accept their roles naturally and they are not eager to change them. Like, for example, a lioness suddenly insisting that it is tired of doing all the killing and that this duty must be shared from now on or that male lions ought to do it. Humans clearly lack these types of instincts and instead keep arguing about their roles, equality, and infidelity. So the idea of monogamy or devotion must have come as part of social ethics (especially in the older times) or for dealing with our psychological needs and deprivations.

Like most creatures, we humans instinctually prefer our autonomy and sense of adventure, especially sexuality. Let's stop pretending otherwise. Our ego (and the urge for independence) prevents us from being dependable instinctually. Referring to the discussions in Chapter Fifteen regarding gender differences, it is reasonable to believe that the instinctual differences between men and women in fact goad them to deflect (or even fight off) each other. Of course, this doesn't mean that they don't fall in love or try to support each other. But many of these conditions are tentative or the residues of cultural norms and religions. Overall, humans have to make special efforts to get along, especially the opposite sexes.

An obvious clue that humans are not instinctually programmed to live together permanently is their amazing craving for sexual freedom. The urge to experience sex with many partners is in almost all human beings. We put too much emphasis on sex with different partners, somewhat instinctually and partly as a means of finding happiness.

A cute *relationship* instinct is that men usually try to avoid commitment while women want to lure them into it. Is this a by-product of the women's instinctual need for procreation? Probably not, because women and men of all ages have these urges. Is this really an instinctual urge or only a 'condition' developed as a result of people's marital experiences throughout the history of mankind? It is hard to say, except for the fact that women seek dependency more naturally, especially during maternity. This condition (to resist commitment) will most likely become even more prevalent in the future as men find it more difficult every day to respond to women's newer demands.

We have accepted the theory of evolution that connects humans to primates and other creatures in general. In the great kingdom of God, the primary role of the male and the female is to reproduce (sexual urge). Their secondary role is to protect one another against adversaries and harsh environments. In particular, the role of the female in protecting and upbringing their offspring is quite prominent. Males are usually less attached to the offspring, and even toward the female, once the initial mating process is complete. Often the female plays a major role in cooling off the relationship too, especially after the offspring gets strong. The male obeys by keeping its distance or moving away altogether. Humans are seemingly driven by similar instincts, despite the social norms devised to keep them focused and tactful. The evidence for similar instincts in humans is not hard to find. We know that:

- Women are more eager to procreate. Their biological clock goads them to get this matter resolved as soon as possible. Women also have a higher urge for parenthood. Thus they are more anxious to find a suitable man and lure him in for the ultimate objective of creating children. Although the women's inherent need for reproduction seems to compete with their career ambitions nowadays, this condition is mostly superficial, as explained below. Deep down, they are more attached to, and protective of, their children than men. Actually, their need for reproduction is more important to them than their urge for independence or career, unlike men. Meanwhile, women's higher urge and urgency for procreation stir their higher need for dependency on men during maternity at least.

- Women show less interest in their husbands when children begin to satiate their emotional needs. Often, children become more important to them than their husbands. Accordingly, their urge and courage for independence grow when the main objective of nature (reproduction) is fulfilled. Of course, if husbands happen to lose their interest or their focus during this confusing process (game), women eventually look for another mate to satisfy their inherent dependency needs and passion.

- Both genders, but particularly men, are lured by other people's charm once their initial attraction to their spouses wears off. Especially when people age, they crave the company of younger people. They feel vibrant and young when they get the attention of the opposite sex and often believe they can revive their youth by pursuing new adventures, instead of continuing the same life routines with an old, nagging spouse. All of us have this weakness—perhaps a natural way of responding to our psychological need for adventure. The fact that some people don't act upon this natural feeling, due to their sense of ethics, fear, or their integrity, doesn't change the basic principle about

people's natural urge to experience love and sex with someone else other than their spouses.
- People resent monotony and get depressed if new adventures are not instilled in their lives rather regularly. Living with the same partner often becomes too monotonous.

So people are not mentally (or instinctually) built to tolerate monogamy for many years, especially in a society like ours, which gives so much value to pleasure and making the best use of our lives.

(b) In terms of partners' personal defects, needs, and misperceptions, the possibility of partners tolerating one another for a long time is constantly decreasing as personal stress and defects increase in society. It was shown, mostly in Part I, that, as our personal needs increase, we become more arrogant and develop a sense of entitlement. Accordingly, our Ego-P prevents us from understanding one another and relating. The trend shows that our personal needs are increasing constantly in the new era and that nowadays we value our independence more than anything else. More independence and emphasis on self-gratification lead to lower longevity of relationships. In some respect, the urge for maternity could be reduced, too, as women put more emphasis on their need for independence, sexuality, and careers.

People's obsession for pleasure, love, and adventure obviously makes them too restless and thus reduces their sense of commitment in relationships. This is a newly emerged need for people that is affecting their perception of life and their relationships. They live longer and want to spend it with people who can give them more pleasure than their existing partners. So they move out of their boring relationships much quicker than it would have probably made sense even a few decades ago.

The kinds of games that couples play nowadays in their relationships for various reasons are also getting more bizarre and destructive every day. The effect of personal idiosyncrasies and superficial needs is making the nature of relationship games too complex and unmanageable for couples. Few people know how to behave and relate to one another naturally in the new world.

(c) In terms of social settings' impact on relationship longevity, we must explore the origin of a 'lifelong relationship' ideology, which can be found in religious and morality gestures of many centuries ago. Although the author advocates relationship longevity, the matter must be tackled realistically according to the new rules, which will be explained shortly. Nonetheless, the present preoccupation about relationship longevity goes back to the outmoded mental conditions of old societies. In modern societies, we have new rules, mainly guided by partners' needs for pleasure, individualism, and freedom. We explained in Chapter Nine why longevity can no longer be an expectation that couples can bring to their relationships. The old social condition for longevity is against our instinctual propensity and it does not fit our new lifestyles, mentality, and the new requirements of relationships.

As a whole, the assumption that humans can learn to get along has so far proven to be inaccurate. On the contrary, humans are probably worse than most other creatures in that regard. Animals at least do not kill their own kinds for such silly reasons that only humans do. We don't hesitate to destroy each other ruthlessly. We have killed over hundred million of our kind in the last century alone, by far the largest number in human history. Apparently, the more civilized we supposedly become, the more ferocious and greedier we get. We have the United Nations and we have all these charitable organizations and generous people, but more people are dying every day in wars, from diseases, and from hunger. The so-called civilized countries and their leaders are pursuing their own interests, especially more wealth and power, regardless of the mayhem they are creating around the world.

In addition to the egotistical nature of all humans, male and female seem to have even a harder time to understand each other and get along. People are not made or prepared to be in relationships. Especially nowadays, they are brought up to focus on finding happiness. To them, companionship is only another means of capturing that elusive happiness; or reversely, an obstacle for finding happiness. Nobody knows that the hardships of life and the agonies of relationships are still out there regardless of our naïve expectations and slogans.

So, at least for relationships, our social mechanisms should be revolutionized in order to match the new social needs and the characteristics of its citizens, especially their increasing arrogance. How? Well, we could say, let's eliminate the need for a marriage certificate and registration. This way partners can get in and out of their relationships as they wish, like the way nature has meant this basic human urge to be managed. But, since we are social beings in need of some rules and statistics, we must find a compromise. Having a basic social order to register our *marriage contracts* has some advantages too. But the main point is to make 'marriage contract' a prerequisite for registering all marriages.

A major discussion about the format and conditions of marriage contracts would be necessary in some other place or book. Nevertheless, a marriage contract must specify all the financial and non-financial terms agreed between partners and then specify *a term* (like five or ten or fifteen years) for the relationship too. Setting a specific term for a relationship is obviously too radical for many people. But it has many advantages as listed on page 352, and also on page 214 in our discussions about reverse psychology. After this initial period, partners may renew the contract for another term, with or without changes to other clauses. Or they could simply allow the contract to expire, in which case their relationship is automatically terminated without a need to burden the court system or cause each other undue stress.

Inserting a term for relationships fits within the new relationship framework quite nicely. It helps partners develop a new mentality that matches their needs for individuality and making decisions with the least amount of hassle and stress. The psychological impact of including a 'term' in our marriage contracts will be tremendous, in the author's opinion. First of all, it sets partners' mindsets properly when they start their relationship. They put more efforts into learning about i) relationship needs in general, ii) the realistic expectations from their relationship based on the terms of their marriage contract, and iii) the relationship model they choose for themselves. They prepare themselves for a relationship that would be fragile (and temporary) unless they show serious interest in keeping it. It would eliminate the artificial needs or motives for getting into a relationship. And most important of all partners respect their partners and their relationship (as R-entity), because at the end of the term they are no longer bound to stay together. The matter of child custody and all other aspects of relationships are worked out in the contract as well. Standard contracts would become available and considered an ordinary process for everybody to adopt. It would no longer be unromantic to sign a contract. Because it is a pre-requisite for all marriages. The only thing partners must do is to make proper adjustments to a standard contract, jot down the terms, and then sign it. And the only thing the government must do, if this process is supported, is to make sure contracts are prepared as a requirement. Courts would review a few legal cases that partners might bring against each other regarding the execution of contract terms.

In addition to a fixed term in contracts for the automatic annulment of relationships (unless renewed), marriage contracts could also include optional clauses for separation or terminating a relationship sooner under pre-specified conditions and subject to a prior notice of let's say a few months or one year by one (or both) partners.

Another radical step that partners should adopt in line with a time-bounded marriage is to celebrate their relationships at the end of each successful term instead of doing it so lavishly at the beginning when there is very little guarantee for partners' ability to really relate to one another successfully. Stop wasting too much effort and money on some event before it is established that partners really deserve to celebrate their ability to live harmoniously together. It is very likely that they are going through this whole shenanigan called marriage because of their naïve image of relationships the way it is misperceived nowadays.

The benefits of having a term specified in relationship contracts are substantial. Just to mention a few, it will:
a) Change the whole social mentality about relationships.
b) Guarantee partners' needs for individualism and independence.
c) Satisfy the instinctual urges of humans (for companionship and procreation) without unnecessary formalities.
d) Free partners from feeling trapped.
e) Keep partners hopeful about future and happiness if their relationship fails.
f) Make partners smarter about life and their relationship decisions.
g) Increase partners' enthusiasm to learn and practice the 'relationship framework' and GARP.
h) Introduce a progressive and productive mindset for partners.
i) Increase love and cooperation in relationships.
j) Enforce teamwork and give it a more crucial role in relationships.
k) Increase longevity of relationships.
l) Make children's lives less stressful and more predictable.
m) Reduce stress in families and society as a whole.
n) Reduce the sense of possessiveness and jealousy.
o) Reduce the burden on court systems substantially.
p) Eliminate the need for couples to spend outrageous legal fees.
q) Reduce the fear of getting into relationships and facing its hassles.

r) Increase economic productivity and social welfare due to reduced stress and time wasted on relationship wars between partners.

5. Support and propagate the idea of relationships being viewed as an independent entity like a business enterprise—R-entity.

Governments should devise all the necessary mechanisms to focus only on R-entity, as if relationships were a kind of business enterprise. In particular, they should require partners to sign a contract before a marriage certificate is issued. This would facilitate partners' acceptance of the new approach and the implementation of the new social mentality.

Just imagine if business partnerships and corporations were created without contracts and shareholders' equity arrangements at the outset. It would have looked ridiculous and extremely expensive to deal with all the claims that partners and shareholders would have wanted to settle in courts. It would have also looked ridiculous if shareholders or business partners had to go to court to ask for a permission to terminate their businesses or partnerships. The matter of settling relationship issues (especially financial ones) in courts is equally ridiculous the way it is done nowadays, especially considering that more than 60% of people in modern societies would have to go through separation and divorce and have some kinds of claims to settle at that point. Some people have to go through this stressful process more than once. Multiple marriages have become too common already for many people. A contract is a must for starting relationships now.

6. Support and propagate the idea of minimizing the government role in relationships.

Governments should gradually abandon their role in regulating, and ruling about, relationships. The more they stay out of this affair, the more couples learn to depend on themselves and teamwork to manage the terms of their contracts. They learn cooperation and tolerance. Couples would start to behave like mature, thinking creatures that humans are supposed to be. All possible conflicts arising from relationships should be dealt with according to the contract in place between partners and nothing more.

7. Support and participate in all kinds of research to enhance the quality of a universal 'relationship framework.' The practical guidelines of the relationship framework would replace the outmoded guidelines of religions and inefficient laws.

As much as governments should stop interfering with relationships and conflicts between partners, they should support universities and scholars to refine the relationship framework and GARP. Governments should find ways of controlling consumerism that is encouraging people to overextend themselves financially. They must teach family budgeting and the relationship framework at high schools very seriously. Governments have a responsibility to protect its citizens against the evils of greed and neediness which are overwhelming all aspects of social life.

I recall Elizabeth Gilbert's witty and succinct observation in her book, *Committed*. I am quoting it here from memory, which is very close, if not the exact, wording she has used to refer to the hectic environment of relationships in the new era: "I'm surprised that they (governments) are still allowing us to get married."

The point is that we all sort of agree that when the society at large faces a major challenge, we hope that some authority (usually the government in democratic societies) steps in to at least play the role of a moderator and induce order before a catastrophe cripples the whole socioeconomic structure. Hopefully we don't have to wait for the boiling point where the government is forced to restrict marriages. Instead, we need the government's and scholar's intervention to bring objectivity back into relationships somehow, because religions and old cultures cannot play that role anymore. Companionship is an immensely important facet of social structure and should not be left unattended for so long.

Chapter Twelve
Relationship Needs Hierarchy

A main objective of the relationship framework is to create a balance between partners' personal needs and the general relationship needs. The relationship needs are reviewed in this chapter, with the aim of ranking them according to their importance for the success of relationships. This ranking can be used as a tentative hierarchy of the relationship needs. Are some relationship needs more urgent than others for making a relationship successful? It would be interesting to study how this relationship hierarchy may coincide with Maslow's personal needs hierarchy.

The relationship needs (success factors) were listed in Table 9.4 in Chapter Nine. Ideally, all of them must be attended to simultaneously as much as possible. But some needs would probably have a higher urgency, in the sense that they must be fulfilled first in most common relationships. We can create this ranking by performing an elaborate 'factor analysis' in the future. But a simple 'relationship needs hierarchy' is needed now for the purpose of this book. One way to go about it is to subjectively develop a tentative list of ranked success factors in relationships. The discussions in this book indicate that partners' knowledge of the relationship framework, commitment to GARP and teamwork, etc. should probably get the highest rankings in this list.

Another approach is to develop a 'relationship needs hierarchy' according to the dependency requirements of partners: That is, we can define a few levels of partners' urge for dependence, and then attach various relationship needs to each 'dependence' level. The lower levels of the hierarchy get a higher rating because partners put the least amount of demands on each other—they are independent individuals. On the other hand, the more partners wish to depend on each other, the more complex (but also complete) their relationship would become. How well each 'relationship need' is satisfied affects the degree of relationship completeness (success) too. So, let's identify five levels of partners' dependency in line with the particular relationship needs as shown in Diagram 12.1 below.

Dependency Level (Relationship Model)	Hierarchy
5	S-love
4	Dependence/Personal Success
3	E-love/Friendship
2	M-love/Compassion
1	Co-existence

Diagram 12.1: Relationship Needs Hierarchy

The five 'dependency' levels signify the complexity of relationship needs that must be satisfied. The higher we go up in the hierarchy, the more dependent partners become on each other. And thus, the more complex relationship needs get. This Relationship Needs model emphasizes that the less complex needs of relationships must be understood and satisfied by partners first before they progress to the higher levels of dependency. The problem in relationships nowadays is that couples actually do the opposite. That is, they naively believe that they can start their relationships at the highest level of dependency and impose all their complex needs, including E-love and S-love, upon each other right away.

The higher we move up in the above hierarchy, the more solid a relationship gets, because more relationship expectations are satisfied. At the upper hierarchies, even the so-called unrealistic expectations (the ones listed in Table 11.2), including S-love, are satisfied. The other main characteristic of the 'relationship needs hierarchy' is that the higher we move up the hierarchy, the more partners are expected to have balanced their needs for dependence and independence personally and in terms of relating to one another. As a whole, in the lower levels of the hierarchy, partners emphasize on their independence. They move up the hierarchy only when they can demonstrate their genuine interest and maturity to respond to each other's dependency needs as well in a proper manner.

Thus, an ironic conclusion from the Relationship Needs Hierarchy is that partners need a high degree maturity to even gain the capacity for grasping the meaning and means of depending on each other. Initially, this conclusion seems rather contrary to the general belief that we need more maturity for being an independent person. But there is no contradiction here if we think about the matter more deeply. Of course, a high degree of maturity and enlightenment is required to achieve personal independence. But at the same time, we need even a higher degree of maturity and enlightenment to become selfless enough to accept some sort of mutual dependency to others and allow others to depend on us too.

This is a very fine point that we should all ponder for understanding our independency needs and gauging the level of our maturity. A great deal of courage and wisdom is required to ask for, or allow, higher dependencies in our lives, and also fulfil the obligations that go with it in the right way. This is a major fact (and hurdle) in relationships that is totally lost to couples with the least amount of maturity and wisdom who also demand a high degree of dependency so selfishly without a sense of the obligations attached to it.

Relationships Models

The 'relationship needs hierarchy' also shows the types of relationships (models) that couples can choose according to their needs, personalities, and compatibility. For our purpose here, five different relationship models are identified in this basic hierarchy, as shown in Diagram 12.1. They demonstrate the concept, but eventually maybe a dozen models can be identified in a more elaborate document.

In all, a dozen relationship models can accommodate the majority of relationships. They enable couples to relate actively or passively, satisfy a good majority of the relationship needs, and induce a relationship environment where the three Es (emotions, effectiveness and efficiency) are present at some degrees.

Relationship Model 1: Co-existence

This is the most basic type of relationship. Partners are familiar with the relationship framework and GARP. They are clear about their *contracted* expectations and stick to them. In this particular model, partners do not have the capacity or interest to fulfil the higher level needs of relationships, e.g., compassion and E-love. They might have wrong perceptions about each other and their relationship. But the level of frictions is minimal because partners adhere to the basic guidelines of GARP and maintain low expectations from their relationship. Nonetheless, the fact that partners are still in this relationship indicates that they have fulfilled some of the realistic expectations listed in Table 11.1, know how to respect each other, and behave civilly according to the relationship framework. In this model, partners are *relating passively*. While all the expectations in Table 11.1 are fulfilled at least at some minimal levels, the emphasis is placed only on certain basic expectations that are *urgently* required, such as sex, independence, communication, and teamwork.

Relationship Model 2: M-love/Compassion

This is the most common type of relationship model that couples try to adopt (and the one that most couples are realistically capable of handling). In this kind of relationship, partners try to respond to some of their partners' need for compassion. They know how to use Model-P effectively to express their emotions and needs. In the process, they satisfy each other's need for M-love—a sense of being loved. They are still relating rather passively, but they know how to maintain their relationship boundaries and not hurt each other's feelings. They try to curb their Ego-P urges to force their opinions or needs. The additional expectations satisfied in this model more *urgently* are: social acceptance, compassion, M-love, peace, and personal freedom.

Relationship Model 3: E-love/Friendship

In this kind of relationship, partners are able to show more compassion and relate better. They know better how to satisfy each other's needs. They are able and willing to satisfy some of their partners' (unrealistic) needs in Table 11.2 as well, e.g., E-love. They also know how to be true friends. The strength of their friendship actually helps them respond to some of each other's unrealistic demands for attention and E-love. Although E-love is an unrealistic expectation in relationships, it helps in the development of relationships when it is partially satisfied (through partners' friendship and Model-P). In this model, partners are *relating rather actively*. The additional expectations satisfied in this model more *urgently* are: security, friendship, E-love, and a small dose of commitment.

Relationship Model 4: Dependence/Personal Success

In this kind of relationship, partners are really in sync with each other. They are *relating actively*. They can truly depend on each other and contribute effectively to each other's personal goals. They know how to support each other compassionately to succeed in their personal pursuits. The additional expectations satisfied in this model more *urgently* are: dependence, personal success, commitment, and longevity.

Relationship Model 5: S-love

This is the highest level of achievement for a relationship. This is the level where partners become true soul mates. It basically gives partners the opportunity to feel and satisfy their spirituality needs and everything else that one could ideally expect from a relationship. They reach love that is heavenly, selfless, and eternal. In this model, all the expectations in both Tables 11.1 and 11.2 are satisfied. They are totally relating.

Although some or all of the unrealistic expectations of partners (as shown in Table 11.2) can be satisfied by some of the above noted models, those expectations must still reflect partners' authentic needs. The minute partners' expectations are contaminated by their obsessions or erratic demands, the relationship model becomes dysfunctional. This applies to higher level relationship models even more strictly. Of course, forgiveness, tolerance, and using Self-P to deal with our partners' obsessions and flaws are always helpful in reducing frictions. But the more authentic partners' needs and demands are, the better would be their chances to move up the 'relationship needs hierarchy.' In all, 'unrealistic expectations' should not imply or be equated with 'unauthentic needs.' The former refers to certain expectations that should not be normally sought by couples under most common conditions (but could be attained at higher levels of the relationships needs hierarchy). Unauthentic needs, on the other hand, refer to such desires and obsessions that are never acceptable in any type of relationship. More elaboration about relationship models is offered on page 371.

Personal Needs versus Relationship Needs

By combining Diagrams 12.1 and 1.1 (Chapter One), we can compare the relationship needs with couples' personal needs. Diagram 12.2 shows this comparison. In this diagram, partners' relationship needs are depicted as a 'social need' on the personal needs hierarchy. It shows 'companionship' a part of social needs of partners. However, as noted before, companionship and compassion are extremely important needs even for a starving, homeless person. Later in this chapter, this point is further explained while the topic of 'Need Urgency' is discussed in more details.

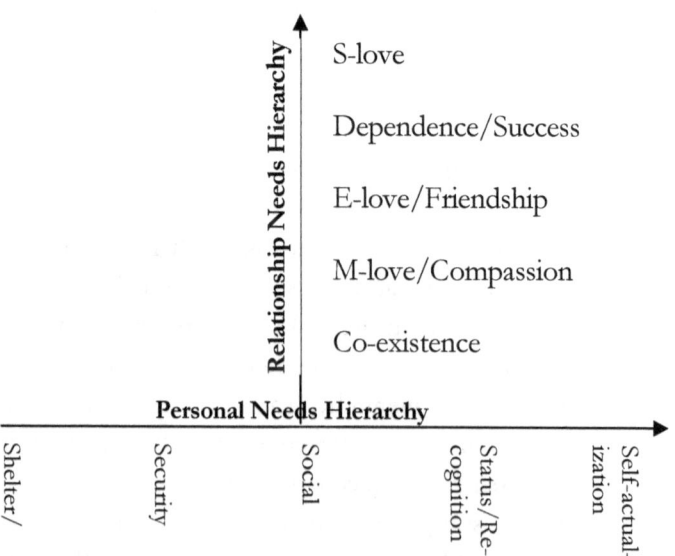

Diagram 12.2: Relationship Needs Hierarchy Shown as a Social Need

In all, it seems more realistic to move the vertical axis, the 'relationship needs hierarchy,' to the beginning of the horizontal axis (i.e., personal needs hierarchy axis), where shelter and food is—Diagram 12.3.

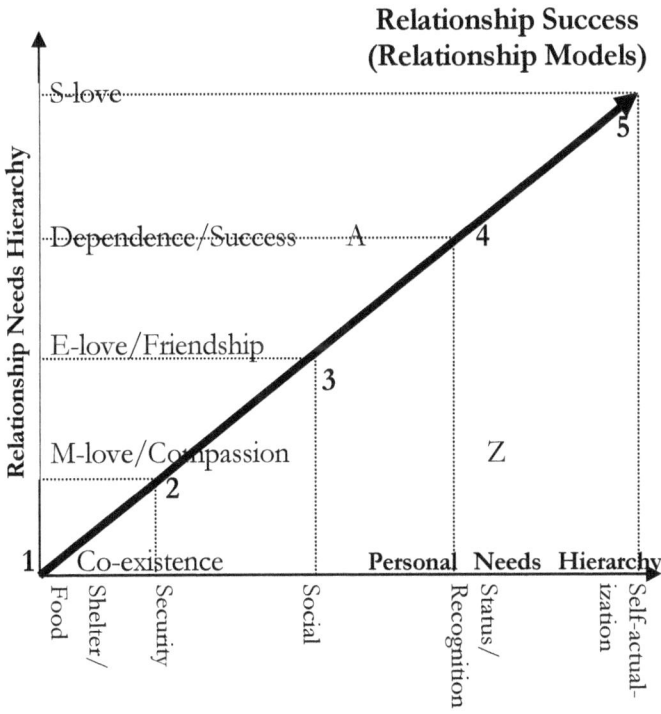

Diagram 12.3: Relationship Needs Hierarchy Shown as a Basic Personal Need

Obviously, the need for a companion has found the highest value in modern societies. (This might sound like an odd statement considering the chaotic situation of relationships in the new era. But the fact that we have so much difficulty finding a companion is actually turning 'relationships' into a more scarce and urgent need.) Anyway, finding a companion is perceived by the majority of us as a basic need—at least in affluent countries where basic needs for food and shelter are not as prominently felt as they were in the older times or as they are felt in poorer countries. Need for a reliable companion has found a profound psychological importance for the majority of people. The unfortunate reality is that the need for compassion is increasing, mostly because people are deprived of it more every day in our hectic social settings. It is also because they have less of it themselves to offer—because arrogance has become a social norm.

The other correct implication of Diagram 12.3 is that even couples striving for their basic personal needs can possibly build a good relationship, even as high as S-love. So, we will adopt Diagram 12.3 as the final presentation for comparing partners' personal needs with the relationship needs. Many other interesting points are noted and discussed in the following pages.

The Interpretation of the 'Relationship Needs Hierarchy'

Diagram 12.3 reveals a lot of information consistent with our daily observations. The most significant interpretations are as follows:
1. 'Companionship' is a basic need according to the discussions in the previous chapters (mainly Chapter One) and also the forthcoming ones on pages 374-375. It is not merely a social need.
2. Many types of balanced relationships exist, where partners are in agreement about their relationship model, their

level of independence, and the level of personal needs that this model normally supports.
3. All couples represented by a point in this diagram can relate somehow (passively or actively) to make their relationships work. Relationships that are dysfunctional for some reason normally induce too many conflicts to allow the kind of balance represented by the points in Diagram 12.3.
4. All the points in this diagram represent those cases where partners' expectations (from their relationship) are somewhat fulfilled by a certain relationship model, simply because 1) their expectations are realistic, 2) their relationship expectations somewhat coincide with their personal needs, and 3) they know the restrictions of the model they have chosen, and stay within its boundaries.
5. Regardless of the relationship model that partners have chosen, they adhere to the relationship framework and observe GARP.
6. The highlighted arrow shows the most ideal types of relationships, because partners' personal needs coincide with their relationship needs perfectly. This arrow signifies 'Relationship Success,' as every point on the arrow is a perfect relationship. Partners have created a successful balance in their relationship without sacrificing their personal needs too much or allowing their personal needs affect their relationship.
7. Other points in the diagram (such as points A and Z) are less perfect, but still manageable, relationships. A is obviously a more successful relationship than Z.
8. Point A reflects the case where partners are more successful in their relationship than they are in achieving their

personal needs. They have sacrificed some of their personal needs to improve their relationship. Conversely, point Z reflects that partners have sacrificed some aspects of their relationship in order to pursue their personal goals. Anyway, both points A and Z reflect working relationships, as long as partners continue their teamwork, agree on the relationship model they have chosen, and know how much emphasis they wish to put on personal needs. The relationship contract they have signed and other aspects of the relationship framework would ensure that this agreed balance is maintained. The cases where disagreements exist between partners are explained in the next chapter when compatibility issues are addressed. The cases explained here are based on the assumption that partners are compatible and have agreed on the relationship model.

9. Point A also indicates that these partners are probably not too ambitious. The reason is that although partners can support each other to pursue their personal goals, they are somehow not taking advantage of this opportunity to better themselves. They seem stuck with their personal needs for social acceptance and security, and emphasizing on keeping each other happy.

10. Point Z, on the other hand, reflects a relationship where partners' personal needs and ambitions are getting the priority. So their relationship is not going to higher levels and they cannot depend on each other as much as couple A does. Couple Z is distracted by personal needs such as work, friends, or even spirituality. Therefore, they cannot give enough attention to their partners and enhance their friendship. While they are relating somewhat actively,

their relationship is only fulfilling their needs for E-love and compassion.
11. The higher we move up the Success Arrow, the more successful (complete) the relationship is, the stronger the bonding of partners is, and the more personal needs of partners are satisfied.
12. Personal needs and relationship needs are reconcilable if partners are mature and sincere about their needs and agree on the relationship model that can best fit their personal lifestyle and authentic needs. The points in Diagram 12.3 can fit a variety of personal preferences of couples. The only requirement is for each partner to know exactly what he/she wants, express them in their contract, and then honour his/her words.
13. The higher levels in the relationship needs hierarchy, e.g., friendship, can better support partners to achieve their personal needs. But we don't take advantage of this opportunity because we are obsessed with our lower personal needs, such as rivalry and greed. Our Ego-P prevents us from seeing the larger picture; to cooperate for achieving our higher personal needs. The higher we climb up the relationship needs hierarchy, a higher sense of partners' dependability and maturity is required. Accordingly, people's rising urge for independence means that they should stick to relationship models in the lower levels.
14. In 'co-existence' (relationship model 1), partners can devote themselves totally to achieve their personal needs. This means that even couples who give a high priority to personal needs and individualism can be in manageable relationships. In this particular model, only minimum ex-

pectations are placed on partners, just to maintain the relationship according to GARP and partners' initial contract. All partners must do is to make sure they have similar objectives and tempers.
15. Moving up the relationship needs hierarchy is not something that partners can negotiate on. They must be really mature in terms of personality, lifestyle, and priorities in order to reach a higher level in the relationship needs hierarchy. This progression is not by partners' desire or choice, but rather an automatic one, as a natural consequence of partners' compatibility, personality, and needs. Therefore, partners should be realistic about the relationship model they choose. They shouldn't demand a high level of dependency until they are sure about their capacity to remain humble and free from ego. Especially, newlyweds must choose the lowest relationship model at the beginning and hope to move upward according to their actual encounters. In reality, however, they do just the opposite. That is, they assume they are equipped to deal with each other's high dependency needs from the beginning.

Table 12.1 lists the grids shown in Diagram 12.3. They are the intersecting points where each relationship type (model) corresponds with a level of personal need. The following discussions highlight these relations, but they also supplement the discussions on pages 360-364 about relationship models. They offer a complementary view of relationship models.

Table 12.1: Main Relationship Models

Relationship Model (Grid)	Relationship Needs Hierarchy	Personal Needs Hierarchy
1	Co-existence	Food, Shelter, Sex
2	M-love/Compassion	Security
3	E-love/Friendship	Social
4	Dependence/Success	Status, Ambitions
5	S-love	Self-actualization

Relationship Model 1: In this type of relationship, partners co-exist in the sense that their obligations toward each other are complete as long as their needs for **food and shelter and sex** are satisfied. This model represents a couple of interesting situations: First, partners have the highest level of freedom to pursue their personal needs as long as a minimum level of relationship need (Co-existence) is satisfied. Partners agree and succeed in co-existing without placing higher demands on each other. In this relationship model, the emphasis is placed on the independence of partners while they benefit from their partnership in a civilized manner. Therefore, they have the opportunity to develop even their highest personal aspirations without being bound or burdened by their partner's erratic demands. This opportunity begins to deteriorate fast at the middle levels of the relationship hierarchy, as partners place more demands on each other, and they must also balance their needs for independence and dependence more precisely. Thus, as relationship expectations increase, partners' ability to pursue their personal needs is restricted—a commonplace observation. They must give more attention to their partners and their relationship. The higher the expectations from relationships, the more necessary and difficult it gets to balance personal needs with the relationship needs. The Success Arrow in Diagram 12.3 shows the balance between the relationship needs and personal needs of partners. The intersecting vertical and horizontal lines for each model get longer as we move up the relationship needs hierarchy, which reflects the degree of difficulty to create a balance between the relationship needs and personal needs of partners. It also gets harder for partners to reach the required balance between their personal needs for dependence and independence.

The second implication of this relationship model is that even people satisfying only their basic needs (i.e., food and shelter) can reach the highest level in the relationship hierarchy; even S-love, if they are humble and selfless (and are willing to devote themselves totally to their partners instead of pursuing their personal needs and goals).

Relationship Model 2: In this type of relationship, partners are mainly looking for some sense of **security** in their relationship. They expect their partners to show compassion, too, although it may not be quite sincere. The focus on 'security' is often a reflection of one or both partners' psychological or financial insecurity. Partners use some Model-P and M-love to relate and reflect passion and security. They wisely start their relationship with caution, try to keep certain boundaries, and curtail their demands for excessive attention (E-love). Their occasional attempt to fulfil more of their personal needs results in conflicts. In particular, if a partner attends to his/her social needs unilaterally, the other partner feels threatened and arguments begin. The balance in their relationship is shaky and threatened if they begin to move beyond their comfort zone too often. So they limit their pursuit of personal needs and stop asking for too much affection beyond M-love.

Relationship Model 3: In this type of relationship, partners relate more constructively with a focus on **friendship**. Thus they find the strength and motivation to satisfy some of their unrealistic needs such as E-love too. Their friendship gives them a higher capacity for teamwork and making compromises. They support each other to explore their personal needs more actively. They have freer social interactions without their attitude or actions coming across as threatening for their relationship. They use Model-P and M-love more effectively to express their emotions to enhance their friendship and the quality of their relationship.

In this relationship model, partners get a chance to fulfil their social needs fully. Still, they might feel some limitations in pursuing their more advanced personal goals without threatening the stability of their relationship. They might find the task of creating the balance between their needs for dependence and independence difficult on some occasions, but overall they have a good grasp of them.

Relationship Model 4: In this type of relationship, partners have proven their maturity to balance their personal needs and the relationship needs. The emphasis is on **supporting** each other to fulfil their personal ambitions. They also balance their personal needs for dependence and independence effectively. A higher sense of dependence on their partners occurs naturally while each partner feels a thorough sense of independence as well. The joy of their relationship empowers partners to accomplish even their highest aspirations while maintaining a fulfilling relationship too.

Relationship Model 5: This is the most successful, complex, and complete type of relationship. It empowers partners to experience enlightenment, tranquility, **S-love**, and they relate naturally.

A reason for so much conflict in relationships is that couples do not have a particular relationship model to guide them. Yet most couples imagine they can start and maintain a relationship at the highest level of the relationship needs hierarchy automatically and fulfil all its complex requirements. It is obvious by now how unreasonable this expectation is.

Need Urgency Implications

This book has drawn on Maslow's needs hierarchy theorem to explain many points regarding relationships. A related concept, Need Urgency, can also help in understanding couples' damaging behaviour in relationships. Need urgency is discussed in scientific journals and books. For the purpose of this book, however, need urgency is studied only to the extent it affects the health of relationships. This pertains to couples' peculiar obsessions when they prioritize their personal needs outside Maslow's needs hierarchy. Need urgency implications will also be a factor for reviewing partners' compatibility measures in the next chapter.

According to Maslow, people inherently try to satisfy their basic needs, starting with their need for 'shelter and food,' before moving up to the next higher group (level) of needs. That is, people have usually satisfied all their previous needs in the hierarchy before devoting themselves to the pursuit of their higher level needs. The theory also stipulates that if a person's lower needs are suddenly disrupted, he/she moves down the needs hierarchy again. He/she would have to satisfy those lower needs before climbing back up the hierarchy again.

The need urgency concept adds another dimension to this general theorem. It basically introduces the cases where a person's urgent need disregards the orderly progression or regression of needs as suggested by the personal needs hierarchy. A few examples may help:

- Overachievers usually ignore the lower needs, e.g., social or security, because their need for success is too urgent and important for them. They are so obsessively drawn to self-actualizing endeavours they might stop caring about their social needs, security, or even food. People with this mentality are plenty in society at all levels of needs hierarchy. They sacrifice their lives and basic needs in order to fulfil their unique urges, ideologies, or their spiritual missions on earth.
- We expect that our need for a companion falls in the category of social needs on Maslow's needs hierarchy. But, in reality, this is not the case, at least in the present social setting. Nowadays, we are too needy for compassion and companionship. On many occasions, even a starving homeless might prefer a companion to food or shelter. This is an example of our psychological and physiological needs competing for attention. A person overwhelmed by love might stop caring about food or security. Some even commit suicide for love or their political ideologies. Very often a person's 'psychological construct' determines the urgency of his/her needs. This could be a permanent condition or a temporary

setback. So, the 'need urgency' concept suggests that for many of us being at a certain level of the needs hierarchy is so urgent we can ignore all other needs. This condition is usually referred to as an obsession, but could have other sources too, such as addiction, fanaticism, false pride, etc. Some people crave 'social acceptance' or 'status' more than 'self-actualization' even when they know that their health and happiness depends on achieving some level of tranquility.

- Ambitious people (or workaholics) actually realize, and suffer from, the lack of enough time for a social life or family. And still they cannot bring themselves to change their priorities. They know they are missing a good slice of life and all the fun out there. They get over-conscious and anxious about their choices. Yet their ambition and need for creativity prevent them from wasting time on anything else.
- Sometimes we settle for friends and companions who are not up to our standards or compatible with us. We do this because of our urgent need to socialize instead of waiting for a perfect friend or partner.
- Even reaching the height of Maslow's needs hierarchy doesn't guarantee long-lasting tranquility. For one thing, self-actualizers must create new things all the time to keep the cycle of actualization alive and potent. On some occasions, they might not be happy even though they are at the height of their creativity. So many reasons exist for this. For example, when they are not getting the recognition they think they deserve. In all, satisfying our needs, even self-actualization, would not automatically turn into happiness or freedom from erratic needs.

Need urgency usually indicates the intensity of a certain need, too, which could be labelled as obsession, which might even lead to insanity. For example, a partner might be obsessed with socializing. He/she is happy only when friends or family are around. This need may cause a major conflict, especially when the other partner prefers a quieter lifestyle. People are often too absorbed in their obsessions to consider them excessive or unnatural. So they argue about the sources of tension in their relationships uselessly. Some people have an obsession for shopping or controlling everything and everyone. Like some kind of addiction, these need urgencies or obsessions can drain the person and people around him/her. Even a simple obsession for cleanliness or tidiness can quickly override love when partners start to get on each other's nerves. And then we keep insisting that love alone can hold our relationships together.

Partners' need urgencies could be short or long term depending on circumstances. It could manifest in terms of mood swings or a complete change of one's lifestyle altogether. Often partners even fall out of love quickly, because of their sudden obsession to pursue a new priority, e.g., to get the university degree they had left incomplete thirty years before. Or a sudden sense of urgency to reclaim one's identity, or attend to one's awakened ambitions. These types of sudden need urgencies ruin the relative balance within a relationship. Partners suddenly face an unfamiliar and intimidating atmosphere and they don't know how to deal with it.

Mood swings are the outcome of need urgencies shifting from one thing to another rather quickly and illogically. Often, they are simply the outcome of a partner's defence mechanism trying to cope with relationship conundrums or to retaliate. Another reason is that couples often get tired of the status quo or get bored with their partners. So they invent an urgent need to escape boredom and depression. The change is usually radical and drastic, because it must overcome their boredom or irritate their partners. Under these circumstances, partners appear neurotic and irrational to each other. Their relationship remains unbalanced, too, because partners have difficulty grasping the meaning and purpose of each other's erratic needs and moods. They don't know what has caused them, when they would reappear, and how to react to them. This is a prevalent situation considering people's immensely emotional need urgencies nowadays. This kind of relationship atmosphere heightens partners' confusion, misperceptions, and frustration. Most of these need urgencies are psychological and impulsive, and thus hard to deal with.

Need urgency shows people's psychological construct. For some people, their need urgency reflects a deep-rooted obsession that stays with them throughout their lives. This is a static type of need urgency, e.g., obsession for cleanliness or an artist's need for self-actualization. It is a reflection of one's personality. This type of permanent obsessions is at least predictable. Partners can learn to either live with these obsessions or get out of the relationship. But often, need urgencies are the symptoms of partners' mood swings and self-defence. These types of erratic behaviour are more difficult to deal with.

Sometimes people's need urgencies become critically time-restrained, too, e.g., to pursue one's ambitions or have children before a certain age. In the new era, the urgency to find a better relationship than the existing one is becoming a time-restrained need too. In particular, when a person is getting old or has left a relationship, he/she suddenly feels an urgent need to find love in a new companion at all cost as soon as possible. The fear of loneliness suddenly makes him/her too anxious. And the need for a companion finds an exceptionally high urgency. He/she employs Model-P relentlessly and sacrifices many other personal needs to satisfy this urgent need as soon as possible. Sometimes a person is so desperate he/she looks totally lost and pathetic.

As a whole, another complexity of relationships lies in the fact that people's unique need urgencies (obsessions) usually do not follow any logic. They could go up or down the personal needs hierarchy quickly without any specific order or reason. Time-restrained urgencies (e.g., an urge to be loved again) obviously are quite stressful for the person and people around him/her. Other than lifestyle and personality differences of partners, their unpredictable need urgencies and obsessions create many additional conflicts in relationships.

The Impact of Need Urgency on Relationships

Several situations were discussed in this chapter about the way 'need urgency' supersedes the principles of Maslow's personal needs hierarchy. A few other points must also be mentioned about the need urgency briefly here. First, as noted before, the need for a companion appears to impose a particular urgency on our lives. All of our 'personal needs' demand our attention at some degree and time. But the need for a companion seems to be an everlasting and imposing one. It seemingly places the highest level of urgency throughout our lives. In fact, our other personal needs often appear pale and inconsequential compared with our need for a companion. Our emotional needs put the highest psychological demand on our existence. So finding solutions for our relationship issues has become a particularly urgent matter for modern societies.

Another point deserving a quick mention is that 'need urgencies' of partners impact their compatibility and thus the health of their relationships. This happens when one or both partners remain uncertain about their expectations from their relationship and their true personal needs. When they cannot stir a good balance between their relationship needs and personal needs, they feel a lingering tension, which then affects their relationship too. So it is important for partners to convince themselves personally about their real needs and the suitable relationship model for them. Any kind of phony balance would only hurt them personally, as well as their partners. They must be flexible, but not at the cost of sacrificing their natural personal needs or real expectations from a relationship, all for the sake of fitting themselves into a particular relationship model. They should negotiate to find a clear position for themselves on the 'relationship needs hierarchy.' And they must feel truly comfortable with that compromise and the relationship model they have adopted. Since partners' need urgencies impact their compatibility in a major way, assessing their need urgencies is another important factor for measuring the compatibility of couples, as explained in the next chapter.

Even though couples should have the option of choosing the best relationship model for their type of personality and needs, they should start from the simplest relationship model, which is the lowest in the relationship hierarchy—

with a low level of dependency on their partner. They could then try to climb up the hierarchy according to their actual experiences in their relationship and by showing their maturity and personality strengths. This policy to start from the lowest level of the relationship hierarchy should replace our existing mentality to start at the highest level. This would be a substantial social challenge.

The 'relationship needs hierarchy' and the relationship models presented in this book are simple ones. They are offered here only for the purpose of making the discussions in this chapter clear. Yet these simple models can be expanded and explained in a full-fledged working manual. Couples can use this manual to identify the specific type of relationship that suits them. Instead of the five models suggested in this book, we could possibly come up with a hierarchy that supports probably a dozen relationship models. These relationship models can possibly contain all types of successful relationships that we could reasonably conceive. Couples could use the manual to identify the suitable relationship model for them by matching their personalities to the requirements of various models. The characteristics and requirements of the models would be easy to understand and follow.

Diagram 12.3 can also be expanded to show the balance between personal needs and relationship needs in much more detail. This can further facilitate couples ability to choose the kind of balance they like to create. Eventually all these details will be available for the lucky couples of the 22nd century. Development of these concepts and models is another type of radical mechanism that we need, the topic which was presented in the previous chapter.

The Impact of Instinctual Needs

The impact of our instinctual needs in decision making and social encounters is enormous as they are the least tameable needs. More importantly, instinctual urges find a high urgency in our personal lives and relationships. Five of these types of needs were discussed in Chapter Two due to their special impact on relationships. They are:

- Need for dependence
- Need for independence
- Need for control
- Need for sex
- Need for love

These instinctual needs become too urgent in almost all relationships nowadays. Yet it is not clear how they fall within the overall 'personal needs hierarchy' of Maslow. In the context of Maslow's model, 'need for control' might be considered a symptom of personal need for security. 'Need for sex' might be seen as a basic physiological need. As explained in Chapter Two, our conflicting needs for dependence and independence actually seem to be impacting our perceptions of all our other needs. 'Need for love' seems to be driven by many other personal needs, as it manifests in terms of E-love, M-love, and S-love. Nonetheless, the real implications of the above instinctual needs are quite complex. More importantly, it is their roles in relationships that are of interest in this book, e.g., when two partners end up using sex as a mechanism for retaliation or manipulating each other. Or in the way individuals' need for independence is impacting the whole spectrum of relationships, especially partners' need for compassion and dependence. It appears that these types of instinctual needs have found a true urgency and importance in relationships in the new era. As such, companionship is no longer a 'social need' on Maslow's needs hierarchy. Rather, it is an essential (basic) need as claimed in the previous section.

The Impact of Need Urgency (NU) on Need Setback Hysteria (NSH)

NSH was discussed briefly in Chapter One. Need urgency and obsessions make the matter of NSH even more troublesome. As noted before, the personal needs hierarchy of Maslow imply that people go about satisfying their needs in an orderly and calm manner. It is assumed they are rational and set their expectations according to their abilities and efforts. Obviously, moving up the personal needs hierarchy and striving for a higher level of need satisfaction is not easy. But traditionally and logically we do not expect people to torture themselves mentally when their higher needs are not yet satisfied. These days, however, it appears that people are excessively obsessed with achieving some unattainable goals. Everybody has become overambitious nowadays. Positive thinking and the idea that everybody can achieve any goal have screwed up their minds. Nowadays, people perceive all kinds of artificial needs, especially the needs for fame and wealth, as their imperative (basic) needs. They are even seen as 'urgent needs' by some. When these highly unattainable goals fail, people take it as a sign of major failure and unworthiness. They take the matter too seriously and suffer when their artificial needs are not satisfied. Both at the personal level and in relationships, the unattained goals are envisioned as catastrophes and shameful. Simple matters that were traditionally considered inconsequential for personal welfare or the health of relationships have nowadays become a source of major frustration and hysteria. People's reactions are sometimes too drastic. They get hysterical sometimes. They might even show signs of insanity when a simple need remains unfulfilled. The impact of people's oversensitivity regarding their unfulfilled needs is destructive personally and for society. In relationships, too, the impact is quite devastating when unrealistic relationship expectations remain unfulfilled. This happens when couples keep imagining and pushing for relationship models beyond their mental ability. Sometime they are imagining some kind of a relationship arrangement that cannot fit within any of the reasonable models presented in this book anyway.

Chapter Thirteen
Compatibility Measures

According to the relationship framework and mechanisms suggested in this book, couples should view 'relationships' in a new light. For one thing, they must consider it a temporary arrangement, unless partners can prove their expertise and sincerity to work together to make their union prosper, which would not be an easy task for most people. Couples should also learn to measure the viability of their relationships more objectively. Relationships should no longer be viewed as a whimsical set of needs and activities to mainly fulfil partners' emotional deficiencies. Being in a relationship is a serious *business* and must be viewed as such by partners. This mentality wouldn't make us less sensitive, sentimental, or compassionate. It only brings caution into relationships in order to minimize future hassles, animosity, and nervous breakdown. The irony is that we would actually take relationships more seriously when we consider them a temporary arrangement. This is a major improvement over the present situation where relationships are taken for granted because we consider them a permanent setup. In this new setting, couples are systematically encouraged to have a proactive and progressive mindset.

Even though the proposed new setup would facilitate the annulment of relationships with the least amount of hassle, still partners are expected to be cautious in two major areas: One area, as discussed in Chapter Eleven, is with regard to the contract that partners must prepare carefully before starting their relationship. The other area of importance is to ensure that partners have the right characteristics for the kind of relationship model they choose. The first question is whether a couple can balance their personal needs and the relationship needs in order to fit within one of the relationship models suggested in the previous chapter. Another question is whether partners have adequate understanding of the relationship model they have chosen, including its operational requirements. Each partner must assess all these factors before starting a relationship. For most relationships, it is only a matter of partners agreeing to start from the lowest relationship model, in which partners maintain their total independence and set the lowest level of expectations from their relationship. They agree that they would only move up to the higher levels of the relationship needs hierarchy once they prove their maturity and a mutual capacity to increase their expectations from their relationship.

The objective of choosing a partner is not to find the illusive happiness. Couples must learn and remember that 'relationships are not for the purposes of finding happiness or love, but only for sharing the hardships of life, including the matter of tolerating their partner's shortfalls.' This is a tough mentality that couples must adopt wholeheartedly if they are truly serious about a relationship. Accordingly, some compatibility tests can be developed to help couples assess the viability of their relationships objectively. The emphasis in these tests is placed on measuring each partner's capacity for being in a relationship and much less on how two people are compatible. The idea is to keep the inevitable relationship conflicts at bare minimum. In particular, with the new approach to relationships, the criteria for the success of relationships are different. So partners must ensure they are qualified (compatible) in terms of satisfying the specific relationship needs outlined in Table 9.4. The old methods of matching some personal traits of partners and calling it a compatibility test would not guarantee a successful relationship. Obviously, depending on gut feeling or love would not work anymore within the new relationship framework either.

In all, the traditional compatibility tests and factors are not applicable to the new relationship framework. So this chapter is intended to propose some new factors and methods to measure partners' qualifications, and thus determine the chances of success of a particular relationship. In the future, we must measure partners' compatibility in three major areas:

1. Partners' Personality
2. Partners' Needs
3. Partners' Perceptions

Partners' Personality measures the psychological fitness of each partner. These tests must in particular measure partners' overall understanding and suitability for being in a relationship. These tests also measure partners' personality aspects: Ego-P, Model-P, and Self-P.

Partners' Needs measures partners' need urgencies and choose the relationship model suitable for them. These tests also measure the suitability of two individuals for being in a certain relationship model.

Partners' Perceptions measures partners' perceptions of themselves, their partners, and their relationship. These tests also measure the impact of partners' perceptions and misperception on their relationship.

Once these three types (sets) of tests are performed, they should be interrelated, correlated, and combined into a final set of results. They would offer a picture of reality about that particular relationship and its partners.

The overall compatibility tests proposed here must actually be applied on a regular basis to measure the progress and health of relationships. These tests, especially Partners' Perceptions, can identify the areas that require some realignment.

Of course, these three types of compatibility tests are useful only when couples adopt the relationship framework and GARP. Compatibility tests in general, and the format proposed in this chapter in particular, cannot have much value for relationships that are based on partners' loose definitions and arbitrary values about relationships.

The objective in this chapter is only to suggest the factors that must be measured and the methods that can be used to do so. It is not intended to actually design the tests of compatibility. That would be a special project all by itself. But creating such compatibility tests, according to the format offered in this chapter, would not be difficult. The remainder of this chapter will explain the working parameters of the three types of compatibility tests noted above.

Type One Measures: Partners' Personality

The three personality aspects of partners, i.e., Ego-P, Model-P, and Self-P, are mostly measured in order to establish the overall personality of each partner. Then these measures are also used to determine the way the personality aspects of partners might interact in their relationship. To make this job more objective and manageable, developing a personality framework, like the one presented in Diagram 13.1 might help.

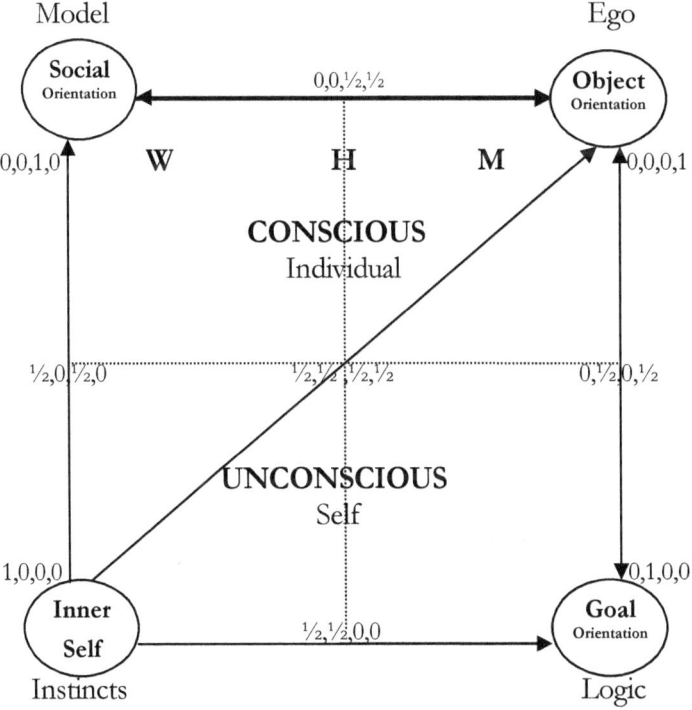

Diagram 13.1: Personality Chart

Personality Factors

Diagram 13.1 offers a reasonable presentation of a person's personality. Once we develop the methods and means of measuring the factors noted on this chart, we can obtain a good understanding of a person's personality. To understand this personality model, its parameters are listed below:

1. A person's personality can be identified and measured in terms of how effectively he/she can:
   a) apply his/her **instincts**,
   b) reason and use his/her **logic**,
   c) connect with people and society—**Model**, and
   d) manage his/her **ego** for his/her own benefit.

These four personality factors are shown in the four corners of Diagram 13.1. They reflect people's major urges to go around and do the things they do:
- **Instincts** drive many of our urges expanding from the basic urge for sex all the way to the complex urge for spirituality. This factor reflects the *inner self* of a person.
- **Model** drives our urges to socialize and adapt. This factor reflects the *social orientation* of a person and his/her need for acceptance.
- **Ego** drives our urges to defend ourselves and to push our desires on others. This factor reflects the *object orientation* of a person, i.e., greed and a need to succeed in acquiring objects or dominating them.

- **Logic** drives our urges for decision making and planning. It reflects our ability to use our brain. This factor reflects the *goal orientation* of a person.
2. A combination of these four factors makes up a person's personality. The intensity of each factor in the mix makes his/her personality unique.
3. The personality aspects, i.e., Self-P, Model-P, and Ego-P, are closely related to the personality factors noted in the above model. The minor difference is the inclusion of 'logic' as an additional factor in the above model. This particular factor impacts individuals' decisions and actions. It manifests itself in our Self-P, Model-P, and Ego-P in different ways. Overall, personality *factors* define those urges that make one's personality, whereas personality *aspects* reflect the manifestation of all those urges (factors).
4. The ratings shown in the Chart (Diagram 13.1) reflect a person's orientation. For example, the rating 1,0,0,0 in the left lower corner of the Chart reflects a hypothetical personality who depends solely on his/her instincts to live. The number '1' means 100%. As another example, a person's personality inside the diagram could possibly be identified as (0.4, 0.6, 0.3, 0.8). This means that this person draws on his/her instincts, logic, model, and ego at 40%, 60%, 30%, and 80% of their total capacities (for that specific individual) respectively. He/she is a rather logical person but mostly an egoist.
5. A similar diagram and rating system can be prepared to rate each person on these factors, but in relation to the total population in each type of society. For example, a person who is using 40% of his instinctual capacity

could be actually using only 25% of a typical instinctual capacity of his fellow citizens living in the same or similar environment. For ease of communication, these relative measures are not explored or explained in the remainder of this chapter. But it should be picked up as part of the compatibility measures that are developed in the future.

6. The ratings are designed in such a way that they are relative, in the sense that if a person uses both his/her logic and Ego-P, the score would be 0,½,0,½. This means that a person using his/her logic is somewhat in control of his Ego-P, but Ego-P is also blocking his ability to stay totally logical or impartial.

7. A person with a rating of ½, ½, ½, ½ (shown at the centre of the graph) has a balanced personality suitable for the present society. 'Suitable for the present society' reflects that the rating is subjective in terms of defining the *ideal personality*. In this sense, the personality model is a dynamic one in order to keep up with social changes and the ideal personality balance at the time. All other ratings are in relation to this standard. It could be a rather difficult job to set a basic 'ideal personality standard.' But it is necessary to have a dynamic yardstick to compare personalities against it. The objective is only to make comparative measures of personalities. The intention is not to define who is better than the other. It would be difficult to even define a 'normal person,' which is obviously not the same as the 'ideal personality.'

Referring to point 6 above, it is emphasised again that a perfect personality means that this person is making

the best use of his/her instincts, has great common sense, knows how best to adapt to the environment, and applies his/her ego in the most effective manner.
8. The lower rectangular of the Chart shows the 'Unconscious Self.' Our instincts and logic are inner urges that drive us to live and do things intuitively, most often without being conscious of how they (instincts and common sense) are operating within us. Sometimes we are aware and pay attention to our instincts and logic. This indicates that accessing our 'unconscious self' is not totally out of our reach. It simply requires more meditation and self-awareness.
9. The upper rectangular of the graph shows the 'Conscious Individual.' We portray our identity and individuality consciously through Model-P and Ego-P.
10. Men and women with all types of personality ratings could be found anywhere on the Chart. But it is probably safe to suggest (hypothesize) the average ratings of (0.3, 0.2, 0.8, 0.7) and (0.1, 0.4, 0.6, 0.9) for women and men respectively. These two ratings are shown in the Chart at points 'W' and 'M'.

These ratings reflect that women are depending more (compared to men) on their instincts in their decisions and actions (0.3 for women versus 0.1 for men). On the other hand, men depend more on their logic (0.2 for women versus 0.4 for men). Their intuitiveness makes women more capable of applying their Model-P to their advantage in a natural way and adapt easier in social settings. Model-P makes them more charming than men (0.8 for women versus 0.6 for men). Also it helps them to rebound after a relationship breakdown much better and faster. Use of their instincts and Model-P also makes women more assertive and decisive. They also are better equipped to bond together more naturally and deeply than men. Men are weaker in all these respects. Men are more aggressive because they are more Ego-P oriented than women (0.7 for women versus 0.9 for men). Also, due to their higher passivity in general, their Model-P is less natural and developed compared to women. They supposedly get together and bond, but their efforts are not deep and reliable. Women are noted to be 'emotional.' The reason is that they are more driven by their instincts and also they have better control of Model-P. They can charm or even shed tears naturally to influence others. On the other hand, men are less capable of being charming or manipulative due to their supposedly logical minds and higher arrogance. Dependence on Model-P and intuition obviously makes women more emotional and vulnerable. So they have been forced to develop some type of defence mechanism to compensate for their emotionality—to become a bit more practical than they are by nature. To do so, they have become more cautious, calculating, and clever. This necessity has made them alert to devise preventative measures for protecting themselves. This is another reason for them to become assertive. Then when they push the limits, of course, this assertiveness might lead to aggressiveness because the art of being assertive is not easy to master.

Due to their higher instinctual tendency and natural handling of Model-P, women are satiated with all three types of love, i.e., E-love, M-love, and S-love. Also, they can maintain a practical balance among these three types of love, better than men. Men usually have no or very little M-love to begin with due to their lower potentiality for Model-P or even perceiving (validating) it. So they know less about stirring, or responding to, romance. Then they suffer more also at the time of separation because of their lower adaptability to change and relationship failure, again due to their lower Model-P and higher Ego-P. Due to their lower capacity for M-love, men are also less capable of creating a balance between their E-love and S-love needs (or using their M-love to make up for the lack of E-love and S-love).

Men are usually more doubtful about their actions and decisions because they depend on their logic for decision making. This is true even though they have higher ego and an urge to come across as decisive. Logic always requires an assessment of alternatives, which causes delays and uncertainty. On the other hand, women are decisive because they mostly act based on their intuition (which is a definite point of view), but also because their strong Model-P tells them that being indecisive is unattractive. However, this decisiveness makes women less patient and more stubborn with their positions or opinions. Then they are also sensitive when their decisions and viewpoints are not understood or acted upon immediately. Women's sensitivity, on the other hand, leads to their higher expectations from relationships. They expect their spouses to understand their needs better, respond to their expectations more readily, etc. Since men are not equipped to understand and respond properly to this oversensitivity, more clashes and retaliations are introduced in relationships. Actually men cannot understand why women are so sensitive and react to simplest things so seriously. Women come across as too demanding nowadays because of their raw oversensitivity.

Women are more emotional partially due to their higher levels of the three love components, i.e., E-love, M-love, and S-love, again due to their instinctual urges. But they are emotional also because they know better how to use M-love to express love better than men can. Men have little or no M-love aptitude, but they are equally suffering from the deprivations caused by their unfulfilled E-love and S-love. Men's natural resistance (due to their logical tendency) toward M-love sometimes frustrates themselves too. But not as much as it frustrates women, because they don't understand why their M-love is unanswered, and why men are so incapable of M-love—romance.

Now the question is whether these differences between men and women are biological or conditional. Probably both. Can it change in the future? These are again topics beyond the scope of this book. But it seems reasonable, for example, to expect M-love increasing in men in the future after several decades of proper exposure to environments that might boost such a need in an authentic manner. They must build up trust gradually instead of being forced to play certain roles without a deep conviction. Whether the situation in relationships would improve and bolster trust between men and women is a big question though.

The reason women complain more often is because they make their decisions quickly intuitively and they don't have patience for men to fuss around projects or be lazy with their decisions (due to their contemplation habits), especially when women feel something should get done right away.

Intuition does not always provide the best answers for the problems of our modern societies. Instincts were good tools for primitive humans. Many of those instincts are still good guides for us in some instances. But some of the instinctual urges are no longer effective for dealing with all sorts of artificial parameters and values that are introduced into our daily lives. Nowadays, instincts alone cannot respond to complex situations in society. And our logic, which men like to depend on a lot, is often contaminated by Ego-P anyway. Obviously, everybody tries to use logic and patience to make better decisions instead of solely depending on instincts and allowing haste to take the best of them. But men do it a little bit more than it seems necessary to women. It is plausible that men have always been in a more direct contact with external forces and threats. So they have got more 'logic orientation' than women. Also women might've remained in closer contact with their instincts due to their maternal urges. A more detailed analysis of gender differences is provided in Chapter Fifteen.

11. Point 'H' in Personality Chart (Diagram 13.1) represents the author's best guess of an average personality rating for humans in modern societies. The rating is probably around (0.2, 0.3, 0.7, 0.8), which means that the personality of an average human in modern society is only

slightly influenced by instincts (20% of all his/her instinctual capacities), he/she benefits from logic and common sense to some extent (30% of his/her total potential), he/she knows how to adapt to his/her environment by using his Model-P (in 70% of occasions), and he/she is highly self-centred and object-oriented (in 80% of his/her dealings with people). This rating is obviously too far off the ideal personality shown in the centre of Diagram 13.1.

12. The arrows in the Personality Chart indicate the following facts:
    - Our instincts drive us to develop 'goal, social, and object' orientations. Thus, we develop Model-P and Ego-P and an ability to think and use logic.
    - Our urges for goal orientation and object orientation constantly exchange information to empower each other.
    - Our urges for social orientation and object orientation constantly exchange information to empower each other.
    - Social orientation and goal orientation constantly exchange information as well, but it is mostly through object orientation. Nonetheless, all factors of personality constantly exchange information amongst themselves.

The above personality model can hopefully help experts to develop:
   a) Tests for measuring each person's personality along the dimensions specified in the model.

b) A standard for the 'balanced personality' only for the sake of making comparisons possible.
c) Hypotheses and principles about the ways that personality ratings of individuals relate to their behaviour in relationships.
d) Average ratings for a common person and across the genders.
e) Hypotheses and principles about the compatibility of couples' personalities for the sake of maximizing the effectiveness of their relationship. Most likely a relationship becomes successful if the couple has high personality ratings, i.e., close to $½,½,½,½$. But it is interesting to develop theories about the possibility of other kinds of complementary or contradictory personalities corresponding in some types of relationships. Couples might be considered compatible for a particular relationship model according to their personality ratings.

Type Two Measures: Partners' Needs

In these tests, compatibility of partners are measured in two complementary ways in terms of their (i) *need urgencies,* and (ii) *personality traits.*

A. Need Urgency Compatibility

Diagram 13.2 on the next page shows those special cases where each partners' personal needs are mostly balanced with his/her expectations from their relationship, even though they might have different personal needs. This normally happens when partners are compatible to some extent and agree to make enough compromises to fit within a particular relationship model. Obviously, partners' personal needs vary and their expectations from a relationship are also different. So, in order to determine the compatibility of two individuals, it would be helpful to measure how, for example, each partner defines and rates his/her need urgency on Diagram 13.2 and whether they could cause conflicts in a particular relationship model.

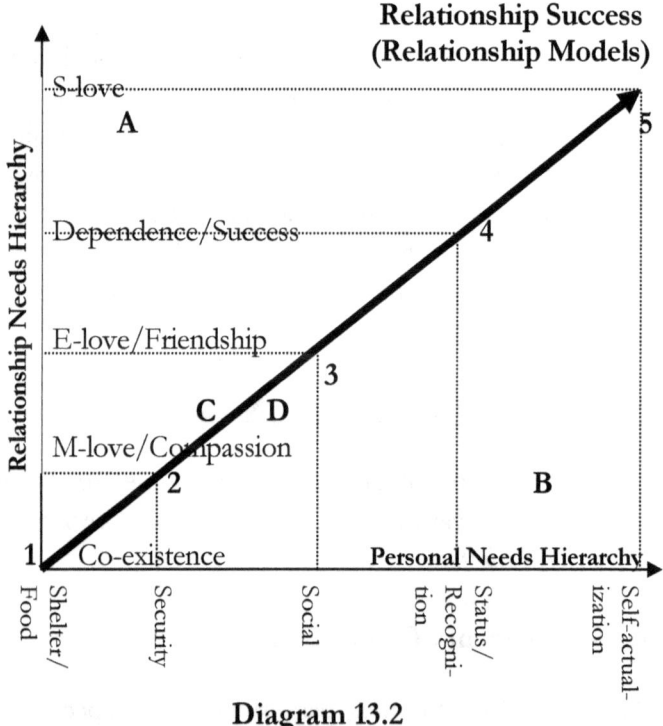

Diagram 13.2

Need Urgency of Partner A vs. Partner B (and C vs. D)

We have two couples in this graph: A&B are the first couple, and C&D are the second couple. Both couples have agreed to adopt a certain relationship model that they find suitable for them. But each partner still has his personal needs and relationship expectations as defined by points A, B, C, and D. Obviously, the second couple (C&D) is more compatible than the first couple. C and D have very close need urgencies. But A and B are too far apart in terms of their need urgencies, which presents a higher likelihood for relationship conflicts. This indicates that their job to make their chosen relationship model a success is more difficult for A&B compared to C&D. So, a test to measure each partners' need urgency can provide valuable information. Not only A and B are too far apart from one another, they are both too far away from the Relationship Success Arrow as well. So both of these factors should be measured:

(1) How far apart the need urgencies of partners are.
(2) How far each partner is from the Relationship Success Arrow.

The idea of partners' compatibility in terms of lifestyle and life priorities is not a new one. But measuring the right factors, and alongside the 'relationship needs hierarchy,' would make our judgments more concrete and useful for various purposes.

B. Personality Traits' Compatibility

Another set of tests should measure partners' personality traits in some detail. These tests would be somewhat in line with the way compatibility tests are run nowadays. The trick is, of course, to choose the right factors and traits for measuring compatibility. The list of factors and traits suggested below seem most relevant for determining couples' compatibility:

Compatibility to increase life enjoyment:

- Physical attraction
- Communication method and content
- Sharing activities (common interests)

Compatibility to increase cooperation and support one another:

- Teamwork capacity
- Ability to support and encourage personal goals
- Ability to provide physical and emotional support
- Ability for joint problem solving and decision making

Compatibility to enhance a sense of commitment:

- Tolerance
- Forgiveness
- Maturity, Patience
- Compassion
- Awareness of the self and the relationship needs
- Ability to express personal needs and expectations tactfully

Type Three Measures: Partners' Perceptions

Compatibility tests of Type One and Type Two, as presented above, are designed to measure the actual ratings of factors included in those tests. For example, measuring a partner's 'capacity for teamwork' would show the expected strength of that partner for teamwork. In Type Three tests, the perceptions of partners are measured, e.g., a partner's assessment of his/her own, or his/her partner's, capacity for teamwork. A great deal of information becomes available when a person's capacity for teamwork is compared with his/her own, as well as his/her partner's, perceptions of that person's actual teamwork in a particular relationship. Chapter Four explained the intricacy and impact of perceptions in relationships. Perceptions are extremely important because people make judgments and decisions according to their perceptions and not facts. Besides, if someone scores high, for example on his/her ability for teamwork, it doesn't necessarily mean that he/she practices it properly in a particular relationship. Even if he/she does a good job of it, if his/her partner doesn't see it that way, then the teamwork is not really effective. Therefore, measuring partners' perceptions of themselves, their partners, and their relationship is extremely important for measuring the compatibility of partners and the health of their relationship.

Partners' perceptions about every compatibility factor (as listed in Type Two Measures, pages 401-402), e.g., teamwork capacity, can be measured and analysed. Furthermore, partners' perceptions about each personality factor (as defined in Type One Measures) can be measured according to the comparisons outlined in Tables 4.1 and 4.2 (Chapter Four). For example, we can measure partner A's perception of himself compared with his/her partner's (B's) perception of him/her (A), let's say in terms of Ego-P. Both of these perceptions are in fact different from the actual measure of A's Ego-P. Let's depict these points in Diagram 13.3.

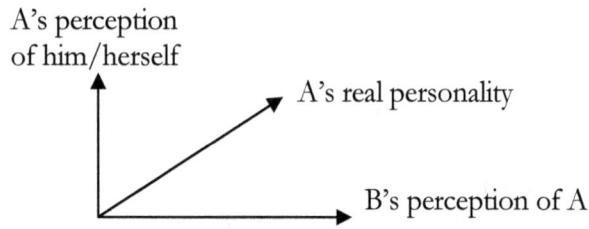

Diagram 13.3: An Example of Perception Measurement

The above compatibility tests are most useful for measuring the state of relationships on a regular basis and identifying the areas that weaknesses are becoming apparent. These tests are also very useful to identity the areas of partners' clear incompatibility at the outset, and to pinpoint the risks of getting in that relationship despite the best relationship model that partners can choose.

PART III

Final Observations
and Recap

Chapter Fourteen
The Destiny of Relationships

Relationship problems are too complex and widespread to overcome quickly. But what makes the situation most difficult is that we are not even prepared to acknowledge that this pandemic has deep-seated roots, which can be remedied only by radical changes. With this kind of passive mindset, we are not making systematic efforts to explore the underlying hurdles of relationships. The complexity of the relationship environment and our passivity about the existing chaos are the main reasons why it will take at least a century to find real solutions for relationships.

Proposing any kind of time estimate for reversing the deteriorating trends in relationships would be totally subjective. But if someone really insisted to know the author's personal opinion about a timeframe, he would offer the following dates:

1) By the year 2115, couples and society develop a good grasp of relationship hurdles and implement the needed radical changes.

2) By 2150, tangible progress in relationships is witnessed globally, provided that more catastrophic events don't distract us altogether.

Suggesting these, or any kind of, dates sounds ridiculous, even to the author himself, considering the dismal future of humanity in general if we follow our present path. The social challenges facing us in terms of water and food shortage, global warming effects, the rising sea levels, seemingly inevitable wars, and numerous other natural and man-made catastrophes might bring humanity to its knees in only a few decades anyway. Being bugged down by various social issues is indeed another reason that relationship problems might not be dealt with in any speeder manner. On the other hand, it is possible that the scope of social catastrophes automatically reduces our expectations from relationships to a large extent when we are forced to concentrate on the matter of survival, somewhat like the humans of the Stone Age. In that kind of environment, all the present fuss about relationships would be thrown out the window. Nonetheless, we must plan according to our most optimistic assumptions about the future of humanity. We should put some relative faith in humans' resilience and eventual awakening to deal with the variety of problems we have created for ourselves, including relationships.

The criteria to gauge progress consist of lower percentage of divorces, less dysfunctional and stressful families, a better balance between personal needs and the relationship needs, and longer lasting relationships.

Is Year 2115 a Good Target?

Considering the fast deteriorating situation of relationships and the rising personal stress due to socioeconomic conditions, the year 2115 is probably a reasonable ballpark to see an active change of attitude toward relationships. Some readers may find 2115 too pessimistic. They could argue that if there were problems with relationships, people would tackle them quickly rather than wait more than a century to help themselves. Actually, they might suggest that the situation would auto-correct itself if there were a real need for change. But the various discussions in this book show why our personal interests and flawed reasoning stand in our way of giving a higher priority to sanitising our relationships. It would probably take us a long time to eventually see the need for GARP and other relationship mechanisms. The situation is not going to auto-correct itself, either, because nowadays relationships are overwhelmed by many conflicting forces, which disallow any kind of straightforward development of ideas. Rather, a direct, solid intervention is required to enhance everybody's awareness and willingness to study and improve relationships. Even then it will take a long time before GARP and other relationship ideas are adopted and functional. The reasons are obvious: Basically people are nowadays too preoccupied with many complex, daily routines to take GARP seriously. They are not experts in finding solutions, and they have rigid mindsets to accept radical changes. Few of us really appreciate the depth of relationship problems despite the overwhelming evidence before our eyes and the suffering we endure. It appears that we have a great appetite for denial in order to sustain our hopes for finding love sooner or later. Our past experiences with love-affairs are not teaching us much about the repercussions of our romanticism. On top of this, social mechanisms are not progressive enough yet in line with social changes and couples' demand for independence and individuality. Social mechanisms, mostly legal systems, must be adapted to the new social realities so that people can adjust their mindsets too.

Some magical forces might cause rapid improvement in the state of relationships. Some people or scholars might even believe that the existing situation would become tolerable with some minor modifications that couples can learn to incorporate in their relationships quickly. But the author doubts these possibilities. Again, the chance for some kind of auto-correction looks dismal to the author. On the contrary, the need for some drastic intervention seems to be inevitable if we wish to suffer less.

On the other hand, some people and scholars may find the suggested dates of 2115 and 2150 too optimistic. They probably have lots of good arguments to support their claims. The author is rather inclined to agree with them. But let's take a middle ground and hope that some kinds of solutions can be found by the next century. Nonetheless, choosing a certain date is not meant to be scientific or essential, but rather a scheme to reflect the difficulty of the job at hand as far as the author can say.

In order to be a little bit more specific about the question 'Why 2115,' however, the facts discussed in the previous chapters must be outlined and assessed. This recap has another value too. It will provide the highlights of the topics reiterated throughout this book. Nonetheless, this chapter will provide more than one hundred points in the following categories:

- a list of the main *facts and trends* regarding relationships,
- short discussions about the *emerging relationship circumstances* in the new era, and

- a tentative timetable that seems reasonable for *implementing radical remedies* to bring some order to relationships.

Facts and Trends

The following facts and trends are observed in the new era:
1. Our economic systems, mainly consumerism, are forming our social values. People have gained a great appetite for objects and ideologies, hoping to buy more things and happiness by accumulating wealth.
2. 'Life is too short' and 'you live only once' have become the main mottos for most of us. So people jump out of their relationships to find a better partner and thus enjoy their presumed short lives the best they can. The basic requirements of relationships are ignored in the clouds of confusing slogans, misperceptions, and superficial values.
3. The increase in personal needs (for objects and compassion) has directly resulted in higher expectations from relationships.
4. The impact of higher expectations from relationships has been two folds: First, it has created additional personal stress that infects relationships. Second, we have come to believe that relationships can satisfy many of our emotional and financial needs. Couples assume that their partners are psychologically capable of providing all the love they seek. They demand more attention and affection to soothe their personal hurts and the stress of living in our chaotic societies. So, in effect, they are weakening the potency of their relationships.
5. Couples try to live beyond their means, at a higher standard of living than they can afford or deserve. This is an

added source of pressure, while partners strive to find that elusive happiness at all cost. They demand more regardless of their means. Family debt per capita in relation to their income is at its highest level ever, due to crooked family values and consumerism. Family crises are getting out of hand due to the lack of partners' sensibility about budgeting and their finances.

6. New societies have advocated the concepts of equality and individualism relentlessly. Partners' strive for independence and identity has turned relationships into a battleground for establishing their territory and superiority. Thus the role of teamwork in relationships is not gaining the needed attention.

7. We put our personal needs ahead of the relationship needs. We abandon our relationships more often by the simplest signs of inconvenience. We want to give ourselves the highest chance of finding happiness in another relationship as soon as possible.

8. The traditional principles that guided relationships in the past have been abolished and there are no new principles to guide couples anymore. There are no standards for couples to measure the health of their relationships against. So they depend on their own subjective viewpoints or the advice of friends and family to justify their crooked conclusions about the state of their relationships.

9. Couples consider 'love' the main factor for relationship success, not only for starting one, but also for sustaining it. The problem with this approach has been discussed in detail in Chapter Six and other parts of this book.

10. Relationships have become too complex and more demanding. Couples are unaware of the relationship needs, the psychological effects of their encounters, and how deeply they are affected by their genes and rearing conditions. They forget that people's mindsets or personalities cannot be changed simply because their partners are expecting them to change.
11. The number of divorces has skyrocketed in the last few decades. At this time, it has passed 50% mark and is approaching 60%.
12. The amount of frustration and stress in the surviving relationships is increasing, too, due to partners' oversensitivity and unfulfilled expectations from relationships. Partners are also burdened by their indecision about staying in or leaving their dysfunctional relationships.
13. Stress levels in society and organizations have risen drastically due to the complexity of work and interactions, employment uncertainties, discriminations, international competition, and the authorities' obsession to serve themselves instead of attending to their social responsibility.
14. The level of stress in families has also increased because, nowadays, usually both partners work outside the house and are exposed to extreme pressures, especially women, who have been subject to more abuse and discrimination in organizations.
15. All the bad values and habits of organizations, such as hypocrisy, power struggle, and arrogance have infected relationships too. Partners follow the same rules to assert themselves at work and at home. Some women might ac-

tually perceive their husbands as abusive bosses in the work environment as well as at home.

16. Personal stress due to social demands and substandard relationships makes couples testy and impatient in their relationships. They bug each other exactly at the time that life is confusing enough and out of control already. And they expect each other to be more romantic too!

17. To remedy relationship problems and enhance communication, counsellors encourage role-playing and love expressions. Yet relationship problems keep rising. This trend shows that the existing schemes, especially role-playing, are not working. Logically, unless partners are naturally convinced about the feelings or words they exchange, their relationship would only worsen. All these role-playings, as well as phony values, have made couples lose their identity and authenticity.

18. Companionship is probably the most important (basic) need of individuals nowadays and the one that is most often left unfulfilled. The importance of 'need for a companion' is evident in the wide range of personal needs it could potentially cover, as discussed in Chapters One and Twelve. Most people think and dream about a good companion as much as they think about food, consciously or subconsciously.

19. A crucial fact that couples ignore when they start their relationships is that, **nowadays the chances of relationships failing are higher than surviving.** The idea of finding a soul mate usually turns into a sour fate when they only end up in substandard relationships. Couples ignore this vital fact at the outset and don't do enough soul-searching and planning in advance.

20. Couples are not trained and prepared to handle the relationship needs and the most likely scenario in their relationships, i.e., separation.

Emerging Relationship Circumstances

The above facts and trends, and other discussions in this book paint the reality of relationships in the new era. The points made in this section are only some of the emerging circumstances of relationships. These examples show the complexity of relationship problems. And yet they hardly scratch the depth of relationship problems. They reflect that reversing the deteriorating situation of relationships would be an uphill struggle and quite time-consuming. **All references like 'people', 'men', 'women' or 'we' don't mean everybody, but rather a significant portion of them.**

21. People seem to be living in a fantasy world with substantial needs and dreams. Their needs for objects don't necessarily match their talents and efforts, and their needs for affection don't match their own capacity to give or receive compassion. Even when they are given wealth and compassion, they abuse it because they are not mentally prepared to handle them responsibly. The more their selfish needs are satisfied, the more arrogant and greedier they become. Everybody believes they deserve more love and things.
22. Accordingly, couples' expectations from relationships have become unrealistic. They have just kept increasing them in line with their rising personal needs.

23. The level of misperceptions and miscommunications in relationships are increasing very fast, too, as explained in Chapters Four and Five.
24. The increasing amount of unfulfilled expectations from relationships has in turn led to a great deal of frustration, retaliation, and hostility in families and society. Partners' oversensitivity due to untamed expectations has obscured even simple communications. For example, we hear often nowadays, especially from women, a phrase such as, "He/she doesn't know how to spoil me!" Many relationships break down every day because of this odd expectation. They don't even mind saying it so bluntly, as if 'spoiling' is a reasonable demand for relationships in the new era. Especially, after years of exploitation by men, now women want to be spoiled as if making up for the lost compassion of past generations. They demand E-love, attention, and obedience, too, sometimes.
25. In all, couples have become too idealistic and emotional about their expectations from relationships. They have lost their sense of objectivity about the purposes and potentials of relationships.
26. Couples continue to jump out of their relationships faster and faster because they believe they can find another partner to fulfil their expectations better and give them the love they deserve. Most of us struggle all our lives in search of an ideal relationship. Only a few of us might eventually realize our naivety after repeated failures.
27. Both single and married people envy each other's position and lifestyle. Everybody wishes to have the advantages of both lifestyles. Married people jump out of their

relationships fast because of their misperceptions about a single (independent) life and the possibility of finding a more appropriate mate. And unmarried people look for an ideal partner obsessively while they also brag about their freedom as a single person. Besides our pleasure seeking mentality in the new era, our erratic urges for both dependence and independence are obviously playing a role in creating these misperceptions about relationships too.

28. We have turned into a special (spoiled) generation—asking for more love while becoming more arrogant at the same time. We don't realize that with more arrogance, we keep losing our capacity to give and receive love. Our children are even more spoiled in terms of idealism and not appreciating the real nature of life, which is full of hardships. So the deteriorating trend in relationships would go downhill for some time to come.

29. Couples are unaware of the true success factors for relationships. So they continue to insist on love and objects as the main requirements.

30. Couples judge the health of their relationships arbitrarily or based on phony values, because there are no authentic yardsticks for setting practical standards and measuring the success of relationships.

31. Couples have little patience and interest to learn about the basic problems of relationships in a serious manner, e.g., reading books like this one. At best, people have only time and patience for the possible quick fixes that have no ultimate value. People read those kinds of books or follow a few of counsellors' advices only to show that

they did something to improve their relationships and still it didn't work.
32. The increasing rivalry and clashes between men and women look like some kind of all out gender warfare. The level of insults, belittling, retaliations, intimidations, abuse, manipulation, games, badmouthing, power struggles, competition, crying, making a scene, screaming, blackmailing, and trying to outsmart one another just keep increasing.
33. Men and women are becoming increasingly alienated due to the changing social values and couples' strive to establish their gender identities better (usually by aiming to weaken the other gender's identity). It appears that some inherent gender differences are also adding fuel to the matter of couples' alienation in relationships. Some of these gender differences are briefly noted in this chapter as part of the emerging relationship circumstances. However, the main hypotheses and analyses of gender differences are discussed in the next chapter.
34. Many of clashes between men and women are due to women's higher instinctual tendency challenging men's higher logical predisposition. In reality, however, both our instincts and logic are usually flawed anyway. So, often, nobody is right due to their erroneous perceptions and lack of objectivity. Then problems increase because men and women want to change each other's decision processes, i.e., to make them more logical or intuitive—more like themselves. They fail because the instinctual urges of women and the logical tendencies of men are too deep to change quickly even if they realized the need

for it. Their inherent personality traits often hinder this change to happen.

35. Personal failures in relationships, ongoing clashes, and sad statistics have led to a deep sense of mistrust among partners. But people still ask for more love as a means of strengthening their relationships. The big contrast is obvious when people insist on more love as the overall trust about love and relationships is fading fast in society. Love in the absence of trust! How could couples really be sincere about their love expressions when deep down, in their subconscious, their sense of mistrust about people, including their partners, linger?

36. It is hard to believe that 'trust' can be rebuilt into relationships as a general social norm in the near future and couples become truly convinced about it. Although couples pretend to start their relationships based on trust, deep down they remain justifiably sceptical about it. This is true despite their convincing expressions of love and the roles they play mostly through M-love. Overall, it is naïve to depend on 'love' or 'trust' to build a relationship. Instead, couples need objective mechanisms and a relationship framework to map their joint life.

37. All those sleeping around with different partners and then talking about finding love are not congruent values or plans. It does not matter how we consider our behaviour a reflection of modernity, our brains cannot handle these high levels of contradictions and still feel love and trust. Satisfying the sexual urge is a practical choice in modern society, but confusing it with love is hypocritical and impractical. The meanings of love, lust, and trust

have become too intermingled and convoluted. This is causing additional mistrust and shakier social values.

38. The conflict caused by less trust and more demand for love is felt deeper by men. This is because men supposedly have higher logical tendencies than women who are more emotional according to the personality chart in Diagram 13.1. With their lower M-love and Model-P, men are already handicapped in expressing love, but when trust is gone, the matter of expressing love becomes even more awkward for them. Women are more capable of expressing love, even when their trust is not high. This is due to their higher M-love and Model-P, of course. Men lack this flexibility but women have a hard time accepting this fact and wonder why men are so passive most often.

The level of trust in relationships, and about our partners' words, would keep declining in line with the upward trend in relationship failures. Thus expressing love with honesty would become even more difficult, especially for men. Accordingly, men usually give up the possibility of finding a soul mate sooner than women. They continue to look for a companion nonetheless, but not with the aim of finding love. Women continue to remain more romantic and optimistic about finding a soul mate due to their higher intuitiveness and Model-P.

39. Couples are unaware of their personal flaws and also how badly everybody gets damaged psychologically during their relationship experiences. They believe that not only they are flawless, but also there are enough perfect people out there to choose for companionship. So they keep searching for some untenable ideal life that matches

their fantasies. In the older times, people used to believe that marriage's most important objective was for partners to share the hardships of life together. Couples knew how difficult life really is. They were ready and willing to sacrifice and help each other sincerely. They played their angelic roles to reduce each other's burdens. But nowadays many couples do just the opposite. First of all, people are pushing themselves to stay positive and believe that life is splendid and manageable. So, instead of sharing life's hardships, they create more burdens for each other with a slight sign of inconvenience. Their unrealistic expectations and dreams about happiness make them view any nuisance an unacceptable barrier in their relationships. And they want to abandon their partners rather quickly for the greener pastures. Today's marital objectives are mainly revolving around partners' fixation for love, sexuality, and happiness.

40. Women have a harder time in satisfying their conflicting needs for dependence and independence than men do. This is due to the emphasis nowadays for women to seek independence as a means of establishing their identity. This pressure aggravates their already conflicting (instinctual) urges for both dependence and independence.

Instinctually, women strive for security and dependence more than men do. Also, the more independence they acquire, the more dependence they crave. This is because their exaggerated search for independence hinders the natural fulfilment of their need for dependence. For example, women are more eager to find love and a social partner, not only because they crave it harder instinctually (due to their higher Model-P and the urge for reproduction), but also because they are more optimistic about the possibility of finding their soul mate.

So, on the one hand, women like to depend on men, for procreation and for fulfilling their higher social needs due to their higher Model-P. But, on the other hand, they feel the urgency to assert their identity by proving their independence. Seeking more independence is also a matter of 'life phase' for women, while raising and enjoying their kids. They feel empowered and independent due to their maternal power, but also because they presume their men are sticking around for emergencies anyway. Once their kids are gone, however, their need for dependence takes precedence again, especially if men have strayed. Inherently, women seem to need dependence on men for support and to complete their social identity, though they might not wish to accept this fact.

Men's conflict in terms of dependence/independence is straight forward and simple. They seek independence instinctually, but need to depend on women to fulfil some of their basic needs, including compassion and sex. They appear helpless without women, while inherently they continue to value their own independence highly.

Nonetheless, both genders strive for both dependence and independence regularly, though for completely different reasons. They go through these cycles even more forcefully at some stages of their relationships. They start a relationship to fulfil their need for dependence (mostly their basic needs, e.g., sex and D-love). But soon they take their relationship for granted and press for a complex need like independence (according to their naïve perceptions of independence.)

41. There is a race in society to behave pompously, strive for a lot of things and compassion, and be highly competitive. Everybody must also be highly sociable and pretentious and popular. When people go to work on Mondays, they keep asking each other what they did on the weekend as if gauging a person's worth and completeness.
42. Humans' inner conflicts are responsible for their confusion, stress, and suffering in life, which eventually impact their relationships too. Overall, humans' *elementary* inner forces to be good are always in conflict with the external forces goading them to be bad. The modern society advocates greed, hypocrisy, dominance, and arrogance just to name a few of the crooked trends in the new era.
43. People have become too opportunistic (users) and calculating, due to their negative experiences and conditioning, including their conviction that life is too short and precious. They use various schemes to strengthen their positions and get ahead, and they associate with people whom they find useful to them in some ways. This general perception (about people's hypocrisy, calculating nature, and insincerity) affects relationships, too, because partners judge each other based on their shallow criteria of life, but also their overall mistrust.
44. How can people be romantic when most of them are only trying to be practical (by being so calculating and materialistic) in such a chaotic environment? These are contradictory objectives. Our social setting is ruining people's perceptions of one another and 'love'.
45. Couples are less capable nowadays to perceive and judge their relationships in its totality. They are easily influ-

enced by their own need urgencies, and they are easily irritated by single events. The overall advantages of relationships are largely ignored due to egotistical judgments based on emotional episodes and erroneous perceptions.

46. There is a 'typical woman' image developing in the new era mostly due to women's recent efforts to achieve equality, individualism, and independence. They have created and portrayed a special role and identity for themselves. On the other hand, men have not yet tried to create and propagate an identity for themselves. They have not been active in projecting a picture of a typical man. Yet they are stereotyped as selfish and unromantic. In reality, however, men are simply lost and without identity, nowadays, because they have difficulty understanding and coping with women's new demands. They have difficulty defining and asserting themselves at this time.

47. Women have been able to bond and support one another to set the rules of relationships. They are creating a new culture that might eventually prove quite dysfunctional for maintaining relationships. An advantage of women's bonding is that they get plenty of support when they leave their relationships. On the other hand, because of this bonding, and in line with the women's general attempt to propagate the new culture, they encourage each other to be least tolerant of their relationship flaws and abandon their spouses quickly. So, while they seem to help each other in terms of support after separation, they might also be screwing up each other and causing more separations, *maybe even intentionally*, by provoking one another with their progressive ideas and attitude.

48. Men, on the other hand, don't have a sense of empathy, nor enough Model-P, to soothe each other's hurts once they leave their wives. Part of this deficiency is because men keep their emotions private to protect their pride. Women show their emotions but move on faster.
49. Women are emotionally stronger by nature, and also due to their higher social adaptability and Model-P. This helps them in terms of rebounding quickly after separation. And then the support they receive from other women helps them recover even faster and better. But the same need for social adaptability and Model-P makes them quite anxious to find a new companion.
50. Most women believe in the likelihood of finding love and an ideal partner, compared with men who give up faster and thus seek a companion mostly out of loneliness and for satisfying their basic needs. In fact, women appear to have a higher need and talent for all three levels of love, i.e., E-love, M-love, and S-love than men.
51. Women's intuitiveness, higher Model-P, and bonding ability give them more resilience and optimism about life and love, which help them adapt better to changes and disappointments. Generally, they don't get too discouraged by their failures in past relationships. Yet the number of women on anti-depressants is twice that of men.
52. Conversely, it usually takes longer for men to heal their wounds and recommit themselves to another relationship, due to their lesser resilience and the lack of support after separation. This additional agony teaches them better lessons. So they usually delay getting into serious relationships. Their logic and mistrust usually override their emotional needs, unlike women. Yet their lower social

adaptability makes them more vulnerable in terms of submitting to women's whims out of loneliness—but not necessarily out of love.

53. Due to their pessimism about finding a soul mate, men are becoming passive and this is making women frustrated, and more assertive.

54. Women are more social instinctually. They seek a companion to fit and feel better in social gatherings, to complete their identity, and for support. So they don't seek men necessarily out of love, loneliness, or merely for the sake of having a companion. They already have many companions in other women. Satisfying their social and security needs often takes precedence over their craving for love. A cynical observation about relationships in the new era is that sometimes women seek men mostly to exert their power over them; to prove their superiority. Conversely, men prefer some seclusion. Thus their need for a companion is more for avoiding total loneliness. Men like socializing too, of course, but it is not their main motivation for finding a companion. Men socialize mostly to make their mates happy, to be perceived as a sociable person, or to create variety in their lives.

55. Despite the women's urge for a companion, and their obsession to enjoy life at its fullest, the welfare of their children often gets a higher priority. Many women postpone their serious relationships with another man, after a marriage breakdown, until they feel their children's relative independence or readiness. So, considering the sacrifice most women make for their children, they believe they deserve their higher love, which they usually receive more than fathers do.

56. Fathers' traditional respect has diminished in families. There are several reasons for this. First, women have assumed the ultimate role and responsibility for raising children and they perform this difficult task with absolute authority and decisiveness. Children find their mothers in charge and their fathers passive with much less authority around the family. Second, mothers really dedicate themselves to their kids, who in turn take a keen note of their mothers' devotion. Children feel a higher bond with their mothers instinctually, too, the same way mothers feel toward their children. Third, children see their mothers more vulnerable and needy for attention, especially because women can show their vulnerability through Model-P cleverly. So children feel obliged to take care of their mothers more than they see a need to sympathize with their fathers. The bottom line is that men feel less involved with children and not receiving adequate love and respect. Their wives actually treat them a lot like another one of the children, including the use of an authoritative tone in their conversations with their husbands. Nonetheless, the lower level of respect and power for fathers has made a negative impact on the health of the whole family.

57. It was emphasized that women are striving to create and express their new strong identity after many decades of oppression by men. They have learned to be assertive and support one another to establish their individuality and identity. Conversely, men are losing theirs due to the ambiguity of the gender roles and new relationship expectations. This is an accurate picture overall, yet the final outcome is questionable. For one thing, women's

success to enforce their identity depends a lot on men's reaction to their demands and the roles that women expect of them to play. But more importantly, both men and women can truly attain, and feel comfortable with, their identities only if they have a companion. Our everlasting, inherent urge to find our soul mates is the best indication of our sense of incompleteness (lack of full identity) without a good companion. Discussions in Chapter Twelve demonstrated that our need for a companion is an urgent and important need. It can potentially satisfy a large number of personal needs of humans stretching from the basic need for sex to the spiritual need for S-love. When these needs are not satisfied, few humans might attain enough psychological independency to affirm their identity in the new era. Women may pretend that they understand, and are happy with, their emerging identity. But when they reflect on their lives, they notice that their identity is incomplete and hurtful without a companion. Indeed, they need a man in their lives more than ever nowadays; more than men need a woman. This is due to women's higher Model-P and eagerness for social activity. So women's identity is questionable without a man or as long as they are not happy with their companion. For one thing, they would be too preoccupied with the task of finding their soul mate, as they are optimistic about finding an ideal partner. As stated before, men are not so optimistic about finding a soul mate, and they are less obsessed about having a companion (or even an identity) due to their lower Model-P. So, if women's strive for identity reduces their chances of finding or keeping *competent* men in their lives, they would never find their true identity. 'Competent' refers to men who supposedly have a strong character (identity). No woman would enjoy a man with a weak character. A man without a strong identity is worthless even for women. Yet many women don't mind weakening their husbands' spirits. It is absurd that all these conflicting forces are somehow corrupting relationship environments. Men are confused and lost for the time being anyway. But their innate resistance and passivity are indeed damaging women's attempt to assert their own identity. This is especially true when the end result is women's lesser access to *competent* men to support them mentally and physically.

58. Having stressed enough on the fact that both men and women need a companion to find their true identity, a more distressing fact must be stressed again as well. That is, even when they are in a relationship, neither gender can find their identities because of all their clashes. They cannot find their identities in relationships either, unless they adopt a more practical relationship framework. The reason is that as long as the parameters for creating their identities are not pure and unselfish, partners continue to fight in order to enforce their perceptions of ideal identities for their genders. Partners' misperceptions of themselves and their partners, as well as their erroneous impression of ideal identities for their genders, prevent them from finding their true and practical identities. Besides, their continuous clashes suck the energy out of them to find and exert their true identity.

59. Two types of role-playing are introduced in relationships, both with adverse effects. First, the role-playing schemes

that marriage counsellors advocate in order to stir up communication and love in relationships. The weakness of this technique is that as long as the real problems of a relationship are not understood by partners, playing roles only frustrates them. They must somehow grasp and tackle the main sources of their problems directly. All the superficial communications actually confuse them more and drive them away from the reality of their relationship.

The second type of role-playing has even a harsher impact on relationships. It begins from the minute partners meet and it continues throughout their relationship. They play all kinds of roles and games to impress, entice, or deceive each other. They exaggerate in all respects in order to succeed: by flattering, getting too emotional, showing indifference, proving their independence and power, retaliating, and so many other games that go on throughout the process of dating and in their relationship too. People like to play certain roles in order to set precedence and enforce their needs. They strive to set artificial boundaries to establish their superiority from the beginning. So it is becoming impossible to sense sincerity and the true personality of people nowadays. This role-playing (including retaliations or reactions as defence mechanisms) might be somewhat justified considering that everybody gets hurt in relationships at some point. They play games to prevent more headaches. But then, they lose the chance of relaxing and being natural. By playing games, couples have minimized their own level of objectivity as well as their partners'. So they suffer personally while their relationships follow a destructive course too. By role-playing, couples are also losing the opportunity of finding companions who appreciate them for who they really are. Instead they only struggle with their own phony personalities (to appear natural), as well as with their partners' (to understand them perhaps).

Nowadays, most people like to depend on their clever Model-P to play appealing roles for attracting love and sympathy. At the same time, they also try to hide their strong Ego-P and haughtiness behind Model-P. In a society where arrogance has found such a strong value, even Model-P often advocates pomposity. So it is becoming difficult to understand who a person really is.

60. Women are becoming more active socially and placing a high value on living life to its fullest. They need to do more things, go to various functions, and travel extensively. At the same time, men are becoming more passive, content, and couch potatoes.

61. Referring to the Personality Chart on page 389, it is suggested that women are the stronger gender overall (see also Chapter Fifteen for a detailed discussion of gender differences). Men are a weaker gender, in terms of emotional vulnerability (personality), despite the fact that women are more emotional. The reasons for this seeming contradiction are explained throughout this chapter. Actually, men's weakness is widely known and propagated regularly in the new era. Even advertising agencies exploit this perception whenever they can benefit from it (see note 71 below). Women are also aware of the men's vulnerability. So it is natural that they might attempt to use this information to push their ideologies and obtain everything they believe they deserve.

62. Due to their higher reliance on intuition, decisiveness, and the teachings of the new culture, women are trying to be in charge of the family. They seem to be good at it, too, in many respects. But, in the process, they also feel the need to prove their superiority to men. Well, since women are the stronger gender in reality, why should not they be in charge or try to show off their superiority occasionally? The problem is that any type of superiority by either gender cannot work in the new era where the emphasis must be placed on equity, individualism, independence, and satisfying personal needs. So when women try to prove their superiority, it leads to further deterioration of relationships and more mistrust. Except, of course, in the cases where husbands really prefer to be completely passive and/or submissive. Many women actually don't mind turning their spouses into submissive men in order to feed their own ego and E-love. Some women might think: "Why not give it a try anyway and see if it works." But, in the end, this situation cannot prevail in progressive relationships.
63. Relationships would go through a lengthy, unpredictable transition period while women try to assert themselves and find their identity.
64. During this transitional period, women have difficulty being a modest (content) wife in an environment which advocates a domineering attitude to enforce equality and identity. Many women have been successful in practicing a dominance approach in their relationships already. They present very appealing role models for the rest of them. Women's influence over one another is too strong to be ignored, by either women or men. Mothers, daugh-

ters, female colleagues and friends are all placing a lot of pressure on one another nowadays to behave assertively. Any woman who attempts to behave differently might be ousted. But more importantly, she would feel miserable for not being a typical (assertive) woman like others.

65. It is quite likely that many men have become modest and submissive, because they have less capability for bonding together and are thus becoming weaker. Furthermore, they are less eager to develop and maintain a strong identity for themselves. Their logical minds, passivity, and neediness for a companion are keeping them the weaker gender they have probably always been. Men's resort to violence and physical domination are indeed good clues about their inability to keep up with the kind of games that women are better at playing so naturally. Men's frustration is also due to their inability to keep up with women's needs, which they often find illogical anyway.

66. Women seem to be winning most of the battles in relationships, but it is doubtful that any gender can win the war that is going on. The point is that, as long as one gender or one partner is weaker than the other, their relationship remains dysfunctional. There would not be enough respect and challenge for the stronger partner to stay in the relationship or take it serious enough. This fact is indeed most relevant in our new culture where individualism and self-esteem have found such a high value. So, women's urge to establish their superiority in the new era would not benefit anybody in the long run. Women are behaving naturally, of course, according to their inherent personality strengths and strong bonding capability. Nonetheless, their effort is already putting re-

lationships in great jeopardy. They would be (are) the ones suffering the most from the repercussions of the existing situation, because they are more sensitive and they believe in love.

67. Obviously relationships get into trouble because both partners are at fault in some respects. And also because the whole society is losing control over both the economy and relationship norms. Even when a partner is smart, patient, and humble to make the relationship work, the prospects of saving his/her relationship might still be gloomy. The reason is that his/her modest behaviour is perceived as a sign of weakness instead of goodness. He/she is treated poorly or ignored. So both partners are normally forced to be assertive, which usually turns into aggressiveness and quarrels.

68. The situation with relationships resembles the global warming mayhem. Nobody is willing to accept the existence of a fundamental problem or do anything about it. The main reason, also like global warming, is the economy. Materialism and hypocrisy wouldn't allow partners to become more realistic about the values surrounding them.

69. Women go into their next relationships with even more expectations instead of less. They believe that their reasons for leaving their past relationships (e.g., need for more love or compassion) had been justified and thus their new relationships must make up for everything they had missed before. They want to prove to themselves and others that they made a right decision to leave their previous relationships. So they look for more love, luxury, and security. Conversely, men usually prepare them-

selves for less authority and set lower expectations if they decide to get into another serious relationship.

70. An effect of women's intuitiveness is that their priorities somewhat change after having their children. For one thing, they are forced to exhibit a lot of authority to make their children follow their rules. A mother is driven instinctually to manage her life as well as her children's. Therefore she becomes authoritative, commanding, and demanding. These are mostly instinctual traits that surface when her life begins to get hectic with children, and maybe a lazy husband, testing her patience. She also finds less time for her husband after children are born. He is suddenly given a lower priority and importance, maybe not intentionally but rather practically. Furthermore, she learns eventually that it is more efficient and natural to treat her husband like another one of her children. Decisively, she has to get things organized and done quickly the way she has found productive through her child-rearing experiences. She finds these tactics, i.e., commanding, demanding, and impatience, most natural and effective for running the family affair. For men, however, this gradual (but drastic) change gets unnatural and annoying eventually. They attribute it to their wives' loss of interest and romance. In this environment, women look rather insensitive, impatient, and sometimes even cruel, in the way they run the whole household, including their husbands.

71. Some partners, especially men, learn to stay passive in order to cope with their substandard relationship situation. Overall, women play a more active role in shaping the relationship atmosphere and imposing the rules due

to their decisiveness. Men, on the other hand, are lazy to argue or fuss too much. So more women are becoming in charge of relationships while men are becoming more submissive.

The existing culture does not give too much room for teamwork. Actually, an image of men's submissiveness (and maybe their idiocy) is propagated regularly even in TV commercials to sell products to women. For example, while writing this chapter, a couple of TV commercials caught the author's eyes. They reflect how social trends regarding relationships are grasped and exploited even by advertisers:

The first commercial was about Multigrain Cheerios. The box apparently refers to 120 calories per serving. The husband makes an innocent comment to his wife: "Are you trying to watch your diet?"

"Do I look like I need to watch my diet?" the wife asks with irritation and sarcasm.

"No, honey, I'm just stating what the box says (about its low calories)," the poor husband replies with a guilty tone in absolute panic.

"What else the box says?" the wife demands.

"The box says, 'Shut up, Steve.'" the husband replies with shame and misery. The wife smirks.

The second commercial was about McCain's Deep and Delicious frozen cake. The wife is enjoying the cake. And the husband is trying to draw his wife's support about his dream of becoming a mime. But she is not paying attention to his comments and enactment of some miming gestures, because she is absorbed by the taste of the cake. When she notices him finally, she demands with impatience: "What're you doing?"

The husband freezes in his miming gesture like a lamb suddenly facing a lion. "I'm living my dream," he replies with total panic and desperation again. "Stop it," the wife orders him.

The husband stops, scared stiff and mute. The commercial ends. The wife makes the ruling and that is the end of the story for the husband who likes to live his dream of becoming a mime.

Humour is supposedly the intention of these commercials, to sell their products. But they are propagating men's passivity and subordination in relationships in the new era—which is largely true but not a proper viewpoint. They exploit the fact that men are put down by women and they can't do a darn thing about it. They advocate women's power, all for the sake of flattering and encouraging them to buy their products. These episodes reflect the reality of relationships, but also propagate arrogance. They find it funny that women's superiority is becoming part of our acceptable culture, including aggression toward men. How are we going to convince ourselves that these values are destructive for both men and women? How many years will we need to be convinced? Probably a century is a good guess!

72. If someone asks the author to identify the most destructive force damaging relationships, he would suggest 'Hollywood.' Those naïve love stories, senseless gender confrontations, and meaningless conclusions have been contaminating the brains of the general public all over the world. Some ignorant writers are doing everybody a dis-

service by their unrealistic, simple-minded scripts. A scene in the movie *Two Weeks Notice* with Sandra Bullock and Hugh Grant is really confusing and interesting: Sometime in the middle of the night, Sandra is returning a pair of shoes that she had borrowed from her friend—a weird timing all by itself. After the friend goes down and opens the door, they sit down near the curb to talk. The friend's husband appears at the window of their apartment, looks down into the street with concern, and says: "Everything's okay?" The wife yells at him with unbelievable attitude, "Not now! Everything is not about you!" Her comment and tone of voice has no relevance and meaning in that scene or in the context of the whole movie. It only reflects the absurdity of relationships' atmosphere. "Okay," the husband mumbles with apprehension as he withdraws away from the window.

73. Women's higher intuition leads to other obstacles too. First, it makes them hasty and adamant in their judgments. Second, it increases their tendency to see and feel things without too much communication. Often they believe they can somehow read their husbands' minds and detect the hidden clues in their conversations. They also assume that their husbands have the same level of intuition to understand their wishes without communicating the ideas to them clearly. They say something and expect their husbands to read between the lines and grasp their intentions. Then they get surprised and frustrated when their husbands don't comprehend their messages. Often they actually believe that their husbands have gotten the message, but are refusing to accept it or do something about it. Women believe that men are (or should be) as

careful and intuitive as they are. They don't recognize that men's lower intuitiveness cannot be helped. Besides, men's logic dictates their need for clear communication instead of guessing the meaning of a vague message.

Overall, women do not believe in, and actually resist, an open and detailed communication, maybe because they feel their husband is not listening, anyway, or is not interested. But women have also become oversensitive and react harshly when men cannot understand their vague messages. As noted above, women's intuition is filling the gap that hinders men's understanding of a message without full communication. Men require clarity and women resist it since they find it unnecessary and unromantic, or they stay vague merely out of spite occasionally too. They simply expect their husbands to understand their meanings and intentions. For example, a husband was complaining to the author that whenever his wife realized her mistake, she only tried to make up for it by preparing his favourite meal, buying him a pair of socks, or making some kind of an indirect gesture of these natures. But she never apologized directly or admitted that she had made a mistake. She simply expected to get the matter resolved without acknowledging the problem or discussing it. He said that, without an open discussion about the problem and a sincere apology, the matter never got resolved in his mind and his wounds never healed. Actually, he considered his wife's behaviour (i.e., the gesture of buying him a present or cooking a fine meal) another type of manipulation.

74. Couples are unaware of the hurdles of finding a new companion after getting out of their existing relation-

ships. They are naïvely too optimistic about their chances of finding a reasonable match, even in the older ages. This is in particular difficult for women who are seeking men of higher qualities after their past relationships fail. Accordingly, couples' problems and frustrations would keep increasing in their second and third relationships. The only exception is when one or both partners become somewhat passive in their new relationship.

75. Many couples prefer to deal with the imperfections of their existing relationships rather than a new one. This is because they get used to its flaws and their partners' shortfalls after many years of sharing both good memories and life's hardships together. They learn to bear their relationship flaws by always recalling its merits. They admit that both partners in almost all relationships are most likely annoyed by each other's quirks. They feel that bearing the imperfections of their existing relationship is easier than learning about, and accepting, the new imperfections of a stranger (a new companion) all of a sudden. Men are particularly lazy, too, to go through the hassle of finding a new companion if the existing relationship is not too bad.

76. People usually expect peace in a new relationship after tolerating their previous partners' imperfections. For men especially, staying lonely seems preferable to living with a person who brings different kinds of idiosyncrasies and childish demands. People hate learning new stuff and adjusting, especially at the later stages of their lives. With old age, they need less sex and usually have less patience or incentives, anyway, while getting more grouchy and demanding too.

77. We seek relationships to relieve our loneliness, but soon find out the absurdity of our dreams and efforts, because relationships actually make us feel the ultimate depth of loneliness and helplessness.
78. Everybody is getting more defensive in their interactions with others due to their past experiences and the increasing level of aggressiveness in society. This is, of course, an added psychological pressure in relationships. We speak with people and our partners with apprehension (superficially), in order to not trigger their defence mechanisms and starting an argument. This situation keeps relationships too edgy and unnatural. At the same time, people are also becoming more aggressive and offensive in order to counterbalance their partners' assertiveness; as the saying goes: the best defence is offence.
79. Often relationships get into trouble because partners are unhappy with themselves and the life they are leading. So they depress their partners with their attitude too. Often they blame their partners for their own career failures, unhappiness, boredom, or unfulfilled dreams. Sometimes they nag at each other to conceal their own shortfalls, e.g., in socializing. Then they gradually hate each other because they believe that their partner is in fact responsible for their unhappiness.
80. Partners waste a lot of time and energy on faultfinding and blaming each other supposedly for the sake of improving their relationship. If only they realized that in the end it doesn't matter whose fault the problems are as long as those problems remain irreconcilable. The bottom line is that they must either find mutually agreeable solutions (a suitable relationship model) to relate some-

how or separate. When relationship problems go beyond certain levels, the only solution is to find ways of relating (living together) passively at a lower level of the relationship hierarchy (model), and stop trying to solve the problems per se. Problems are often unsolvable, because they are caused by irreversible idiosyncrasies of partners. We humans have proven that not even our logic and common sense can help us solve our personal or social (including economic and political) problems.

81. The gender struggles to reach some illusory balance of power and equality is continuing at many levels, and the situation would most likely get out of hand in the future with global destructive outcomes.

82. We have difficulty learning from our mistakes and from the pains that our relationships are causing us. We prefer to suffer than change our perspective about the inherent limitations of relationships, especially within the context of the existing lifestyles. Accordingly, it would be hard for the controversial messages of this book to find popularity amidst the mass of beautifully packaged messages (and social values) promising prosperity and happiness to everybody.

83. One of the main goals of a relationship framework is to bring *objectivity* back into relationships. But a main hurdle is selling the idea of objectivity to women who are used to dealing with issues intuitively, and to men whose sense of logic has already made them dogmatic. Nonetheless, society must gradually propagate the guidelines of a relationship framework. A more logical atmosphere must replace gender struggles for superiority. Reaching a balance of power and identity would require some form of

objectivity eventually. Otherwise chaos would bring family relationships to a halt.

84. A puzzling point is, 'What kind of a partner are couples looking for when they insist on breaking each other's pride and spirit, mainly by competing with each other relentlessly?' In particular, a relevant question is, "Whether women can ever find submissive men attractive and trustworthy at all?" How could women enjoy or respect weak men?

85. Another major conflict is emerging: Couples are expecting their partners to be strong, competitive, and assertive outside the house to maximize families' welfare, but be submissive and passive at home to accommodate them.

86. The emerging trends in society, especially couples' needs for individuality and independence, are irreversible. And people's psychological attributes cannot be changed either. So, the only solution for our relationships is to find new mechanisms and relationship principles to match our new needs.

87. Also couples should get more serious about modifying their mindsets and viewing relationships in a new perspective. They should do so for increasing their chances of building a reliable relationship.

88. Partners' strive for independence leads to more distance between them. But working within a relationship framework, while advocating partners' independence, rectifies this problem to a large extent. Couples learn to respect and deal with their partners' need for independence and view 'independence' as a major requirement of teamwork. Meanwhile, more detailed mechanisms of teamwork must be developed too.

89. The way we behave nowadays, hardly can anybody find their soul mates. Even if we happen to find them by accident, we just keep losing them due to our phony personalities and ideologies, not to mention our idiotic games and ego. It is interesting that even couples with similar values, lifestyle, and priorities keep rejecting one another since they don't give themselves a chance to relate authentically. They don't know how to be natural instead of phony.
90. Some couples have indeed found their soul mates, but they lose them when their own oversensitivity gives them wrong impressions about the health of their relationship and the purpose of relationships in general. They lose their partners due to their fantasies, such as a better life with a different partner, love, money, etc. High expectations and misperceptions are making couples lose the soul mates they have already found.
91. Partners get too intimate too early as a sign of love, trust, and loyalty, instead of proving all of these high qualities gradually through real actions and right attitude. Often, partners actually try to manipulate each other by showing off a polished image of themselves. Nevertheless, statistics show that most couples end up losing their love, trust, and loyalty in their relationships.
92. Partners try to exploit each other (knowingly or inadvertently) by *activating their M-love to fake S-love to get E-love.*
93. People assume they are (or can be) loving, trustworthy, or loyal. But all evidences indicate that humans are impure by nature, and then environment makes them even more cruel and aggressive.

94. Relationships suffer from humans' inherent defects more than anything else. Some artificial expressions of passion, as a result of attraction or other needs of partners, don't change their true nature as humans with all their inherent defects.
95. Our rampant relationship issues are causing more mistrust amongst youth. Thus, each generation is causing more damages for the relationships of the future generations. We are making our children more sceptical about marriage and less prepared to deal with its requirements, especially its most likely consequence, i.e., separation.
96. Driven by the recent popular ideologies, including positive thinking slogans, people like to believe that life is beautiful and that happiness is within reach. Yet, most prominent philosophies and our personal experiences indicate the opposite: That life is nothing but a place for suffering and paying for our past or present sins. The point is that our idealism and search for this phantom happiness are misleading many couples; they just put too much demand on each other recklessly and then finally separate. It is a pity that our misguided perceptions stop us from taking advantage of our only opportunity to suffer less in this world: That is, by bringing more objectivity into our relationships and enjoying one another, instead of arguing about our inconsequential needs and obsessions, especially this illusive 'happiness.' We are actually proving the philosophers right about life being only a place for suffering. For one thing, we suffer from our relationships (or lack of them) due to our own naïve expectations and games.

97. Being optimistic and positive about life are useful tools. But when they cause gross misperceptions and raise our naïve expectations, e.g., for more love or a better partner, they must be construed as another cause of partners' confusion and relationship failures. The bottom line is that if positive thinking and 'living in the now' schemes worked, by now everybody would have joined in to reap its rewards. Everybody would have benefited from these magical cures by now and we could see all those happy faces around us. But all we see is more depression and desperation. We need the highest level of antidepressants to help us continue living and suffering. If positive thinking schemes worked, relationship problems had disappeared and everybody was living happily with their soul mates. Instead, we see more unrealizable expectations and self-pity. Many people are edgy these days because their positive thinking alone, even when they combine it with a great deal of personal efforts, does not seem to get them anywhere. They still lose their companions to the phony life philosophies that are misleading people, and they still lose their life savings in financial markets as a result of other people's greed or incompetence.

98. Many philosophers suggest that life cannot be a happy affair, because the minute we have nothing to do, and can supposedly enjoy life, we get bored. So we look for adventure, work, or a new companion to rejuvenate our lives. But they all make us suffer, too, especially our relationships. In all, we struggle all our lives to find something creative to do or a worthy companion to give us some moments of happiness. Some spiritualists, of course, believe that we could help ourselves a little if we

learned to be a better human being and stayed content, which is a tough mission for most of us.

99. Nowadays, being a good human does not always pay off anyway. He/she is often perceived as a weak and passive individual and not taken seriously. It might not help (actually damage) his/her relationship, anyway, if his/her partner is not an equally good human being. So, being a good person may not be necessarily useful for drawing other people's compassion or achieving tangible benefits.

100. The only benefit of being good is to mitigate one's suffering and possibly get a better chance to relate to one's partner unselfishly.

The Timetable to Implement Radical Remedies

To reverse the deteriorating trends in relationships, it seems that we must wait for the following events and conditions to take their natural courses. During this timeframe, a large number of radical remedies, like the ones suggested in Chapter Eleven, are implemented gradually according to the following facts and timeline:

101. The scope of relationship problems is not still pressing people enough to take serious steps. So the situation will continue to get worse before people begin to appreciate the need for changing their mentalities and approaches. Couples' expectations keep rising not only from relationships, but also in terms of finding the right partner for themselves. Everybody looks for a partner with higher qualities than themselves and better than their past spouses. This is a mathematically unattainable demand that is emerging in society. The matter gets especially im-

practical when they seek love in a partner who must also be trustworthy, attractive, patient, and intelligent.

102. In addition to the egotistical nature of all humans, people seem to have even a harder time to get along with the opposite genders. People are not prepared to be in relationships. Especially, nowadays, they have been brought up to seek happiness, and to them companionship is only another means of capturing that elusive happiness. They like to ignore that the hardships of life and relationships are there regardless of their naïve expectations and slogans.

103. So, for the next 40-50 years, gender equality wars and conflicts will escalate and prevent people from finding common grounds for negotiating their needs and lowering their expectations from relationships.

104. The deterioration is measured by the divorce rate (including separations). But other indicators would assist as well, such as people's stress in relationships and society, and the rate of unmarried people in various age categories. A divorce rate of 75% will probably be reached in 2060s. Then the upsetting trends might start an initial interest to study relationships more seriously and to consider some radical solutions more systematically. Governments and scholars will get involved more actively. Various types of research will be needed to define a workable relationship framework and GARP. Of course, the progress depends on the global economic condition at that time, as it will deeply affect the state of relationships in the future. With the high likelihood of a global economic collapse and the demise of consumerism, relationship issues might become of secondary importance when people must strug-

gle for the basic means of survival. On the other hand, economic gloom might inject some sense of reality into relationships. Couples might learn to revert to their traditional mentality and lower their expectations from both life and relationships. But let's assume that we can succeed to continue with some form of 'a better managed' capitalism and moderate consumerism. We have at least learned that deregulation and completely 'free enterprise' leads to chaos. The debt crises in the fall of 2008 and the summer of 2011, which will haunt us for many years to come, might change our mentality. Yet, considering humans' appetite for greed and corruption, we might be heading for big troubles. This means more relationship problems, too, due to stressful economic conditions and uncertainties.

105. Probably by 2080s, with a divorce rate around 80%, the general public will acknowledge the need for change. It will be a period of reflection and realizing that the roles and games that couples are playing (e.g., to demand both dependence and independence) are only hurting them. They will understand the need to adjust their expectations from relationships. Then, the relationship framework, and the GARP proposed by scholars, might find wide support.

106. GARP must fit the requirements of the society and the emerging progressive norms. Most likely the need for independence and individuality will still be a dominant factor and thus set the tone for the upcoming relationship guidelines. A foundation is created to oversee the development and dissemination of GARP.

107. Aside from interest and patience, it will take couples a few decades to digest the need for radical changes and adopt a more progressive mindset about relationships. More education is provided to the general public, especially at high schools, to propagate the relationship needs and framework. By the end of the 21st century, people might eventually learn the art of being independent financially and emotionally instead of only pretending it. More natural communication, and less role-playing and games, will find common appeal in order to reinstate trust and integrity in relationships.
108. It will take another couple of decades for people to get comfortable with the relationship framework and GARP. The new mindset will gradually find full acceptance and couples feel comfortable using the new processes and guidelines. Social mechanisms, including court systems, will be equipped to handle the new setup. This will bring us to the year 2115.
109. It will take 30-40 years for GARP and the relationship framework to become a natural setting for relationships. This will bring us to 2150.
110. Good luck, that's the best the author can hope for. Yet he would be thrilled to be proven wrong if by some miracle the state of relationships begins to improve much faster than the above depressing dates.

Chapter Fifteen
Gender Differences

The way men and women perceive the world, set their priorities in life, and make decisions are quite different. These differences become more vivid in modern societies where self-worth, equality, and independence find the highest value. Along with humans' inherent ego and low capacity for compromise, gender differences make the tasks of communicating and relating so much more difficult in relationships. Gender differences are discussed in other parts of this book as obstacles for bringing objectivity back into relationships. This problem will persist until couples' mindsets are hopefully aligned with the relationship needs within the next few decades. In this chapter, the foundation of gender differences and their impact on relationships are explained further.

Diagram 15.1 (next page) outlines some of the plausible personality characteristics of men and women. It is developed based on the discussions on page 353 (item 10) and the Personality Chart in Diagram 13.1.

As noted in Chapter Thirteen, men and women are found everywhere on the Personality Chart with large variations in terms of their personality traits. But it might be possible to say that, on the average, men and women have some noticeable personality differences. These gender differences reflect people's natural (instinctual) and acquired urges according to the emerging social circumstances.

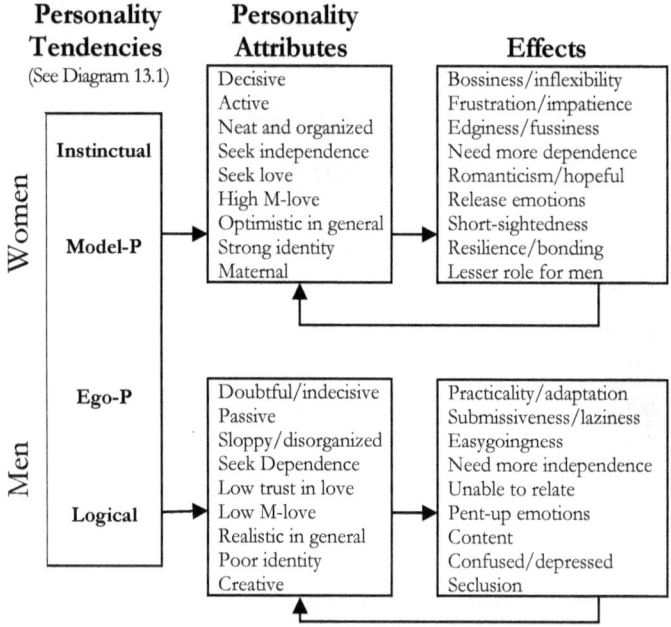

Diagram 15.1: Gender Differences

Everybody holds all of the four main dimensions of personality as listed under the column 'Personality Tendencies' in Diagram 15.1, i.e., instincts, logic, Model-P and Ego-P. However women have a bit higher instinctual tendencies while men have a bit more logical tendencies. Women are more Model-P oriented whereas men are more Ego-P oriented. These unique tendencies impact relationships more intensely as people become more obsessed with individualism.

The 'personality attributes' and 'effects' listed in diagram 15.1 must be viewed only as working hypotheses and not proven theorems. It is impossible to generalize anything easily in social sciences, especially about human behaviour and personality. The gender tendencies and differences noted here are by no means complete either. They are only some examples of the most common observations about genders' encounters and communications. With this disclaimer, the following hypotheses are offered by the author. They are presented in the same order of the items listed in Diagram 15.1. Yet some points may be repeated when they apply to more than one item in the diagram. Also, the discussions in other chapters of this book (especially the last two chapters) about gender differences are based on the working hypotheses presented in this chapter.

1. Due to their higher intuitiveness, women are more decisive than men.
2. The effect of their decisiveness is that women appear bossy and inflexible with their viewpoints. Inflexibility is a symptom of their intuitiveness, which makes them more certain about their conclusions. And they are bossy and inflexible simply because they are frustrated with their procrastinating husbands. Often, however, their inflexibility is perceived by men as a sign of insensitivity. The perceived low sensitivity is, of course, not contradictory to the fact that women are usually better in expressing their emotions with their higher Model-P and M-love when necessary.
3. Due to their higher logical tendencies, men are hesitant to draw conclusions and make decisions before they've

spent enough time to review all the alternatives. This method of decision making portrays them as indecisive and lacking spontaneity.
4. Of course, men are trying to be practical by disallowing spontaneity dictate their decisions and cause tragedy. Some men actually realize their partial responsibility for their wives' anxiety (due to men's indecisiveness) and thus try to make up for it by patience and adaptation. That is, to make up for their indecisiveness, they learn to absorb and tolerate their partners' reactions, including their bossiness.
5. Contrary to women, who are intuitively decisive, men must be forced into making a decision by timelines, business obligations, desperation, etc. Their indecisiveness manifest in the way they hesitate in choosing and proposing to a woman too. Women usually make a decision about the suitability of a man rather quickly.
6. Higher instinctual urges have given women higher emotional tendencies and a higher Model-P aptitude.
7. Higher logical tendencies of men have led to their higher analytical ability, creativity, and philosophizing during the history of mankind. Within this type of environment, men have acquired a higher Ego-P aptitude and become more arrogant.
8. Their higher Model-P and decisiveness encourage women to be more active in social settings, relationships, and family life.
9. Their higher Ego-P and analytical tendency encourage men to become rather passive, isolated, and to strive for self-actualization.

10. Men's excess Ego-P over Model-P ultimately turns them more inwardly and inactive in their relationships too. They must try hard to adapt themselves to this environment in order to minimize the amount of family clashes.
11. Women are more action orientated also due to their decisiveness. They wish to organize and manage things quickly and move on. The effect of their action orientation is that they get frustrated and show impatience when their plans or desires are put on hold. This situation is another factor for becoming bossy to get things going.
12. Men's passivity portrays them as lazy and uncaring. Their passivity is then further reinforced and proven when they eventually let their wives run the family affairs, mostly because they (men) are actually lazy, even for arguments.
13. Women have a high tendency (bordering obsession) for the cleanliness and tidiness of their households.
14. The effect of their obsession for cleanliness and tidiness is that women come across as uptight and fussy. Their tendency to depend so much on their intuition also contributes to their edginess.
15. Men are sloppy and disorganized in general. Their system of setting their life priorities becomes substantially vivid in the way they consider cleanliness and tidiness a waste of their precious time; yet they can easily waste that time on odd hobbies, watching sports, or drinking beer.
16. The effect of their sloppiness is that men come across as too careless and easygoing about issues that their wives give much higher priority to, mainly in terms of household appearance and cleanliness.
17. Women seek more independence in order to assert their identity in modern society after many years of inequity,

inequality, and oppression by men. But inherently they need dependence on a partner at least for emotional support more than ever. Independence is obviously synonymous with needlessness. So, the more women play the role of needless partners, the more men find themselves alienated in terms of helping women with their dependence need. There are so many reasons for this. But one obvious reason is that, as civilized people, we try to help someone or interfere in his/her affairs only when he/she asks for help. In particular, it feels awkward to interfere with the affairs of a spouse who insists on being needless at so many levels all the time. Unfortunately, partners are getting confused about when to provide or seek help, especially emotional support. Misperceptions and misinterpretations about help sought or provided are making couples both anxious and oversensitive about their relationships. The bottom line is that the women's need for dependence on a reliable partner is left increasingly unfulfilled. Meanwhile, their higher Model-P and emotional tendencies reinforce their need for dependence even more.

18. An argument opposite to the previous point can be made about men. That is, men seek dependence, but they need more independence. Men have always sought dependence on a partner for sex, companionship, and support in maintaining a household. They are simply too lazy and incompetent in keeping the household shipshape. Their search for dependence is even more prominent nowadays where women insist on their independence and thus reduce the supply of reliable and consistent source of support for men. Men have a harder time to fulfil this objec-

tive and thus they seek dependence even more desperately—almost at the same level that women seek more independence.

But men, by nature and their higher Ego-P, need more independence psychologically. They like to be left alone to spend time on their own contemplations, creating, and feeding their Ego-P. So men seek dependence (by looking for a companion) in order to find the opportunity of fulfilling their need for independence. In the older times, men got the dependence they sought rather easily. Thus they could fulfil their need for independence easier too. But they have now lost the means of satisfying both their dependence and independence needs. Nowadays, they must pay a high price to obtain the dependence they seek in a companion. The price is paid in the form of giving up more and more of their independence, which they crave instinctually and had always enjoyed easily in the past. The amount of independence they must forgo to gain a relative dependence often seems out of proportion (to them at least) and thus they are losing some of their identities, as will be discussed later in this chapter.

A reasonable question based on the above discussions is, 'Why men and women have difficulty relating to one another when their needs are indeed so nicely complementary?' While women seek more independence and men seek more dependence, why cannot they just fulfil each other's exact needs? The answer is that even though each gender struggles for one particular need more prominently, their real needs (for dependence and independence) are exactly opposite to what they express openly. They just hide them from their partners.

19. Neither gender has yet decided about a right balance between their dependence/independence needs, which they need in order to minimize their inner conflicts. In particular, they must balance their gender-oriented needs in order to communicate effectively with each other. Besides, it is questionable whether the natural properties of genders would ever allow them reach a practical balance for their dependence and independence needs that are also acceptable to the other gender.

20. As noted mostly in Chapter Fourteen, women believe in love and seek it more actively due to their instinctual and emotional tendencies. They also seem to have a higher need for things including fashion, art, and household decorations. Women's search for love and things appear deep and instinctual, as if these needs were totally authentic and heartfelt—often even reaching the level of obsession. Relative to women, men's need for love and things appear to be moderate and mostly for feeding their Ego-P (power) and for attracting women anyway. Of course, men's ego and greed goads them to make more money to prove themselves. Like all other males in the animal kingdom, men fight, compete, and try to fulfil women's needs, mostly for reaping the rewards of their company and feeding their own ego. Men's obsessions relate more to power, pleasure, and creativity instead of love and objects per se. Yet, due to their passive attitude about love, and higher deprivation of love, men are inherently more vulnerable emotionally.

21. One effect of the gender differences noted above is the rather obvious conclusion that women are more romantic and needy for a companion despite their efforts to appear

independent, bossy, and needless. Or at least they are more open about their search for love than men. They live in a world of fantasy with many dreams, especially about love and the possibility of finding a prince. Men's high Ego-P, and low Model-P, curtails their ability to seek love as openly as they need. They are more practical and realize soon that finding a princess is merely a myth. But as noted above they are more vulnerable emotionally.

22. Men have less faith in love due to their logical tendencies, and because they apply the existing information about relationship failures more analytically. In the older cultures, love had much less value for men, and that mentality has been passed on to men in the new generations to a great extent as well. They have always been less romantic, anyway, and thus the effect of the new culture and the movies about romance and love has been lesser on men than it has been on women. Yet men are equally sensitive and very much emotional, if not more than women in many instances. Their lack of trust in love and their inability, or the lack of opportunity, to express their emotions reduce their ability to relate to their partners, which then leads to deep inner conflicts for them too.

23. Again due to their high Model-P, women have a higher M-love as well. This means that they do express their feelings easier and more masterfully. This ability increases their charm and chances of fulfilling their needs much better. In a way, one might say that women are better equipped to manipulate men.

24. Men's lower Model-P and M-love result in pent-up emotions and aggression, especially when they insist on push-

ing logic while their spouses are seeking support and affection.

25. Women are more optimistic about life and love. They live longer perhaps because of their positive attitude too. (Although the stress from working outside the house and love deprivation would most likely reduce women's life expectancy in the years to come.) Women's positive attitude helps them rebound faster than men after a separation, since they keep hoping for good things and love coming their ways soon.

26. Women's optimism makes them less concerned about the potential risks ahead. They seem to concentrate mostly on the near future, perhaps now. For example, they seem to show an obsession to own a house regardless of the financial justifications. Their short-sightedness is a symptom of too much optimism.

27. Men are more realistic about life and love because they make better use of past information due to their logical tendencies. They lose hope rather soon in order to reach a state of contentment. They are more doubtful and submissive.

28. Women have been able to portray a strong identity for themselves. They know what they want and are learning fast how to get it. They are focused and determined. This is obviously easy for them to achieve because they only have to identify the things they were missing in the past, such as equality and independence. Now, all they must do is to find the ways of getting those seemingly precious things. They have proven capable of supporting one another and bonding for their common objectives. They have developed many new techniques and games to

achieve what they want and stay vigilant about the progress of their plans. They have learned to make money and be independent and of course they are more optimistic about life in general too. To ensure their plans aren't jeopardized, they have become calculating and assertive, and sometimes even aggressive. As a whole, women have developed a specific and concrete identity (or at least an image of it) for themselves and are bonding together to make sure this identity is promoted and protected. Women's cohesiveness and lower Ego-P have been helping them in reinforcing their new identity.

29. For men the situation has been just the opposite. Due to their lower intuition and lower Model-P, they have not been able to understand the new culture introduced by women. They have been somewhat caught off-guard and they have not yet been able to formulate a new identity for themselves to satisfy women's needs without losing even more of their own identity. At this point, the shock and confusion are keeping men divided and unorganized. Their higher Ego-P prevents them from organizing their thoughts and finding common grounds. They are passive and lazy about this matter too, of course. They have so far not taken women's strive for a new identity seriously enough either. They naively imagined that the situation was under control. But now they must forgo a lot of their independence to acquire the dependence they seek in a companion. They don't know how to develop a new identity to cope with the emerging environment. Instead, they are becoming more submissive and passive. So the effect of this situation is that men are becoming more isolated and frustrated with their relationships. Women are

also frustrated but for different reasons, mainly men's passivity.

30. The stronger identity for women at the cost of men losing theirs would damage relationships and both genders would suffer from this imbalance. Meanwhile, neither gender would find its true identity, because in the final analyses they need each other to create their real identities. (Points 57 and 58 on pages 427-9 offer more insight about this issue.)

31. The effect of women forcing their new progressive identity and men losing theirs would be interesting. One could argue that men's Ego-P would be curbed eventually and thus a new relationship atmosphere might emerge. It is a possibility. But the change, if any, would not be felt in this century. There are many reasons for this. First, Ego-P is an inherent trait for men built throughout a long history of humanity and it cannot be undermined easily despite the women's attempt to tame it. It would take many decades to tone down men's Ego-P tendencies, if at all possible. Second, the force of Ego-P in men would not allow the existing situation, i.e., loss of identity, continue for too long. Even the existing passive reactions by men could result in the emergence of new relationship approaches. Men are equally intelligent and maybe even capable of colluding in order to reclaim some kind of identity for themselves. Nonetheless, both men and women would realize the necessity of creating the needed balances and attitudes. Men's loss of identity is, thus, a temporary situation. A new identity for men would emerge eventually within a century or so. The question is how passive and submissive it would be!

32. A similar comment can be made about women's present Model-P tendency. With their new approach, they already seem (or pretend) to be gaining a great deal of Ego-P. If this happens, many of the above personality traits would no longer remain valid. They would erode naturally. But again, the reality is that women's instinctual tendencies are too deep to be drastically subdued by their attempt to create a man-like identity for themselves. They would always be the tender mother that nature has meant them to be, despite the perceived image of their insensitivity on many occasions (see point 2 on page 453). Nonetheless, the existing state of transition would hopefully come to a practical equilibrium sooner or later. In that steady state, both genders have clear identities that lead to a higher synergy in relationships.

33. Mothers' powerful urge for maternity pushes them not only in terms of seducing men for the ultimate purpose of procreation, but also finding a lesser value in men afterward. Nature is possibly making women more demanding and commanding to take care of the whole family efficiently. So they treat men like another child. They keep nagging and pushing them away into an emotional standby, at least temporarily. To women, babies are their ultimate creations that satisfy their need for self-actualization and dependence to a great extent. Thus children become the centre of their focus. Although women would continue to have a strong need for dependency on men (mostly for socializing and E-love), this urge is somewhat dampened at least while their children keep them busy and while they know that their faithful husbands are still around at a safe distance.

34. Women's natural (historical) tendency to treat men like another child might have contributed a lot to men's seclusion. They became more self-reliant and developed a higher need for self-actualization, creativity, and Ego-P. Conversely, women became more Model-P oriented to support one another and their offspring with lesser need for males. On the other hand, men's perception of (and frustration about) women's insensitivity toward them might have contributed to men's seclusion and aggressiveness toward women.
35. As noted before, women encourage one another to be assertive with their husbands and leave them if they cannot respond to their desires. The question here is women's motives. Do they provoke one another out of kindness, malice, ignorance, or a combination of these incentives? A cynical viewpoint is that they often do it to screw up one another intentionally, either for personal reasons or to promote women's presumed identity. The jury is out on this one. Yet there are some good explanations why they might be doing it for their own benefit and not necessarily out of kindness. Getting into these discussions is beyond the purpose of this book, however. Nonetheless, women believe that by propagating a low-tolerance attitude, they would enforce their identity and feminism and keep their husbands under control. This mentality might backfire and deteriorate the chances of harmony in relationships.
36. Despite their high aptitude for bonding, women have a higher tendency for jealousy and rivalry. In particular, they are very competitive amongst themselves in terms of objects and the passion they seek from their husbands or other men. They also compete amongst themselves in

terms of pushing their identity. They struggle to demonstrate their individuality and dominance in their relationships in order to excel other women on these factors. All these competitions infect their relationships.

37. The human hormones and their cyclical changes impact the brain activity of genders differently. Especially women are more susceptible to depression, anxiety, and mood swings due to hormonal changes during childbirth, menstrual cycle, and menopause.

38. The genders' distinct 'brain functions' make them react to various life conditions and stress quite differently. For example, the cortisol level, which measures stress intensity, is typically two times higher in women compared with men. This is due to the way women perceive pain much deeper and the way they must go about calming themselves.

39. While men try to deal with their stress by solving the problem or ignoring it altogether, women need to talk about their problems. The chance to talk releases serotonin in their brains that calms their limbic system. There are also twice as many women on antidepressants as men based on recent statistics.

40. In all, hormones usually make women more decisive and optimistic about life, and thus they set high expectations for their relationships. Along with new slogans and approaches in society, women are nowadays more idealistic and seek love and happiness more obsessively, too, which then lead to their higher depression and uptightness. Hormones have also increased women's ability to bond and be outgoing.

The above rudimentary observations about gender differences have been made based on the hypotheses suggested in Diagram 15.1 and the author's understanding of studies about human hormones. These observations also signify and verify the emergence of a peculiar trend in relationships. For example, they reflect that women are more optimistic about life and the possibility of finding real love regardless of their age and their past negative experiences. Their optimism goads them to live in their fantasy world and keep looking for romance and beautiful things. Furthermore, they are very active nowadays in encouraging one another to seek perfection, love, independence and individuality. They encourage and support one another to leave their relationships when they cannot give them all the things and compassion they believe they deserve. They naively assume, all along, that men are psychologically capable of delivering all those things and compassion. And so when they don't, it is out of spite and stupidity.

On the other hand, men are more practical and give up on the idea of finding the perfect mate. Thus they try to be a little more tolerant and accept mediocre relationships longer. Their minds are basically preoccupied with more immediate responsibilities or silly hobbies like sports. Their Ego-P and passivity, of course, cause relationship conflicts. But the bottom line is that men cannot change themselves too much, not enough for the liking of women. So couples face undue conflicts and separations. Women in particular keep saying that life is too short and you live only once. So they keep chasing their fantasy about men who can fulfil their dreams. They don't take notice that, while wasting their lives in search of acceptable men (if not ideal ones), they might be depriving themselves from the simple privileges of companionship and accomplishing certain objectives that two people can attain better together if they stopped arguing too much. So more loneliness and depression are emerging in society, while women keep searching for their imaginary mates, and men are becoming more sceptical about getting into relationships. Obviously, if couples weren't so adamant (needy) about controlling their partners, and if people stopped encouraging one another to look for a perfect relationship and love, they could enjoy all the more important benefits of relationships. The obsession for love, things, power, and domination is hindering the possibility of enjoying our relationships. Both genders are responsible for some aspects of these shortfalls in some ways.

Gender differences have become more obvious and prevalent in the new era and they will continue to be responsible for more relationship conflicts. Accordingly, partners' struggles to establish their gender identities and balance their needs for dependence and independence lead to their increasing inner conflicts and frustration. In addition to gender differences and genders' search for their identities, many other relationship and personal issues (as discussed in this book) also make it difficult for partners to relate to each other. This vast scope of potential problems has made relationship environments too complex and unmanageable. All these deteriorating trends will continue to get more out of control in the future decades, unless couples change their mentalities about the purposes and potentials of relationships and realign their expectations accordingly.

Love is to give…

Chapter Sixteen
Summary and Conclusions

The facts and interpretations presented in this book are based on statistics, daily experiences, and methodical analyses. This chapter provides an outline of these findings without repeating the points noted in the last two chapters. It includes a collection of the author's thoughts, hypotheses, scattered notes, and the highlights of this book's discussions. Many of these points may actually be refined and included in GARP when it is being prepared. So another purpose of this chapter is to provide some useful material for GARP. The highlights are provided in two parts:

- A high-level summary of topics and discussions in Parts I and II
- A summary of observations, analyses, and findings

For more elaboration about the following conclusions, please refer to the main text (Chapters One through Thirteen) to find the related topics.

A high-level summary of the topics and discussions

1. We are somewhat ignoring the fundamental fact that more than 50% of marriages in modern societies lead to divorce and separation. Furthermore, a large population has difficulty even starting a relationship. And a good majority of couples consider their relationships unsatisfactory. They simply tolerate the situation because they are sceptical about the consequences of ending their marginal relationships.
2. We consider 'companionship' a basic need and not a medium range social need. Most of us consider it the best prize God could bestow upon humans, not to mention the sexual benefits of relationships. This belief has evolved somewhat instinctually but also through social conditioning.
3. The above facts show that most people suffer due to relationships (whether they are in one or not), because they consider having a companion an essential need. Yet couples are not trained to anticipate even the basic hurdles of relationships or assess them realistically.
4. Couples starting a relationship have a wrong perception about the purposes and potentials of relationships. They are also unconscious about the high chance of marriage breakdowns, or prefer to ignore it.
5. Couples are not trained to work proactively from day one to protect their marriage from going on a wrong course.

6. The old principles that kept marriages together are long gone and no new principles have been designed to fit the needs of the new era.
7. Societies are expanding and getting more complex every day. The new social values have drastically changed our lifestyles and convictions. Accordingly, our relationships have become quite difficult to understand and manage.
8. Our personal needs, insecurities, and idiosyncrasies are increasing rapidly in line with changes in social values, and we are getting more obsessed every day about finding happiness and love.
9. We have become more demanding of ourselves, society, and our marriage partners.
10. Partners' personal needs, especially individualism, is placing undue pressure on relationships and causing more frictions.
11. Conversely, personal stress from relationships is putting enormous pressure on society and the economy too.
12. Social mechanisms and laws are not efficient anymore to respond to the newer needs of relationships.
13. Partners' personal defects are natural consequences of their genetic and upbringing conditions, all beyond their control. We have a hard time accepting this fact and instead keep pushing our partners to change, or we retaliate to make them suffer.
14. Family health and values should be studied more seriously and given a higher priority by people and governments.
15. Couples need a new mindset and a set of guidelines to help them relate in their relationships.

16. Radical solutions are needed to make relationships more manageable in the new world.
17. New relationship principles (GARP) should be developed to match social changes in the new era.
18. GARP must be propagated actively in order to change couples' mentality about the nature of love and relationships.
19. Creating a new atmosphere for relationships would not be easy and quick. People are not ready to give up their personal convictions and pleasures to improve their relationships.
20. Nonetheless, the need for developing a new relationship framework is certain. Maybe we can hope to get there by the year 2115, if by then humanity still exists in a functional way.

A summary of observations, analyses, and findings

21. Too many relationships are nowadays ruined due to partners' subjective assessments and hasty decisions.
22. Out of necessity, everybody would realize eventually that relationship decisions must become less arbitrary and emotional.
23. The increasing complexity of relationships cannot be handled loosely anymore. It would be too risky to depend on erratic perceptions and interpretations of people to define relationships randomly. We need a rather universal relationship framework.
24. Couples' unique personalities obviously lead to a large variety of relationship types. But still it is possible for all

of them to work from within a similar framework to maximize relationships' effectiveness. Trusting some generally acceptable norms for assessing our relationships would be preferable to depending on our subjective (and often misleading) views of our relationships.

25. The sense of failure to find our soul mate, despite our lifelong search and struggles, causes deep psychological scars and stress.
26. The ultimate goal of this book is to bring objectivity back into relationships.
27. The simpler books that focus on quick fixes cannot help couples with their relationships. It is like building a house without a foundation. The matters of love and relationships in modern societies are more complex than the laws of physics, because they hardly submit to any logic or formula.
28. A major hurdle in relationships is that people trust one another less every day due to bad personal experiences and rampant socioeconomic corruption in modern societies.
29. Experts suggest all kinds of solutions for relationship problems and still relationships keep failing more than ever. This indicates that none of those solutions really works. The mere fact that there are so many incongruent solutions (all these variations) reflects that counsellors have not been able to come up with reasonably dependable solutions.
30. The worst kind of therapy is when couples are encouraged to play phony roles to express passion or compassion as a mechanism for saving their relationships. Role-playing is obviously an artificial activity that might induce

more frustration in the end if partners are not intellectually (and emotionally) convinced about the authenticity of their own (or their partner's) feelings and words.
31. The fact that some people cannot express their feelings is often not due to a lack of communication skill. In most instances, the problem lies deep in the psyche of individuals and it is often beyond repair.
32. It is time for a more comprehensive approach to study the nature of relationship problems. We must study the needs of our new society and scrutinize all the emerging facts.
33. Basically, we must study *what* has changed in society, *how* they are affecting relationships, and *why* radical changes are needed.
34. Our perception of reality (and life) is severely damaged nowadays as we have introduced more artificial needs in our lives and because we have been propagating a lot of jargons about life and happiness. So our challenge is to develop relationship principles that fit the new reality of relationships.
35. The major assumption for couples must be that the likelihood of their relationship failing is much higher than succeeding.
36. Accordingly, couples must be able to prove that they deserve to stay in their relationships. Now couples must carry a high burden of proof (by showing their aptitude) for prolonging their relationships beyond their preliminary romance and as partners' patience begin to falter.
37. We must plan and behave according to the statistics and experiences around us. They all indicate that *marriage is a*

temporary arrangement unless a miracle makes it last as long as we hope it should.

38. On the other hand, this highlighted awareness might actually motivate us to extend realistic efforts and save our relationships. Our new approach to see relationships as a temporary arrangement can actually help couples make it last longer.
39. This book has intended to demonstrate a dozen essential facts about relationships in the new era, as listed on page 23.
40. Learning about the nature and authenticity of our personal needs, and motivations behind them, can help our relationships, mainly through self-awareness.
41. Contrary to our naïve presumptions, our personal needs usually get frustrated instead of fulfilled when we start a relationship.
42. It seems that the only way couples may save their relationships is to enhance their awareness about the complexity of human needs and behaviour and how they infect their relationships.
43. We must reconsider our view of relationships, redefine our expectations sensibly, and be prepared for the worst scenario, i.e., separation.
44. The meaning of the word 'love' has become too ambiguous.
45. Our crusade to find happiness revolves mainly around the notion of finding that special person who fits the image of a mate who can make our dreams come true. We hope to complete our existence through him/her. This crusade is partly the symptom of people's instinctual need for spiritual love (S-love)—the selfless kind of love

that falls at the highest level of Maslow's personal needs hierarchy. However, we are mostly seeking E-love (deficiency love)—the selfish need to be loved by someone who solves our insecurities too.

46. People have the following motives for expressing or expecting love:
    - To *communicate* with their partners.
    - To express their basic *feelings*.
    - To release *psychological* pressures.
    - To mimic their *spiritual* needs.
    - To *control* their partners.
    - To manipulate (abuse) their partners.

47. Love has become such a precious commodity nowadays because it can satisfy a variety of personal needs and motives. Although people seek love to share a spiritual experience with their soul mate, many people are inherently incapable of giving love. They merely want to be loved to heal their insecurities and to control their partners.

48. Possessiveness and jealousy are not the reflections of true love. They only represent a person's rampant emotions and the urge to control someone for E-love, money, friendship, sex, etc.

49. The complex 'need for a companion' comprise of many personal needs that extend over the full spectrum of Maslow's personal needs hierarchy, from the basic need for sex, extends over a wide medium range needs, including compassion, and encompass our high-level need for spirituality through S-love (self-less love).

50. Our challenge in relationships is to learn about sharing compassion without imagining and expecting S-love.

51. Sex is taking on a rather complex role in relationships nowadays as couples' strive for E-love (deficiency love) is getting out of control.
52. Sex is often treated nowadays as a regulating tool rather than a basic need.
53. Both our basic need for sex (including the urge for reproduction, especially for women) and our high-level need for love (S-love) are instinctual needs. So, it appears that we have created most of the medium-range personal needs through evolution and according to cultural conditions.
54. Naively, we assume that relationships can magically fulfil our most prominent personal needs.
55. We also assume that relationships can somehow deal with all the idiosyncrasies that partners bring with them to this environment.
56. Naively, we assume that our partners are capable of making us happy.
57. We ignore the high likelihood that our partners haven't been able to make themselves happy (even though nowadays everybody likes to shout how happy and mature they are and how beautiful life is). So how can we expect others to make us happy?
58. Even if both partners have good intentions, are good-natured, and realize that give and take in a relationship may provide a relative sense of comfort (not necessarily happiness) for both partners, they still don't know how to relate fairly. So we need a *relationship framework* and a set of *principles* to show how partners may relate with the least amount of frictions.

59. Couples are living in such an imaginary world they can't even grasp the nature of their relationship problems, let alone finding solutions within that imaginary setting.
60. Couples ignore that often it is their own personal needs and expectations that require adjusting; and not the attitude of their partners.
61. Our needs for more things and more compassion are what we have imposed upon ourselves by habit and imitation.
62. We must find ways of fulfilling our personal needs (e.g., happiness) independently so that the burden on relationships is reduced.
63. Our personal needs are becoming too complex because the authentic and artificial ones are getting mixed up and creating new meanings and expectations beyond our apprehension and ability to satisfy. Yet we must somehow learn to deal with all these needs.
64. It is depressing to see that finding a suitable companion has become such a challenging and frustrating endeavour despite the increasing number of matchmaking services and meeting places.
65. Nowadays, nobody knows the needs and demands of relationships.
66. Couples fail because there is no realistic definition of 'relationship needs' to prepare them for the challenges of companionship in the new era amidst all other daily life demands.
67. No uniform set of objectives is available for relationships to guide couples; to tame their wild perceptions of relationships' potentials and purposes.

68. We must learn to view 'relationships' as a unique entity, which has specific needs very different from the conflicting needs of two partners.
69. Of course, every relationship has its unique characteristics and setting. And there should be some level of flexibility in relationships to accommodate all personalities. But only a handful relationship models can support partners to relate to each other effectively.
70. Couples must evaluate their personal needs in comparison to the relationship needs objectively and then choose the relationship model that best fits their personalities.
71. Without guidelines, even compatible couples are subject to gross misperceptions and loose interpretations about their relationships.
72. The lack of knowledge about the specific needs of relationships has caused many of the problems we are witnessing nowadays.
73. The atmosphere for personal need fulfilment is not calm and logical nowadays. People get hysterical when their imaginary needs are not satisfied.
74. Increasingly, we witness people's hysteria for not succeeding to climb up the personal needs hierarchy quickly enough.
75. Our personal needs are developed and triggered by a wide range of inner and outer forces.
76. Inner forces comprise of:
    - Instincts
    - Genetics
    - Habits (conditioning)
    - Reactions (impulses)

Summary and Conclusions

77. Outer forces refer to socioeconomic environment, upbringing, etc.
78. The purpose of studying the inner forces is to increase self-awareness and thus stir objectivity into relationships. Then, through self-awareness, couples learn that so much of their partners' personalities are also developed by forces beyond their control.
79. Our gravest misperception is that our partners are in control of their personalities.
80. Inner forces basically refer to our inherent or absorbed characteristics. We hardly have any control over these traits.
81. As a symbol of civilization, we have developed laws, ethics, and etiquettes because we believe that people's urges and actions are often fuelled by erratic forces mostly beyond their control.
82. We have little patience for people's imperfections because we arrogantly assume that we are perfect ourselves. Furthermore, we expect others to be perfect like us, too, according to our perceived definition of perfection, of course. These two misleading presumptions are actually caused by our inner forces dictating our judgment and dulling our objectivity.
83. One particular inner conflict stays with us for the rest of our lives. It arises when our two fundamental needs for dependence and independence keep competing and clashing constantly in our mind.
84. In fact, any of Maslow's hierarchical needs are often at the mercy of our needs for dependence and independence. Our other needs (even need for food) are boosted

or dampened by our prominent need for independence (or dependence) regardless of the consequences.

85. As we proceed through life, the number of our dependencies keeps rising, while we keep struggling to develop our unique identity and independence. We get frustrated often when our independence is tainted by our need for dependence on other people and society.

86. We hate the way our partner is squashing our independence. But we also hate that we cannot depend on them enough. The level of conflict between our needs for dependence and independence keeps rising and putting pressure on relationships.

87. Especially, with the added emphasis on individualism and independence in modern societies, personal conflicts due to the inner needs for both dependence and independence have become too prominent and more widespread in society.

88. Creating and maintaining a balance between our conflicting needs for both independence and dependence is a tough job, even if we assume such a balance can be found.

89. In general, independence requires (and leads to) a lot of isolation and self-sacrifice. Dependence is mostly synonymous with compassion.

90. Our partners and society in general do not know how to cope with our need for dependence. Often, they actually ridicule and take advantage of our perceived weakness, i.e., our inability to be independent.

91. Our inner conflicts actually heighten when we try to pretend to be more independent than we really feel we are, or can handle.

92. By exaggerating our need for independence, we are in effect imposing another set of artificial expectations on ourselves, which are unachievable. At the same time, we are jeopardizing our chances to fulfil our need for dependence. We keep alienating our partners by our exaggerated show of independence. These superficial needs and situations cause more inner conflicts as well as clashes between partners.
93. People become aggressive in order to show assertiveness, mostly because they don't know the delicate art of assertiveness.
94. The artificial need to *show off* our independence, as a symbol of freedom and identity, has in effect become counter productive for both our individuality and relationships.
95. The bottom line is that partners' need for dependence is undervalued at so many levels by our modern lifestyles, values, and social pressures. It is trendier to show one's aptitude for individualism. So, people pretend to be independent in order to fit and survive.
96. Obviously, the smart thing nowadays is to not depend on others or their words. They simply cannot deliver because of the limitations in their own lives and personality, and not necessarily out of malice.
97. There is an ongoing struggle between partners to maintain a balance of power in order to stop the other from dominating them.
98. Everybody likes more independence for themselves but less for their partners.
99. With freedom (and independence), most people are mainly thinking about freedom to explore sexuality and

love. This is an automatic reaction to our philosophy about life being short and living only once.//
100. A bizarre trend is emerging as a result of couples' struggle to cope with their needs for dependence and independence: Some couples seek separation with the slightest inconvenience in their relationships; and some couples accept abuse and adultery because they are too apprehensive about loneliness and isolation. These prevalent extremes show the extent of value changes in new societies.
101. Overall, we are not as strong individuals as we often pretend to be in our exaggerated show of independence and individuality.
102. We are not equipped and strong enough to create a reasonable balance between our needs for dependence and independence in our relationships either.
103. The contentious issues in regard to our personal needs for dependence and independence are summarized on page 72.
104. The longer partners stay in a relationship, the more substantial and incompatible their needs for both dependence and independence become. Accordingly, this condition increases both the level of personal conflict and the pressure placed on their relationship.
105. The more complex our societies and interactions get, the more we feel a need to control the sources of potential threats to our physical and mental welfare. This is particularly true because nowadays we trust people much less than we did a few decades ago.
106. When we get into relationships, the need for control becomes even more crucial.

107. We try to control our partners in order to minimize the possibility of getting hurt by them, but also because we believe this would be the best way to protect our relationships.
108. While both genders have equal sexual drives, they often have different motives for acting upon it.
109. Women's natural superiority in creating and safeguarding their offspring appears to contribute to the fact that men lose their priority in relationships when children are born.
110. It appears that our destinies are largely mapped for us in our genes. We think and act in certain ways that finally lead to a certain destiny.
111. Genetics formulates a good portion of our personality and destiny. Even our conscious attempts to adjust our personality cannot override the effect of genetics easily.
112. We never recognize the source of our crooked behaviour, or we deny its destructive force and impact on our relationships. But even if we accept our flaws, we can hardly do much with them.
113. The scars, hurt feelings, and bad experiences cannot be forgotten easily. Their deep effect can always be traced in our personality and unexpected aggression, hatred, and self-pity.
114. Conditional forces are those habits and values that we have adopted wholeheartedly. They are the absorbed effects of *outer forces*, e.g., society.
115. Conditional forces also entail our doubts, quirks, and insecurities.
116. Conditional forces severely impact couples' perceptions and priorities in relationships. And, together with the ef-

fect of genetics, they make the likelihood of partners' compatibility very remote.
117. Reactional forces (defence mechanisms) reside in our unconscious and subconscious minds and then suddenly activate our nervous system with a strong blow.
118. External (outer) forces, e.g., nature, society, economy, and work environment, impact our mood and reaction to events regularly. Accordingly, they impact our long-term view of life and our relationships.
119. Another outer force affecting relationships adversely without anyone's fault is that women are in a state of transition in terms of the progressive role they would like to play in society and relationships.
120. Women's new role in relationships is not understood even by the majority of women, let alone by men who are expected to know what the new format should be and respond positively too.
121. A special situation seems to have emerged: Due to men's passivity, women find it necessary to become aggressive in order to attain the assertiveness they need urgently.
122. When couples meet, they want to set the tone of their relationships by playing all kinds of games, all in hopes of manipulating and controlling their relationship at the end.
123. It would be an inherently difficult task, for men especially, to achieve the changes required in terms of gender roles, even in a timelier manner, even if they agreed to the changes women are asking.
124. Within this confusing situation, all kinds of destructive aggressions by both men and women are convoluting the transition process. Instead of progress, we witness sabo-

tages and retaliation, more games, more divorces, and family murder suicides.

125. The bottom line is that men have lost their identity (whatever it was, good or bad) and don't understand the sensibility of what is expected of them. And women are frustrated, too, because they can't prove and enforce a new identity, which they believe they know what it is.

126. The result of the current confusion (about gender identities) is that partners finally get fed up with their struggles to convince each other logically. So they try to dominate each other or resort to divorce.

127. Obviously, under the hostile environment of relationships, each one of us turns into another destructive *outer force* for our partners.

128. There are a lot of anger and stress out there in society due to people's inability to find a suitable companion or enjoy their existing relationships. Partners just keep blaming each other's lack of common sense to understand their seemingly justified needs.

129. Logic and common sense do not help solve conflicts, because everybody has his/her unique perception of logic and common sense. Nowadays, there seems to be as many varieties of logic and common sense in relationships as the people in them. So only some guidelines can keep relationships in some kind of order.

130. The way we go about satisfying our personal needs portrays our 'personality.' Personality reveals i) our efforts to relate to the world, and ii) other people's perception of our efforts to relate to the world.

131. 'Personality' is an abstract concept, because it is only a reflection of who we want to be or try to be, not the true

person we are. And, also, because personality remains largely a matter of judgment by others about who we are, again not the person that we really are. In all, 'personality' remains an obscure, complex dimension of human with very peculiar characteristics that are hard to pinpoint or predict, let alone manage.

132. Personality is the main tool and motivator to go about satisfying our personal needs.
133. Personality also contains a large inventory of emotions and cognition.
134. We love *who we believe we are* and thus avoid any advice or clues about the way our personality is hurting us or people around us. So we seldom give ourselves a chance to really find out *who we are*.
135. Studying human personality, and its impact on our lives, is highly urgent because we are all striving to establish our identities individually and in relationships.
136. Unfortunately, we hate to agree that our new values and our personalities are too ambiguous (and shallow too), and they are becoming drastically detrimental to our happiness and health.
137. The distinction between good and bad is becoming too subjective nowadays. We depend on the authorities, celebrities, and propagandas to decide about good and bad.
138. The personality model presented in this book has three components:
    a. **Ego-P** reflects (and drives) our desires, ambitions, sense of responsibility, defence mechanism, and all other traits that enable us to assert ourselves and protect our lives.

b. **Self-P** contains our inner urges, love, integrity, inquisitiveness, potentialities, creativity and spirituality. This aspect of our personality reflects humans' soul and vulnerability.

c. **Model-P** is basically the most practical aspect of our personality in the way it tries to help us adapt to social norms and get accepted and admired if possible. It is driven mainly by our conditional and adaptation needs.

139. Depending upon our genetics and experiences, each person's personality manifests by a different degree of Ego-P, Model-P, and Self-P.

140. Although we may apply any mix of the personality aspects in a special instance for a special purpose, we often adopt a fix personality profile that reflects a certain proportion of each aspect of personality.

141. Our actions and attitude reflect some degree of all three aspects of our unique personalities. However, every one of our daily interactions can be noted to have a tone particular to one aspect of our personality.

142. People often behave under the influence of a main personality aspect.

143. Our personality aspects create misperceptions when we are sending a message and also when we are receiving a message.

144. The complexity of relationship interactions and communications is due to the way different personality aspects of partners react to one another in every situation without proper attention or intention.

145. The irony is that we believe or pretend to be communicating with total honesty and integrity. We believe we are

communicating with our Self-P. But in reality all communications are normally contaminated by Ego-P and Model-P.
146. It helps our relationships, and life as a whole, if we learn to gauge and adjust the volume of these personality aspects regularly. We can make a habit of monitoring and distinguishing the personality aspects in our encounters and pinpoint the one usually in control.
147. Keeping track of the interworking and manifestation of our personality aspects is the most important step toward self-awareness. And this awareness is obviously the best tool for improving our relationships.
148. All three personality aspects have both good and bad sides.
149. A useful process of self-awareness and also minimizing relationship clashes is to pursue the steps outlined on page 112.
150. The following hypotheses seem reasonable:
    - Self-P is driven mostly by the inner force A (instincts and spirit).
    - Ego-P is driven mostly by the inner force B (genetics, chemistry, and nervous system). But Ego-P is also affected by the inner forces C and D (conditioning and defence mechanisms).
    - Model-P is driven mostly by the inner forces C and D as well as external forces.
    - 'Human nature' is mostly a combination of Self-P and that part of Ego-P that is driven by the inner force B.
151. For building an ideal relationship, partners should be *good and enlightened* persons first.

Summary and Conclusions

152. Being a 'good' person mostly refers to individual's personality dominance. Obviously, the more a partner is driven by Self-P, and the less he/she is influenced by Ego-P, the better he/she is, with a higher chance to build an ideal relationship. Goodness is a reflection of a person's level of naturalness and integrity.
153. But, in reality, most people are becoming more crooked, phony, spoiled, and demanding every day. As a result, they become more incompatible with one another. Personality flaws, insecurities, and evilness reduce the chances of success for relationships drastically.
154. People perceive the world and people according to their unique personalities. But it also appears that men and women have major differences in terms of perceiving events and people. They have a rather uniform way of interpreting the world and setting their priorities.
155. Considering the high volume of misperceptions, it seems safe to say that they play the most destructive role in our relationships. This is not only due to the consequences of miscommunications between partners in relationships, but also because we are confused personally about who we are, what we need, and what can really make us happy.
156. Our misperceptions create obstacles for building our relationships. But the main point is that we, including our partners, cannot overcome our misperceptions readily, due to our deep psychological constructs. Our dogmatic perceptions are driven by our firm *inner forces*.
157. The bottom line is that we cannot perceive our own personality accurately. And we have difficulty judging each other's personality too.

158. It seems that we have become the most snobbish people on earth throughout the entire history of mankind.
159. We lose our identity when our perceptions of our personality and the world contradict reality to a large extent. Meanwhile, the lack of identity causes more confusion and misperceptions. It makes the job of adapting to our environment difficult and frustrating. This vicious cycle continues until we are totally out of touch with reality and our purpose of living.
160. The fact is that we never know who we are despite our lifelong struggle to establish our identity. The reason is that we perceive ourselves and our personality according to the inner forces A to D, a biased perception of the world, and also according to bogus social standards.
161. In relationships, the task of developing our identity faces even a tougher challenge. This is because being in a relationship imposes a new puzzling role for partners just for the sake of making the best of the situation. And also because partners like to influence each other.
162. Aside from its spiritual connotation, 'Who am I?', as a philosophical question, reflects the complexity of our personality and perceptions. We have all realized the difficulty of answering this question.
163. But the question 'Who am I?' also reflects the existence of another dimension of us, the self, which is unknown to us. The self, we agree, is different from either our perceptions of ourselves or other people's perceptions of us.
164. We are responsible for misperceptions between us and our partners when we keep insisting that we know who we are instead of trying to learn more about ourselves through self-awareness. We are also guilty for letting our

misperceptions cripple our understanding of our partners, our means of communicating, and our ability to solve our conflicts.

165. As intelligent humans, we are not used to self-analysis to understand the extent of our defects and faulty perceptions.

166. Not only we assume and insist that we know who we are, but also we insist that our partners are fully aware of who they are (mostly as we perceive them!).

167. Once we set our minds about 'who they are,' positively or negatively, it becomes close to impossible to accept any counter argument about the validity of our opinions and perceptions.

168. If only we learn that our partners cannot learn what we insist they should learn, we may be able to better manage our relationships and assess our options realistically.

169. We are completely self-centred not only in terms of thinking mostly about our needs, but also in terms of imposing all those needs on our relationships.

170. Conflicts are inevitable as long as relationships are viewed and measured according to partners' misperceptions of themselves and their partners.

171. The drastic rise in relationship conflicts is due to couples' misperceptions about 'who they are and who they can be.' They just keep portraying a pompous identity to prove their strong individuality.

172. Our communications are driven by many conscious, subconscious, and unconscious motives or impulses. Thus, the level of consciousness is a major psychological factor in communications.

173. Mind and body are only tools. They are used by this powerful entity called 'the Self' or 'Cognition' to run our affairs, partly consciously and partly unconsciously.
174. Cognition and consciousness are the locus of all human attributes, behaviour, and decisions.
175. Our weaknesses and strengths are stored at all levels of consciousness. They affect us and people around us positively or negatively depending on our awareness. Awareness is simply the level of our cognition that we have learned to master.
176. The importance of self-awareness becomes evident when we consider its objective to dig into our subconscious and unconscious territories and gradually explore the causes of our deep-rooted behaviour.
177. We are apprehensive about the repercussions of independent thinking and behaving, including rejection and loneliness.
178. Most likely the idea of human purity is only a fantasy. Humans, like most other creatures in nature, are probably supposed to be wild and offensive to protect themselves and their own species. Except that humans are often careless about their own kind, anyway, as they keep killing one another in millions as a routine human lifestyle—a justified habit. So far we have only proven human impurity.
179. The idea of the search for tranquility and purity has emerged from humans' struggle to escape constant suffering and stress.
180. In fact we might have an easier task proving that humans become more arrogant and unreliable as time goes by.

181. These depressing conclusions about human nature further confirm the earlier assertions about human limitations to understand the requirements of relationships and coping with them.
182. Still some level of active involvement with life is better than neglecting ourselves and losing the opportunity of being a more conscious and conscientious person.
183. Most of our thoughts and decisions are processed beyond our control (in the subconscious and unconscious). The first benefit of this knowledge is that we appreciate the difficulty of effective communication more clearly. We understand the obstacles that everybody faces in communicating and running their relationships.
184. The desire for wealth and power has ruined our capacity to grasp our very basic need for true independence, to free ourselves from people and symbols that constrict our ability to think straight and unselfishly. We pretend to be independent and free, but these gestures are usually too far from reality (our daily routines) and how we really feel.
185. Learning about the levels of consciousness can enhance our objectivity, to judge our own and other people's behaviour better. More importantly, a few people may also acquire a capacity to tap the enormous power of subconscious and unconscious—toward enlightenment.
186. The three personality aspects of an individual match the three levels of consciousness very nicely. This reflects the correlation of a person's level of consciousness with his/her personality and behaviour.
    - The **Model-P** aspect of personality mostly operates from within the **conscious** level of one's mind. It

represents mostly our sense of adaptation, playfulness, and sociability.
- The **Ego-P** aspect of personality represents our **subconscious** mind, which reflects our private and selfish traits and motives.
- The **Self-P** aspect of personality represents mostly our **unconscious** urges, instincts, potentialities, and spirituality inclinations.

187. The five main causes of misperceptions, as discussed in Chapter Four, are also the main causes of miscommunications. They are:
    - Equivocation
    - Misrepresentation
    - Transference
    - Apprehension
    - Identity

   Miscommunications and misperceptions keep impacting one another and piling up dangerously in the early stages of relationships. Once these misperceptions are deposited in various levels of couples' consciousness, there is very little anybody can do to reverse the deteriorating state of their relationships.

188. Our communications, perceptions, and consciousness (including the three personality aspects) are highly interrelated impulses. Collectively, they instigate our reactions and behaviour in any circumstance.

189. Since love has become the locus of relationships in modern societies, we must at least know what it is and understand the role it can realistically play in relationships.

190. To really appreciate love and possibly enjoy it, we should remove the ambiguities surrounding our present impression of it.
191. Chapter One highlighted two crucial points: (a) a good companion can *potentially* satisfy a wide range of partners' personal needs, and (b) we are programmed, instinctually and culturally, to look for a soul mate, because we believe he/she can relieve our loneliness and satisfy our personal needs. In a sense, we intuitively put too much faith in the potentials of companionship.
192. The word 'love,' in the context used nowadays, basically consists of people's impression (and expression) of their 1) urges, 2) feelings, and 3) moods during their search for a companion.
193. The **Urges** that drive humans to find a mate are Sex, Compassion, and S-love. Compassion by itself includes many other urges such as E-love, security, dependence, respect, and recognition.
194. The **Feelings** related to humans' search for a mate are numerous, including delight, elation, lust, jealousy, possessiveness, hatred, anger, and all other feelings that humans face while chasing any desire. A variety of feelings emerge during their love affairs, success, or failure.
195. The **Moods** that emerge during humans' search for a companion are comprised of: Attraction, Romance, and Attachment. They are fed by a mix of urges and feelings, but also by conscious assessments.
196. **Attraction** is triggered by physical appeal, lust, but also our careful evaluation of a person's attributes and resources. Our instinctual criteria for selecting a mate,

mostly for the purpose of bearing a child with this person, often play its role too.

197. **Romance** is our innate impression of S-love and our calculating expressions of passion in order to lure in our beloved. So, again, we are using both our instinctual and logical assets to find a companion.
198. **Attachment** is the effect of closeness to a person and enjoying the compassion satisfied by this union.
199. We have historically combined all these urges, feelings, and moods and called it love, thus creating such a vague definition to deal with.
200. People suffer because of love for two main reasons: First, the forces behind their love urges, feelings, and moods aren't clear to them in order to deal with the sources of their anxieties directly. Second, they assume love is a lasting condition.
201. Understanding the true meaning and implications of love might help us curb our initial unwarranted enthusiasm and prepare ourselves better for its heartbreaking consequences.
202. The *urges, moods, and feelings* related to 'finding a companion' should be studied as psychological reactions—symptoms of love—but not love itself.
203. True love is that one instinctual urge that we have identified as S-love. Love, in its purest sense, is just a simple, selfless appreciation for the mere 'being' of another person without having any selfish urges to own, control, or impose one's needs upon that person.
204. This pure feeling of S-love, which is engraved in our unconscious, is occasionally directed toward our beloved, too, but usually for a short period. This is because we

usually have a hard time internalizing S-love unless we learn to become a selfless individual.

205. We create all kinds of images and love moods (in the form of attraction and romance) in our minds when we are struck by some flickers of S-love. But these love moods are the outcome of our urgent urges for 'sex' and 'compassion,' as we struggle to find a companion.

206. Overall, it is our strong 'need for a companion' (once directed toward a particular person) that creates all those urges, feelings, and moods that we customarily (and wrongly) attribute to love.

207. This subtle understanding about love is important because it makes us reflect and put our love related urges and feelings into a proper perspective. We remember that it is our 'need for a companion' and 'sense of loneliness' that often makes us behave in strange ways.

208. The real cause of our restlessness and loneliness is not love (or lack of it), although we crave more love the lonelier we get. The real cause of our loneliness is our rising inability to *relate* to one another, while our obsession to find a soul mate keeps growing at the same time.

209. This awareness might goad us to adopt a new mentality: to either give less importance to having a companion, or go about finding him/her in a more honest and productive manner.

210. Our 'need for a companion' is actually so strong it has turned into *'desperation* for a companion' in recent decades.

211. We remain hopeful all our lives to find a soul mate who would fulfil most of our personal needs. But our chances for actually finding a soul mate is quite remote, and then

realizing the 'potentialities' of a companion (and maintaining good relationships) is even smaller for all the reasons enumerated in this book.

212. Nowadays, partners have difficulty even fulfilling each other's basic need for sex on a long-term basis, let alone all those more complex needs for E-love, compassion, and S-love.

213. Yet people seem to have a chronic optimism about the potentialities of relationships despite their repeated failures, frustration, anger, and desperation.

214. Our desperation for a companion would keep rising because we cannot maintain a relationship or trust our partners in the long run.

215. We have become too idealistic. Instead of understanding the roots of relationship problems and our role in causing many of them, we keep dreaming about a soul mate and an ideal relationship with another partner. We don't see the futility of our search for love or a soul mate.

216. Naturally, the more relationships fail, the more desperate people get, which ironically only heightens their craving for love even more. It is easy to notice that the more a person is desperate to find a companion, the faster and deeper he/she falls in love.

217. In all, our obsession for love nowadays is a reflection of our loneliness and desperation for a companion, but our exaggerated expectations (including love) ruin our relationships and we become even more desperate and lonely. This vicious cycle is destroying people's trust in one another and their expressions of love.

218. If we realize that love cannot be the success factor for relationships, we might redirect our focus to our own per-

sonalities, lifestyles, needs, demands, and methods of going about finding a companion.
219. The way we have become—so haughty and oversensitive—is to be blamed for the failure of relationships, not the lack of love or couple's inability to be romantic.
220. Attraction has been a rather instinctual mood (process) for selecting a mate going back millions of years in the history of evolution. Nowadays we get attracted, or pretend to be attracted, to someone based on many other factors, too, such as his/her wealth, social standing, etc.
221. Romance has always existed in nature, too, yet its role has also been tentative (like 'Attraction') for both animals and humans. But we like to have lots of it nowadays—a naive demand that is increasing expectations and clashes when couples cannot deliver romance naturally.
222. Attachment has evolved in humans as the need for support to raise offspring emerged for our ancestors several million years ago. It was mostly a temporary arrangement, too, and then partners went their own ways when children could live on their own.
223. Nowadays we have got used to the idea of having a long-term commitment with a partner. This new mentality has grown stronger as a result of humans becoming more insecure, calculating, and needy for love and compassion in recent history.
224. At the same time, we have become too arrogant and choosy and thus sabotage our chances to sustain long commitments with anybody.
225. Nonetheless, our yearning for both romance and attachment appears to be largely self-imposed moods and

also a reflection of humans' insecurities as well as struggle for social morality.
226. Love has always been addressed as a combination of many feelings, urges, and moods related to humans' search for a companion. If the ancient Greek had defined ten different kinds of love, now psychologist come up with six or eight types again based on its symptoms.
227. Dividing love into certain categories by attaching certain feelings to each category would not help the existing chaos in relationships. It only convolutes the meaning of a simple concept like love even more.
228. In the final analysis, the essence of love is always that notion of selflessness toward another being regardless of all the feelings and urges that are manifesting in that particular case, e.g., love toward our children, parents, a person, or even objects such as nature, artistic passion, etc. Love is always the unique feeling of S-love regardless of all the emotions that get attached to it.
229. Sometimes we make a big fuss about the way a lover becomes restless, jealous, depressed, sleepless, etc. But these symptoms are common in many other situations, too, when any particular plan or desire of a person is threatened. People lose sleep and become restless about any matter that occupies their minds, e.g., a project, a catastrophe, etc., or get jealous if a job promotion is given to another person.
230. The symptoms of love shouldn't affect the nature of love, if it's true love. Even compassion, which is noble and often more precious than even love, should not be mixed up with love.

231. Pure, unselfish S-love satisfies some peaceful emotions and urges of humans, but it doesn't lead to self-destruction or war with our beloved. This is the simple definition of love adopted in this book.
232. Hatred and rage, when love fails, clearly show that our perception of 'love' hadn't been pure (S-love). Obviously, many of our selfish and destructive urges and feelings get attached to our *impression and expression* of love. And it helps to know the real motives behind these urges and feelings.
233. In all, people's sense of love nowadays consists of some kind of mixed urges for sex, compassion, and an impression of S-love. Then they express some feelings and moods, all in an attempt to find a companion.
234. Hormones that rule human urges do not seem to support people's excessive expectations from love and relationships.
235. Human hormones can be blamed for many facts listed on pages 178-180 regarding the inherent vulnerabilities of love and relationships.
236. In the past, love had little impact on people's daily lives and their relationships, simply because people didn't read many books and weren't exposed to such relentless amount of misleading propaganda about love. They had real life hardships to worry about. They weren't so obsessed about expressing themselves as much either.
237. The new social values have brainwashed us to make love the locus of relationships and thus inflict enormous pressure upon ourselves and our partners.
238. Love has become confused with attraction and mixed up with many other urges and feelings of humans. The ob-

jectives of love and relationships are also muddled up in people's minds in a destructive way.

239. Three types of love satisfy the three aspects of our personality:
- **S-love** is Self-P driven and reflects the most **spiritual** and selfless way of loving someone. This is what Maslow refers to as B-love.
- **E-love** is Ego-P driven and reflects our **deficiency** need for love and attention. This is what Maslow refers to as D-love.
- **M-love** is Model-P driven and reflects our most **practical** way of communicating our passion to another person.

240. People's three personality aspects perceive 'love' differently and make them react to it differently too.

241. The commonplace love consists of i) physical attraction and lust, and ii) a combination of S-love, M-love, and E-love. Therefore:
- A person's 'need for a companion' affects all the three aspects of his/her personality, and each personality aspect plays a role when someone expresses love to another person.
- Seeking love reflects both our instinctual and conditional urges.
- Each person is influenced by a certain level of S-love, M-love, and E-love at the time he/she expresses his/her love. Thus, the meaning of love is different for each person depending on the level of each love aspect he/she has applied to perceive love.
- Inventing an imaginary meaning for love (anything other than for defining S-love, E-love, M-love) and

spreading it for common use is pointless—except for writing fiction and making movies.

242. On most occasions, our initial perception and impression of S-love fades away after we get into relationships. The reason is very simple: Self-P is needed to protect S-love. Also, S-love deteriorates when new perceptions override the initial ones.

243. Overall, the destiny of love doesn't look to be very bright because:
    - The meaning of love is getting more ambiguous and useless, especially for building relationships. But, then, we usually like to make a big deal about the phrase "I love you." In effect, the use of the word love has become too hypocritical considering that people have a variety of purposes for, and understanding of, love.
    - The general increase in social complexity, sexuality, and corruption makes people less and less trustful of one another and their expressions of love. But, at the same time, people insist that relationships and love must be built on absolute trust and honesty.

244. Our limited options to face the reality of love and relationships are:
    - To become selfless and internalize S-love,
    - To pursue love affairs here and there if we are lucky,
    - To live alone while waiting for love,
    - To use M-love to instil mutual respect and civility in relationships.

245. An advantage of M-love is that expressing one's feelings through M-love would partially respond to partners' need for S-love.

246. Using M-love in relationships has other advantages too: It provides a venue for partners to be romantic without raising relationship expectations or creating misunderstandings about their love expressions.
247. M-love also fulfils some of partners' E-love needs. This happens because people's *subconscious* can easily substitute M-love for E-love, while their *conscious* minds remember the purpose of M-love.
248. M-love is a voluntary and possibly periodical gesture by one or both partners. It shouldn't be turned into an expectation by a partner; otherwise it would be E-love and not M-love anymore.
249. Love has no definite meaning to draw upon or set expectations for. We can apply it arbitrarily only to soothe our need for compassion without making an issue out of it or expecting long-term commitment on that basis. "You said you loved me!" is a common complaint when couples interpret 'love' based on their random and vague perceptions.
250. Obviously, the word 'love' covers a large variety of meanings and none of them really reflects true love (S-love).
251. Couples get hurt because of their wrong impressions of love, and because they annoy each other with their exaggerated expectations for love and attention. People destroy not only their chances for building manageable relationships, but also the opportunity of understanding the meaning of S-love.
252. 'Love' is perceived and applied differently by each individual according to his/her psychological and circumstantial needs.

253. Happiness is a myth all by itself, but finding it in relationships is plain utopian—only a wishful thinking cultivated in our imaginations.
254. We want happiness to fit our contaminated lifestyles, instead of a lifestyle that could induce peace of mind as the closest state of happiness.
255. Unfortunately, human nature does not support happiness and tranquility because of innate human urges for challenge, controversy, power, domination, competition, greed, struggle for survival, etc. Anger, hatred, jealousy, spite, and aggressiveness come to us so naturally, but we must try really hard to be honest, compassionate, sincere, etc.
256. Most relationships become instable soon enough, only because they fail to satisfy our fantastic desires for happiness and sexuality.
257. The slogan 'life's purpose is to find happiness' is in fact causing more suffering than guiding people toward happiness. The reason is that it makes people believe that such a myth (happiness) actually exists, and it is due to their stupidity or relationships they cannot find it.
258. The purpose of life is neither to find and spread happiness nor to create good human beings. Life doesn't have any particular meaning, nor is it about anything in particular. Life is merely a collection of events and moments that transpires in people's lives according to natural laws and chances and affects them based on their cognition.
259. Humans have many other ambitions in life, which they often pursue with greater passion than their desire for happiness or even pleasures, e.g., need for love, power,

or recognition. Most people just cannot sit idle and be happy with their contentment.
260. Happiness and goodness are the likely outcomes of our choices to set the right balance between our ambitions and contentment.
261. The fact that we have to try so hard to become better human beings and find happiness shows that humans are not pure by nature.
262. The simple fact that ego is an inherent part of the human psyche is enough to cause human bias, selfishness, hypocrisy, and hundreds of other impurities and flaws.
263. Human purity is not a matter of comparing the number of good deeds versus bad ones either, even if people did more good than bad. Purity is an absolute fact and not an algebraic equation. It either exists or not. The only question is how often humans' impurity approaches evilness. Too often and universally, it usually feels!
264. Propagating that humans are good by nature would only create a false expectation in society, and people get even more disappointed and frustrated regularly when facing reality. The more we consider people's malice unnatural, the more deliberate their actions appear.
265. On the other hand, if we accept that humans are flawed and impure by nature, we would develop more tolerance and compassion, because we understand that human actions are mostly beyond their control or are pushed by greed and social corruption. We might even smarten up and correct the social causes of human corruption.
266. Our reaction to people's claims of purity and happiness shows our major scepticism. We need a lot of evidence to believe in even one person's goodness and happiness.

267. Once we accept that human nature is impure, we would also keep our expectations from people and relationships low. We get less surprised and angry while we develop some form of understanding and compassion toward our partners and the helpless humanity.
268. As social values and personal needs of couples change during the course of history, the meaning, objectives, and format of their relationships should be reassessed and redefined as well.
269. Basically, we have three options regarding relationships:
    a. **Continue with the status quo,** which means we just hope that nature, will take its course and eventually some kind of a format will emerge for relationships.
    b. **Hope that one gender will eventually dominate the other** so that order may return to relationships.
    c. **Create a relationship framework** to guide couples in running their relationships while they attempt to test their abilities to relate.
270. We can say that *a relationship is a collection of partners' actions and feelings.* But a relationship must also be viewed as a *system or atmosphere for facilitating partners' cooperation to achieve certain goals.*
271. The basic nature of relationships nowadays and the emerging trends are outlined on pages 195-6.
272. The stress caused by new lifestyles is crippling a good majority of relationships and also threatening the foundation of our societies in general. The situation is only going to get worse if new solutions and a framework for relationships are not found soon.
273. Without a framework, the state of relationships would deteriorate beyond control very soon.

274. The first step for developing a framework is to see relationships as an *independent* setting, and not a collection of partners' whims.
275. The framework can help partners learn and follow some guidelines to 'relate' to each other. They should stop hoping that the task of *relating* can happen automatically or by a lifelong trial and error. The framework would help couples set their objectives and expectations from relationships more realistically.
276. Another objective of the relationship framework is to identify a handful relationship models that can fit the variety of individuals' personalities, while providing the advantages of being in relationships.
277. People are paranoid about fairness nowadays. A 'relationship framework' can replace the need for couples' constant fight for 'equality.'
278. The main objectives of a relationship framework are:
    A. To enforce teamwork,
    B. To bring objectivity back into relationships,
    C. To increase communication effectiveness,
    D. To reduce partners' expectations from relationships, and
    E. To overhaul individuals' mentality and social mechanisms.
279. Knowing about teamwork and actually being committed to it as the only solution for relationships are two different things.
280. For the mere reason that individuality is becoming the most important requirement of relationships, creating new methods of teamwork is imperative more than ever.

281. New methods of teamwork might contain a variety of tools, including a simple agreement between partners about sharing responsibilities and finances of the household and sticking to the plan.
282. Another role of teamwork would be to maintain some kind of balance between partners' personal needs and the relationship needs.
283. Once partners learn to focus on teamwork, their obsession for *equality* feels and becomes obsolete. Instead of depending on equality, or superiority, the success of relationships would be measured only by the smooth operation and outcome of teamwork.
284. Indeed, the strength of teamwork lies on its emphasis on partners' independence and objectivity.
285. In line with our personal obsession for more things and affection, we have reduced the capacity of our relationships to be objective.
286. Without relationship guidelines and principles, partners' communications have become too subjective, Ego-P oriented, and destructive.
287. The logic dictates that the more we promote individuality and personal rights, the less we should expect from relationships. We should become more self-reliant to maintain our independence.
288. Personal needs and relationship needs aren't the same or coincidental.
289. Most relationship problems emerge because couples perceive relationship needs as an extension of their personal needs.

290. A major purpose of developing a framework is to discuss and eliminate some of the misperceptions about relationships.
291. A great deal of soul searching and mental adjustments is needed in order to adapt our relationships to the new social framework.
292. One major misperception in society and people's minds is that relationships should last forever.
293. It is time to perceive relationships more in terms of an open-ended arrangement rather than a long-term commitment. The advantages of such a relationship arrangement might amaze us at the end.
294. By establishing new mechanisms like the ones suggested in Chapter Eleven, reverse psychology would help couples and their relationships in at least four ways:
    - Couples get into their relationships more carefully based on intelligent analyses of their needs, compatibility, and the relationship models that are most suitable for them.
    - Couples work harder and more consciously to prolong their relationships instead of allowing it to expire. This would increase the longevity of most relationships.
    - Couples become mentally prepared to leave their relationships with the least amount of shock and hassle when it isn't working. They know that separation is a good and acceptable possibility.
    - Ending relationships would be automatic and hassle free.
295. We need modern thinking and principles for relationships to match the modern life we are so eagerly embracing.

296. Our culture permeates many invalid myths about love that are listed on page 218.
297. We are ignoring the fact that almost all relationships in the modern world have started based on love and they still keep failing miserably.
298. Nowadays, couples have become both too romantic and antagonistic.
299. Many couples are frustrated and confused, as they feel trapped in their loveless (maybe hostile) relationships. This is especially stressful for those who are adamant that love is the essence of relationships.
300. Hypocrisy and deceit overwhelm our love affairs and relationships when we constantly draw on Model-P aspect of our personality to play games and manipulate our partners.
301. Being natural requires keeping Model-P at the minimum level needed only for etiquette and tactfulness, before it leads to phoniness.
302. Even 'love' is contaminated by selfishness and gross misperceptions nowadays.
303. A simple fact about the meaning of love has been ignored in our new culture: We don't appreciate that the more one seeks S-love, the more one must be honest and sincere in character. Yet we have lost our ability to be natural and sincere because of all the complex games that have been introduced in relationships in recent decades.
304. Like other aspects of social life these days, a superficial (embellished) love is acceptable and preferred to sincerity and reality.

305. Partners look for unconditional (selfless) love from each other, but impose a lot of conditions to ensure *equality*, even in terms of the level of love they exchange.
306. While equality, in the sense of *fairness*, is the foundation of democratic societies, the concept of equality has turned into a socio-political platform to further spread our demented social values.
307. The concept of love is often confused in the minds of couples who not only make the equality of love a relationship requirement, but also *retaliate* harshly when their love is not returned equally.
308. We imagine that we can hide our insincerity, mistrust, and dishonesty from the rest of the world. But this mentality only shows our arrogance and high belief in Model-P to bail us out. The good news is that people can see each other's true nature despite all the elaborate games they play to pretend a false personality of themselves and to conceal their calculating nature.
309. The games and retaliation schemes in relationships show how ridiculous the idea of measuring the strength of our relationships by 'love' is. We just ignore all these contradictions and keep looking for S-love in such a contaminated environment.
310. Loving someone requires a special knowledge and awareness.
311. For true love, partners need a highly developed character. For example, only a fool might believe in love expressions by a naïve person.
312. The hoopla around positive thinking in recent decades has had some disturbing consequences on our perception of life. For one thing, we have lost touch with the

harsh reality of life and believe that we deserve to have all the best of everything including a flawless, loving relationship. We have all become too idealistic.

313. So, all our lives, we look for an imaginary idol to accept as our companion, or we try to rebuild our partners to fit that image. Especially there is a trend out there to make men softer so that they can respond better to women's desires and perceptions of relationships.

314. Everybody is quite unique (and most likely damaged) due to his/her nature, needs, and perceptions. So, people's expectation to find or create their ideal partners is just too naïve. It is amazing how partners expect each other to behave the same way they think and feel themselves, as if such transformation was feasible or even desirable.

315. The question partners should ask themselves is whether they can find the right formula—relationship model—to relate to each other effectively and live a quiet life without trying to change each other.

316. The complexity of relationships is evident in the manner couples use various aspects of their personality, i.e., Ego-P, Mode-P, and Self-P, to communicate their perceived feelings of love.

317. Since love is nowadays the glue that holds couples together, all other aspects of their relationship become difficult to manage and appreciate, as well, when love begins to lose its intensity.

318. Promises and wedding vows actually create many problems in relationships. For one thing, promises raise partners' expectations from each other unrealistically. But the main problem is that partners get a wrong impression about the security and permanence of their relationship.

They ignore that all relationships are vulnerable and require constant attention and work in order to survive one more day.

319. What we call love in our relationships is often only a combination of lust, possessiveness, and psychological deficiencies we've compiled through social interactions. Besides, not even S-love is necessarily a success factor for relationships anyway.

320. We seldom get an opportunity to learn about some of the finer means of thinking and living. Even when we do, we have extreme difficulty staying on a path of awareness when people around us are consumed with superficial needs and spread phony values.

321. Instead of looking for an ideal, imaginary relationship environment, maybe our new goal should be to make relationships only manageable and tolerable. This requires conscious efforts to lower our personal expectations and define new objectives for our relationships.

322. At two extremes, a relationship may be viewed as a spiritual connection between two individuals, or as some boring activities and interactions between them to share life's hardships.

323. For our relationships, we don't seem to have captured the sense for the right balance between practicality and romance. For example, most people have realized that signing a prenuptial agreement is necessary as a practical measure, but doing so still appears businesslike and unromantic to them.

324. The truth is that our *urgent* emotional *needs* (e.g., need for sex, E-love, and security) overpower our ability to think practically about the potential catastrophes of relation-

ships. This is particularly true because our spirits is usually weakened by other harsh realities of modern lifestyles.

325. Tension is increasing in relationships not only due to people's higher emphasis on independence, but also their ongoing self-pity for not having an ideal partner in their lives.
326. Nowadays people have a high opinion of themselves (often unrealistically) and thus set a high standard for their ideal partner and their needs from relationships.
327. For one thing, people like to exaggerate their self-worth to themselves and others in order to prove their identity.
328. People's struggle for independence (identity) and their tendency to play phony roles to be popular create a lot of inner conflicts for them, because the more they try to prove their identity, the more they lose it.
329. Life is getting harder to adapt to every day, and the fast deterioration of relationships' environment is the most direct (and costly) effect of our inability to adapt in a natural way.
330. People seem obsessed with their search for a soul mate nowadays, as they consider it a necessity and a right.
331. But having a companion feels like a lot of work these days too.
332. The level and complexity of partners' expectations have kept increasing as society promotes phonier lifestyles.
333. Realistically, though, the level of expectations from relationships should be reduced to compensate for the increasing pressures that society is placing on the personal life of people already.

334. As normal human beings, we are unable to respond to the rotating demands of our partners for independence and dependence. So we must adopt a relationship model to handle the situation consistently.
335. The existing social fervour for independence indicates that, as a general rule, couples should place their emphasis on a relationship model that best guarantees partners' independence.
336. The higher we climb up the relationships hierarchy, a higher sense of dependence and maturity is required from partners. Accordingly, couples' increasing urge for independence means that they should stick to models in the lower levels of the relationship needs hierarchy.
337. Advocating independence in relationships might appear inconsistent with the objective of 'enforcing teamwork.' But there is no conflict here, as 'teamwork' must be viewed as an objective negotiation process between two independent partners, and not their dependency.
338. As we insist on more independence and individualism, the need for teamwork and communication becomes greater for keeping our egos under a leash. At the same time, for teamwork, partners should have some genuine qualities, including modesty and objectivity. Though, modesty and the obsession for individualism often don't go together.
339. The supply and demand for compassion are drastically unbalanced in societies. There is a large demand for it and so little supply.
340. The rising level of stress in society has made us vulnerable and too needy for sympathy, but there is nobody out there to give it to us.

341. Whether we can find happiness in relationships or not depends on a large number of factors, mainly our mental capacity to interpret, absorb, and reflect happiness. In all, happiness is more a subjective perception than a tangible commodity to expect from relationships.
342. We usually think that relationships can bring us happiness because it can solve our personal problems. This is a false assumption and an unrealistic expectation.
343. Actually, instead of expecting relationships to solve our problems, we should expect and prepare ourselves to deal with the hardships of relationships and the high likelihood of separation.
344. People behave neurotically and randomly to find happiness in a variety of things or events, like going to yoga, travelling, shopping excessively, looking for love, dancing, getting into art, etc. But these random searches for relief or happiness bring us only more frustration, unless we settle with our inner selves and relax naturally.
345. Why partners wait until they hate each other so much they cannot even look into each other's eyes? Why not separate civilly as soon as they realize they cannot relate to each other realistically. Why don't they remember that in most cases people cannot change?
346. Many people don't have the patience or time for friendship, but still insist on building a 'love' relationship. They disregard the basic principles, like courtesy and respect, to allow their friendship grow in a natural way. Instead, they depend on their weird games to incite a phony love. How can people trust each other for a serious relationship if they don't even know how to be good friends?

347. The main feature of successful friendships, which is missing in relationships, is that friends' limited expectations come naturally, without pressure or demand. Then even if those expectations are not fulfilled, they usually don't argue or fight, but rather moderate their own expectations to sustain their friendship.
348. As a practical step, partners should begin to realize that nowadays the sense of commitment is vastly eroded by the need for individualism.
349. Most relationships would have been considered acceptable if couples were not misled by their superficial needs. For example, partners believe that they deserve to get a lot of attention from their companions and actually be 'spoiled' by them rather regularly. Or as they get old, they only see the aging of their partner and not their own. So they try to revive their youthful memories with another person who is not so old and cranky like their spouses, and flatters them too.
350. Couples' ability to give and receive compassion in their relationships depends on how humble and enlightened they really are.
351. Due to our high expectations from life nowadays, and positive thinking, we always imagine that we can find (or could have found) a better partner than the one we have. We believe we deserve a better one and that he/she can be found if we look around for him/her. But any seeming desirable partner proves inadequate again soon enough.
352. With the constant increase of relationship conflicts nowadays, only a proactive (preventative) approach

might stop breakdowns. We now need to foresee and prevent relationship conflicts as much as possible.

353. Instead of depending on partners to imagine the purposes of relationships and behave randomly according to their interpretations, a workable framework based on social conditions of the time must be made available to everybody.

354. Instead of measuring the success of relationships objectively, we let the selfishness and neediness of partners make this critical judgment. It is only their arrogance that is being measured then.

355. Instead of relying on random criteria of couples or their in-laws, an objective set of modest criteria should define the success of relationships. In this sense, 'relationships' is viewed as an independent *entity* free from random judgments and perceptions of partners.

356. We are placing a lot of pressure on society and our partners with our rampant needs for things, sympathy, and security. This is limiting the chances of relationships to pursue a practical path.

357. Someday we must realize and agree that relationship expectations set beyond some modest, humanistic levels are artificial and imposed by psychologically distressed and deprived people. Then, we will rush to redefine relationships as an independent entity with unique needs.

358. The obvious first step for assessing relationship conflicts is to establish whether they are genuine or only created based on partners' exaggerated expectations, unfulfilled personal needs, or idiosyncrasies. But the question is who would be doing this assessment for couples and society as a whole, and according to what yardsticks?

359. Viewing 'relationships' as an independent entity (R-entity), like a business enterprise, doesn't undermine its emotional importance.
360. R-entity is only a concept with the important task of reminding couples that relationship needs are unique and not an extension of their personal needs.
361. R-entity can be viewed as an important third party (the third leg of a tripod) in relationships to keep partners stable and objective.
362. A marital partnership is many folds more complex and demanding than any business partnership, because the cost of failure is much higher.
363. R-entity simply provides the opportunity of bringing a similar level of discipline that exists in business to the concept we call *relationships*.
364. Relationships are now too complex, we need companions more urgently than ever, and we have become less patient too. These conditions are creating major dilemmas for everybody. Meanwhile, we continue to be too obsessed with love and an idealistic perception of relationships in the new era.
365. We don't realize that, in fact, we have created more limitations for our relationships by our exaggerated perception of its high potential, especially in terms of bringing us happiness.
366. Because we have not still determined the acceptable level of tolerance, and because we have kept rising our expectations from relationships, suddenly our level of patience has become too low.
367. Our options about relationships seem to be clear. They are:

Summary and Conclusions

- Keep fighting and struggling in relationships, or live in solitude, while sticking to some rigid perceptions of an ideal relationship.
- Learn to accept the new reality about relationships, reduce expectations from them, fulfil as much of personal needs outside the relationship, tolerate some level of relationship imperfections, and separate peacefully when it proves unmanageable.

368. The ultimate objective of a relationship framework is to *enable partners relate to each other emotionally, effectively, and efficiently (the three Es)* even when a variety of their personal expectations cannot be fulfilled in their relationship.

369. Relating emotionally doesn't mean love. Rather, it means understanding other people's limitations, inherent hurts, and inability to change, and our capacity to still show sympathy toward them.

370. People are oversensitive but lack compassion. Often they are careless and heartless themselves, but are hurt by the simplest comments or inadequate attention. This is of course a symptom of their high Ego-P too.

371. The complexity of relationships is easy to grasp when we appreciate the complexity of human nature. We must realize how hopelessly helpless we are due to our psychological defects and idiosyncrasies.

372. Relationships would always remain a demanding and confusing aspect of our lives. Accordingly, we must begin to see and accept relationships in a different light, as a temporary union. And we should also learn to become humbler humans and modify our life values.

373. Not having a relationship sounds ridiculous to a large majority of the population who seeks a companion as a

basic need. Both our instincts and culture constantly force us to attend to this need actively.

374. In all, we must modify our mindset to deal with the relationships' specific demands. The particular relationship model that couples choose should keep their affairs and communications manageable, while allowing them to deal with their personal needs individually.

375. A couple relates actively when they can maintain positive emotions, effectiveness, and efficiency in their relationship—the three Es.

376. Couples relate passively when they learn to live with minimum expectations from their relationship while it still remains manageable. The three Es are somewhat necessary in 'passive relating' too.

377. It is important for partners to know about the way they are 'relating,' if at all, and acknowledge it too.

378. The absence of some kind of relationship principles is preventing partners to relate. This is a frustrating shortfall of relationships nowadays. In all, there are no Generally Acceptable Relationship Principles (GARP) to guide couples and provide an effective relationship framework.

379. GARP can help partners understand and respect each other's boundaries. Also, couples need GARP to recognize how humans' inherent shortfalls are affecting their behaviour. Unfortunately, the present state of relationships is mostly dominated by partners' phony roles, games, and retaliations—instead of being managed by GARP.

380. The bottom line is that we must be willing to sacrifice in some respects to gain the tranquility of manageable rela-

tionships, and we must learn how to tame our egos to accept and honour GARP.
381. GARP will be an easy-to-read document for the general public. It will list all the facts and guidelines about relationships according to the social setting of the time.
382. GARP's objectives are explained on pages 298-305.
383. GARP is urgently needed because couples are unaware of the scope of conflicts that their demand for large levels of both dependence and independence has created in their relationships.
384. Convincing people to replace their emotional decision processes with GARP would be difficult.
385. The process of implementing GARP would require a lot of learning and adjusting. This would take time and patience.
386. Logically, a fair and sensible GARP should be adopted quickly by everybody for their own benefit. But overcoming our old habits and urges to entertain GARP or other mechanisms would be difficult.
387. GARP might appear doomed at the outset by its attempt to introduce reasoning and formulate some principles about relationships. Reasoning in the emotional environment of relationships sounds too absurd.
388. GARP appears like a bizarre approach in a society where objectivity and logic seem to have lost their meanings a long time ago.
389. Nonetheless, the idea of introducing GARP appears to be the only option left for society to study the deteriorating state of relationships.
390. Most of us, with a manageable amount of psychological defects and destructive urges, eventually appreciate the

potential of GARP. We must become more open-minded and realistic about our expectations from relationships by adopting GARP.

391. We must identify a practical balance between couples' personal needs and the relationship needs in the new era and define those boundaries in GARP.
392. Once a platform is defined and accepted by prominent sociologists, psychologists, and the population at large, modifying and expanding GARP would be an automatic process like all other social processes in progressive societies of the future.
393. Scholars and experts must find creative ways to inform the general public of the flaws of our existing ways. They must do more research and be more proactive in terms of changing couples' mindsets about relationships.
394. As human beings, with the objective of reaching our deep potentials and tranquility, we are wasting too much time and energy on the petty problems of relationships. This is absurd and a sin.
395. Partners usually question each other's logic regarding their relationship approaches and needs and ask each other "Who said that?" GARP can provide a point of reference (an authority) for many of those questionable personal preferences that partners find arbitrary at the present time.
396. This book has little value for those readers who believe the situation with relationships is fine as it is. But for those of us who are tired of the existing atmosphere, we must prepare ourselves for drastic changes if we are really looking for tangible results. The bottom line is that

we need a framework to redefine relationships and reassess socioeconomic conditions in our modern society.
397. Unfortunately, it appears that only radical solutions might reverse the fast-deteriorating state of relationships.
398. In the present atmosphere, the first thought for any person looking for a companion should be whether they both understand the intricacies and risks of relationships, have developed the right mindset for facing the inevitable setbacks, and are enough mature, independent, and strong to deal with both the inevitable headaches of being in a relationship and when it falls apart.
399. The main mental adjustments required for couples are listed on page 327.
400. Furthermore, social mechanisms must be revamped to support the new social mentality and relationship needs.
401. The overall adjustments required for social mechanisms are listed on page 328.
402. The existing asset distribution mechanism at the time of separation is a silly copout. It has evolved only because courts are not equipped to make a fair assessment of relationship issues and financial assets.
403. People and governments are unaware of the ambiguity, confusion, and damages (both financial and emotional) that the existing social mechanisms are causing for relationships and society as a whole.
404. Governments are busy with so many socioeconomic matters already to worry about relationship failures. So they just deal with the symptoms of this social chaos the best they can at a high cost to taxpayers.
405. If couples didn't depend on courts to grant them financial compensation for being in a relationship, their true

mentality would be revealed before entering their relationships and many couples wouldn't have ended up in bad relationships merely based on trust.

406. The absence of government to meddle with relationship decisions would strengthen the concept of individualism. It would empower couples' sense of independence when the responsibility of taking care of their personal interests is left to them.

407. With less government intervention, suddenly partners realize the need to become more proactive and blunt. They would try to find ways to protect themselves in case their relationship fails. They would now really exercise their authority as independent individuals and write a *contract* that outlines their expectations. It particularly provides the clear terms of settlement in case of terminating their relationship.

408. The concept of couples signing a contract for their relationship is not new or unromantic. In the older and more practical cultures and religions, for many centuries, a form of contract has helped couples stipulate their expectations and boundaries. It is only in the new cultures where most people consider signing a contract unromantic.

409. Whether couples' decisions at the time of signing a contract would be perfect or not is irrelevant because they, as independent individuals, make those decisions. Of course, couples can always depend on professional advice to prepare the right contract for them. Also, when new mechanisms are in place, many standard documents will be available for couples to choose a proper relation-

ship model and the type of contract that best suits their needs.

410. The absence of government makes couples smarter and more cautious about their relationships. This new approach would change people's mindset and attitude. There will be less unsuitable relationships. And couples stay in their relationships longer, because they have initially thought through the stages of their relationships more realistically, especially the sad ending that most relationships must face nowadays.

411. The modification of government role in relationships has the highest impact on the financial independence of partners. Instead of letting courts decide about the distribution of assets at the time of separation, partners should have independently and objectively agreed on a system that fits their expectations in their initial marriage contract.

412. The welfare of the public and the prosperity of society are the main objectives of any government. As such, it has a stake in supporting a type of relationship framework that can help partners' needs most effectively and efficiently. Governments cannot leave this important task to chance and hope that things would work out nicely on their own in society.

413. The relationship framework, models, needs, and mechanisms, must be taught in high-schools. There should be strict rules for passing these mandatory courses. They are more important than sex education and many other courses.

414. Governments should become a lot more conscientious and active in teaching people how to budget and live

within their means. Governments' role to push consumerism to strengthen the economy is coming at the cost of family destructions and imminent social catastrophe.

415. Of course, the longevity of relationships has many advantages if it can be properly mastered. But three main questions can be asked:

   a. Are humans instinctually equipped to live together for the length of their long lives (especially now that life-expectancy is increasing so drastically)?

   b. Do partners' personalities and needs support the possibility of living together forever?

   c. Do our new social values and settings encourage the possibility of relationship longevity?

   On pages 343-351, the author argues that the answer to all the three above questions is no.

416. One clue that humans are not instinctually programmed to live together permanently is their amazing craving for sexual freedom. The urge to experience sex with many partners is in almost all human beings. As a means of happiness or psychological remedy, sex has become too important for us to remain content with only one partner. Sex is the first refuge we seek when our relationships face a calamity.

417. Another major hurdle for relationship longevity is that humans have to struggle hard to get along, especially the opposite sexes.

418. In all, it seems that humans are inherently not made to be in relationships. A good portion of people has even less capacity (including patience) to be in relationships due to their intense self-centredness and deep idiosyncrasies.

Yet we all try to force the idea of longevity out of habit, loneliness, urge for procreation, etc.

419. Men and women are so incompatible in general that when, by chance, they match and really love one another for a long time, it appears like a magical and spiritual sensation beyond our normal (expected) worldly experiences. It is such an odd event and coincidence. And still we are too naïve to believe it should happen to all of us and thus we pursue it like a reasonable expectation.

420. The benefits of having a specific term (for automatic annulment) in relationship contracts are substantial. See the list on page 352.

421. Governments should abandon their role in regulating, and ruling about, relationships. This would make couples depend on themselves and teamwork to manage the terms of their contracts.

422. While governments should stay clear of direct interference with relationship conflicts, they must support universities and other scholars to develop the relationship framework and GARP.

423. Although many couples use nannies, still the matter of raising children, versus following one's career, has become sensitive these days. One way to settle this issue is to make the partner who insists on having children accept the main role in raising them while the methods and degree of the other partner's involvement are also negotiated in advance and recorded in the marriage contract.

424. The question of having kids at all would become even more crucial in the future. It will become essential to decide carefully whether partners are prepared and capable of raising children.

425. Sometime in the far future, people might even be given a right to sue their parents for bringing them into this world or the way they have raised them. This would be a good policy for making people more responsible for creating children, who might suffer in dysfunctional families, corrupt societies, and polluted environments.
426. Making children should become a calculated decision by intelligent parents rather than a selfish act to enrich their own lives, or even for the socioeconomic purposes of governments.
427. Often our 'psychological construct' dictates the urgency of our needs. So, basically, the 'need urgency' concept suggests that for many of us being at a certain level of needs hierarchy is so urgent and important we can ignore all other needs, even if we face starvation or death.
428. All of our personal needs demand our attention at some degree and time. But the need to be in a relationship seems to be an everlasting, urgent, and imposing need.
429. When couples cannot create a good balance between their personal needs and the relationship needs, they feel tension. Thus, each partner must convince him/herself honestly about his/her real needs, instead of agreeing to be in a certain type of relationship (model) hastily.
430. Partners may leave some room for leniency in terms of the relationship model they are comfortable with, but not too much at the cost of going against their natural needs. If one or both partners cannot find a reasonable compromise about a suitable model, that would be the best indication that they are not made to be in a relationship together.

431. Even though couples should have the option of choosing the best relationship model for their type of personality and needs, normally they should start from the simplest relationship model, which is the lowest in the relationship hierarchy. They could then try to climb up the hierarchy according to their actual experiences in their relationship and by showing their aptitude and personality strengths.
432. The 'relationship needs hierarchy' and the relationship models presented in this book are simple ones. Yet they can be expanded and explained in a working manual. Couples can use this manual to identify the relationship model that suits them. Instead of the five models suggested in this book, we could possibly come up with a hierarchy that supports about a dozen relationship models.
433. The relationship framework and mechanisms proposed in this book put the onus on partners to be extra vigilant about their relationships. It is their own fault if they get themselves involved in faulty relationships or don't end them quickly and peacefully.
434. In this setting, partners must have a proactive and progressive mindset. Partners must view their relationship as a temporary arrangement, unless they can prove their expertise and sincerity to work together.
435. Relationships can no longer be viewed as a whimsical set of activities and needs to merely fulfil our emotional deficiencies. Being in a relationship is a serious *business* and must be viewed as such by partners.
436. The factors for success in relationships are quite different nowadays.

437. A person's personality can be identified and measured in terms of how effectively he/she can:
    - apply his/her **instincts**,
    - reason and use his/her **logic**,
    - connect with people and society—**Model**, and
    - manage his **ego** for his/her own benefit.
438. A unique mix of the above four factors makes up a person's personality.
439. The personality aspects, i.e., Self-P, Model-P, and Ego-P, are closely related to the personality factors. The minor difference is the inclusion of 'logic' as another factor in the personality model (page 389).
440. Relationship problems are too complex and widespread to overcome quickly. But what makes the situation more troublesome is that we are not even prepared to acknowledge that this pandemic has fundamentally destructive roots and requires radical changes.
441. A disturbing feature of relationships in the new era is partners' ever-increasing appetite to play games in order to manipulate each other. The nature and extent of these games are becoming too complex to handle and thus make partners even more jittery and incompatible for building a relationship together. A main motive for these games is partners' need for personal expression or retaliation. They are the newly developed defence mechanisms that couples adopt in order to supposedly protect themselves.
442. Men and women are inherently incompatible in terms of nature. So partners' effort to find their compatible companion is mostly a shot in the dark anyway. And still the

new relationship approaches and games make the job of finding our soul mate even tougher.

443. Peculiar signals that men and women send to one another by their attitude and games are causing more distance between them. These games are too difficult to understand or respond to.

444. The games couples play to maintain the balance of power is an ongoing, exhausting process. Partners simply seem incapable of putting down their guards, to live and relate naturally.

445. Another problem is that even when a partner decides to stop playing games and behave naturally, he/she still cannot deal with his/her partner who is addicted to these relationship games.

446. The irony is that people always notice and criticize other people's games and phoniness, but not their own. Most often they are aware of the games and roles they are playing, but naively assume that people don't notice them. They believe in their playacting too much. Or even worse, they think people are too simple or busy to see through them.

447. People play roles and games in order to maximize their chances for success in their relationships. But, by doing so, they actually increase the chances of being rejected and dumped.

448. A frustrating situation in relationships develops when a partner insists on playing a role or game and the other partner is not falling for it.

449. Relationships fail because too many of partners' games keep clashing. The more games they play to cope with

social and relationship issues, the more conflicts arise, which then lead to even more games.

450. Usually one partner starts a game with a special intention. Then the other partner starts his/her own game instead of playing along. The first partner is astonished that his/her game is detected and resisted. They keep introducing more games until they are exhausted and angry.

451. People consider charming and manipulating others their absolute right and an effective tool, while they believe they are good at it too. So when they fail, they just get too angry and nasty about it. All that charm turns suddenly into hostility and ruins even their basic friendships.

452. The way people snub each other as a way of relating—to set the tone of their friendships and relationships—is funny.

453. It appears that, nowadays, too many people are always struggling to either find a companion or get rid of him/her.

454. Instead of expecting happiness as a reward of being in a relationship, couples should actually be willing to pay a big price for it. This is a major fact they must accept before entering a relationship. Always a high price must be paid for the few fringe benefits of relationships.

455. Anyone who is capable of retaliating harshly is inherently empty of compassion. In particular, it is quite silly when someone retaliates in order to force compassion in their relationships.

456. Love and anger are not compatible, and whoever uses anger to force (or keep) love is simply incapable of giving or receiving love.

457. With the advent of various dating facilities, people meet and learn about many candidates for dating. While this flexibility seems helpful to find a match, it also increases people's false hopes about the possibility of finding a qualified person soon. So they become too fussy and keep joggling a bunch of relationships. Of course, people who are truly suitable for being in relationships are becoming scarcer too.
458. People keep multiple relationships because they are doubtful about the viability of any of them. Also, it is more efficient to study a few prospect partners simultaneously, as it usually takes many years to get to know someone. Having multiple relationships can also help a person rebound faster if one of his/her favourite relationships fails. He/she has other relationships to lean on at least temporarily. All these justifications sound reasonable, but what a world we have created.
459. Our hope to eventually find a soul mate is a crooked incentive that stops us from making (or keeping) our commitments in a relationship.
460. Perhaps the best definition for a soul mate is: 'Someone we can get along with, finally!'
461. Another cause of the increasing mistrust in society and relationships is that people are aware of the games being played, including multiple dating. So it is hard for people to take their relationships seriously. And yet everybody seems to be racing against time to find a reliable companion. People's struggle and hope to find love, trust, and happiness appear both admirable and depressing.
462. Many people, especially women, take the flattery they receive a sign of their chances to find a better mate once

they leave their present partners. Then after separation, they realize how they have been misled.

463. Many men are enjoying the present situation with multiple dating and all, while women are getting more frustrated due to their failure to find a qualified partner and also facing men's increasing passivity.

464. People's reaction to the present relationship conditions is just to do more of the same, i.e., more games, multiple dating, lying and mistrust, more shallow relationships, and rising frustration.

465. The complexity of the relationship environment and our passivity about it are the reasons why it will take at least a century to find real solutions for relationships.

466. Many humble individuals are out there who could be in good relationships together if they weren't deterred by their (often justified) paranoia about the state of relationships and their lack of trust in people.

467. Our accurate perceptions of corruption and duplicity in society cause cynicism about people's truthfulness and authenticity. This personal wisdom and warranted defence mechanism might inadvertently lead to a large amount of misperceptions in relationships, because every simple clue is misunderstood. But a great deal of misperceptions is also caused by our idiosyncrasies or communication hurdles.

468. The high percentage of marriage breakdowns and subsequent headaches make relationships too risky nowadays. So absolute caution regarding the words and promises of our partners is warranted.

469. The cost (consequences) of trusting our partners is high because they disappoint us sooner or later. But the cost

of not showing full trust in them is also too high, as they find it insulting and a sign of our indifference toward them.

470. Mistrust is a natural (and often necessary) condition in relationships in the new era. This is a logical consequence of social life and not a sign of a person's weakness or selfishness.

471. People's mistrust is often caused by their own oversensitivity and misperceptions, too, which then affects their behaviour and their partner's added mistrust in them. In all, partners must remain conscious of the high possibility and causes of misjudging each other.

472. We shouldn't expect our partners to trust us completely, especially when we feel the difficulty of trusting them completely ourselves.

473. We can never know *who we are* or *who they are* and they can never know *who they are* or *who we are*. This is a fact we must honour with open minds. We struggle all our lives to find ourselves and happiness, to no avail. So, how can we expect others to know us and trust us when even we don't? It is simply impossible to build trust based on our doubtful perceptions of ourselves and others.

474. We shouldn't consider love and trust as main factors of relationships' health anymore. These are misleading, illogical yardsticks. People often lie about their love or trust to avoid confrontations, or to be tactful and wise. Demanding trust or love beyond people's natural capacity would only bring more duplicity and phoniness into relationships.

475. We must come to terms with two major facts in the new era: 1) it is natural that partners lose trust in each other to

some extent eventually, and 2) we should learn to live in relationships with imperfect trust levels instead of making a big issue about it. We should be ultra cautious at the time of starting our relationships, but then remain flexible about inevitable mistrust and disappointments later on.

476. People don't know how to be tactful or observe even simple etiquettes, but keep insisting on the purity of their soul.
477. While everybody is obsessed about finding his/her soul mate, the chance of it ever happening is slim. But we all have difficulty accepting this fact, since we want to stay positive. Our romantic search for a soul mate is preventing us from perceiving relationships realistically.
478. Couples' promises or commitment are not reliable. Especially, taking the phrase 'I love you' seriously, as a sign of commitment, is naïve.
479. People don't change unless they feel the need for it through years of meditation and self-awareness. So, partners' retaliations and intimidations to change each other are just a reflection of their own naivety.
480. People, especially women, are nowadays too idealistic, ambitious, neurotic, and stressed out due to their new lifestyles and fantasies.
481. Women make a lot of fuss about their need for independence, but also demand to be spoiled. Ironically they don't see the conflict either.
482. People are getting more insecure due to our crooked social structure and values and thus they have become needier for attention and love. When they don't get it at the desired level, they feel even more lost and frustrated.

483. Relationships have become too important nowadays because people's basic needs are easily satisfied in modern societies. Without pressing issues and hardship, they fuss too much about love and happiness.
484. Relationships appear like the best antidote for loneliness, too, because we cannot live independently anymore despite all our pretensions.
485. But providing constant attention to our insecure partners is also a major responsibility that causes anxiety besides all the extra work.
486. Relationships also force lifestyle changes and adaptation, often for fitting with our partners' family habits and conflicting preferences.
487. Couples' insecurity and need for retaliation have reached such extremes that they kidnap, terrorize, or harm their own children just for intimidating their estranged partners. The intensity of child custody battles also shows how ineffective our relationship mechanisms are.
488. What works for women in a relationship doesn't work for men anymore, and vice versa. In particular, men and women mistrust the opposite genders much more than their own. The increasing same-sex relationships might be partly due to the fact that they get along better.
489. In all, it appears that we are reaching an era where men can no longer be what women want (in terms of character) and vice versa.
490. Nowadays, most people don't look for a partner to merely satisfy their basic companionship need. Rather, they want their relationships to satisfy a host of their personal needs and/or solve their personal problems. They also expect it to bring them happiness. Accordingly, they

blame their relationships for their personal failure to figure out life or find happiness. In all, couples are facing a transition period.

491. The transition period mainly refers to the process of men and women learning their relationship roles in the new era. But in reality it refers to the long period for couples, especially women, to realize that their expectations from relationships are not logical and feasible.

492. Greed and ego don't disappear when people marry, not even when they happen to be in love. In fact, greed and ego are the main forces behind all other pressing needs of individuals in relationships, including their needs for identity, control, recognition, love, and retaliation.

493. We are forced to play games and roles all our lives. We are somehow dragged into situations beyond our control where we must play along with others and assert ourselves. This condition is infecting relationships, too, as partners constantly play games and roles—out of necessity unfortunately. Hardly anybody is natural these days.

494. We spend most of our lives playing games and roles to: 1) impress (charm), 2) flatter, 3) intimidate, or 4) snub someone. So, the amount of time we are natural and sincere is quite minimal.

495. Personal idiosyncrasies would keep increasing as social values deteriorate, and vice versa. This is another vicious cycle that would keep spinning out of control and make more relationships fail every year.

496. Hope is an innate urge that keeps us motivated in our boring lives, but it mustn't make us dogmatic, e.g., about the possibility of finding our soul mate. Hope is a useful urge for survival but not a reliable reality.

497. Most often, partners actually end up destroying each other's lives instead of enriching it. This is because life is getting more complex and stressful every year and people have more difficulty coping with social pressures while they live longer too. People are too stressed and impatient to handle their excessive relationship demands effectively.
498. For relative tranquility, we must know the art of living independently instead of looking for a soul mate to bring us happiness.
499. We always face a major trade off in life: companionship brings us headaches, and tranquility requires loneliness and self-reliance. The question is how to make a decision according to one's personality.
500. The ultimate question is whether we can develop relationship models that fit couples' personalities and provide an atmosphere for a relatively tranquil and effective companionship. This book suggests that this option is plausible if we develop a relationship framework and its corresponding principles to bring objectivity back into relationships.

Epilogue
The Mystery of Love

This has been a book of analyses, statistics, trends, and logic. It has even attempted to dissect the meaning and implications of love in our modern world—such a naïve, bold undertaking! Yet the reasons for viewing relationships in some kind of a scientific light were explained in a few parts of this book. They are valid reasons. Furthermore, some radical changes were suggested for alleviating the runaway conflicts of relationships in the recent era. All those discussions gave a much lower importance to love for the success of relationships. But the role of love in relationships remains a haunting reality for most of us forever. Despite our arrogance, flaws, and lessons of failing relationships, love continues to overwhelm our lives like a heavenly impression, a myth, a craving, a helplessness. So, some kind of a reality check about the mystery of love and human's compelling romanticism is necessary before we close this book. After all, most people seek romance instinctively, and then become even more helpless when they eventually face it. We simply inflict more misery upon ourselves by our obsession for love; as if God has deliberately forced such a horrendous punishment upon humans to counterbalance the joy of love that He bestows upon them occasionally. We are driven to fall in love and then pay a high price for its bliss in the way lovers torture each other. The situation is quite frustrating because we, such intelligent creatures, cannot decide between the heartache of being in love or the suffering of a loveless life. By the way, the question of being in a relationship or not (with or without love) is a different dilemma all by itself—separate from the headaches of love altogether.

Our lifelong struggle to find love or suffer because of it is becoming more prevalent in the new era. On the one hand, economic growth is giving us more time and money to spend on our social needs. On the other hand, the high stress from social chaos and our dashed ambitions make us more susceptible to fall victim to love, or at least an impression of love, which has even harsher effects. Be it a reflection of our instinctual, social, or psychological needs, love is such a beautiful and yet hurtful phenomenon beyond human logic and explanation. As Rumi says:

> "The sign of love is in the misery of heart,
> No sickness is worse than the illness of heart.
> The lover's reasoning is apart from all reasons,
> Love is the astrolabe of God's mysteries."

Why would anybody be crazy to seek love then? The answer is that, love is such a penetrating and gratifying experience nobody can elude its traps. We simply get hypnotized. And once in love, we lose all our willpower, motives, and sleep. We face the mystery of love—the harshest challenge that God has imposed upon humans. So what is the point of suggesting guidelines, relationship models, and a framework when love affliction makes us so helpless we forget even ourselves and our basic needs?

This book suggests the means of bringing objectivity back into relationships. But, love defies any sense of logic. The sweetness of love simply knocks one's socks off. We lose ourselves, our minds and consciousness, when we fall in love. Any advice for love or relationships (such as the guidelines proposed in this book) would be the first thing we forget in this circumstance. Yet a small voice keeps nagging in our heads: "Is it wise to chase love and lose my identity in the process? Should I try to get hold of my emotions somehow?" Sometimes we eventually succeed to elude love when it cripples our normal routines, reasoning, and behaving. We try to get our sanity back. But more often than not, as an inevitable consequence of love, its power grabs us by the throat and drags us to the bottom of the pit. By the time we grasp the absurdity of our position, so much of our life and energy is consumed by love—one or many of them. Of course, we seldom feel sorry about any of these inconveniences and losses. The rewards of love seem worth all the pain we endure. Yet, eventually, we are somehow forced to let go of love in order to get hold of our self. We can be selfless awhile but not indefinitely. We can hold our breath to love someone temporarily, but we can never stop breathing altogether and not dying. Sometimes, one might prefer to die than live without one's beloved. And once in a while, someone learns to live selflessly regardless of his/her lover's response to all that love. Nonetheless, when in love, we become just too ignorant and helpless about how things usually go wrong in relationships. This is one important truth we can always remember in order to remain vigilant about our relationships and love affairs.

Another important point is that we seldom have the wisdom and willpower to separate love from relationships. In fact, we normally believe we can turn love into a permanent relationship and we insist on defining relationships mostly by love. Naively we assume that love can make a good relationship. These unrealistic expectations, however, only bring us disappointment. We don't like to separate love from relationships, and even when we do, we have a hard time deciding which one to choose. Each one of these two adventures fulfils a part of our natural needs. However, our eagerness for love usually supersedes our logical pursuit of a relationship. We even leave our not-so-bad relationships for love, or even for the chance of finding love. Like all other myths, love brings us a temporary relief from boredom and life's burdens. It provides a precious remedy for our empty hearts living in such phony societies. Its soothing warmth overrides any kind of logic. We accept the humiliation and agony that comes with it, which could possibly even lead to insanity. We cannot pick a time to love. We have no say about whom we fall in love with and we cannot avoid love traps either. Love just pops out of nowhere accidentally and overwhelms us quickly. On the other hand, we feel the need for a manageable relationship to sustain our routine lives and our sanity. We might come to our senses eventually and abandon our romantic fantasies. This usually happens when love finally fades away or we suffer enough. Then we start to think of a companion to bring us some peace and stability—the virtues that love usually lacks.

But relationships, too, are quite difficult to manage nowadays for all the reasons counted in this book, which in turn goad us to seek relief in love again, elsewhere, with a different person. The bottom line is that both our love affairs and relationships have become so important, yet agonizing, for reasons of their own. Obviously, there is not much that can be done about the symptoms of love. Often we try to reconcile our needs for both love and a long-term relationship. But the task of keeping love in relationships is often too difficult, as shown in this book. In all, a vicious cycle consumes all the fibres of our existence as a result of our search for love and a reliable companion.

Yet love is a good remedy to forget ourselves and life's hardships, despite (or because of) the agony it eventually imposes upon us. Even this brief discussion of love in these final pages is only for the purpose of bringing some relief to the readers after all the pessimistic points made throughout this book about the harsh reality of relationships. I believe that reciting the mystery and the joy of love is a good way to end this depressing book. If the readers thought all along that the author is against love, I hope these last few lines show how I indeed advocate and enjoy love whenever I can find it. Love is a highly intoxicating feeling that I have enjoyed a few times personally, always with devastating conclusions. Yet, I believe, love is a precious potion and rather manageable as long as one nurtures it solely within him/herself. The anguish begins only when we try to share love with someone else. 'Giving' is a natural symptom of love. We give ourselves, our soul, our wealth, and sometimes our integrity to our partners as a price of nourishing love. But often our partners misunderstand the meaning of our giving. They don't know how to return love with their own authentic feelings and behaviour. On the other hand, a true lover shouldn't care if his/her lover is incapable or unwilling to love him/her back, or behave according to the perfect picture he/she had imagined for his/her beloved. This is the only way to love without getting hurt all the time, which is of course a very difficult proposition for most people. In all, despite my share of disappointments and suffering, I cannot imagine turning away from love if and when it presents itself to me. I hope my last breath is drawn with the feeling and thought of a particular love. As you can see, I remain optimistic about love. This is because I know of some exceptions where lovers have been mature enough to sustain their passion for their entire lives. Actually, I feel lucky these days to be in love again—God knows for how long. I met this beautiful, sophisticated lady while I was editing this book and my new novel, *Midnight Gate-opener*. I'm glad I'd almost finished these books. Otherwise, the excitement of the new passion would've hindered my thoughts and the completion of the books. I am glad she has come into my life. But also I think, "God help me!" It is already reducing my ability to focus on work anyway. Let's blame all the editing imperfections in these two books on love! Anyhow, I'll embrace this new love and adventure. It is giving me some vitality after many years of loveless, stagnant existence. I am hoping that, this time, the new affair would prove to be one of those exceptions where love and tranquility merge within an everlasting relationship. The only trick I am hoping to implement successfully this time is to love her without expecting too much in return. I am hoping to use my new wisdom to make it last a bit longer. I have learned, possibly, to welcome love in its mythical context to satisfy my spiritual needs. I must, however, forget about all my other expectations from love. How am I going to avoid the destructive symptoms of love, I wonder? I need immense willpower to do so. But I won't be surprised if someday I feel the need to leave her too!

At the same time, of course, I know the challenge, especially for young couples, to understand and pursue relationships with open minds away from love. I hope they keep an eye on the heartbreaking facts of relationships. They must remember to assess their partners' personality and incentives for starting or staying in a relationship. I have felt sad all along when writing this book and suggesting such radical solutions, but I believe they are absolutely necessary. It hasn't been easy for me to generalize the state of relationships so negatively and to stress the obvious fact that a majority of them would fail due to the lack of compassion, logic, trust, or objectivity. I am sorry if my pessimism has broken so many people's (especially women's) delicate hearts, as they see life mainly through love. I am sad that we have so much difficulty nowadays to build our relationships. But there is nothing else we can do. It is a sickness that requires a bitter medicine. I just hope that I have succeeded in convincing you that we must change our mentality about the potentials and purposes of love and relationships, and that social mechanisms must be revamped drastically too.

Meanwhile, enjoy love selflessly, with open eyes and minds about its severe limitations and most likely a sad ending.

www.ingramcontent.com/pod-product-compliance
Lightning Source LLC
Chambersburg PA
CBHW071641160426
43195CB00012B/1320